Reclaiming Identity

Reclaiming Identity

*Realist Theory
and the
Predicament of
Postmodernism*

EDITED BY

Paula M. L. Moya and
Michael R. Hames-García

UNIVERSITY OF CALIFORNIA PRESS
Berkeley · Los Angeles · London

The following chapters are revised versions of materials published elsewhere: chapter 1, Satya P. Mohanty, "The Epistemic Status of Cultural Identity: On *Beloved* and the Postcolonial Condition," *Cultural Critique* 24 (Spring 1993): 41–80; chapter 2, Paula M. L. Moya, "Postmodernism, 'Realism,' and the Politics of Identity: Cherríe Moraga and Chicana Feminism," in *Feminist Genealogies, Colonial Legacies, Democratic Futures,* ed. M. Jacqui Alexander and Chandra Talpade Mohanty (New York: Routledge, 1997): 125–50, 379–84; chapter 4, Caroline S. Hau, "On Representing Others: Intellectuals, Pedagogy, and the Uses of Error," *Journal of English Studies and Comparative Literature* (University of the Philippines) 1, no. 2 (January 1998): 3–36.

University of California Press
Berkeley and Los Angeles, California

University of California Press, Ltd.
London, England

Library of Congress Cataloging-in-Publication Data

Reclaiming identity : realist theory and the predicament of postmodernism / edited by Paula M. L. Moya and Michael R. Hames-García.
    p.   cm.
    Includes bibliographical references and index.
    ISBN 0-520-22348-9 (cloth : alk. paper)—
ISBN 0-520-22349-7 (pbk. : alk. paper)
    1. Group identity.   2. Social perception.
3. Postmodernism.   I. Moya, Paula M. L.
II. Hames-García, Michael Roy.

HM753.R43   2000
305—dc21   00-022788
                                       CIP

Manufactured in the United States of America

09 08 07 06 05 04 03 02 01 00
10 9 8 7 6 5 4 3 2 1

The paper used in this publication meets the minimum requirements of ANSI / NISO Z39.48-1992 (R 1997) (*Permanence of Paper*).♾

For Tim Young

and

for Alpha Baldé, Terrence Calhoun,
and Tiffany Willoughby-Herard

Contents

Acknowledgments   *ix*

Introduction: Reclaiming Identity
   Paula M. L. Moya   *1*

THE REALIST THEORY OF IDENTITY AND
THE PREDICAMENT OF POSTMODERNISM

  1. The Epistemic Status of Cultural Identity:
     On *Beloved* and the Postcolonial Condition
     Satya P. Mohanty   29

  2. Postmodernism, "Realism," and the Politics of
     Identity: Cherríe Moraga and Chicana Feminism
     Paula M. L. Moya   67

  3. "Who Are Our Own People?": Challenges for
     a Theory of Social Identity
     Michael R. Hames-García   102

POSTPOSITIVIST OBJECTIVITY:
USES OF ERROR, VALUES, AND IDENTITY

4. On Representing Others: Intellectuals, Pedagogy,
   and the Uses of Error
   Caroline S. Hau   *133*

5. "It Matters to Get the Facts Straight": Joy Kogawa, Realism,
   and Objectivity of Values
   Minh T. Nguyen   *171*

6. Racial Authenticity and White Separatism: The Future
   of Racial Program Housing on College Campuses
   Amie A. Macdonald   *205*

REALIST CONCEPTIONS OF AGENCY, EXPERIENCE, AND IDENTITY

7. Who Says Who Says?: The Epistemological Grounds
   for Agency in Liberatory Political Projects
   Brent R. Henze   *229*

8. Is There Something You Need to Tell Me?: Coming Out
   and the Ambiguity of Experience
   William S. Wilkerson   *251*

9. Reading "Experience": The Debate in Intellectual History
   among Scott, Toews, and LaCapra
   John H. Zammito   *279*

10. Who's Afraid of Identity Politics?
    Linda Martín Alcoff   *312*

Contributors   *345*

Index   *347*

Acknowledgments

The editors of this volume would like to extend our deepest gratitude to Satya Mohanty, Linda Alcoff, Bill Wilkerson, and Tim Young for their crucial assistance and encouragement across the span of this project.

Ernesto Martínez's friendship, editorial advice, and assistance in formatting and proofreading have been invaluable. We would also like to acknowledge Elizabeth Minnich for her helpful suggestions and strong support and Leslie Roman for her encouragement early in the project. Special recognition and appreciation are due to Linda Norton for her faith in our intellectual vision and her steadfast support. The entire University of California Press team has been phenomenal, in particular, Lynn Meinhardt and Mary Koon. Sheila Berg's close inspection of the final manuscript has been invaluable.

In addition, we want to say thank you to the following people who have helped us in crucially important ways: Rosaura Sánchez and José David Saldívar for letting this volume go to print; Associate Dean David Holloway and Assistant Dean Stephanie Kalfayan at Stanford University and the Binghamton Research Foundation at Binghamton University for providing needed funding; and Ramón Saldívar and Dominick LaCapra for engaging with our ideas and asking hard questions. We are also grateful for the comments and questions from the audience at panels in which portions of this work were presented, including the annual meeting of the American Studies Association in 1998, the conference Hispanics: Cultural Locations at the University of San Francisco in 1998, the annual meeting of the Society for Phenomenology and Existential Philosophy in 1999, and a forum at Cornell University in 1999.

Michael Hames-García would also like to acknowledge David Bartine for his support and advice, María Lugones and members of the Methodologies of Resistant Negotiation Working Group at SUNY Binghamton for their encouragement and support, and students in his Queer Theory and its Discontents graduate seminar.

Paula M. L. Moya expresses her gratitude to Al Camarillo and the other members of the Inequalities and Identities workshop at Stanford University, Alyce Boster and Dagmar Logie for their unstinting administrative support, and the students in her graduate courses Introduction to Feminist Theory and Realist Theory and the Predicament of Postmodernism.

Finally, we would both like to extend our most heartfelt thanks to the contributors to this volume for their patience and cooperation in realizing this vision.

Reclaiming Identity

Paula M. L. Moya

WHY IDENTITY?

> The bitter truth is that in a racist society where a brown
> skin (along with other colors) can cost lives, people will em-
> brace any ideology that seems to offer the hope of change.
> Even when that ideology proves counter-productive, the
> hope persists. . . . [N]ationalism, then, has to be seen as
> a complicated, two-edged sword. It can't be fully under-
> stood if we just dismiss it as "identity politics."
>
> Elizabeth Martínez,
De Colores Means All of Us

"Identity" remains one of the most urgent—as well as hotly disputed—
topics in literary and cultural studies. For nearly two decades, it has been
a central focus of debate for psychoanalytic, poststructuralist, and cultural materialist criticism in areas ranging from postcolonial and ethnic
studies to feminism and queer theory.[1] Oddly enough, much of what has

---

I would like to gratefully acknowledge the helpful comments and suggestions of Johnnella
Butler, Michael Hames-García, Marcial Gonzalez, Ernesto Martinez, Gonzalo Martinez,
Satya Mohanty, Robert Warrior, and Tim Young.

1. Because detailed bibliographic leads pointing to the debates about identity are available in the essays in this volume, I will not attempt to provide comprehensive citations in
the notes to this introduction. Instead, I will provide a few important references for the
purpose of assisting an interested reader. For fairly comprehensive bibliographies together

been written about identity during this period seeks to delegitimate, and
in some cases eliminate, the concept itself by revealing its ontological, epistemological, and political limitations. Activists and academics alike have
responded to essentialist tendencies in the cultural nationalist and feminist movements of the 1960s and 1970s[2] and to the violent ethnic conflicts
of the 1980s and 1990s by concluding that (social or cultural) identity,
as a basis for political action, is theoretically incoherent and politically
pernicious.[3] Because we intend to reevaluate—even to reclaim—identity
and because we want to rescue identity from the disrepute into which it
has fallen, the authors and editors of this volume take seriously the criticisms that have been directed against the concept of identity. Therefore,
I begin by reviewing the substance of the critiques to which identity has
been subjected before I explain how French poststructuralism—arguably
the most influential intellectual trend in the humanities during the past
twenty-five years—has provided crucial theoretical support to scholars
attempting to dismantle the concept of identity. I then address the question of why we feel the need to recuperate such a troublesome concept
and introduce the postpositivist realist framework from which we have
attempted to do so.[4]

---

with helpful analyses of the issues at stake in debates about identity, see Fuss; Dean. Important collections that highlight debates about identity include Gates; Smith, *Home Girls;*
LaCapra; Mohanty, Russo, and Torres; Nicholson; Anzaldúa; Moraga and Anzaldúa; Appiah and Gates; Abelove, Barale, and Halperin; Nicholson and Seidman; McCarthy and
Crichlow; and Calhoun, *Social Theory and the Politics of Identity.*
    2. In fact, the judgment regarding whether the different social movements of the 1960s
and 1970s were truly "essentialist" deserves further consideration. Alcoff, for instance, argues in this volume that what is often seen as the locus classicus of identity politics, the
"Black Feminist Statement" by the Combahee River Collective, is more realist than essentialist. Similarly, Henze, also in this volume, uses the examples of two identity-related
feminist projects from the 1970s to disprove the validity of essentialism. The various projects involved in maintaining an allegiance to a racial or gender identity for the purpose of
honoring and engaging lived experience may have been too summarily reduced and dismissed by poststructuralist-inspired critics without a sympathetic understanding of the epistemological processes involved. I do not mean that essentialist notions of identity do not
exist (certainly nineteenth-century scientific racism depended on an essentialist notion of
identity), nor do I deny that some social movements of the 1970s had essentialist tendencies. Consider, for example, the claim in "El Plan de Aztlán," "We, the Chicano inhabi-
tants and civilizers of the northern land of Aztlán . . . *declare* that the call of our blood is
our power, our responsibility, and our inevitable destiny," and the assertion, "Nationalism as the key to organization transcends all religious, political, class, and economic fac-
tions or boundaries. Nationalism is the common denominator that all members of La Raza
can agree on" (Alurista et al. 4, 5). I do mean to suggest that not all projects involving
claims to identity are the same, nor are all the claims they might make equally justified.
    3. For a discussion of this phenomenon, see Alcoff's essay in this volume, esp. the sec-
tion "Problems with Identity."
    4. The postpositivist realist theory of identity, as it has been formulated, elaborated,
and tested in this anthology, emerged from a collective of scholars working together in and

The first problem with essentialist conceptions of identity, according to critics, is the tendency to posit one aspect of identity (say, gender) as the sole cause or determinant constituting the social meanings of an individual's experience. The difficulty, critics of identity point out, is that identities are constituted differently in different historical contexts. So, for example, a slave woman living in antebellum America might experience her "womanness" very differently from a middle-class housewife living in Victorian England. Moreover, the social meanings attached to each woman's gender might be so different as to render the project of describing one woman in terms of the other meaningless. Even two women living in close proximity to each other (such as a Zulu maid and her Afrikaner madam) might be so differently situated in relation to the category of gender that their experiences, and the social meanings inscribed in those experiences, cannot be usefully described in the same terms. These examples illustrate that, contrary to an essentialist view, identity categories are neither stable nor internally homogenous.

The instability and internal heterogeneity of identity categories (such as gender) have prompted critics of identity to point to a range of additional problems. They remind us that insofar as every woman differs from every other woman in more or less significant ways, it is impossible to determine the (racial, class, cultural, etc.) identity of the "authentic woman" and thus to unify different women under the signifier "woman." And because women's experiences are so varied, there can be no such thing as an authentic or exemplary "woman's experience." This situation, the critic of identity suggests, creates an epistemological difficulty: as we do not know exactly what experiences of women can be taken as exemplary, we cannot know with certainty what criteria to apply in analyzing and understanding women's actions, intentions, and emotions. As a result, "women's experience" can only be understood as an arbitrary construct. Indeed, any account of "women's experience" risks naturalizing one group of women's experience as normative and thereby marginalizing that of another group's.

This difficulty, in turn, gives rise to a variety of political predicaments: if no one woman can know and represent the experiences of all women, on what authority can she speak "as a woman"? At best, she might be

<hr>

around Cornell University during the 1990s. The scholars who initially came together did so partly in response to the excesses of the widespread skepticism and constructivism in literary theory and cultural studies and partly because they were interested in formulating a complex and rigorous theory of identity that could be put to work in the service of progressive politics.

able to speak accurately of her own unique experience of being a woman (and some postmodernist critics would deny even this)—but then she would be speaking as an individual, not as a woman. The issue of authority of experience is thus intimately tied to the problem of representation: if even a woman cannot be trusted to speak accurately for and about "women," then how is it possible to speak for or about "women" at all? In fact, some critics of identity tell us, it is not possible: to speak of "women" in a substantive way is to risk projecting onto all women one socially dominant construction of "woman," thereby distorting the meanings of the lives of more marginalized women. It is to engage, they warn us, in the practice of ideological normalization and exclusion.[5]

These critiques of identity have been articulated by activists and academics coming from a wide range of perspectives. Activist women of color, conservative pundits, postmodernist theorists, and feminists of all colors and theoretical perspectives have noted the very real challenges posed by the concept of identity. The answer to the question of how to respond to these challenges, however, has varied widely. Some critics have retained an allegiance to the concept of identity and have attempted to reformulate or complicate their understandings of it. Ethnic studies scholars and members of various student groups, for example, continue to deploy identity as an organizing principle in their scholarly, political, and activist endeavors. Such scholars and activists have insisted that identity categories do not devolve into essentialist programs. Instead, identity categories provide modes of articulating and examining significant correlations between lived experience and social location. Other critics have advocated the abandonment of the whole enterprise of determining who belongs to what group or what that belonging might mean to the lives of social group members. On the one hand, conservative critics argue for this abandonment on the grounds that paying attention to particular identities will unnecessarily balkanize our society and obscure our shared human attributes. On the other hand, postmodernists claim that it is an error to grant ontological or epistemological significance to identity categories.

The centrality of French poststructuralism for postmodernist critiques

5. For some academic critiques of identity that point to the problems I have just enumerated, see Fuss; Butler, *Gender Trouble;* Culler; Spelman; Nicholson and Fraser; Spivak, "Can the Subaltern Speak?"; Alarcón; Michaels; Suleri; Martin and Mohanty. For an essay that presents a way of going beyond some of these critiques of identity in feminist theory, see my "Chicana Feminism and Postmodernist Theory." Popular press critiques of identity include autobiographical accounts written by neoconservative minorities. See, e.g., Rodriguez; Steele; Carter.

of the concept of identity is exemplified by the way deconstruction has been applied in social and cultural theory.[6] Postmodernist critics inspired by deconstruction, for example, have tended to analogize and thus understand social relations with reference to linguistic structures. The deconstructionist thesis about the arbitrariness and indeed indeterminacy of linguistic reference led many U.S. literary theorists and cultural critics to understand concepts like experience and identity (which are fundamentally about social relations) as similarly indeterminate and hence epistemically unreliable. Such critics argue that, inasmuch as meaning is constituted by systems of differences purely internal to the languages through which humans interpret the world, meaning is inescapably relative. Meaning is never fully present because it is constituted by the endless possibilities of what it is not and is therefore at least always partially deferred. Because meaning exists only in a shifting and unstable relationship to the webs of signification through which it comes into being and because humans have no access to anything meaningful outside these sometimes disparate webs, there can be no "objective" truth. The desire for "truth" or "objective" knowledge is therefore seen as resting on a naively representational theory of language that relies on the following mistaken assumptions: first, that there is a one-to-one correspondence between signs and their extralinguistic real-world referents; and second, that some kind of intrinsic meaning dwells in those real-world referents, independent of human thought or action. Knowledge, insofar as it is mediated by language, cannot be said to be objective.

As a result of the influence of poststructuralism, the terms of the debate in the academy regarding selves and cultural identities have shifted considerably. Broadly speaking, U.S. scholars in the humanities who have been influenced by poststructuralist theory have undermined conven-

---

6. Poststructuralism is a philosophical movement that emerged in France in the late 1960s as a critique of phenomenology and structuralism. It is primarily associated with theorists (who were themselves trained by phenomenologists and structuralists) like Derrida, Kristeva, Lacan, Foucault, and Barthes. Although poststructuralism includes a variety of perspectives deriving from the different theories of its principal thinkers, it is characterized by an opposition to structuralist principles (condemned as "totalizing" and "deterministic") and a focus on (sometimes a celebration of) difference and multiplicity. It has been credited with the textualizing of the social world, the critique of subject-centered thought, and the demise of grand narratives and general truth claims. It is distinguishable from postmodernism insofar as it is an "essentially theoretical shift, not a claim that anything in the external world had changed to necessitate a new theory" (Calhoun, *Critical Social Theory* 114). The significance of poststructuralism for my discussion is that postmodernism, as a theoretical and/or critical position, derives substantially from it (Calhoun, *Critical Social Theory* 100).

tional understandings of identity by discounting the possibility of objective knowledge. Instead of asking how we know who we are, poststructuralist-inspired critics are inclined to suggest that we cannot know; rather than investigate the nature of the self, they are likely to suggest that it has no nature. The self, the argument goes, can have no nature because subjectivity does not exist outside the grammatical structures that govern our thought; rather, it is produced by those structures. Because subjects exist only in relation to ever-evolving webs of signification and because they constantly differ from themselves as time passes and meanings change, the self—as a unified, stable, and knowable entity existing prior to or outside language—is merely a fiction of language, an effect of discourse. Social and cultural identities, it is argued, are similarly fictitious because the selves they claim to designate cannot be pinned down, fixed, or definitively identified. Moreover, identities are not simply fictitious; they are dangerously mystifying. They are mystifying precisely because they treat fictions as facts and cover over the fissures, contradictions, and differences internal to the social construct we call a "self." Inasmuch as the desire to identify ourselves and others remains complicit with positivist assumptions about a fully knowable world—a world that can be described, hierarchized, named, and mastered—identity as a concept will serve oppressive and reductive ideological functions. In this view, to speak of identities as "real" is to naturalize them and to disguise the structures of power involved in their production and maintenance.

This "postmodernist" critique of identity that I am describing[7] should be understood in part as a corrective to a prior social and intellectual

7. Postmodernism is a more diffuse, and so harder to define, cultural phenomenon than poststructuralism. Most critics agree that it can be characterized in at least three (analytically separable) ways: (1) as an aesthetic practice; (2) as a historical stage in the development of late capitalism; and (3) as a theoretical or critical position. I am not concerned here with postmodernism as either a historical period or an aesthetic movement. While I will describe the (often implicit) epistemological underpinnings of "postmodernist" theoretical conceptions of identity, I am aware that postmodernist theory does not constitute a unified intellectual movement. Nevertheless, the arguments of many prominent figures in contemporary feminist, postcolonial, antiracist, and queer theory (some of whom reject the term I am using to describe them) share important commonalities; they are characterized by a strong epistemological skepticism, a valorization of flux and mobility, and a general suspicion of, or hostility toward, all normative and/or universalist claims. It is this theoretical bias, recognizable in much of the work done in the humanities today, that I am pointing to with the use of the adjective "postmodernist." Readers interested in learning more about postmodernist theory and the critiques to which it has been subjected should consult Nicholson, esp. introd.; Nicholson and Seidman, esp. introd.; Eagleton; McGowan; Calhoun, *Critical Social Theory*, esp. chap. 4. For more about postmodernism as a historical or cultural phenomenon, see Jameson; Harvey; Best and Kellner; Waugh; Anderson.

tendency toward "essentialism."[8] Cultural critics drawn to the postmodernist approach had seen the epistemological and political limitations of essentialist conceptions of identity; in the absence of attractive
alternatives, postmodernist deconstructions of identity seemed to be the
safest, most progressive, way to go.[9] The progressive political activist's
or theorist's task, postmodernists have insisted, should be to undermine
or "subvert" identities in order to destabilize the normalizing forces that
bring them into being.[10]

Why, then, do the authors and editors of this volume want to reclaim
the concept of identity? How, if the concept has been deconstructed and
debunked, if it has been shown to be conceptually flawed and politically
pernicious, is there anything left to say? There are several answers to
these questions, but the brief response is that prevailing theories of identity lack the intellectual resources to distinguish between different kinds
of identities. We contend that a theory of identity is inadequate unless
it allows a social theorist to analyze the epistemic status and political
salience of any given identity and provides her with the resources to as-
certain and evaluate the possibilities and limits of different identities.
Neither "essentialist" nor "postmodernist" theories of identity can do
this. As a result, critics who have adopted either of these two approaches
have tended to overestimate or underestimate the political salience of

8. "Essentialism" here refers to the notion that individuals or groups have an immutable and discoverable "essence"—a basic, unvariable, and presocial nature. As a theoretical concept, essentialism expresses itself through the tendency to see *one* social category (class, gender, race, sexuality, etc.) as determinate in the last instance for the cultural
identity of the individual or group in question. As a political strategy, essentialism has had
both liberatory and reactionary effects.
  9. It would be an impossible task to determine the true motives of all critics who attack identity. A generous reading demands that we take postmodernist critics at their word
and that we accept the possibility that they believe all but the most strategic claims to identity to be essentialist and therefore politically pernicious. A less generous reading, but one
that also deserves consideration, is that the charge of essentialism might also result from
a racist counterstance to the agency of newly politicized minorities.
  10. This was the program advanced by Butler in her influential book, *Gender Trouble*. See especially her last chapter where she argues the following: "The critical task for
feminism is not to establish a point of view outside of constructed identities; that conceit
is the construction of an epistemological model that would disavow its own cultural location and, hence, promote itself as a global subject, a position that deploys precisely the
imperialist strategies that feminism ought to criticize. The critical task is, rather, to affirm
the local possibilities of intervention through participating in precisely those practices of
repetition that constitute identity and, therefore, present the immanent possibility of contesting them. . . . The task is not whether to repeat, but how to repeat or, indeed, to repeat
and, through a radical proliferation of gender, to *displace* the very gender norms that enable the repetition itself" (147, 148).

actual identities. I will return to this point when I discuss the postpositivist realist alternative in the next section. Let me first discuss additional responses—some practical/political, some epistemological—to the questions I posed above.

The contributors to this book have undertaken this collective project at least partly because we believe that the recent negative emphasis on the violence of identification/subjectivation is overstated. Cultural identities are not only and always "wounded attachments."[11] They can also be enabling, enlightening, and enriching structures of attachment and feeling. Much of the postmodernist writing on identity loses sight of this and, consequently, fails to explain significant modes by which people experience, understand, and know the world. The significance of identity depends partly on the fact that goods and resources are still distributed according to identity categories. Who we are—that is, who we perceive ourselves or are perceived by others to be—will significantly affect our life chances: where we can live, whom we will marry (or whether we can marry), and what kinds of educational and employment opportunities will be available to us. Another reason we are working on this issue is because we contend that an ability to take effective steps toward progressive social change is predicated on an acknowledgment of, and a familiarity with, past and present structures of inequality—structures that are often highly correlated with categories of identity. This correlation undoubtedly accounts for why identity has been a fundamental element of social liberation as well as of social oppression.

Finally, we have undertaken the task of reclaiming identity because "identities" are evaluatable theoretical claims that have epistemic consequences. Who we understand ourselves to be will have consequences for how we experience and understand the world. Our conceptions of who we are as social beings (our identities) influence—and in turn are influenced by—our understandings of how our society is structured and what our particular experiences in that society are likely to be. The point, however, is that our different views about how our society is structured and where we and others fit into that totality are not all equally accu-

---

11. This formulation derives from Brown's book *States of Injury*, in which she draws on Nietzsche to argue that politicized identities are structured by *ressentiment*. In Brown's view, people who organize on the basis of identity become invested in their own subjection through their paradoxical attempts to relieve their suffering. They are fueled by humiliation and driven by impotence to exact revenge on those who, by virtue of superior strength and good fortune, do not suffer the "unendurable pain" of the historically subordinated. Revenge, by this account, is achieved through the production of guilt and by making a social virtue of suffering. See chap. 3, esp. 66–76.

rate. So, for example, a white man who identifies as a white supremacist might experience his job layoff as a direct consequence of a federal
government or Jewish conspiracy rather than as a result of corporate con-
solidation or economic restructuring. In this case, his understanding about
the way society is structured is more erroneous than accurate—as are
his ideas about his putative racial superiority. Identities are thus not simply products of structures of power; they are often assumed or chosen
for complex subjective reasons that can be objectively evaluated. Moreover, identities have consequences for the kinds of associations human
beings form (such as white supremacist churches along the lines of Christian Identity) and the sorts of activities they engage in (such as blowing
up federal buildings or shooting random nonwhite or Jewish people).[12]
So, while the authors and editors of this book do not take the reification
of existing identities as our goal, we insist they must be thoroughly understood before they can be either transformed or dismantled. To understand them, we need to be able to distinguish those identities that provide more promising perspectives on the underlying structures of social
conflict from those that do not. We need to take the epistemic status of
identities seriously enough to make such distinctions.[13]

12. Within four months of the time of this writing, in 1999, white boys and men espousing white supremacist ideology were charged with the following crimes. On June 18
arsonists set fire to three synagogues around Sacramento, California, leaving behind anti-
Semitic literature. Two brothers, Benjamin Williams, 31, and James Williams, 29, were
later accused of the crime. These same two brothers have also been accused of the July 1
murder of a gay couple, who were found slain in their bed in Redding, California. On July
3 Benjamin Smith, 21, killed an African American father walking with his two small children and a Korean graduate student leaving church. He wounded nine other nonwhite or
Jewish people in a series of attacks in Illinois before killing himself the next day as police
tried to arrest him. On July 5 a soldier at Fort Campbell, Kentucky, who had been harassed
by his fellow soldiers because he was gay, was beaten so severely that he died the next day.
Pvt. Calvin Glover, 18, and Spec. Justin Fisher, 25, have been accused of the crime. On
August 10 Buford Furrow, Jr., 37, allegedly fired seventy shots at a Jewish community center in Los Angeles, wounding four people, before killing a Filipino American postal worker.
Furrow turned himself in to the FBI in Las Vegas the next day, saying he wanted the attack "to be a wake-up call to America to kill Jews." On August 29 Vincent Prodberger,
19, and two 17-year-old juveniles allegedly fire-bombed the home of Judge Jack Komar in
San Jose, California. According to police, Judge Komar's home was targeted because the
three suspects believed him to be Jewish. Judge Komar is Catholic.
   13. The argument here is that postmodernist theory does not provide the intellectual
resources to either acknowledge the epistemic significance of actual identities or distinguish
between those identities that provide more promising perspectives on our social world from
those that do not. This deficiency, in turn, seriously limits postmodernist theorists' ability
to formulate effective projects for political change. The difficulty postmodernist theorists
have had in formulating and/or justifying their political and intellectual projects has led
some theorists to advocate the practice of "strategic essentialisms" (Spivak, "Subaltern Studies") or the invocation of "contingent foundations" (Butler, "Contingent Foundations").
While the solution of a pragmatic appeal to a framework- or tradition-specific justification

WHY REALISM?

When we say that a thing is real we are simply expressing
a sort of respect. We mean that the thing must be taken
seriously because it can affect us in ways that are not
entirely in our control and because we cannot learn about
it without making an effort that goes beyond our imagination. . . . As a physicist I perceive scientific explanations
and laws as things that are what they are and cannot be
made up as I go along. . . . [A]nd I therefore accord the
laws of nature (to which our present laws are an approximation) the honor of being real.

> Steven Weinberg, *Dreams of a Final Theory*

Recently, discussions about identity have become predictable and unil-
luminating, partly because their terms have remained fixed within the
opposing "postmodernist" and "essentialist" positions (where the latter
is construed as the basis for naive identity politics). Neither of the two
opposing positions has proved adequate to the task of explaining the social, political, and epistemic significance of identities. Essentialist conceptions, which tend to see the meanings generated by experience as "self-
evident" and existing identities as "natural," are unable to account for
some of the most salient features of actual identities. They have been unable to explain the internal heterogeneity of groups, the multiple and
sometimes contradictory constitution of individuals, and the possibility
of change—both cultural and at the level of individual personal identity.
In turn, postmodernist conceptions—which tend to deny that identities
either refer to or are causally influenced by the social world—have been
unable to evaluate the legitimacy or illegitimacy of different identity

---

tends to satisfy those critics already committed to postmodernist precepts, others remain un-
convinced that postmodernist theory can be politically efficacious or intellectually useful.

For an illustration of the poverty of postmodernist theory for formulating an intellectual project, consider Keith Jenkins's attempt in *The Postmodern History Reader*. In his
introduction to that anthology, Jenkins admits that he does not know what a postmodern
history would actually look like. All he can tell us is that postmodern histories "(if they
exist) . . . will not be like 'histories in the upper case' [or] much like lower case histories
either in their old realist, 'for its own sake' formulations" (28). My point here is that someone who wants to dismiss (as ideologically misguided) the tested methodologies of a discipline should do more than gesture toward some "postmodern-type histories" that have
been identified by a few "trend-spotters" (28). At the very least, Jenkins should show that
postmodern methodologies enable historians to produce better histories than do the "realist, empiricist, objectivist, documentarist, and liberal-pluralist" methodologies that he
likes to deprecate.

claims. Because postmodernists are reluctant to admit that identities refer outward (with varying degrees of accuracy) to our shared world, they
see all identities as arbitrary and as unconnected to social and economic
structures. This renders postmodernists incapable of judging the male
patriarch (whose identity claims might include a belief in his own gender superiority) as being more or less credible than, say, a woman (whose
identity claims might include a belief in her own disadvantaged position
vis-à-vis a "glass ceiling"). My point (at least for now) is not to say which
one of these individuals' identity claims is more justified but simply to
suggest that the issue is at least partly an empirical one: the different identity claims cannot be examined, tested, and judged without reference to
existing social and economic structures. Although increasing numbers of
theorists have voiced their concerns about the poverty of the opposition
between these essentialist and postmodernist approaches to identity,[14]
no one has offered a richly elaborated alternative theoretical framework
that can transcend it—until now. This volume represents the first coor-
dinated effort to present an alternative theoretical approach to identity
that can take debates about the concept to a new level.

The alternative approach to identity that this volume develops and
expands was first articulated by the literary theorist Satya P. Mohanty
in his 1993 essay, "The Epistemic Status of Cultural Identity: On
Beloved and the Postcolonial Condition." Both in that essay and in his
subsequent book, *Literary Theory and the Claims of History*, Mohanty
draws on the tradition of American pragmatism and recent developments
in analytic philosophy (in particular, epistemology, social theory, and the
philosophy of science) to explore the contours of a "postpositivist realist" approach to identity.[15] In the process of working out a sophisticated
and nuanced alternative to current conceptions that see identity either
in a deterministic way or as purely arbitrary (or, at most, "strategic"),
Mohanty reveals the opposition between "postmodernist" and "essentialist" theories of identity to be both false and unhelpful. His postpositivist realist theory of identity solves the central challenge confronting

---

14. See, e.g., Alcoff; Sedgwick; hooks; Singer; Zammito; Lugones; de Lauretis.
15. As an intellectual trend, the postpositivist realism Mohanty defends emerges
partly from within the philosophy of science and from analytic epistemology more generally and is particularly indebted to the work of Charles Peirce, W. V. O. Quine, Donald Davidson, Hilary Putnam, and Richard Boyd. In extending postpositivist realism into
the realm of identity, Mohanty also draws extensively on the work of Toni Morrison,
Immanuel Kant, Charles Taylor, Naomi Scheman, and Sandra Harding. For more specific
bibliographical references, see S. Mohanty's essay in this volume and *Literary Theory*,
esp. chaps. 6, 7.

theorists of identity today. It shows how identities can be both real and constructed: how they can be politically and epistemically significant, on the one hand, and variable, nonessential, and radically historical, on the other.

Just as the postmodernist dismissal of identity is based on a denial of the possibility of objectivity, so Mohanty's realist reclaiming of identity is based on a reaffirmation of the possibility of (a postpositivist) objectivity. Contra postmodernists, realists contend that humans can develop reliable knowledge about their world and about how and where they fit into that world.[16] But postpositivist realists are not naive empiricists; they do not hope to flip the poststructuralist critique on its head and return to an uncritical belief in the possibility of theoretically unmediated knowledge. Rather, they refuse the definition of terms such as "objectivity" and "knowledge" as postmodernists have conceptualized them. Postpositivist realists assert both that (1) all observation and knowledge are theory mediated and that (2) a theory-mediated objective knowledge is both possible and desirable. They replace a simple correspondence theory of truth with a more dialectical causal theory of reference in which linguistic structures both shape our perceptions of and refer (in more or less partial and accurate ways) to causal features of a real world.[17] And they endorse a conception of objectivity as an ideal of inquiry rather than as a condition of absolute and achieved certainty.

What really distinguishes postpositivist realists from postmodernists (and, for that matter, positivists) is that realists have a different understanding of what "objectivity" is. The reason postmodernists deny the possibility of objectivity is that they have an impoverished view of what can count as objective. For postmodernists (as for positivists), objective knowledge is knowledge that is completely free of theoretically mediated bias. And because postmodernists rightly conclude that there is no such thing as a context-transcendent, subject-independent, and theoretically

16. While disagreement exists among those who would call themselves realists, the most sophisticated and nuanced versions of realism today entail a postpositivist conception of objectivity, together with an acknowledgment that the world cannot be reduced to our ideas about it. Indeed, realists argue, "the real world" is causally relevant to our epistemic endeavors, since it shapes and limits our knowledge of what is around us. For an exceptionally clear exposition on what makes a theory realist, see Collier, esp. pp. 6–7. See also Boyd, "How to Be a Moral Realist." For a discussion in this volume, see Alcoff's essay, esp. the section "Realisms."

17. For more on causal theories of reference, see chap. 2 of Mohanty, *Literary Theory,* esp. 66–72; Devitt and Sterelny, esp. pt. 2; Boyd, "Metaphor and Theory Change"; Putnam, "The Meaning of 'Meaning'" and "Explanation and Reference"; Field. For a short but helpful discussion in this volume, see Hames-Garcia's essay, esp. the section "Realism."

unmediated knowledge, they therefore conclude that there can be no such thing as objective knowledge.[18] Defenders of a postpositivist conception of objectivity, by contrast, stake out a less absolutist and more theoretically productive position. They suggest that objective knowledge can be built on an analysis of the different kinds of subjective or theoretical bias or interest. Such an analysis "distinguishes those biases that are limiting or counterproductive from those that are in fact necessary for knowledge, that are epistemically productive and useful" (Mohanty, "Can Our Values Be Objective?").[19] Realists thus do not shy away from making truth claims, but (following C. S. Peirce) they understand those claims to be "fallibilistic"—that is, like even the best discoveries of the natural sciences, open to revision on the basis of new or relevant information. In fact, it is realists' willingness to admit the (in principle, endless) possibility of error in the quest for knowledge that enables them to avoid positivist assumptions about certainty and unrevisability that inform the (postmodernist) skeptic's doubts about the possibility of arriving at a more accurate account of the world. Just as it is possible to be wrong about one's experience, postpositivist realists insist, so it is possible to arrive at more accurate interpretations of it.[20]

Another feature of realists' understanding of objectivity is their rejection of the positivist idea that objective knowledge should be sought by attempting to separate the realm of hard facts from the realm of

18. The postmodernist critic Barbara Hernstein Smith, for example, employs a positivist conception of objectivity in her discussion of the feminist legal scholar Robin West's response to Smith's earlier book, *Contingencies of Value*. In that discussion, Smith understands the "rhetoric of objectivism" as involving "the invocation of self-evident truth and objective fact, of intrinsic value and absolute right, of that which is universal, total, and transcendent" (5). Later in the book, Smith defends a standard for evaluating theories that is similar, in some crucial ways, to a postpositivist conception of objectivity. She suggests that theories can be "found better or worse than others in relation to measures such as applicability, coherence, connectibility, and so forth." She notes that these "measures are not objective in the classic sense, since they depend on matters of perspective, interpretation, and judgment, and will vary under different conditions" (77–78). She insists, however, that her standards are "non-'objective.'" Unfortunately, because Smith lacks a complex theory of reference, she is unable to fully exploit the implications of her insight regarding the epistemically normative significance of "applicability, coherence, and connectibility." After all, in order for a theory to be "applicable," or "connectible," it must be applicable or connectible *to*—that is, *with reference to*—something outside. As long as Smith retains her extreme and limited notions of objectivity and reference, she will be limited to the defensive posture she adopts in *Belief and Resistance* and will be unable to develop further even the contingent standards she thinks are necessary for deciding between different theories or political or ethical positions.

19. For a fuller discussion about postpositivist objectivity, see Mohanty, *Literary Theory*, esp. chap. 6.

20. For a fuller discussion in this volume of the relationship between error and objectivity, see Hau's essay.

values.[21] Because realists understand that all knowledge is the product of particular kinds of social practice, they recognize the causal constraints placed by the social and natural world on what humans can know. Moreover, because humans' biologically and temporally limited bodies enable and constrain what we are able to think, feel, and believe and because our bodies are themselves subject to the (more or less regular) laws of the natural and social world, realists know that what humans are able to think of as "good" is intimately related to (although not monocausally determined by) the social and natural "facts" of the world.[22] Consequently, realists contend, humans' subjective and evaluative judgments are neither fundamentally "arbitrary" nor merely "conventional." Rather, they are based on structures of belief that can be justified (or not) with reference to their own and others' well-being. These judgments and beliefs, thus, have the potential to contribute to objective knowledge about the world.

Over the past few years, a number of scholars have responded to Mohanty's work by taking up, from within a postpositivist realist framework, the challenge posed by the concept of identity.[23] These responses to Mohanty's work incorporate the best insights of challenges to older theories of identity (e.g., the social construction of identities, the challenge of multiplicity, the epistemic status of identity) while theorizing new and critical conceptions of objectivity, epistemic privilege, and universalism. In reply to postmodernist contentions that the process of identification is arbitrary and illusory, they demonstrate that such critiques fail to provide an adequate account of the causal and referential relationship between a subject's social location (e.g., race, class, gender, sexuality) and her identity. As part of this effort, the editors of this anthology have collected a number of these essays here to make this emerging "postpositivist realist" approach more accessible to academic and activist communities.

21. For more on the realist position regarding the necessary interdependence of facts and values, see Putnam, *Reason, Truth, and History,* esp. chap. 6; Putnam, *Realism with a Human Face,* esp. chaps. 9–12; Collier, esp. chap. 6; Mohanty, *Literary Theory,* esp. chap. 7; Nguyen (this vol.). Nguyen provides additional bibliographical references regarding the relationship of facts to values.

22. The social theorist Craig Calhoun, whose epistemological approach is substantially similar to the postpositivist realist approach we advocate in this volume, provides a pithy example of how knowledge is tied to social practice when he says that "it is not imaginable that Marx would have developed his theory of capitalism had he lived in the ninth and not the nineteenth century" (*Critical Social Theory* 86).

23. Published examples of this response include my essays, "Postmodernism, 'Realism,' and the Politics of Identity" (reprinted this vol.) and "Chicana Feminism and Postmodernist Theory," as well as Hames-García, "Dr. Gonzo's Carnival." Other essays that take a postpositivist realist approach to identity include Roman; Babbitt; Barad.

GOALS OF THE ANTHOLOGY

I am speaking my small piece of truth, as best as I can. . . .
[W]e each have only a piece of the truth. So here it is: I'm
putting it down for you to see if our fragments match anywhere, if our pieces, together, make another larger piece
of the truth that can be part of the map we are making together to show us the way to get to the longed-for world.

Minnie Bruce Pratt,
"Identity: Skin, Blood, Heart"

One of the intentions of this volume is to meet the challenges posed by
the concept of identity by introducing the postpositivist realist theory
of identity to scholars working in a variety of fields. In addition, this
volume seeks to contribute to the theory's development and elaboration. We do this by bringing together essays written by scholars in several disciplines (literature, philosophy, and history) and a variety of fields
of study (Chicana/o studies, Asian American studies, feminist theory,
African American literature, gay and lesbian studies, intellectual history,
postcolonial theory, political philosophy, and continental philosophy).
All the essays proceed from a postpositivist realist theoretical framework and elaborate one or more aspects of the theory, even as they explore the implications of the postpositivist realist approach for a variety
of issues and concerns. Some essays also explore the compatibility of postpositivist realism with other critical traditions. Readers will discover a
unique feature of this multiauthor book: each essay builds on the work
of Satya Mohanty and engages with the other essays to achieve a kind
of intellectual synthesis that is usually attained only in single-author
volumes.

The editors have chosen this systematic approach for several reasons.
As a practical matter, we sought to put together a volume on identity
appropriate for use in an upper-level undergraduate or graduate seminar in literary theory, feminist theory, political philosophy, literary criticism, women's studies, ethnic studies, or cultural studies. The volume
is also meant as a critical commentary on postmodernist (and essentialist) accounts of identity, since, in elaborating an alternative theory of identity, the essays highlight those features of the earlier theories that are inadequate. What we hope to make evident is that understandings of the
concept of identity derive from (often tacit) theoretical assumptions about
experience, knowledge, and the possibility and nature of objectivity.
Whether or not a critic thinks identities should be celebrated or subverted,

paid attention to or ignored, will depend to a great extent on the epistemological underpinnings of his or her work.

Moreover, by theorizing in a variety of contexts the political and epistemic value of identity and nonessentialist identity politics, the authors and editors of this book hope to advance discussions about identity in literary and cultural studies, social theory, and the humanities in general. We have chosen this interdisciplinary and multifield format to demonstrate the potential theoretical reach of the postpositivist realist theory of identity. Because our approach defines the concepts of identity, experience, and knowledge in ways that go beyond the understandings of those concepts widely accepted within the humanities today, it has the potential to bring the humanities back into conversation with the social and natural sciences. We thus position postpositivist realism to stand alongside competing theoretical paradigms—to show ours as a viable alternative approach to a variety of practical and theoretical issues. So, while this volume focuses on the concept of identity, the consequences of our work are potentially quite far-reaching and extend beyond the consideration of identity as such.

Although scholars in literary criticism and theory have been deeply influenced by strains of continental philosophy, the field as a whole has been unfamiliar with the theoretical contributions of analytic philosophy. As a result, some very productive approaches to understanding natural and social phenomena have been ignored or prematurely rejected by literary scholars. There have, of course, been exceptions to this trend: Paisley Livingston's 1988 book, *Literary Knowledge,* and George Levine's edited collection, *Realism and Representation* (which grew out of a 1989 conference of the same name), are two notable examples. Both volumes make valuable contributions to the field by exploring the relevance of various forms of critical (as opposed to positivist) realism to the practice of literary criticism. In *Literary Theory and the Claims of History,* Mohanty advances this project and extends it by demonstrating (in the essay reprinted in this volume) the relevance of a postpositivist realist approach for the question of identity. In "The Epistemic Status of Cultural Identity," Mohanty provides a nuanced reading of Toni Morrison's novel in which he shows how postpositivist objectivity, theory-mediated experience, and a causal theory of reference are relevant to something as personal and everyday as cultural identity. Transcending the limitations of both postmodernist and essentialist approaches, Mohanty makes a powerful argument for the epistemic significance of identity. He argues that we can adjudicate the validity and usefulness of different identities by viewing them as theoretical claims that attempt to account for causal features of the social world. In the process, he demonstrates that a good theory of identity does more than simply celebrate or dismiss the various uses of identity—rather, it enables cultural critics to explain where and why identities are problematic and where and why they are empowering.

One of the central claims of this anthology is that the realist theory of identity provides a better account of what identity is and how it is formed. In his essay, "Is There Something You Need to Tell Me? Coming Out and the Ambiguity of Experience," William S. Wilkerson demonstrates this and contributes to a postpositivist realist understanding of the relationship among social location, experience, and identity. He does this by presenting some phenomenological considerations about the experience of coming out as lesbian or gay. He shows how experience is not immediate and self-evident but mediated and ambiguous, so that it is possible to be wrong about one's experience as well as to arrive at more accurate interpretations of it. His discussion reveals how a "gay identity" is tied to existing social and political structures and enables an accurate understanding of a "pre-gay" individual's experience. Bridging the divide between contemporary continental philosophy and the Anglo-analytic philosophical tradition, Wilkerson explains how the realist theory avoids the pitfalls of foundationalist epistemologies without having to go the route of postmodernism.

Realists about identity believe that subjectivity or particularity is not antithetical to objective knowledge but is constitutive of it. From a realist perspective, particular (i.e., racial or gender) identities are not something to transcend or subvert but something we need to engage with and attend to. This necessity is elegantly demonstrated in Michael R. Hames-García's essay, "'Who Are Our Own People?' Challenges for a Theory of Social Identity." Hames-García seeks to understand the challenges made to the theorization of identity by "multiplicity," for example, the multiple construction of the self by race, gender, and sexuality. He develops the notion of "restriction" to describe the social processes by which selves come to be (falsely) understood in relation to a single aspect of identity. In showing how a postpositivist realist theory of identity better accounts for multiplicity than do other theories of identity, Hames-García indicates the knowledge-generating value of paying attention to how certain identity categories are privileged and others are occluded. He shows that realism provides a subtler, more complex, and more complete picture of how any given identity is formed—a picture that includes that identity's excluded other, its formative context, and its historical character and social function. Hames-García includes in his essay realist readings of Michael Nava's book *The Hidden Law* and the House of Color video *I Object* in which he demonstrates that, when their messages are taken seriously, cultural productions by people of color can offer transcultural insights into ethical questions of human value, community, and solidarity.

Realists also contend that knowledge is not disembodied, or somewhere "out there" to be had, but rather that it comes into being in and through embodied selves. In other words, humans generate knowledge, and our ability to do so is causally dependent on both our cognitive capacities and our historical and social locations. In my own essay, "Postmodernism, 'Realism,' and the Politics of Identity: Cherríe Moraga and Chicana Feminism," I draw on Mohanty's work to extract the basic claims of a postpositivist realist theory of identity. I then situate and effectively "test" the realist theory within the realm of Chicana/o studies by articulating a realist account of Chicana identity that theorizes the connections among social location, experience, and cultural identity. Through an analysis of Moraga's "theory in the flesh," I show how the historically constituted social categories that make up an individual's particular social location are causally relevant for the experiences she will have and demonstrate how identities both condition and are conditioned by individuals' interpretations of their experiences. I then develop the implications of the realist theory of identity for the notion of epistemic privilege and use it to argue for the significance of the embodied knowledge of women of color.

A consequence of the realist acknowledgment of embodied knowledge is a recognition of the importance of individual agency. In his essay, "Who Says Who Says? The Epistemological Grounds for Agency in Liberatory Political Projects," Brent R. Henze argues that a discussion of agency, which is primarily the province of individuals, should not drop out of any discussion of epistemic privilege. He opposes essentialist conceptions of identity—in which the common experiences of the group take priority over the unknown or unique experiences of individual members—on the grounds that such conceptions fail to develop the most accurate frameworks for interpreting experience precisely because they deny individual agency. Using as examples the project entailed in *This Bridge Called My Back* and the feminist consciousness-raising group described by the philosopher Naomi Scheman, Henze shows that it is, in fact, individual agency that provides the most epistemically and politically effective grounds for the collective agency of an identity group. The essay concludes with a programmatic analysis of the role "outsiders" can play in liberation struggles. In keeping with his general project, Henze argues that this role must be one that acknowledges its own position vis-à-vis structures of oppression but that also can participate in the collaborative process without impinging on the agency of oppressed actors to speak for themselves.

The elaboration of the way humans develop reliable knowledge about themselves and their world presented by the essays in this volume deepens the realist understanding of the link between "facts" and "values." In her essay, "'It Matters to Get the Facts Straight': Joy Kogawa, Realism, and Objectivity of Values," Minh T. Nguyen offers a realist reading of Joy Kogawa's novels *Obasan* and *Itsuka* to explore the affective and collective dimension of objective knowledge. Nguyen argues that much recent criticism of Asian American literature has tacitly accepted certain postmodernist premises (including a radically skeptical stance toward the epistemic status of experience) that have resulted in crucial misreadings of many Asian American texts, particularly those of Kogawa. Against postmodernist interpretations, Nguyen reads the uncertainty of Naomi (the central character) not as leading to a postmodernist skepticism regarding her ability to know the world but rather as being a necessary position in a dialectic that leads her to a fuller and more objective understanding of her situation. According to Nguyen, Kogawa's novels offer a postpositivist conception of objectivity, especially objectivity of knowledge and values. Using Kogawa's work as an example, Nguyen argues that the personal experiences and racialized perspectives of people of color should be seen as significant social and political theories—and that, as theories, they provide fallible normative accounts of social reality and values.

The insights generated by a postpositivist realist approach to culture and identity present interesting implications for how we might act in the service of progressive social change. In her essay, "Racial Authenticity and White Separatism: The Future of Racial Program Housing on College Campuses," Amie A. Macdonald addresses the controversy surrounding racial program housing on college and university campuses. She traces arguments in opposition to racial program housing to misleading theoretical premises that fail to elucidate the links among cultural identity, objectivity, and knowledge. Grounding her argument in liberatory struggles such as the civil rights movement, Macdonald revisits the unique features of race-based program housing by providing a post-positivist realist examination of the political and epistemic significance of self-segregation and cultural identity. She argues that we can better understand the role ethnic community houses play—not only in regard to the affective needs of ethnic community members but also in regard to the epistemic needs of racially diverse university communities—when we remember that such houses can foster the preservation of alternative communities of meaning. In the course of her argument, Macdonald makes two crucial points: (1) that the existence of a plurality of perspectives secures the continued diversity of interpretations of the social world and ensures a richer array of knowledges from which to construct social, political, aesthetic, spiritual, and scientific accounts of our experience; and (2) that as long as social subordination is a central feature of our society, the intellectual analyses of people who are marginalized and oppressed are crucial to an accurate account of social power and the possibility of political transformation. On the basis of these two contentions, Macdonald defends voluntary self-segregation of people of color as the best social condition in a white-dominated society for creating alternative and affirmative cultures.

One of the most troubling issues for progressive political and social activists, especially for those influenced by poststructuralism, has remained the problem of representing, or speaking for, others. Caroline S. Hau addresses this issue directly in her essay, "On Representing Others: Intellectuals, Pedagogy, and the Uses of Error." She begins by tracing a theoretical trajectory through the writings of Mao, Fanon, and Cabral to show that the role these three thinkers assign to the intellectual in a struggle for liberation is informed by varying assumptions about the possibility of representational error—the ineradicable risk of intellectual activity. Hau connects this problematization of intellectual authority within the discourse of decolonization to broader contemporary concerns, commonly articulated by poststructuralist and postmodernist theorists, about the impossibility of objectivity and the social constructedness of truth. She argues that a postpositivist realist account of knowledge (with its corresponding accounts of objectivity, experience, and error) provides a way of resolving some of these problems by transforming error into an important component of the evaluation of theory-dependent knowledges. Hau concludes by suggesting that the task of the progressive intellectual is not to abjure the responsibility of representing others but to work toward the gradual identification and accommodation of error by continually interacting with (and learning about) the people she hopes to represent or influence. Only through her social practices and her active theorizing about the world, Hau argues, can an intellectual develop a more accurate understanding of how she is related to the others she is attempting to represent.

The methodological implications of postpositivist realism for intellectual inquiry are usefully demonstrated in John H. Zammito's essay, "Reading 'Experience': The Debate in Intellectual History among Scott, Toews, and LaCapra." Zammito draws on the postpositivist conception of objectivity he finds in Mohanty's work to suggest a workable and defensible standard of historical inquiry that could form a shared horizon of understanding for intellectual history. He begins by resituating the historian Joan Scott's influential essay "The Evidence of Experience" within the intellectual and historical milieu out of which it emerged. By putting it back in dialogue with John Toews's earlier essay, "Intellectual History after the Linguistic Turn" (to which Scott was responding), Zammito makes a crucial contribution to the debate in intellectual history concerning the significance of experience to the formulation of shared disciplinary standards. He takes issue with Scott's hyperbolic poststructuralist claims about experience in order to defend a postpositivist conception of objectivity that allows both for the "historicization of the historical subject" and for the dialogic search for a commonality of critical appraisal among historians. He argues, contra Scott, that the practice of attending to the linguistic constitution of experience need not entail rejecting the possibility that experiences can provide evidence either about the past or about the world we currently share. In the process, Zammito proposes a postpositivist standard of empirical inquiry that could provide points of mediation between his own hermeneutic-historicist concerns and the poststructuralist approach of Dominick LaCapra.

In the volume's final essay, "Who's Afraid of Identity Politics?" Linda Martín Alcoff makes a philosophical clarification and defense of the new realist account of identity developed by the other essays in the anthology. By tracing what "went wrong," that is, how an antiessentialist theoretical trend created a situation in which the links among identity, politics, and knowledge became increasingly nebulous until it looked as if none existed at all, Alcoff clarifies what is metaphysically and epistemologically in dispute between theorists who have been associated with postmodernism and those who call themselves realists. By discussing approaches to the self developed by Hegel, Freud, Sartre, and Foucault, among others, that have had a major influence on current accounts of identity, Alcoff helps us to understand how the critique of identity in contemporary literary and cultural criticism can be traced to a desire to deflect the power of the other over the self. She concludes that the solution to essentialism is not the rejection of identity but a more robust formulation of identity such as that offered by a postpositivist realist theory.

FUTURE DIRECTIONS

As we discover (or uncover) things a theory as formulated
did not know about or attend to, we have occasion to
further elaborate or develop the theory in the light of
what we now know. Sometimes a theory can absorb new
things; sometimes not. Whichever, we do best if we make
the effort and see what happens to the theory under strain.
Its success may suggest we have misunderstood the theory
all along. Its failure can only instruct if we are scrupulous
in finding the source of the fault. The fact that a theory as
traditionally understood omits something should be the
beginning, not the end, of inquiry.

Barbara Herman,
The Practice of Moral Judgment

Realists about identity have begun the difficult project of figuring out not only which identity claims (and identities) they should accept as justified but also what related methodological and political strategies might lead to progressive outcomes. In the process, they have had to abandon the role of the skeptic to the postmodernist, and the mantle of certainty to the essentialist, in order to undertake a difficult and uncertain task. The task is difficult not only because to defend identity, as Alcoff reminds us in her contribution to this volume, is to swim upstream of strong academic currents but also and primarily because deciding between different identity claims is a deeply contextual and theoretically and empirically complex enterprise. Judging well requires an appreciation for the situatedness and embodiedness of knowledge, together with an ability to abstract from relevant cultural particularities. The task is uncertain because, as Hau reminds us in her essay in this volume, error is the ineradicable risk of intellectual activity: to posit something is to risk being wrong about it. But to say either that all identities are epistemically valid or that none of them are is to take "the easy way out" (Mohanty, *Literary Theory* 238). Realists understand that as long as identities remain economically, politically, and socially significant, determining the justifiability of particular identity claims will remain a necessary part of progressive politics. Taking the easy way out is thus not something they are willing to do.

The contributors to this volume do not imagine that we will have the last word on matters of identity. We do, however, believe that this volume succeeds in presenting an alternative theory of identity that solves some of the key problems of current theories of identity. Moreover, we believe that the postpositivist realist epistemology that underlies our conception of identity has the potential to push intellectual inquiry (especially in the humanities) in theoretically productive directions. In the spirit of cooperation, then, we invite our readers to take seriously our various claims and to show us where we—individually or collectively—might amend, revise, or advance our thinking about the task we have undertaken.

WORKS CITED

Abelove, Henry, Michele Aina Barale, and David M. Halperin, eds. *The Lesbian and Gay Studies Reader.* New York: Routledge, 1993.

Alarcón, Norma. "The Theoretical Subject(s) of *This Bridge Called My Back* and Anglo-American Feminism." *Criticism in the Borderlands: Studies in Chicano Literature, Culture, and Ideology.* Ed. Hector Calderón and José David Saldívar. Durham: Duke University Press, 1990. 28–39.

Alcoff, Linda. "Cultural Feminism versus Post-structuralism: The Identity Crisis in Feminist Theory." *Signs: Journal of Women in Culture and Society* 13.31 (1988): 405–36.

Alurista, et al. "El Plan de Aztlán." *Documents of the Chicano Struggle.* Rpt. New York: Pathfinder Press, 1971. 4–6.

Anderson, Perry. *The Origins of Postmodernity.* London: Verso, 1998.

Anzaldúa, Gloria, ed. *Making Face, Making Soul—Haciendo Caras: Creative and Critical Perspectives by Women of Color.* San Francisco: Aunt Lute Books, 1990.

Appiah, Kwame Anthony, and Henry Louis Gates, Jr., eds. *Identities.* Special issue. *Critical Inquiry* 18.4 (1992).

Babbitt, Susan E. "Identity, Knowledge, and Toni Morrison's *Beloved:* Questions about Understanding Racism." *Hypatia* 9.3 (1994): 1–18.

Barad, Karen. "Meeting the Universe Halfway: Realism and Social Construction without Contradiction." *Feminism, Science, and the Philosophy of Science.* Ed. Lynn Hankinson Nelson and Jack Nelson. Dordrecht: Kluwer Academic Publishers, 1996. 161–94.

Best, Steven, and Douglas Kellner, eds. *The Postmodern Turn.* New York: Guilford Press, 1997.

Boyd, Richard N. "How to Be a Moral Realist." *Essays on Moral Realism.* Ed. Geoffrey Sayre-McCord. Ithaca: Cornell University Press, 1988. 181–228.

———. "Metaphor and Theory Change: What Is a 'Metaphor' a Metaphor For?"

Metaphor and Thought. Ed. Andrew Ortony. 2d ed. Cambridge: Cambridge University Press, 1993. 481–532.

Brown, Wendy. *States of Injury: Power and Freedom in Late Modernity.* Princeton: Princeton University Press, 1995.

Butler, Judith. "Contingent Foundations: Feminism and the Question of 'Postmodernism.'" *Feminists Theorize the Political.* Ed. Judith Butler and Joan Scott. New York: Routledge, 1992. 3–21.

———. *Gender Trouble: Feminism and the Subversion of Identity.* New York: Routledge, 1990.

Calhoun, Craig. *Critical Social Theory: Culture, History, and the Challenge of Difference.* Cambridge, MA: Blackwell, 1995.

———, ed. *Social Theory and the Politics of Identity.* Oxford: Blackwell, 1994.

Carter, Stephen. *Reflections of an Affirmative Action Baby.* New York: Basic-Books, 1991.

Collier, Andrew. *Critical Realism: An Introduction to Roy Bhaskar's Philosophy.* London: Verso, 1994.

Culler, Jonathan. *On Deconstruction: Theory and Criticism after Structuralism.* Ithaca: Cornell University Press, 1982.

Dean, Jodi. *Solidarity of Strangers: Feminism after Identity Politics.* Berkeley: University of California Press, 1996.

de Lauretis, Teresa. "Fem/Les Scramble." *Cross Purposes: Lesbians, Feminists, and the Limits of Alliance.* Ed. Dana Heller. Bloomington: Indiana University Press, 1997. 42–48.

Devitt, Michael, and Kim Sterelny, eds. *Language and Reality: An Introduction to the Philosophy of Language.* 2d ed. Cambridge, MA: MIT Press, 1999.

Eagleton, Terry. *The Illusions of Postmodernism.* London: Blackwell, 1996.

Field, Hartry. "Theory Change and the Indeterminacy of Reference." *Journal of Philosophy* 70 (1973): 462–81.

Fuss, Diana. *Essentially Speaking: Feminism, Nature & Difference.* New York: Routledge, 1989.

Gates, Henry Louis, ed. *"Race," Writing, and Difference.* Chicago: University of Chicago Press, 1985.

Hames-García, Michael R. "Dr. Gonzo's Carnival: The Testimonial Satires of Oscar Zeta Acosta, Chicano Lawyer." *American Literature* 72.3 (2000).

Harvey, David. *The Condition of Postmodernity: An Enquiry Into the Origins of Cultural Change.* New York: Blackwell, 1989.

Herman, Barbara. *The Practice of Moral Judgment.* Cambridge, MA: Harvard University Press, 1993.

hooks, bell. "Essentialism and Experience." *American Literary History* 3.1 (1991): 172–83.

Jameson, Fredric. *Postmodernism, or, The Cultural Logic of Late Capitalism.* Durham: Duke University Press, 1991.

Jenkins, Keith. Introduction. *The Postmodern History Reader.* London: Routledge, 1997.

LaCapra, Dominick, ed. *The Bounds of Race.* Ithaca: Cornell University Press, 1991.

Levine, George, ed. *Realism and Representation: Essays on the Problem of Re-*

alism in Relation to Science, Literature, and Culture. Madison: University of Wisconsin Press, 1993.

Livingston, Paisley. *Literary Knowledge: Humanistic Inquiry and the Philosophy of Science.* Ithaca: Cornell University Press, 1988.

Lugones, Maria. "Purity, Impurity, and Separation." *Signs: Journal of Women in Culture and Society* (Winter 1994): 458–79.

Martin, Biddy, and Chandra Talpade Mohanty. "Feminist Politics: What's Home Got to Do with It?" *Feminist Studies / Critical Studies.* Ed. Teresa de Lauretis. Bloomington: Indiana University Press, 1986. 191–212.

Martínez, Elizabeth. *De Colores Means All of Us: Latina Views for a Multi-Colored Century.* Cambridge, MA: South End Press, 1998.

Michaels, Walter Benn. "Race into Culture: A Critical Genealogy of Cultural Identity." *Critical Inquiry* 18.4 (1992): 655–85.

McCarthy, Cameron, and Warren Crichlow, eds. *Race, Identity, and Representation in Education.* New York: Routledge, 1993.

McGowan, John. *Postmodernism and Its Critics.* Ithaca: Cornell University Press, 1991.

Mohanty, Chandra Talpade, Ann Russo, and Lourdes Torres, eds. *Third World Women and the Politics of Feminism.* Bloomington: Indiana University Press, 1991.

Mohanty, Satya P. "Can Our Values Be Objective? On Ethics, Aesthetics, and Progressive Politics." *New Literary History* (forthcoming).

———. *Literary Theory and the Claims of History: Postmodernism, Objectivity, Multicultural Politics.* Ithaca: Cornell University Press, 1997.

Moraga, Cherríe, and Gloria Anzaldúa, eds. *This Bridge Called My Back: Writings by Radical Women of Color.* New York: Kitchen Table: Women of Color Press, 1983.

Moya, Paula M. L. "Chicana Feminism and Postmodernist Theory." *Signs: Journal of Women in Culture and Society* 26.2 (2001).

———. "Postmodernism, 'Realism,' and the Politics of Identity: Cherríe Moraga and Chicana Feminism." *Feminist Genealogies, Colonial Legacies, Democratic Futures.* Ed. M. Jacqui Alexander and Chandra Talpade Mohanty. New York: Routledge, 1997. 125–50, 379–85. [Reprinted as chapter 2 in this volume.]

Nicholson, Linda J., ed. *Feminism/Postmodernism.* New York: Routledge, 1990.

Nicholson, Linda J., and Nancy Fraser. "Social Criticism without Philosophy: An Encounter between Feminism and Postmodernism." *Feminism/Postmodernism.* Ed. Linda J. Nicholson. New York: Routledge, 1990. 19–38.

Nicholson, Linda, and Steven Seidman. Introduction. *Social Postmodernism: Beyond Identity Politics.* Ed. Linda Nicholson and Steven Seidman. Cambridge: Cambridge University Press. 1–35.

Pratt, Minnie Bruce. "Identity: Skin, Blood, Heart." *Yours in Struggle: Three Feminist Perspectives on Anti-Semitism and Racism.* Ed. Elly Bulkin, Minnie Bruce Pratt, and Barbara Smith. Ithaca: Firebrand Books, 1988. 11–63.

Putnam, Hilary. "Explanation and Reference." *Mind, Language, and Reality.* Cambridge: Cambridge University Press, 1975.

———. "The Meaning of 'Meaning.'" *Mind, Language, and Reality.* Cambridge: Cambridge University Press, 1975.

————. *Realism with a Human Face.* Cambridge, MA: Harvard University Press, 1990.

————. *Reason, Truth, and History.* Cambridge: Cambridge University Press, 1981.

Rodriguez, Richard. *Hunger of Memory: The Education of Richard Rodriguez.* New York: Bantam Books, 1983.

Roman, Leslie. "White Is a Color! White Defensiveness, Postmodernism, and Anti-racist Pedagogy." *Race, Identity, and Representation in Education.* Ed. Cameron McCarthy and Warren Crichlow. New York: Routledge, 1993. 71–88.

Sedgwick, Eve. *Epistemology of the Closet.* Berkeley: University of California Press, 1990.

Singer, Linda. "Feminism and Postmodernism." *Feminists Theorize the Political.* Ed. Judith Butler and Joan Scott. New York: Routledge, 1992. 464–75.

Smith, Barbara, ed. *Home Girls: A Black Feminist Anthology.* New York: Kitchen Table: Women of Color Press, 1983.

Smith, Barbara Hernstein. *Belief and Resistance: Dynamics of Contemporary Intellectual Controversy.* Cambridge, MA: Harvard University Press, 1997.

————. *Contingencies of Value: Alternative Perspectives for Critical Theory.* Cambridge, MA: Harvard University Press, 1988.

Spelman, Elizabeth. *Inessential Woman: Problems of Exclusion in Feminist Thought.* Boston: Beacon Press, 1988.

Spivak, Gayatri Chakravorty. "Can the Subaltern Speak?" *Marxism and the Interpretation of Culture.* Ed. Cary Nelson and Lawrence Grossberg. Urbana: University of Illinois Press, 1988. 271–313.

————. "Subaltern Studies: Deconstructing Historiography." *In Other Worlds: Essays in Cultural Politics.* New York: Routledge, 1987.

Steele, Shelby. *The Content of Our Character: A New Vision of Race in America.* New York: St. Martin's Press, 1990.

Suleri, Sara. "Woman Skin Deep: Feminism and the Postcolonial Condition." *Critical Inquiry* 18.4 (1992): 756–69.

Waugh, Patricia. Introduction. *Postmodernism: A Reader.* Ed. Patricia Waugh. London: Edward Arnold, 1992. 1–10.

Weinberg, Steven. *Dreams of a Final Theory.* New York: Pantheon Books, 1993.

Zammito, John H. "Are We Being Theoretical Yet? The New Historicism, the New Philosophy of History, and 'Practicing Historians.'" *Journal of Modern History* 65 (December 1993): 783–814.

THE REALIST THEORY OF IDENTITY

AND THE PREDICAMENT

OF POSTMODERNISM

The Epistemic Status of Cultural Identity

On Beloved *and the Postcolonial Condition*

Satya P. Mohanty

Several closely related practical and theoretical questions concerning identity emerge from current debates about cultural diversity. If multiculturalism is to be a goal of educational and political institutions, we need a workable notion of how a social group is unified by a common culture, as well as the ability to identify genuine cultural differences (and similarities) across groups. Whether cultures are inherited or consciously and deliberately created, basic problems of definition—who belongs where or with whom, who belongs and who doesn't—are unavoidable the moment we translate our dreams of diversity into social visions and agendas. Debates about minority literatures, for instance, often get bogged down in tedious disputes over genuineness or authenticity, but it is difficult to eliminate these disputes entirely. That is because they point to what is in many cases a practical problem: who can be trusted to represent the real interests of the group without fear of betrayal or misrepresentation? Every "obvious" answer (such as "It'll have to be one of us, of course!") begs the question, indicating why our views about cultural identity always involve theoretical presuppositions. The most basic questions about identity call for a more general reexamination of the relation between personal experience and public meanings—subjective

This chapter has been excerpted from Satya P. Mohanty's *Literary Theory and the Claims of History*. An earlier version, without the concluding remarks, appeared in *Cultural Critique* 24 (Spring 1993): 41–80.

choices and evaluations, on the one hand, and objective social location, on the other.

So it is not surprising that recent theoretical writings on cultural identity have focused on the status of our personal experiences, examining the claims to representativeness we might make on their behalf. The two dominant alternative views on cultural identity—the view associated with identity politics and characterized as essentialism and the position of postmodernism—are in fact seen as providing conflicting definitions of identity because they understand the relation between the experiences of social actors and the theoretical construct we call "their identity" very differently. Simply put, the essentialist view would be that the identity common to members of a social group is stable and more or less unchanging, since it is based on the experiences they share. Opponents of essentialism often find this view seriously misleading, since it ignores historical changes and glosses over internal differences within a group by privileging only the experiences that are common to everyone. Postmodernists in particular insist that identities are fabricated and constructed rather than self-evidently deduced from experience, since—they claim—experience cannot be a source of objective knowledge.[1]

My central task here is to show, first, that the relation between experience and identity is a genuine philosophical or theoretical issue, and, second, that there is a better way to think about identity than might be suggested by the alternatives provided by the essentialists and the postmodernists. I develop this view by examining what I shall call the epistemic status of cultural identity. After outlining some of the key theoretical issues implied in discussions of identity, I explore these questions further through an analysis of Toni Morrison's remarkable novel, *Beloved,* which is directly concerned with the relations among personal experience, social meanings, and cultural identities.

One of the main components of the postmodernist case against identity politics is the charge that "experience" is not a self-evident or even reliable source of knowledge and cannot be seen as grounding a social identity. Postmodernists typically warn against the desire to consider ex-

---

1. Diana Fuss, in *Essentially Speaking,* provides an intelligent discussion of various kinds of essentialism and identity politics. Since my focus here is primarily on postmodernism, I have found it expedient to initially accept the simple definition of identity politics in terms of an ahistorical essentialism. Later, however, I attempt to answer some of the fundamental questions raised by proponents of identity politics (e.g., the status of experience, the epistemological privilege that the oppressed might have, etc.) in terms that are not available through the postmodernist-essentialist debate as it is currently understood, even in resourceful reinterpretations such as the one Fuss provides.

perience a foundation of other social meanings; they point out that personal experiences are basically rather unstable or slippery, and since they can only be interpreted in terms of linguistic or other signs, they must be heir to all the exegetical and interpretive problems that accompany social signification. This specifically poststructuralist view contains an epistemological thesis. Jonathan Culler's formulation of the thesis in his 1982 discussion of experience and "reading" is one that is most frequently cited: "'Experience' always has [a] divided, duplicitous character: it has always already occurred and yet is still to be produced—an indispensable point of reference, yet never simply there" (*On Deconstruction* 63). This claim, with its Derridean allusions (Derrida usually couches it as a critique of specifically idealist or phenomenological notions of experience), leads to the following conclusion about the relation between experience and identity: "For a woman to read as a woman is not to repeat an identity or an experience that is given but to play a role she constructs with reference to her identity as a woman, which is also a construct, so that the series can continue: a woman reading as a woman reading as a woman. The noncoincidence reveals an interval, a division within woman or within any reading subject and the 'experience' of that subject" (64; emphasis added).[2]

I think, however, that this argument about the relation between experience and cultural identity can be best appreciated as part of the more general suspicion of foundationalism in contemporary thought, for there is nothing peculiar to experience as such which warrants its rejection on epistemological grounds. The critique of epistemological foundationalism contains the suggestion that we naturalize epistemology, that is, ex-

---

2. For a selective survey of the various critiques of experience in modern European philosophy, see Jardine 145–55. Jardine is however not too helpful when it comes to basic distinctions such as that between Hegel's *Erfahrung* and the ordinary idea of everyday experience Culler and other poststructuralist critics wish to question. For a useful account of some of the responses to Culler's position, see Fuss 23–37. For a postmodernist position on identity that draws on a variety of sources and identifies itself as "postcolonial," see Bhabha 183–209; the relevant epistemological claims (as I understand them) are presented on pp. 191–94.

The current skepticism about the claims of experience can be traced back to Nietzsche, especially his critique of idealist notions of consciousness and subjectivity as self-sufficient and self-authorizing (see, e.g., *The Will to Power* 263–67, secs. 477–80). Nietzsche's central argument is an antipositivist one about the theory dependence of experience and facts. Whether recognition of theory dependence should lead to a denial of objectivity is one of the main questions I am addressing here. Postmodernists say that it does; Nietzsche was at least ambiguous on the subject. For Nietzsche's conception of objectivity (through the mediation of theories or perspectives), see *On the Genealogy of Morals* 555, Third Essay, sec. 12, a conception that is compatible with the antirelativist theory I am outlining here.

amine the production, justification, and regulation of belief as social processes. Many antifoundationalists contend that the growth of empirical knowledge about the practices and protocols of justification in the various sciences ought to shape our understanding of epistemological questions. In this sense, neither a "method" of justification nor some privileged class of foundational beliefs can be seen as existing outside the social contexts of inquiry.[3]

I suggest that we consider the postmodernist critique of identity politics in analogous terms, as a critique of experiential foundationalism. If we were not to specify the critique in this way, the general postmodernist skepticism toward experience could lead to the strange conclusion that the experiences of social actors are irrelevant to explain, say, their moral or political growth. Alternatively, we could be led to conclude that moral or political change (growth or decline) is never real because it is tied to experience and can thus never be justified. The antifoundationalist thesis I have tried to retrieve from postmodernism brings into focus the accurate and damaging critique that postmodernists can make of identity politics, but by itself it does not entail either of the two extreme conclusions to which their skepticism can lead us. The naturalist-realist account of experience I defend here is neither foundationalist nor skeptical; it maintains that experience, properly interpreted, can yield reliable and genuine knowledge, just as it can point up instances and sources of real mystification. Central to this account is the claim that the experience of social subjects has a cognitive component. Experiences can be "true" or "false," can be evaluated as justified or illegitimate in relation to the subject and his world, for "experience" refers very simply to the variety of ways humans process information. (This conception carries none of the normative baggage that comes with Hegelian *Erfahrung*, which is always tied to a particular model of ethical development. Neither does it presuppose, as Dilthey's conception of *Erlebnis* does, a necessary opposition between "lived experience" and scientific thinking.) It is on the basis of this revised understanding of experience that we can construct a realist theory of social or cultural identity, in which experiences would not serve as foundations because of their self-evident authenticity but would provide some of the raw material with which we construct identities. As we shall see, to say that experiences and identities are constructed

3. For a brief statement of the naturalistic view of philosophy as "continuous with science" rather than an "a priori propaedutic or groundwork for science," see Quine, *Ontological Relativity* 126–28.

is not to prejudge the question of their epistemic status.[4] Radical skepticism about the cognitive implications of cultural identity is not the only alternative to an ahistorical essentialism.

A REALIST APPROACH TO CULTURE AND POLITICS

The first claim I wish to advance is that "personal experience" is socially and "theoretically" constructed, and it is precisely in this mediated way that it yields knowledge. Let me develop this idea by drawing in part on work done by feminist theorists in the last decade and a half, beginning with an insightful essay by the philosopher Naomi Scheman.[5]

Writing from an explicitly anti-individualist perspective on such things as emotions and feelings, Scheman explains how the notion of our emotions as our own "inner" possessions is fundamentally misleading. She focuses on the anger that women who have been members of feminist consciousness-raising groups often come to feel. This anger, Scheman says, should not be seen as a fully formed emotion that was waiting to be released or expressed in the context of the group. Rather, the emotion becomes what it is through the mediation of the social and emotional environment that the consciousness-raising group provides. Part of what constitutes this environment is an alternative narrative or ac-

4. I think it is a belief in the cognitive component of experience (and the knowledge it can give us about our social location) that is behind Houston Baker's impatience with Anthony Appiah's "debunking" account of the reality of race (both in Gates, "Race," Writing, and Difference). Appiah's critique of racial essentialism is not based on postmodernist premises, but his response to Baker on the question of experience is evasive (see "The Conservation of 'Race'" 39–44) and might point to a vagueness in his conception of identity.

One way of evaluating my theory of experience and identity is to see how it responds to the challenge the historian Joan Scott has formulated quite well: "Experience is not a word we can do without, although it is tempting, given its usage to essentialize identity and reify the subject, to abandon it altogether. . . . But [experience] serves as a way of talking about what happened, of establishing difference and similarity, of claiming knowledge. . . . Given the ubiquity of the term, it seems to me more useful to work with it, to analyze its operations and redefine its meaning. . . . The study of experience . . . must call into question its originary status in historical explanation" (37). Scott points out that postmodernist attacks on experience are a critique of a certain kind of epistemological view. I am not sure, however, that I agree with her assumption that a "genuinely non-foundational[ist] history" is possible only "when historians take as their project not the reproduction and transmission of knowledge said to be arrived at through experience, but the analysis of the production of that knowledge itself" (37). I would suggest that once we acknowledge the cognitive status of experience, as well as the way it is necessarily theory dependent, we can conceive of legitimate ways of reproducing and transmitting "knowledge said to be arrived at through experience." As will be clear from what I argue below, this is in fact the best way to understand the "epistemic privilege" of, say, the oppressed, as well as how it demands hermeneutical respect from the historian.

5. See Scheman, "Anger and the Politics of Naming."

count of the individual's relationship with the world, and these alternative accounts are unavoidably theoretical. They involve notions of what a woman is supposed to be angry about, what she should not tolerate, what is worth valuing, notions that are not merely moral but also social-theoretical in nature. They imply social visions and critiques of what exists; at the very least they suggest that it is perfectly okay to feel dissatisfied about certain relationships and social arrangements. Scheman's point is that in many important instances such alternative accounts and notions help organize inchoate or confused feelings to produce an emotion that is experienced more directly and fully. It follows, then, that this new emotion, say, anger, and the ways it is experienced are not purely personal or individual. A necessary part of its form and shape is determined by the nonindividual social meanings that the theories and accounts supply. It would be false to say that this emotion is the individual's own "inner" possession and that she alone has "privileged access" to its meaning or significance ("Anger" 179). Rather, our emotions provide evidence of the extent to which even our deepest personal experiences are socially constructed, mediated by visions and values that are "political" in nature, that refer outward to the world beyond the individual.

> The structure that consciousness-raising groups provide for the interpretation of feelings and behavior is overtly political; it should be immediately obvious that one is presented with a particular way of making sense of one's experience, a way intimately linked with certain controversial political views. Consciousness-raising groups are not, however, unique in this respect. What they are is unusually honest: the political framework is explicit (though often vague) and openly argued for. The alternative is not "a clear space in which to get your head together" but a hidden political framework that pretends not to be one. (186)

There are different ways of making sense of an experience, and the way we make sense of it can in fact create a new experience.

Consider Scheman's example, Alice, who joins a consciousness-raising group and in the safe and supportive environment provided by other women like her learns to recognize that her depression and guilt, though sincerely felt, may not be legitimate. In fact, they hide from her her real needs and feelings, as well as the real nature of her situation. "The guilt and depression," the group might argue and Alice might come to acknowledge, "are a response to and a cover for those other feelings, notably feelings of anger. Alice is urged to recognize her anger as legitimate and justifiable in this situation" (177). Here is where the "political" nature of the views Alice is now asked to ponder comes in: she is not seen as merely bringing to the surface something she, as a lone individual, knew and felt all along. Rather, her emotion (the anger) is constituted in part by the "views" about the world, about herself in it, and the details of what is acceptable and unacceptable in this new theoretical picture. She comes to experience anger by reinterpreting her old feelings of depression, guilt, and so on, but she does so unavoidably with the aid of theory, an alternative, socially produced construction of herself and the world. Now, "we may describe [Alice] as having discovered that she had been angry, though she hadn't previously recognized it. She would, in fact, have denied it if she were asked: 'Why *should* I be angry?'" "It is significant," Scheman goes on, "that a denial that one is angry often takes the form of a denial that one would be justified in being angry. Thus one's discovery of anger can often occur not from focusing on one's feelings but from a political redescription of one's situation" (177). The reason we say that Alice "discovers" she has been angry is that the anger underlay her vague or confused feelings of depression or guilt; now it organizes these feelings, giving them coherence and clarity. And our judgment that the anger is deeper than the depression or guilt is derived from (and corroborated by) our understanding of Alice's changing personal and social situation, an understanding that is based in part on a "theory."[6]

Here we discern what might be the strongest argument against the essentialist picture of cultural identity. The constructed nature of experience shows why there is no guarantee that my experiences will lead me to some common core of values or beliefs that link me with every other member of my cultural group. Our experiences do not have self-evident meanings, for they are in part theoretical affairs, and our access to our remotest personal feelings is dependent on social narratives, paradigms, and even ideologies. In fact, drawing on a Nietzschean theme, the postmodernist might declare that we need to go further, that the kind of theory dependence I have just identified leads to a radical perspectivism or relativism. When we choose among these alternative ways of organizing and interpreting experience, we make a purely arbitrary choice, determined by our social locations or our prerational ideological commitments. "Experience" remains unstable and unreliable. Why, then, speak

---

6. This theory-mediated process of coming to acknowledge one's genuine feelings is central to any form of political consciousness raising. The antiracist work done by the "freedom schools" in the South also drew on normative theories of personhood and racial justice in order to enable victims of racism to accurately interpret their experiences and their needs. Such "interpretations" are, as I hope to suggest, never purely intellectual.

of the cognitive component of personal experience, as though we might be able to glean objective knowledge from it?[7]

Oddly enough, this postmodernist response turns out to reveal a disguised form of foundationalism, for it remains within a specifically positivist conception of objectivity and knowledge. It assumes that the only kind of objective knowledge we can have is independent of (socially produced and revisable) theoretical presuppositions and concludes that the theory dependence of experience is evidence that it is always epistemically suspect. But what if we reject as overly abstract and limiting this conception of objectivity as presupposition-free knowledge? What if we give up both radical perspectivism and the dream of a "view from nowhere" in order to grant that all the knowledge we can ever have is necessarily dependent on theories and perspectives? We might then be able to see that there are different kinds and degrees of theory dependence and understand how theory-laden and socially constructed experiences can lead to a knowledge that is accurate and reliable.

Consider Scheman's example again. Alice's emotion, "anger," is the result of a political redescription of herself and her world, but if that new description happens to explain adequately and cogently—as social, psychological, and moral theory—the constituent features of Alice's situation, then Alice's experience of the emotion anger leads us to conclude that she has just come to know something, something not merely about her repressed feelings but also about her self, her personhood, and the range of its moral and political claims and needs. She comes to this knowledge by discovering or understanding features of the social and cultural arrangements of her world that define her sense of self, the choices she is taught to have, the range of personal capacities she is expected to exploit and exercise. And she does so in the process of learning to trust her judgments about herself, recognizing how others like her have done so as well. If this is the case, Alice's anger is not merely a personal or private thing inside, as it were, her own "innermost" self; rather, her anger is the theoretical prism through which she views her world and herself in it correctly. Hers is then an objective as-

7. I am thinking here of the kind of extreme thesis about "drives" and "needs" that Nietzsche sometimes combined with his valid antipositivist insights: "Against positivism, which halts at phenomena—'There are only *facts*'—I would say: No, facts [*sic*] is precisely what there is not, only interpretations. We cannot establish any fact 'in itself': perhaps it is folly to want to do such a thing. . . . It is our needs that interpret the world; our drives and their For and Against. Every drive is a kind of lust to rule; each one has its perspective that it would like to compel all the other drives to accept as a norm" (*Will* 267, sec. 481).

sessment of her situation, and in this strong sense, her anger is rational and justified.[8]

The example also suggests why emotions do not have to be seen as fully explicit beliefs or clear processes of reasoning for us to appreciate their cognitive role. We misunderstand the way Alice's anger gives coherence and shape to her previously confused feelings if we do not also appreciate the extent to which her experience of anger is a process whereby she weighs one vaguely felt hunch against another, reinterprets and reevaluates the information she considered relevant to her feelings and her situation, and thus redefines the contours of "her world." This sifting and reinterpretation of information sometimes happens quite suddenly; at other times, it becomes clearer and more lucid slowly and only in retrospect. The emotion is this not-entirely-explicit way Alice learns to reanalyze or even discern crucial features of her situation.

Emotions fall somewhere between conscious reasoning and reflexlike instinctual responses to stimuli. They are, as Ronald de Sousa has proposed, ways of paying attention to the world. They fill the "gaps" between our instinctually driven desires, on the one hand, and our fully developed reasoning faculties, on the other, especially when we need to decide what to do or believe. Emotions are "determinate patterns of salience"; like Kuhn's scientific paradigms, says de Sousa, they provide our half-articulated "questions" about the world. Emotions are "what we see the world 'in terms of,'" and therefore, like the scientific paradigm, they "cannot be articulated propositions" ("The Rationality" 136–38). It is significant that the focus her anger provides allows Alice to discover some of the constitutive features of her world. Emotions enable and encourage specific interpretations or evaluations of the world, and our judgment that Alice's anger is rational, justified, or "appropriate" (de Sousa's term) is a judgment about the accuracy of the interpretation and the objectivity of the evaluation. In Aristotelian terms, an essential component of Alice's moral development would be the increased capacity of her analytical and affective faculties to work together for cognitive

8. In emphasizing the fact that Alice comes to know something about her world through her emotion, I wish to show how Scheman's account of emotion is a realist one. Scheman does not identify her position as realist, perhaps because she thinks (wrongly, to my mind) that realism about emotions can only lead to a sort of physicalism: e.g., "types of psychological states (like being angry or in pain) actually are types of physical states (like certain patterns of neurons firing)" ("Individualism" 225). My interpretation of emotions in this essay should suggest a better conception of the realist view. For a cognitivist-realist understanding of emotions that is compatible with mine, see the many valuable suggestions in Lorde, esp. 54–58.

purposes. Emotional growth would be central to moral growth, and both presuppose the postpositivist notion of theory-mediated objectivity I am defending.[9]

There is no commitment here to the silly idea that all emotions are equally justified or rational. Questions about the legitimacy of emotions are answered by looking at the features of the subject in her world, and it is possible to glean an accurate picture of these features not only through the right theory (or narrative or description) but also through the relevant information that we can examine and share. "The difference between someone who is irrationally angry and someone who is not," Scheman explains, "may not be a difference in what they *feel* so much as a difference in what sorts of feelings, under what sorts of circumstances they are ready to take as anger. When we judge that people are right to deny the name of anger to their irrational reactions, we are often judging that their situation, unlike Alice's, does not really call for anger" (178–79). If Alice's father or husband were to become angry at Alice for supposedly betraying their trust by going to the consciousness-raising group meetings and by becoming dissatisfied with her personal relationships, we would evaluate these emotions as we do Alice's. The anger may be sincerely felt, but whether or not we consider it justified or legitimate would depend on what we think of the underlying political and moral views of these men about the role of women in society, as well as the information (about themselves, about their society, and so on) they draw on—or ignore— to support these views. This kind of assessment is naturally both complex and difficult. But the difficulty is not due to anything peculiar to emotions. All experience—and emotions offer the paradigm case here—is socially constructed, but the constructedness does not make it arbitrary or unstable in advance. Experiences are crucial indexes of our relationships with our world (including our relationships with ourselves), and to stress their cognitive nature is to argue that they can be susceptible to varying degrees of socially constructed truth or error and can serve as sources of objective knowledge or socially produced mystification.

9. "A person of practical insight," writes Martha Nussbaum, imaginatively and resourcefully elaborating Aristotle's view of moral development, "will cultivate emotional openness and responsiveness in approaching a new situation. Frequently, it will be her passional response, rather than detached thinking, that will guide her to the appropriate recognitions. 'Here is a case where a friend needs my help': this will often be 'seen' first by the feelings that are constituent parts of friendship, rather than by pure intellect. Intellect will often want to consult these feelings to get information about the true nature of the situation. Without them its approach to a new situation would be blind and obtuse. . . . Without feeling, a part of the correct perception is missing" (78–79).

This kind of argument about the cognitive component of experience helps strengthen the claim made by feminist standpoint theorists that in a gender-stratified society women's experiences are often significant repositories of oppositional knowledge, but this does not mean that experience serves to ground feminist knowledge. "It is rather," Sandra Harding maintains, "the subsequently articulated observations of and theory about the rest of nature and social relations" which help us make sense of "women's lives" in our sexist social structure (*Whose Science?* 124). "Women's lives" constitute an "objective location" (123) from which feminist research should examine the world, because without it we would not be able to explain a significant feature of our society. "Women's lives" is a theoretical notion or construct, but it involves the kind of social theory without which we could not make sense of—explain—a central feature of our world. The theoretical notion "women's lives" refers not just to the experiences of women but also to a particular social arrangement of gender relations and hierarchies which can be analyzed and evaluated. The standpoint of women in this society is not self-evidently deduced from the "lived experience" of individual women or groups of women. Rather, the standpoint is based in "women's lives" to the extent that it articulates their material and epistemological interests. Such interests are discovered by an explanatory empirical account of the nature of gender stratification, how it is reproduced and regulated, and the particular social groups and values it legitimates. Our definition of social location is thus closely tied to our understanding of social interests.[10]

An important metatheoretical consequence follows from this. Objectivity is inextricably tied to social and historical conditions, and objec-

---

10. This explanatory notion of "objective interests" implies comparison with other competing explanations of the same phenomena. When Marxists talk about the objective interests of the working class, they are trying to explain the location of the class in terms, on the one hand, of the relations of production and, on the other, of their theories about human freedom and social justice. Ernesto Laclau and Chantal Mouffe's criticism of the notion of objective interests thus seems to be either hasty or disingenuous. "In our view," they write, ". . . it is necessary to . . . discard the idea of a perfectly unified and homogeneous agent, such as the working class of classical discourse. . . . [F]undamental interests in socialism cannot be *logically* deduced from determinate positions in the economic process" (84). The theoretical assumption here is that "fundamental interests in socialism" can either be "logically deduced" on the basis of "determinate positions in the economic process" or else not discovered at all. The view that "interests" might be inferred (or deduced, in their stronger language) solely on the basis of "determinate positions" without the mediation of any theory is clearly based on a positivist understanding of explanation. Having rejected this view, Laclau and Mouffe leap to the postmodernist conclusion that a social group's interests cannot be identified through an objective explanation: There is "no constitutive principle for social agents [interests or anything else] which can be fixed in an

tive knowledge is the product not of disinterested theoretical inquiry so much as of particular kinds of social practice. In the case of social phenomena such as sexism and racism, whose distorted representation benefits the powerful and established groups and institutions, an attempt at an objective explanation is necessarily continuous with oppositional political struggles. Objective knowledge of such social phenomena is in fact often dependent on the theoretical knowledge that activism creates, for without these alternative constructions and accounts, Harding notes, our capacity to interpret and understand the dominant ideologies and institutions is limited to those created or sanctioned by these very ideologies and institutions (127). Moreover, as Richard Boyd shows in an important essay, even moral knowledge (for example, knowledge of "fundamental human goods") is to a great extent "experimental knowledge," dependent on social and political experiments. "We would not have been able to explore the dimensions of our needs for artistic expression and appreciation," Boyd points out, "had not social and technological developments made possible cultures in which, for some classes at least, there was the leisure to produce and consume art. We would not have understood the role of political democracy in [shaping our conception of the human] good had the conditions not arisen in which the first limited democracies developed. Only after the moral insights gained from the first democratic experiments were in hand, were we equipped to see the depth of the moral peculiarity of slavery. Only since the establishment of the first socialist societies are we even beginning to obtain the data necessary to assess the role of egalitarian social practices in fostering the good" ("How to Be a Moral Realist" 205).

The claim that political activity is in various ways continuous with attempts to seek scientific, objective explanations of social reality underscores that objective knowledge should not be sought by metatheoretically sundering the realm of "hard facts" from the realm of values. In the postpositivist picture of knowledge I am outlining here, some evaluations—from vaguely felt ethical judgments to more developed normative theories of right and wrong—can in crucial instances enable and facilitate greater accuracy in representing social reality, providing better ways of organizing the relevant or salient facts, urging us to look in newer

---

ultimate class core." This leads to the more general assertion that "unfixity [is] the condition of every social identity" (85). The glib antiobjectivism of many postmodernist positions is based on such positivist presuppositions about the nature of inquiry. For a useful point of contrast, see the accounts of Marx's conception of scientific and moral objectivity in Railton 763–73; and Gilbert 154–83.

and more productive ways. We have seen in the case of Alice how this epistemic reorientation takes place on a very personal level, where an individual's recognition and conscious acceptance of her feelings makes possible the process of search and discovery through which she comes to discern crucial features of her situation. For such emotional growth is a form of epistemic training as well. When we speak of collective political struggles and oppositional social movements, we can see how the political is continuous with the epistemological. In fact one may interpret Marx's famous eleventh thesis on Feuerbach as making just such an epistemological argument. It does not urge us to give up the job of interpreting the world (in the interest of changing it) but instead points out how the possibility of interpreting our world accurately depends fundamentally on our coming to know what it would take to change it, on our identifying the central relations of power and privilege that sustain it and make the world what it is. And we learn to identify these relations through our various attempts to change the world, not merely to contemplate it as it is.[11]

We can thus see how the unavoidability of theory, one of the key ideas of postpositivist intellectual culture, leads to an important nonrelativist insight about the political moorings of knowledge: there are better or worse social and political theories, and we can seek less distorted and more objective knowledge of social phenomena by creating the conditions for the production of better knowledge. Given the pervasiveness of both sexism and individualism in Alice's culture, it is more likely that she will come to discover the reality about herself and her situation in a feminist consciousness-raising group than by herself at home. Research institutions that employ scientists from a wide variety of social backgrounds (and do not confine decision making about research topics or the allocation of funds to a handful of individuals from the socially advantaged groups) will be less likely than other institutions to betray unconscious racial or gender bias in their research agendas. Objectivity is something we struggle for, in a number of direct and not so obvious ways, and this puts into perspective the epistemic privilege "experience" might give us. Feminist standpoint theorists like Harding both develop and clarify Marx's argument about the political bases of knowledge production. A standpoint, says Harding, "is not something that anyone can have simply by claiming it" (127). Since "experience" is only the raw material

11. See Railton, esp. 770–71.

for the kind of political and social knowledge that constitutes a feminist standpoint, it cannot guarantee or ground it. A standpoint is thus "an achievement" (127), both theoretical and political. The objectivity we achieve is thus profoundly theory dependent and thus postpositivist. It is based on our developing understanding of the various causes of distortion and mystification. I believe a naturalistic conception of human inquiry best suits the various examples I have been discussing. An essential part of this conception of inquiry would be an understanding of fallibility which is developed and specified through our explanations of how different kinds and degrees of error arise. Precision and depth in understanding the sources and causes of error or mystification help us define the nature of objectivity, and central to this definition would be the possibility of its revision and improvement on the basis of new information. This conception of fallibility is thus based on a dialectical opposition between objectivity and error. Since error in this view is opposed not to certainty but rather to objectivity as a theory-dependent, socially realizable goal, the possibility of error does not sanction skepticism about the possibility of knowledge. Such skepticism (postmodernist or otherwise) is usually the flip side of the quest for certainty.[12]

My proposal is that we reorient our theorizing of cultural identity in the following way: instead of conceiving identities as self-evidently based on the authentic experiences of members of a cultural or social group

12. One way to evaluate different versions of postmodernism is to examine the conception of objectivity they define themselves against; another is to look carefully at how precisely they develop their notion of fallibility. Donna Haraway has suggested in a well-known essay that we need to go beyond "realism" (by which I think she means positivism) to conceive the world (i.e., the object of knowledge) as a "coding trickster with whom we must learn to converse" (esp. 198–99, 201). "The Coyote or Trickster," she argues, "embodied in American Southwest Indian accounts, suggests our situation when we give up mastery but keep searching for fidelity, knowing all the while we will be hoodwinked" (199). The image suggests the epistemological injunction to acknowledge "the agency of the world" by "mak[ing] room for some unsettling possibilities, including a sense of the world's independent sense of humour" (199). This view is for the most part compatible with the postpositivist epistemology I am developing here, but Haraway's conception of fallibility is not precise enough to be very helpful. It is important to know more than the fact that "we will be hoodwinked," which is here formulated as a generalized possibility. We do not begin to understand the hoodwinking until we appreciate why and where we were wrong in our expectations (or theories). In many situations—many more than Haraway's image suggests—it is barely useful to know that we were wrong unless we are also led to a more precise understanding of the sources of our error. I agree with Haraway that we should give up (foundationalist) "mastery," and opt for (postpositivist) "fidelity"; but our conception of that fidelity will be richer to the extent that we can specify and deepen our understanding of the conditions that lead to our "hoodwinking." Objectivity and error are the products of social practice, and we should attempt to understand as much as we legitimately can about them (in naturalistic terms) before we generalize about our condition of original epistemic sinfulness.

(the conception that underlies identity politics) or as all equally unreal to the extent that they lay any claim to the real experiences of real people because experience is a radically mystifying term (this is the postmodernist alternative), we need to explore the possibility of a theoretical understanding of social and cultural identity in terms of objective social location. To do so, we need a cognitivist conception of experience, as I have been suggesting, a conception that will allow for both legitimate and illegitimate experience, enabling us to see experience as source of both real knowledge and social mystification. Both the knowledge and the mystification are, however, open to analysis on the basis of empirical information about our social situation and a theoretical account of our current social and political arrangements. Whether we inherit an identity—masculinity, being black—or we actively choose one on the basis of our political predilections—radical lesbianism, black nationalism, socialism—our identities are ways of making sense of our experiences. Identities are theoretical constructions that enable us to read the world in specific ways. It is in this sense that they are valuable, and their epistemic status should be taken very seriously. In them, and through them, we learn to define and reshape our values and our commitments, we give texture and form to our collective futures. Both the essentialism of identity politics and the skepticism of the postmodernist position seriously underread the real epistemic and political complexities of our social and cultural identities.

POSTCOLONIAL IDENTITY AND
MORAL EPISTEMOLOGY IN *BELOVED*

These complexities are at the heart of Toni Morrison's postcolonial cultural project in her remarkable novel, *Beloved*. Central to the novel is a vision of the continuity between experience and identity, a vision only partly articulated in the juxtaposition of the dedication ("Sixty Million and more"), with its claim to establish kinship with the unnamed and unremembered who perished in the infamous Middle Passage, together with the epigraph's audacious appropriation of God's voice from Hosea, quoted by Paul in Romans, chapter 9: "I will call them my people, / which were not my people; / and her beloved, / which was not beloved."

Laying claim to a past often serves simply to create an ancestry for oneself. What makes this juxtaposition of allusions in *Beloved* especially significant is that it suggests how the claim is going to be spelled out later in the novel, the terms in which one's relationship with the past is going to be conceived. The community sought in *Beloved* involves as its essence a moral and imaginative expansion of oneself, in particular one's capacity to experience. Only in the context of this expanded capacity can we understand the trajectory of the moral debate that informs and organizes the narrative: the debate between Paul D and Sethe about the nature and limits of Sethe's "mother-love." Is Sethe's killing of her "crawling already?" child to prevent her from being captured and enslaved an instance of a love that's too "thick," as Paul seems to think, an emotional attachment that makes Sethe forget that she is transgressing the limits of what is morally permissible for humans? "You got two feet, Sethe, not four," Paul says uncomprehendingly when he hears what she has done (165). How we evaluate Sethe and this incipient moral debate depends on how we interpret Paul D's growth in the second half of the novel and how we define the relationship between his ability to understand and his emotional capacity to respond to the dead and absent members of the community of the oppressed.

Sethe's defiant maternal cry that she has "milk enough for all"— repeated insistently over the course of the novel—is as much a response to Paul D's specific moral accusation as it is a reminder of her powerful will to survive. For she claims to have had will enough to survive the indignity of the rape in which her owners steal her milk from her, and also the determined love to nourish the generations of children—alive and dead—who will together create the community she seeks. Sethe's argument would be, I suppose, that there is no way to respond to Paul D's question on its own terms. The moral injunction—you are human after all, Sethe, and there are things you simply cannot do!—is too abstract. The political vision of a community of the oppressed, which the novel seeks primarily through the agency of its women characters, provides the context in which Paul's challenge can be specified, given historical resonance and meaning. We should begin, then, by acknowledging the need for this community, a need that is from Sethe's perspective not only affective but also epistemic.

To create this community, the survivor of slavery must begin by facing the immediate past more directly, and neither Sethe nor Paul D is able to do so alone. Only when they are together, and together in a very specific way that I shall describe in a moment, are they able to face the horror of Sweet Home. The act of remembering, Morrison's text insists, is not simply an attempt to know the past by recapitulating its events. The cognitive task of "rememory" is dependent on an emotional achievement, on the labor of trusting—oneself, one's judgments, one's companions. Paul D's arrival at 124 Bluestone Road opens up the possibility of Sethe's renegotiation with her own past, for that past is unavoidably collective. Like Alice's in Naomi Scheman's example, Sethe's capacity to know herself is tied up with her capacity to feel with others: "The morning she woke up next to Paul D . . . she . . . thought . . . of the temptation to trust and remember that gripped her as she stood before the cooking stove in his arms. Would it be all right? Would it be all right to go ahead and feel? Go ahead and *count on something?*" (38). Trusting enables remembering because it organizes and interprets crucial new information about one's life: it might be safe, now, to acknowledge one's feelings; one might be justified in counting on the relative safety of this environment. This safe environment is based on cooperation, on the most basic form of social activity, and it restores to Sethe some of her most intimate and personal experience of herself: "To push busyness into the corners of the room and just stand there a minute or two, naked from shoulder blade to waist, relieved of the weight of her breasts, smelling the stolen milk again and the pleasure of baking bread[.] Maybe this one time she could stop dead still in the middle of a cooking meal—not even leave the stove—and feel the hurt her back ought to. Trust things and remember things because the last of the Sweet Home men was there to catch her if she sank?" (18). Trusting involves emotional labor because Sethe has to reorganize her feelings toward others and herself; she has to come to acknowledge what is appropriate to feel. So trusting depends in part on her ability to judge whether something is appropriate, that is, to appraise relevant information about her changing situation and about her needs and desires. The assurance that Paul would be "there to catch her if she sank" changes her world profoundly, makes possible a cognitive reorientation. Paul is important because he can raise the possibility of trust, because he can help create the emotional conditions in which a new kind of knowing is possible.

Indeed, the main argument for seeing Paul D as a central participant in the moral debate the novel stages is that from the very beginning he reveals a capacity for an extraordinary kind of sympathy. That is in fact why we take his later charge ("You got two feet, Sethe, not four") seriously, acknowledging the potential force of his judgment. Although male and an outsider in Sethe's world of dead and living kinfolk, Paul D has a moral and imaginative life that can take him far beyond what traditional individualist notions of feeling and emotion might lead us to expect.

Notice in the following extraordinary passage how a kind of braiding of consciousnesses is achieved, a weaving together of emotional perspectives, through which a memory is relived and a new meaning created. Sethe and Paul have just finished having sex, and it has been disappointingly short, abrupt, and meaningless. As they lie together in discomfort and embarrassment, a fused memory wells up without having been verbalized. Sethe remembers both her wedding night and the first time she had sex with her husband, Halle, in the cornfields in Sweet Home; Paul's related memory of that not-so-private event adds counterpoint and resonance. The perspectives shift back and forth, occasionally without warning, and "fusion" is achieved gradually. The text points to new knowledge as well as a new way of knowing, both registered in the word "free" and its gentle but deliberate modulation.

> Halle wanted privacy for [Sethe] and got public display. Who could miss a ripple in a cornfield on a quiet cloudless day? He, Sixo and both of the Pauls sat under Brother [the tree] pouring water from a gourd over their heads, and through eyes streaming with well water, they watched the confusion of tassels in the field below. . . .
> How loose the silk. How jailed down the juice.
> The jealous admiration of the watching men melted with the feast of new corn they allowed themselves that night. Plucked from the broken stalks that Mr. Garner could not doubt was the fault of the raccoon. . . . [N]ow Paul D couldn't remember how finally they'd cooked those ears too young to eat. What he did remember was parting the hair to get to the tip, the edge of his fingernail just under, so as not to graze a single kernel.
> The pulling down of the tight sheath, the ripping sound always convinced her it hurt.
> As soon as one strip of husk was down, the rest obeyed and the ear yielded up to him its shy rows, exposed at last. How loose the silk. How quick the jailed-up flavor ran free.
> No matter what all your teeth and wet fingers anticipated, there was no accounting for the way that simple joy could shake you.
> How loose the silk. How fine and loose and free. (27)

Paul's and Sethe's memories fuse in the repeated image of the cornsilk and the juice, and the resonance of the word "free" the second time it appears is much greater than the reference to the loose cornsilk or the jailed-up juice might suggest. The fusion of perspectives suggests something new, something that Sethe and Paul in fact have in common—a concern with the moral implications of being enslaved and being free. After she has arrived in Cincinnati, Sethe realizes that freedom for the slave involves more than a flight from the legal condition of bondage: the colonial condition continues unless it is faced as a fundamental ethical challenge. "Freeing yourself was one thing," she thinks, articulating the constitutive cultural challenge of the postcolonial condition, "claiming ownership of that freed self was another" (95).

In fact the disagreement between her and Paul D is defined by a question about the real implications of political freedom. Can you really be free, Paul seems to ask, if your love is so "thick" that it binds you to the level of the subrational, that it demeans your essential human self by distorting your capacity to determine which actions are simply not morally permissible for humans? Part of Sethe's response to this charge is evident in the passage I have just analyzed. Sethe is not simply reliving the first time she had sex with Halle; she thinks also about her wedding night and her relationship with her husband. Mrs. Garner is surprised that Sethe in fact insists on a ceremony to make her union with Halle a formal event. She sews her own dress, refusing to be lowered to the level of the breeder that slavery insisted she be. For Sethe, freedom—even under slavery—appears as the ineliminable human need for self-determination, with the capacity for moral agency at its core. So it is not enough to be free from legally imposed bondage; one must also claim ownership of one's freed self. And this ownership, Sethe might have argued with Paul, cannot be a purely individual affair. To understand this ownership adequately, we need access to the buried memories and experiences of others who might have shared our experience. We need to reconstruct what our relevant community might have been, appreciate the social and historical dimensions of our innermost selves. Paul's moral accusation is unfair and simplistic to the very extent that it seems like the application of a general law to an isolated individual act; Sethe suggests that Paul's judgment itself needs to be reevaluated in the context of the knowledge of their common historical experience, a knowledge that remains unavailable to the individual by herself.

For both Sethe and Paul, reclaiming community involves personal growth in their rational and affective capacities to deal with their traumatic pasts. In psychoanalytic terms, the novel traces their developing ability to "work through" the implications of their complex cathectic relationships with Sweet Home and everything that followed. In the early chapters both characters reveal a deep resistance to confronting their pasts on any level, which is manifested in their inability to narrate their own personal stories by themselves. If for Sethe surviving was predicated on "keeping the past at bay" (42), keeping it from forming a coherent narrative with the present and the future, the attempt to construct and narrate the story together with Paul can succeed only if the past ceases to be a form of uncontrolled repetition, "acted out" by the subject rather than integrated cognitively and affectively into her life. Even when it is successful, the narrating is at best fitful and uneasy; "working through" the traumatizing past involves dealing with the way it effectively arrests one's agency: "[Sethe] was spinning. Round and round the room. Past the jelly cupboard, past the window, past the front door, another window, the sideboard, the keeping-room door, the dry sink, the stove— back to the jelly cupboard. Paul D sat at the table watching her drift into view then disappear behind his back, turning like a slow but steady wheel. . . . [T]he wheel never stopped" (159). To go beyond this image of motion and energy without real movement, Sethe has to integrate more fully into her emotional life the theoretical knowledge she both has and resists: if her past is not just hers alone, she can regain its meaning only through collective effort—with Paul, with Denver and Beloved. Her anxieties about trusting, herself as well as others, cannot be resolved at a purely intellectual level.[13]

Morrison indicates in several ways why historical memory might be available to human subjects only if we expand our notion of personal experience to refer to ways of both feeling and knowing, and to include collectives as well as individual selves. The braiding and fusing of voices and emotions makes possible the new knowledge we seek about our postcolonial condition. That it does is evident even more clearly in the searching, exploratory quality of the chant of the black women who at the end help Sethe exorcise the ghost, searching for something that is, once again, both the stuff of history and a new knowledge: "When the women assembled outside 124, Sethe was breaking a lump of ice into chunks. . . . When the music entered the window, she was wringing a cool cloth to put on Beloved's forehead. . . . Sethe opened the door and reached for Beloved's hand. Together they stood in the doorway. For Sethe it was as though the Clearing had come to her with all its heat and simmering leaves, where the voices of women searched for the right combination, the key, the code, the sound that broke the back of words. Building voice upon voice until they found it, and when they did it was a wave of sound

---

13. Mae Henderson has provided an insightful analysis of the historiographical project of *Beloved*, focusing on Morrison's views about memory and narrative (see 62–87). For an application of psychoanalytic concepts like "acting out" and "working through" to the historian's relationship with his or her object, see LaCapra, "Representing the Holocaust" 108–27, 356–60. This theme is developed in what is easily one of the most honest and illuminating articles on the de Man controversy, LaCapra's "The Personal, the Political and the Textual" 5–38, where the focus is less on de Man's World War II journalistic writings and their moral implications and more on the responses of some of his more illustrious defenders.

wide enough to sound deep water and knock the pods off chestnut trees. It broke over Sethe and she trembled like the baptized in its wash" (261). The dense allusions in the images bring to mind the varieties of ways people join to transcend their present condition, to re-create past and future through an act of collective imagination and will. And this act is something one learns; one searches for the knowledge to be able to do it right. Images of water evoke both the unremembered dead of the Middle Passage and the power of giving birth; the Clearing brings to mind the collective healing ritual presided over by Sethe's dead mother-in-law, the ritual that makes possible the communal life of the survivors of slavery. In every instance the collective effort produces something new, the fusion of voices (the call and response, the braiding of sounds that breaks the back of words) leads to possibilities that could not have been created by the effort of an individual by herself.

The image of braiding I have been using suggests that in the very way it is written Morrison's novel advocates a specific moral epistemology. If the narrative is organized around a moral debate between Sethe and Paul, we see in crucial passages such as the ones I have been analyzing why the debate cannot be adequately understood in its stark or abstract form as a disagreement in judgment. Rather, Sethe's response to Paul is elaborated by precisely such moments of narrative braiding of perspectives, suggesting how much more Paul will need to know about his communal past, as well as the way he might go about seeking this knowledge. The almost insular world of Sethe, Denver, and Beloved represents the most complex instance of the kind of intersubjective knowing that Paul and the reader must learn to appreciate. For in their search for reconciliation, mother and daughters, victims all, reclaim one another by deepening our understanding of what it means to call something or someone one's own. Again, the narrator often deliberately makes it dificult to separate the voices, but notice in the first passage from Beloved's monologue how the community of the dead from the Middle Passage is invoked in a way that frames and lends meaning to the later passage in which Sethe, Denver, and Beloved acknowledge one another's needs and demands.

> We are not crouching now   we are standing but my legs are like my dead man's eyes   I cannot fall because there is no room to   the men without skin are making loud noises . . . the woman is there with the face I want the face that is mine   they fall into the sea which is the color of the bread she has nothing in her ears   if I had the teeth of the man who died on my face I would bite the circle around her neck   bite it away   I know she

does not like it   now there is room to crouch and to watch the crouching
others   it is the crouching that is now always now inside   the woman
with my face is in the sea   a hot thing (211)

Beloved   -
You are my sister
You are my daughter
You are my face; you are me
I have found you again; you have come back to me
You are my Beloved
You are mine
You are mine
You are mine

I have your milk
I have your smile
I will take care of you

You are my face; I am you. Why did you leave me who am you?
I will never leave you again
Don't ever leave me again
You will never leave me again
You went in the water
I drank your blood
I brought your milk
You forgot to smile
I loved you
You hurt me
You came back to me
You left me

I waited for you
You are mine
You are mine
You are mine (216–17)

Beloved reconnects us with the dead and unremembered of the Middle
Passage but also specifically with Sethe's mother who had come from
Africa. The "face" that Beloved claims is not just her grandmother's, however, for the images of claiming kinship reverberate outward. "The face
I want" becomes "the face that is mine," suggesting the appropriation
of another to oneself. But in the very next lines the distance increases, to
register an other who might need help: she has an iron ring around her
neck that she "does not like" or—more emphatic still—"the woman with
my face is in the sea   a hot thing."

    Loving, forgiving, acknowledging, helping, even making demands or
accusations—all these are woven together through the different voices

in the second passage, suggesting the complexity of coming to know one-self and one's family or community through sustained emotional labor. But the allusion to Sethe's mother in Beloved's monologue opens out from one's immediate purview to include those from the past whose lives frame one's own. If Sethe's mother survived the Middle Passage, she did so only to be hanged later. Sethe remembers her primarily through her absence, and through her struggle to communicate to her daughter a lineage that Sethe would barely register: "She must of nursed me two or three weeks—that's the way the others did. Then she went back in rice and I sucked from another woman whose job it was. She never fixed my hair nor noth-ing. . . . One thing she did do. She picked me up and carried me behind the smokehouse. Back there she opened up her dress and lifted her breast and pointed under it. Right on her rib was a circle and a cross burnt right in the skin. She said, 'This is your ma'am. This,' and she pointed" (60–61). Sethe is too young and ignorant of history to know what the sign meant, and why her mother is hanged later with, as she says uncompre-hendingly, "a whole lot of them" (61). The surrogate mother Nan, whose job it was to nurse babies and who spoke the same African language Sethe's mother spoke, fills in a portion of the lost narrative with a moral insistence that Sethe can appreciate only in retrospect.

> Nighttime. Nan holding her with her good arm, waving the stump of the other in the air. "Telling you. I am telling you, small girl Sethe," and she did that. She told Sethe that her mother and Nan were together from the sea. Both were taken up many times by the crew. "She threw them all way but you. The one from the crew she threw away on the island. The others from more whites she also threw away. Without names, she threw them. You she gave the name of the black man. She put her arms around him. The others she did not put her arms around. Never. Never. Telling you. I am telling you, small girl Sethe." (62)

What Sethe's perspective—mediated through Denver, Beloved, and the dead women characters—offers Paul is a new understanding of the historical achievement of motherhood. It had the function not just of giving birth and nurturing, but—when fatherhood was denied the slave family—the most basic historical role of positing meaning and continu-ity as well. Mothering becomes a central trope in the novel because it is defined as a key feature of the moral and historical imagination. The slave mother persevered to create identity, both personal and familial; in her image—and on her body—were inscribed the twin imperatives to sur-vive and to create new meaning. The recurring images of water, milk, and blood combine in the novel to suggest some of the material conditions in which one creates the conscience of the race, for the race needs to survive, both physically and in our imaginations, before we can examine its moral choices. Sethe insists that the community of the colonized includes not just the living survivors of the slave plantations but also, beyond it, the absent, those who need to be reclaimed, who need in fact to be asked to make their claims on us. The novel's central thesis about black motherhood subtends the moral issue Paul raises; it deepens, qualifies, and historicizes it. It suggests in effect that Paul's question—can a human do that?!—is indeed too abstract, bereft of historical and contextual depth. In order to pose the question appropriately, we need the cognitive context that only the community of the colonized—dead and living, slave and nonslave—can provide. It is this that Paul D begins to realize when he finally returns to 124 Bluestone Road.

Paul achieves this realization by coming to terms with Beloved, the ghost, and the powerful spell she cast on him. By coming to understand that he both needed Beloved and was afraid of her, he learns the historical lesson for which the narrative has prepared us. Before his reconciliation with Sethe, Paul D must acknowledge that his dependency on Beloved is a sign of his connection with the past he has up till now misunderstood, the past of water and death and ocean-deep emotion that threatens to both engulf him and liberate him. Through this reliving of his relationship with the exorcised ghost-child, Paul comes to have faith in the intergenerational lineage of black women whose primordial presence frames his moral questioning because it makes possible his historical and cultural present.

> There is the pallet spread with old newspapers gnawed at the edges by mice. The lard can. The potato sacks too, but empty now, they lie on the dirt floor in heaps. In daylight he can't imagine it in darkness with moonlight seeping through the cracks. Nor the desire that drowned him there and forced him to struggle up, up into that girl like she was the clear air at the top of the sea. Coupling with her wasn't even fun. It was more like a brainless urge to stay alive. Each time she came, pulled up her skirts, a life hunger overwhelmed him and he had no more control over it than over his lungs. And afterward, beached and gobbling air, in the midst of repulsion and personal shame, he was thankful too for having been escorted to some ocean-deep place he once belonged to. (263–64)

If coupling with Beloved is something to which Paul was blindly and "brainless[ly]" driven, it is paradoxically because it evoked a "life hunger" in him which he only now begins to understand. His need for her was like the need for air, the "clear air at the top of the sea," but the life he unwittingly seeks is his own unclaimed history, the "ocean-deep place" of the dead female ancestors to whom he once "belonged." This belonging is what brings Paul to his final moment of reconciliation with Sethe, and this reconciliation is as much an intellectual growth as it is an emotional acknowledgment of his historical indebtedness. It is a moment that emblematizes the general cultural phenomenon Hortense Spillers indicates, the essential moral education through which the African-American male comes to "regain the heritage of the mother" as "an aspect of his own personhood—the power of 'yes' to the female within" (Spillers 80).

Note how in the scene of reconciliation the earlier image about the morality of infanticide gets revised, the stark demand of the abstract moral law—"be human"—is softened and humanized in its turn, for it is located in culture, in history, in life. Sethe is ill and exhausted when Paul returns, and she is lying in Baby Suggs's bed:

> "Don't you die on me! This is Baby Suggs' bed! Is that what you planning?" He is so angry he could kill her. He checks himself, remembering Denver's warning, and whispers, "What you planning, Sethe?"
> "Look," he says, "Denver be here in the day. I be here in the night. I'm a take care of you, you hear? Starting now. First off, you don't smell right. Stay there. Don't move. Let me heat up some water." He stops. "Is it all right, Sethe, if I heat up some water?"
> "And count my feet?" she asks him.
> He steps closer. "Rub your feet." (271–72)

This transformation from law to human understanding, from abstract humanity to real feeling, is predicated on the enlargement of Paul's personal capacity to experience, but if my reading of the novel is convincing it suggests how much historical knowledge, indeed how much theoretical knowledge, is involved in Paul's growth. His new relationship to Sethe and to Beloved is based on a new understanding of his history, of a history constructed and sustained by generations of black mothers. Morrison's novel is one of the most challenging of postcolonial texts because it indicates the extent to which the search for a genuinely noncolonial moral and cultural identity depends on a revisionary historiography.[14] We cannot really claim ourselves morally or politically until we have reconstructed our collective identity, reexamined our dead and our

14. It is of course not only the colonized who need to worry about the way their search for a noncolonial identity depends on an adequate historiography. For an account of the colonizer's identity, and how it might survive in postcolonial contexts precisely to the extent that its genealogy is not traced, see my "Drawing the Color Line," especially the concluding section.

disremembered. This is not simply a project of adding to one's ancestral line, for as we have seen, it often involves fundamental discoveries about what ancestry is, what continuity consists in, how cultural meanings do not just sustain themselves through history but are in fact materially embodied and fought for.

Sethe's act of infanticide resonates differently after we have reconsidered the role of motherhood under slavery. We think, for instance, of Sethe's unnamed mother, who throws all her children except Sethe away as an act of resistance to rape and racial humiliation. It is something of this order that Sethe decides to do in slitting her child's throat. If Paul speaks in terms of the abstraction we call "the human," Sethe's situation and that of other slave mothers reminds us that humanity is itself measured in terms of a moral personhood, a capacity for self-determination, which the institution of slavery denied the slave. "Anybody white could take your whole self for anything that came to mind. Not just work, kill, or maim you, but dirty you. Dirty you so bad you couldn't like yourself any more. Dirty you so bad you forgot who you were and couldn't think it up. And though she and others lived through and got over it, she could never let it happen to her own. The best thing she was, was her children" (251). We may or may not agree with Sethe's argument, but we need to come to terms with the historical community she claims as her own, and reexamine the moral theory we bring with us. That is what Paul does at the end, as he seeks reconciliation with Sethe.

> "Sethe," he says, "me and you, we got more yesterday than anybody. We need some kind of tomorrow."
> "Me? Me?" (273)

He claims her community as his own and, through her, reclaims an aspect of his own personhood, but his words of acceptance and reconciliation suggest a new challenge, a new way of conceiving the postcolonial tomorrow. Sethe's argument had been that she could not let her children be enslaved because they were "her best thing"; Paul does not condemn her action now as he had done in the past, but he suggests a different emphasis: "You your best thing, Sethe. You are." This is not quite a disagreement so much as an indication that the distinctly postcolonial challenge lies in leaving part of the past behind, in working through it to imagine agency and selfhood in positive terms, inventing new dimensions of cultural possibility.

Morrison's novel suggests that the community that defines our cultural identity is constructed through a complex and ongoing process involving both emotional and cognitive effort. Central to this effort is the work of the moral imagination that learns to "remember" with honesty and integrity. Morrison's vision of the writer's historical task, as she described it in a 1987 lecture, is what we would call realist or cognitivist:

> The act of imagination is bound up with memory. You know, they straightened out the Mississippi River in places, to make room for houses and livable acreage. Occasionally the river floods these places. "Floods" is the word they use, but in fact it is not flooding; it is remembering. Remembering where it used to be. All water has a perfect memory and is forever trying to get back to where it was. Writers are like that: remembering where we were, what valley we ran through, what the banks were like, the light that was there and the route back to our original place. It is emotional memory—what the nerves and the skin remember as well as how it appeared.("The Site of Memory" 98–99)

Needless to say, such remembering is never easy, nor is the moral growth that is closely tied with it irreversible, for fallibility, or at least the danger of forgetting what is essential, is always a historical possibility. What we need to recognize is that such forgetting would not be simply a personal failure but rather a loss of community, of necessary social meaning. Hence the tone of loss and mourning that frames the scene of Paul and Sethe's reconcilation. There are images of "dead ivy," "shriveled blossoms," and a "bleak and minus nothing" (270). As the novel ends, it is not just Beloved who is forgotten "but the water too and what it is down there" (275). Integral to the postpositivist realist view of experience and identity is thus the necessary caution that our cultural identities (or the moral and political knowledge we might seek through them) are defined in a way that is historically open-ended, never frozen or settled once and for all: "Down by the stream in back of 124 [Beloved's] footprints come and go, come and go. They are so familiar. Should a child, an adult, place his feet in them, they will fit. Take them out and they disappear again as though nobody walked there" (275).

CULTURAL DIFFERENCE AND SOCIAL POWER

Let me summarize part of my central argument in outlining some of the advantages of the realist view of experience and identity. First, this account of cultural identity explains an important way in which identities can be both constructed (socially, linguistically, theoretically, and so on) and "real" at the same time. Their "reality" consists in their referring outward, to causally significant features of the social world. Alice's gendered identity is theoretically constructed, to be sure, insofar as she elaborates and consolidates it in the context of the consciousness-raising group and the alternative descriptions of the world she encounters and debates there. But if this description happens to be accurate as an explanation of the key causal factors that make this world what it is, that is, make this world this world, then Alice's new feminist cultural and political identity is "real" in the following sense: it refers accurately to her social location and interests. Alice discovers that what defines her life in her society is the fact that she belongs to a group defined by gender. Gender is a social fact that is causally relevant for the experiences she has and the choices and possibilities that are available to her. Her world is what it is because in it social power is sustained through the hierarchical organization of gendered groups, including the cultural meanings they share. The collective identity Alice consciously forges through reexamination of the accepted cultural meanings and values, the given definition of her personal and political interests, is then as much her discovery as it is a construction. For good social and political theories do not only organize pregiven facts about the world; they also make it possible for us to detect new ones. They do so by guiding us to new patterns of salience and relevance, teaching us what to take seriously and what to reinterpret. To say that theories and identities "refer" is thus to understand the complex way they provide us knowledge about the world. Beyond the elementary descriptive relationship that individual signs might have with unique and static objects, "reference," postpositivist realists say, should be understood dialectically and socially as providing us degrees of "epistemic access" to reality. On this view, there can be both partial and successful reference. In some cases, theories (like signs) can fail to refer accurately, but reference should not be conceived as an all-or-nothing affair. Thus, when I say that cultural identities refer, I am suggesting that they can be evaluated using the same complex epistemic criteria we use to evaluate "theories."[15]

So the second advantage a realist theory of identity offers is this: it helps explain how we can distinguish legitimate identities from spurious ones. In fact it gives us the way to appreciate different degrees of legitimacy and spuriousness. It does so by urging us to take the epistemic status of personal experience very seriously, seriously enough in fact to con-

---

15. This way of understanding reference builds on the "causal" account discussed in chapter 2 of my *Literary Theory and the Claims of History.* Also see Boyd, "Metaphor and Theory Change" 356–408, for a useful development of the causal theory.

sider why Alice's anger and her father's are not equally justified, and how Paul D's initial moral judgment of Sethe's action can become subtler and deeper, more adequate to the reality they share. Alice's evolving personal experience plays an epistemic role since it reveals to her some of the determining features of her social location and her world, and where, objectively speaking, her personal interests might lie. To say that Alice (like Paul or Sethe) learns from her experience is to emphasize that under certain conditions personal experience yields reliable knowledge about oneself and one's situation.[16] And since different experiences and identities refer to different aspects of one world, one complex causal structure that we call "social reality," the realist theory of identity implies that we can evaluate them comparatively by considering how adequately they explain this structure. This comparison is often a complex and difficult negotiation (since it can involve competing interpretations and only partially overlapping bodies of information), but it is facilitated by making buried explanations explicit, by examining the social and political views that are involved in what seem like purely personal choices and predilections. Experiences and identities—and theories about them—are bits of social and political theory themselves and are to be evaluated as such.

The cultural radicalism of the postmodernist position I identified earlier is based on the argument that all identities are constructed and are thus contingent and changeable. But it cannot adequately explain what difference different kinds of construction make. Since it refuses to take the epistemic dimension of experience seriously, it cannot explain how (as, say, in the case of Alice or Paul D) changes in our cultural identity reflect moral and political growth, an increase both in our personal capacities and in knowledge. Once we consider the theoretical option to postmodernism provided by the realist account of identity I have proposed here, it might also be clearer why we should not frame our questions about cultural identity in terms of a rigid opposition between essentialism, claiming unchanging "reality," and (social) constructionism, emphasizing social and historical ideology. Both this unhelpful opposition and efforts to transcend it through such weak theoretical compromises as are suggested by such terms as "strategic essentialism"[17] are

16. For two realist accounts that define political identity by reference to social location, common interests, and shared contexts of struggle, see Sivanandan (on "black" people in Britain) and Chandra Talpade Mohanty (on "Third World women"). I discussed Sivandandan's essay briefly in my *Literary Theory and the Claims of History* 17.

17. See Spivak 202–11; and for a position that is both more complex and more lucidly discussed, Fuss, esp. 118–19. I think Fuss's overall project would be better served by

based on an evasion of the difficult but unavoidable epistemological questions that the postmodernist confronts. If the identities of social actors cannot be deduced from experiences whose meanings are self-evident, is there anything objective we can say about these identities? How do we determine that one social identity is more legitimate than another? How do we justify one "strategy" over another? Is such justification purely a matter of pragmatic calculation, or does it obey some epistemic constraints as well? Does what we know about the world (independently of specific questions about identity) have any bearing on our understanding of this justification? I have suggested some answers to these questions by emphasizing the continuity of accounts of cultural identity with accounts of the social justification of knowledge, especially the knowledge involved in our ethical and political claims and commitments.

The third, more specific, advantage of the realist approach to experience and identity is that it explains how the oppressed may have epistemic privilege, but it does so without espousing a self-defeating or dubious kind of relativism with separatist implications. To have a cognitivist view of experience is to claim that its truth content can be evaluated, and thus potentially shared with others. As we saw in my discussion of a theory of emotions, the individualist "privileged access" theory is wrong because it denies that personal experience is fundamentally theory mediated. A realist theory of the kind I have outlined would both acknowledge the constitutive role played by theory and respect the ways specific theories—and social situations, conditions of research,and so on—provide better or worse ways of detecting new and relevant information about our world. I have said (drawing on Harding, Boyd, and Marx) that certain social arrangements and conditions—social struggles of dominated groups, for instance—can help produce more objective knowledge about a world that is constitutively defined by relations of domination. That would help explain why granting the possibility of epistemic privilege to the oppressed might be more than a sentimental gesture; in many cases in fact it is the only way to push us toward greater social objectivity. For granting that the oppressed have this privilege opens up the possibility that our own epistemic perspective is partial, shaped by our social location, and that it needs to be understood and revised hermeneutically. One way to read my account of Paul D's growth over the course of the novel is that he grows because Sethe challenges him to

---

a fully developed realist theory of experience than by the Althusserian one she invokes in her concluding discussion.

become aware of his partiality. His recognition of the nature of his dependence on Beloved—the particular needs she fulfilled, the ocean-deep
place to which he had lost access which she restored—is a historical lesson that is learned by becoming less forgetful and more fully human, more
aware of the cultural sources of his own personhood.

This is a general lesson whose implications every historian confronts,
as theorists have lately been pointing out. Reviewing the recent cultural
debate among German historians about the centrality of the Holocaust
in the writing of objective national history, Dominick LaCapra shows
why the historian of the period must overcome the kind of false objectivity that is derived from a denial of one's "subject position." What is
needed, instead, is an understanding of the variety of affective responses
to the past, responses shaped by one's location. For the historian's interpretation to be more objective than might otherwise be possible, she
must attend to the ethical implications of her discursive stances.

> The Holocaust presents the historian with transference in the most traumatic
> form conceivable—but in a form that will vary with the difference in subject
> position of the analyst. Whether the historian or analyst is a survivor, a rela-
> tive of survivors, a former Nazi, a former collaborator, a relative of former
> Nazis or collaborators, a younger Jew or German distanced from more im-
> mediate contact with survival, participation, or collaboration, or a relative "out-
> sider" to these problems will make a difference even in the meaning of state-
> ments that may be formally identical. Certain statements or even entire
> orientations may seem appropriate for someone in a given subject position but
> not in others. (It would, for example, be ridiculous if I tried to assume the voice
> of Elie Wiesel or Saul Friedlander. There is a sense in which I have no right to
> these voices. There is also a sense in which, experiencing a lack of a viable
> voice, I am constrained to resort to quotation and commentary more often
> than I otherwise might be.) Thus although any historian must be "invested"
> in a distinctive way in the events of the Holocaust, not all investments (or
> cathexes) are the same and not all statements, rhetorics, or orientations are
> equally available to different historians. ("Representing the Holocaust" 110)

LaCapra goes on to characterize "statements, rhetorics, or orientations"
as specific choices about "how language is used" (110), but in the context of my present discussion it is possible to see that they point to epistemic choices and stances as well. They "orient" inquiry by suggesting
where we might be reflexive or critical, where attention to seemingly irrelevant subjective information can lead to greater objectivity. When we
acknowledge that the experiences of victims might be repositories of valuable knowledge, and thus allow that they have epistemic privilege, we
are not thereby reduced to sentimental silence. Entailed in our ac-

knowledgment is the need to pay attention to the way our social locations facilitate or inhibit knowledge by predisposing us to register and
interpret information in certain ways. Our relation to social power produces forms of blindness just as it enables degrees of lucidity. The notion of epistemic privilege is thus inseparable from the cognitivist account
of experience and cultural identity I have sketched, and it explains how
objectivity in historical and moral inquiry can be found not by denying
our perspectives or locations but rather by interrogating their epistemic
consequences.

My arguments should indicate that these consequences are not so severe that we need to retreat into skepticism. Even when we are discussing
such slippery things as personal experiences and cultural meanings, it is
not clear that postmodernist skepticism is warranted. Either to base
definitions of identity on an idealized conception of experience (as essentialists do) or to deny experience any cognitive value whatsoever (as
postmodernists might) is to cut with too blunt a theoretical knife. The
realist-cognitivist account of identity I have proposed here, a definition
implicit in Toni Morrison's novel, might suggest to some a viable alternative to these dominant theoretical positions.

CONCLUDING REMARKS

One implication of the realist account of identity I have provided may
surprise some readers. This theory reconciles the claims of certain forms
of identity politics with moral universalism. Indeed, it enables us to respect social difference while deepening the radical potential of universalist moral and political claims. The notion of epistemic privilege I outlined,
a notion central to the realist understanding of identity, shows us why
this should be the case. If our views about our identities are partly explanations of the world in which we live and these explanations are based
on the knowledge we gather from our social activities, then the claim that
oppressed social groups have a special kind of knowledge about the world
as it affects them is hardly a mysterious one requiring idealist assumptions about cultural essences or inaccessible particularities. Rather it is
an empirical claim, tied to a wider (empirical and theoretical) account of
the society in which these groups live. And therefore any claim about the
epistemic privilege of a particular social group will be only as convincing
as the social theory and description that accompany it. On the view I am
defending, claims about the epistemic privilege of a particular group are
necessarily embedded in wider explanatory theories of history and of the

society in which the group lives. Both the claim of epistemic privilege and the identity politics based on it need to be evaluated as any social and historical explanation should be; they are prone, like all explanatory accounts of the world, to error—both empirical and theoretical.

But when such a claim about a particular social group is true, its implications are general, not merely limited to the subjective experiences of the group in question. The knowledge we gain is "objective." This conclusion shows why we need to be wary of those overly abstract universalist visions of morality or social justice which focus on only the most general features that the various social groups (or individuals) have in common and exclude consideration of relevant particularities, relevant contextual information. Part of Sethe's response to Paul D's moral indignation is that he has inadequate understanding of the social context in which he, as a (black) man, has developed his moral views about infanticide. Paul's understanding is deepened by his recognition of his partiality, his—historically and socially produced—ignorance about the role of motherhood in the slave family. Sethe does not defend infanticide; she widens the focus of the moral debate to include the relevant contexts of her action, and thus makes it more complex.

Paul's growth is predicated on his coming to know Sethe's perspective, on learning to acknowledge both the partiality of his knowledge and the reason Sethe knows something that he does not about the world in which they both live. Sethe's epistemic privilege is not an accident; it derives from her experience of being a slave mother, that is, her resistance to being a reproducer of slaves. Paul comes to recognize that both motherhood and the gendered division of labor on which slavery was built are objective historical and social facts that shape what he knows and what he does not, that—consequently—influence the moral judgment he makes. But Paul's response—in fact the genuineness of his emotional and moral growth—is predicated on his acceptance of Sethe's claim about motherhood as an empirical fact about slave society. I have not argued in this chapter that Paul *has* to accept this claim, and Morrison's novel gives the reader the same option. If the historical claim is seen as cogent, however, it is incumbent upon us to pay attention to the special knowledge that slave mothers have. But in that case such attention would not derive from sentimental respect for motherhood but would rather be sound epistemic practice. Such subjective perspectives often contain deep sources of information and knowledge, or even alternative theoretical pictures and accounts of the world we all share. An adequate appreciation of such "particular" perspectives and viewpoints makes possible a richer general picture, a deeper and more nuanced universalist view of human needs and vulnerabilities, as well as—by implication—human flourishing. In such cases, the (cultural or historical) particular and the (moral) universal complement and substantiate each other.

This explains why, with all their flaws and obvious limitations, identity–based political struggles can be built on genuine political insights. Once we acknowledge, as the realist theory requires, that such struggles cannot be based on a priori claims to political or moral knowledge, we can understand how they can legitimately draw on personal experiences and histories to deepen our knowledge of society. A feminist political consciousness often develops, for instance, through a recognition of the overwhelming significance of the personal, of the way gender relations and inequalities are played out in our most intimate relationships (including our relationships with ourselves). As we saw in Alice's case, an adequate appreciation of the political effects of gender often depends on a personal reorientation or growth, involving both the affective and the deliberative faculties. And the relation between the personal and the political is complex and indeed dialectical. The recovery of an individual's sense of personal worth and the development of her capacity for the right kind of anger or indignation partly depend on finding the right social and political theory. In Alice's case, such a theory or such deeply theoretical hypotheses are what the consciousness-raising group provides. The group also provides Alice with the appropriate epistemic and emotional context in which to examine such hypotheses, and thus Alice's political growth, the growth in her knowledge about herself, her capacities, and her world, is predicated on her acknowledgment of her inherited social identity and its effects.

What cultural and social conditions make identitarian politics a necessary (though certainly not sufficient) form of social struggle, even of social inquiry? Alice's situation is by no means uncommon. What makes Alice's "identity" so central to the process of her moral and political growth is a very crucial feature of the world in which we all live: hierarchical and unequal gender relations are produced and reproduced by a process through which Alice is taught in effect to devalue her personal experiences as a source of knowledge about her world, and even about herself as a person—that is, as someone with genuine needs and capacities, rights and entitlements. Alice learns to value these experiences again and to glean from them—as well as from the fact that she had been taught to ignore them—crucial information about both herself and her world. "Learning" to value and imagine in such new ways is relevant not only for the disadvantaged but also for the historically privileged, for both privilege and privation can produce (different kinds of) moral and political blindness. Cultural decolonization often involves an interrogation of the epistemic and affective consequences of our social location, of historically learned habits of thinking and feeling. For both Alice and Paul D the developing recognition of aspects of their inherited identities amounts to a form of decolonization, a necessary political education. Through his extended dialogue with Sethe, Paul comes to acknowledge both his indebtedness to his community and his own partial knowledge— a partiality fostered at least as much by his gendered identity as by any purely personal trait or idiosyncrasy.

For Paul and Alice, as for so many others in modern society, an identity-based politics becomes a necessary first step in coming to know what an oppressive social and cultural system obscures. Such "obscuring" is often a highly mediated and almost invisible process, implicit in traditional forms of schooling as well as in less formal practices of education and socialization. The institutions of social reproduction and cultural transmission— schools, libraries, newspapers, and museums, for instance—are oriented to the dominant cultural and social perspectives. Much of their bias is often invisible because of the relatively benign form the transmission of cultural information takes: it seems utterly natural, part of the scheme of things. In such instances, cultural assimilation amounts to a repression of alternative sources of experience and value. That repression would explain why the feelings of minority groups about their "racial" or cultural identities are so tenacious, for instance, or why claims about the significance of gender or sexual identity are more than the simple "politics of recognition."[18] Quite often, such claims and feelings embody alternative and antihegemonic accounts of what is significant and in fact necessary for a more accurate understanding of the world we all share.

Thus, in analyzing identity-based politics, claims about the general social significance of a particular identity should be evaluated together with its accompanying assumptions or arguments about how the current social or cultural system makes some experiences intelligible and others obscure or irrelevant, how it treats some as legitimate sources of knowledge about the world while relegating others to the level of the narrowly personal. Both the claims and the underlying assumptions refer to the social

---

18. Charles Taylor sees contemporary demands for multiculturalism as primarily the demand for "recognition"; see "The Politics of Recognition" 25–73. It should be evident by now why I would think that this is an underestimation of the multiculturalist claim.

world; they amount to explanatory theses with both empirical and theoretical content. They need to be engaged as such, and evaluated as we evaluate other such descriptions and theories about society. This realist attitude toward identity politics does not guarantee that a particular version of identity politics is justified; that justification will depend on the details of what is being claimed. We need to ask if these details mesh with the world as we know it, and to see how the accompanying theories compare with our best moral and political accounts. Thus, for instance, parallel claims and assumptions can be made by both the kind of feminist identity politics that Alice practices and a retrograde form of religious fundamentalism, and we have no way of choosing between them in advance. It would be hasty to dismiss both Alice's feminist identity and the fundamentalist religious identity *in the same way*, simply because both appeal to personal experience and make some claim to epistemic privilege. As I have been emphasizing, realism about identity requires that we see identities as complex theories about (and explanations of) the social world, and the only way to evaluate such theories is to look at how well they work as explanations. "Good" social and cultural identities are quite simply (based on) good explanations of the social world. Such explanations are not purely empirical, and what makes them "good" is in part the cogency of the background theories they draw on, which often necessarily have deep moral and evaluative content. But such necessary interdependence of the empirical and the theoretical, the factual and the evaluative, is, the postpositivist realist will point out, not evidence of the unique epistemic status of cultural identities; this interdependence is a feature of all inquiry, scientific and moral, and adjudicating between different identity claims is not fundamentally all that different from adjudicating between two fairly complex accounts of the natural or social world. There simply is no easy way out, for a lot depends on the details. What we lose by looking for an easy way out—for example, by denying all identities validity because they are always tied to personal experience and subjective judgments—is the capacity to make useful and important distinctions between different kinds of identity, different kinds of value and judgment.

WORKS CITED

Appiah, Anthony. "The Conservation of 'Race.'" *Black American Literature Forum* 23.1 (Spring 1989): 37–69.
———. "The Uncompleted Argument: Du Bois and the Illusion of Race." *Critical Inquiry* 12.1 (1985): 21–37.

Baker, Houston A., Jr. "Caliban's Triple Play." *"Race," Writing, and Difference.* Ed. Henry Louis Gates. Vol. 12, no. 1. Chicago: University of Chicago Press. 381–95.

Bhabha, Homi K. "Interrogating Identity: The Postcolonial Prerogative." *Anatomy of Racism.* Ed. David Theo Goldberg. Minneapolis: University of Minnesota Press, 1990. 183–209.

Boyd, Richard N. "How to Be a Moral Realist." *Essays on Moral Realism.* Ed. Geoffrey Sayre-McCord. Ithaca: Cornell University Press, 1988. 181–228.

———. "Metaphor and Theory Change: What Is 'Metaphor' a Metaphor For?" *Metaphor and Thought.* Ed. Andrew Ortony. New York: Cambridge University Press, 1979. 356–408.

Culler, Jonathan. *On Deconstruction: Theory and Criticism after Structuralism.* Ithaca: Cornell University Press, 1982.

de Sousa, Ronald. "The Rationality of Emotions." *Explaining Emotions.* Ed. Amelie O. Rorty. Berkeley: University of California Press, 1980. 127–51.

Fuss, Diana. *Essentially Speaking: Feminism, Nature & Difference.* New York: Routledge, 1989.

Gates, Henry Louis, ed. *"Race," Writing, and Difference.* Vol. 12, no. 1. Chicago: University of Chicago Press, 1985.

Gilbert, Alan. "Marx's Moral Realism: Eudaimonism and Moral Progress." *After Marx.* Ed. Terence Ball and James Farr. New York: Cambridge University Press, 1984. 154–83.

Haraway, Donna J. "Situated Knowledges: The Science Question in Feminism and the Privilege of Partial Perspective." *Simians, Cyborgs, and Women.* New York: Routledge, 1991. 183–201, 248–50.

Harding, Sandra. *Whose Science? Whose Knowledge? Thinking from Women's Lives.* Ithaca: Cornell University Press, 1991.

Henderson, Mae G. "Toni Morrison's *Beloved:* Remembering the Body as Historical Text." *Comparative American Identities.* Ed. Hortense Spillers. New York: Routledge, 1991. 62–87.

Jardine, Alice A. *Gynesis.* Ithaca: Cornell University Press, 1985.

LaCapra, Dominick. "The Personal, the Political and the Textual: Paul de Man as Object of Transference." *History and Memory* 4.1 (1992): 5–38.

———. "Representing the Holocaust: Reflections on Historians' Debate." *Probing the Limits of Representation: Nazism and the "Final Solution."* Ed. Saul Friedlander. Cambridge, MA: Harvard University Press, 1992. 108–27, 356–60.

Laclau, Ernesto, and Chantal Mouffe. *Hegemony & Socialist Strategy: Towards a Radical Democratic Politics.* Trans. Winston Moore and Paul Cammack. London: Verso, 1985.

Lorde, Audre. *Sister Outsider.* Freedom, CA: Crossing Press, 1984.

Mohanty, Chandra Talpade. "Cartographies of Struggle: Third World Women and the Politics of Feminism." *Third World Women and the Politics of Feminism.* Ed. Chandra Talpade Mohanty, Ann Russo, and Lourdes Torres. Bloomington: Indiana University Press, 1991. 1–47.

Mohanty, Satya. "Drawing the Color Line: Kipling and the Culture of Colonial Rule." *The Bounds of Race: Perspectives on Hegemony and Resistance.* Ed. Dominick LaCapra. Ithaca: Cornell University Press, 1991. 311–42.

————. *Literary Theory and the Claims of History: Postmodernism, Objectivity, Multicultural Politics.* Ithaca: Cornell University Press, 1997.

————. "Us and Them: On the Philosophical Basis of Political Criticism." *Yale Journal of Criticism* 2.2 (1989): 1–31.

Mohanty, Satya P., and Jonathan Monroe. "John Ashbery and the Articulation of the Social." *Diacritics* 17.2 (Summer 1987): 37–63.

Morrison, Toni. *Beloved.* New York: Knopf, 1987.

————. "The Site of Memory." *Inventing the Truth: The Art and Craft of Memoir.* Ed. William Zinsser. Boston: Houghton Mifflin, 1987. 103–24.

Nietzsche, Friedrich. *On the Genealogy of Morals. Basic Writings of Nietzsche.* Trans. and ed. Walter Kaufmann. New York: Modern Library, 1969. 449–599.

————. *The Will to Power.* Trans. Walter Kaufmann and R. J. Hollingdale. Ed. Walter Kaufmann. New York: Vintage, 1968.

Nussbaum, Martha. *Love's Knowledge.* New York: Oxford University Press, 1990.

Putnam, Hilary. "Explanation and Reference." *Mind, Language and Reality.* New York: Cambridge University Press, 1975. 196–214.

————. "The Meaning of 'Meaning.'" *Mind, Language and Reality.* 215–71.

Quine, W. V. O. "Epistemology Naturalized." *Naturalizing Epistemology.* Ed. Hilary Kornblith. Cambridge, MA: MIT Press, 1985. 15–29.

————. *Ontological Relativity and Other Essays.* New York: Columbia University Press, 1969. 126–28.

Railton, Peter. "Marx and the Objectivity of Science." *The Philosophy of Science.* Ed. Richard Boyd, Philip Gasper, and J. D. Trout. Cambridge, MA: MIT Press, 1991. 763–73.

Rorty, Richard. *Philosophy and the Mirror of Nature.* Princeton: Princeton University Press, 1979.

Scheman, Naomi. "Anger and the Politics of Naming." *Women and Language in Literature and Society.* Ed. Sally McConnell-Ginet, Ruth Borker, and Nelly Furman. New York: Praeger, 1980. 174–87.

————. "Individualism and the Objects of Psychology." *Discovering Reality.* Ed. Sandra Harding and Merril B. Hintikka. Dordrecht: D. Riedel, 1983. 225–44.

Scott, Joan. "'Experience.'" *Feminists Theorize the Political.* Ed. Judith Butler and Joan Scott. New York: Routledge, 1992. 22–40.

Sivanandan, A. "RAT and the Degradation of Black Struggle." *Communities of Resistance: Writings on Black Struggles for Socialism.* London: Verso, 1990. 77–122.

Spillers, Hortense. "Mama's Baby, Papa's Maybe: An American Grammar Book." *Diacritics* 17.2 (1987): 65–81.

Spivak, Gayatri Chakravorty. *In Other Worlds: Essays in Cultural Politics.* New York: Routledge, 1987.

Taylor, Charles. "The Politics of Recognition." *Multiculturalism and the Politics of Recognition: An Essay by Charles Taylor.* Ed. Amy Gutmann. Princeton: Princeton University Press, 1992. 25–73.

CHAPTER 2

Postmodernism, "Realism," and the Politics of Identity

Cherríe Moraga and Chicana Feminism

Paula M. L. Moya

> If we are interested in building a movement that will not constantly
> be subverted by internal differences, then we must build from the
> insideout, not the other way around. Coming to terms with the
> suffering of others has never meant looking away from our own.
>
> Cherríe Moraga, *This Bridge Called My Back*

In her foreword to the second edition of *This Bridge Called My Back,* co-editor Cherríe Moraga admits to feeling discouraged about the prospects for a Third World feminism. The three years intervening between the first and second editions of *Bridge* have confirmed her insight that "Third World feminism does not provide the kind of easy political framework that women of color" run to in droves. Time has strengthened her awareness that women of color are not a "'natural' affinity group" but are people who, across sometimes painful differences, "come together out of political necessity." However, if Moraga has abandoned an easy optimism, she has not forsaken her dream of building a "broad-based U.S. women of color movement capable of spanning borders of nation and ethnicity." Urging us to "look deeply" within ourselves, Moraga encourages us to come to terms with our own suffering in order to challenge and, if necessary, "change ourselves, even sometimes our most cherished block-hard convictions." In calling for us to look within ourselves, Moraga demonstrates her comprehension that coalitions across difference require a thorough understanding of how we are different from others, as well as how they are different from us. Because differences are relational, our ability to understand an "other" depends largely on our willingness to examine our "self." For Moraga, in the service of a larger project, "difference" is something to be deliberately and respectfully engaged.

In another context, we see a quite contrary treatment of the concept of difference. Within the field of U.S. literary and cultural studies, the institutionalization of a discourse of postmodernism has spawned an approach to difference that ironically erases the distinctiveness and relationality of difference itself. typically, postmodernist theorists either internalize difference so that the individual is herself seen as "fragmented" and "contradictory" (thus disregarding the distinctions that exist between different kinds of people), or they attempt to "subvert" difference by showing that "difference" is merely a discursive illusion (thus leaving no way to contend with the fact that people experience themselves as different from each other). In either case, postmodernists reinscribe, albeit unintentionally, a kind of universalizing sameness (we are all marginal now!) that their celebration of "difference" had tried so hard to avoid. Under the hegemonic influence of postmodernism within U.S. literary and cultural studies, the feminist scholar concerned with engaging difference in the way Moraga suggests will be bound by certain theoretical and methodological constraints. She will be justifiably wary of using categories of analysis (such as "race" or "gender") or invoking concepts (like "experience" or "identity") that have been displaced or "deconstructed" by postmodernist theorists. If, as Judith Butler and Joan Scott claim in their introduction to *Feminists Theorize the Political,* concepts like "experience" and "identity" enact a "silent violence . . . as they have operated not merely to marginalize certain groups, but to erase and exclude them from the notion of 'community' altogether," then any invocation of these "foundational" concepts will be seen as always already tainted with exclusionary and totalizing forms of power (xiv). In the current theoretical climate within U.S. literary and cultural studies, the feminist scholar who persists in using categories such as race or gender can be presumptively charged with essentialism, while her appeals to "experience" or "identity" may cause her to be dismissed as either dangerously reactionary or hopelessly naive. If, on the contrary, she accepts the strictures placed on her by postmodernism, the concerned feminist scholar may well find it difficult to explain why some people experience feelings of racial self-hatred while others feel a sense of racial superiority, some people live in poverty while others live in comfort, and some people have to worry about getting pregnant while others do not. Feminist scholars have begun to note the legislative effect of postmodernism on feminist theorizing. In her essay "Feminism and Postmodernism," Linda Singer points to what she sees as an "impulse" within contemporary feminist discourse "to establish some privileged relationship with postmodern discourse which is intended to have regulative impact on the conduct of feminist theory and practice":

> Both from within and from outside feminist discourse, there re-emerges with regularity these days a cautionary invective with respect to the appropriation of the language concepts and rhetoric—like that of the subject or personal identity—which has been placed in a problematized epistemic suspension by postmodern tactics of deconstruction. While such cautionary considerations are not without merit (and many, at least to my mind, are truly compelling), it is both presumptuous and pre-emptive to assume that such considerations must occupy some privileged position with respect to the development of feminist theory in the range and breadth of its concerns and approaches. (468)

Similarly, in her paper "The Elimination of Experience in Feminist Theory," Linda Martín Alcoff notes that "the rising influence of postmodernism has had a noticeable debilitating effect on [the project of empowering women as knowledge producers], producing a flurry of critical attacks on unproblematized accounts of experience and on identity politics" (4). Such critical attacks have served, in conventional theoretical wisdom, to delegitimize *all* accounts of experience and to undermine all forms of identity politics—unproblematized or not.

The problem posed by postmodernism is particularly acute for U.S. feminist scholars and activists of color, for whom "experience" and "identity" continue to be primary organizing principles around which they theorize and mobilize. Even women of color who readily acknowledge the nonessential nature of their political or theoretical commitments persist in referring to themselves as, for instance, "Chicana" or "black" feminists and continue to join organizations, such as Mujeres Activas en Letras y Cambio Social (MALCS), that are organized around principles of identity. For example, Moraga acknowledges that women of color are not a "'natural' affinity group" even as she works to build a movement around and for people who identify as women of color. She can do this, without contradiction, since her understanding of the identity "women of color" reconceptualizes the notion of "identity" itself. Unlike postmodernist feminists who understand the concept of identity as inherently and perniciously "foundational," Moraga understands identities as relational and grounded in the historically produced social categories that constitute social locations.

Ironically, Moraga and other women of color are often called on in postmodernist feminist accounts of identity to delegitimize any theoretical project that attends to the linkages between identity (with its experiential and cognitive components) and social location (the particular nexus of gender, race, class, and sexuality in which a given individual exists in the world). Such projects are derided by postmodernist feminists as theoretically mistaken and dangerously "exclusionary"—particularly in relation to women of color themselves.[1]

Accordingly, I devote the first section of this chapter to an examination of the theoretical misappropriation of women of color—specifically the Chicana activist and theorist Cherríe Moraga—by the influential postmodernist theorists Judith Butler and Donna Haraway. I criticize these two theorists not only because they appropriate Moraga's words without attending to her theoretical insights but also, and more important, because they employ her work at key moments in their arguments to legitimate their respective theoretical projects. In the second section, I draw on the work of Satya P. Mohanty to articulate a "postpositivist realist" account of Chicana identity that goes beyond essentialism by theorizing the connections among social location, experience, cultural identity, and knowledge.[2]

1. In their introduction to *Feminists Theorize the Political,* Scott and Butler ask the following questions: "What are the points of convergence between a) poststructuralist criticisms of identity and b) recent theory by women of color that critically exposes the unified or coherent subject as a prerogative of white theory?"; "To what extent do the terms used to defend the universal subject encode fears about those cultural minorities excluded in and by the construction of that subject; to what extent is the outcry against the 'postmodern' a defense of culturally privileged epistemic positions that leave unexamined the excluded domains of homosexuality, race, and class?"; "What is the significance of the poststructuralist critique of binary logic for the theorization of the subaltern?"; and "How do universal theories of 'patriarchy' or phallogocentrism need to be rethought in order to avoid the consequences of a white-feminist epistemological/cultural imperialism?" My point is that such questions enact an un-self-critical enlistment of the "woman of color," the "subaltern," and the "cultural minority" to serve as legitimators of the project entailed in "postmodern" or poststructuralist criticisms of identity.

2. When I use the term "realism" in this work, I am not referring to the literary mode in which the details of the plot or characters are "true to life." I refer, instead, to a philosophical (and, in particular, epistemological) position. Broadly speaking, a realist epistemology implies a belief in a "reality" that exists independently of our mental constructions of it. Thus, while our (better or worse) understandings of our world may provide our only access to "reality," our mental constructions of the world do not constitute the totality of what can be considered "real." It ought to be made clear that when the postpositivist realist says that something is "real," she does not mean to say that it is not socially constructed; rather, her point is that it is not only socially constructed. In the case of identity, for instance, the realist claim is that there is a nonarbitrary limit to the range of identities we can "construct" or "choose" for any person in a given social formation. It is that nonarbitrary limit that forms the boundary between (objective) "reality" and our (subjective) construction—or understanding—of it. For more on the implications of "realism" within the context of literary studies, see Satya Mohanty's "Colonial Legacies, Multicultural Futures," esp. 111–15.

By demonstrating the cognitive component of cultural identity, I underscore the possibility that some identities can be more politically progressive than others *not* because they are "transgressive" or "indeterminate" but because they provide us with a critical perspective from which we can disclose the complicated workings of ideology and oppression. Finally, in the last section, I provide my own realist reading of Moraga and show—by resituating her work within the cultural and historical conditions from which it emerged—that Moraga's elaboration of a "theory in the flesh" gestures toward a realist theory of identity. A realist reading of Moraga's work presents a strong case for how and why the theoretical insights of women of color are necessary for understanding fundamental aspects of U.S. society.

POSTMODERNIST CYBORGS AND THE DENIAL OF SOCIAL LOCATION

In her influential essay, "A Manifesto for Cyborgs," Donna Haraway figures Chicanas as exemplary cyborgs and, as such, prototypical postmodern subjects. She identifies two paradigmatic "group of texts" that she sees as constructing cyborg identities: "women of color and monstrous selves in feminist science fiction" (216). Although Haraway usually employs the generic term "women of color," she accords Chicanas a privileged position within her framework. According to Haraway, the primary characteristic of the cyborg is that of a creature who transcends, confuses, or destroys boundaries. Chicanas, as the products of the intermixing of Spaniards, Indians, and Africans, cannot claim racial or cultural purity. Their neither/nor racial status, their unclear genealogical relationship to the history of oppression (as descendants of both colonizer and colonized), and their ambiguous national identity (as neither Mexican nor fully "American") give Chicanas their signifying power within the terms of the cyborgian myth. To demonstrate that Haraway does, in fact, figure Chicanas as exemplary cyborgs, I have juxtaposed below a few passages from Haraway's text that describe characteristics first of cyborgs (I) and then of Chicanas/women of color (II). Notice how Haraway's figuration of Chicanas, instead of liberating them from a historically determined discursive position, ironically traps them—as well as their living counterparts in the real world—within a specific *signifying* function:

   I. Cyborg writing must not be about the Fall, the imagination of a once-upon-a-time wholeness before language, before writing, before Man. (217)

II. Malinche was the mother here, not Eve before eating the forbidden fruit. Writing affirms Sister Outsider, not the Woman-before-the-Fall-into-Writing needed by the phallogocentric Family of Man. (218)

I. A cyborg body is not innocent; it was not born in a garden; it does not seek unitary identity and so generates antagonistic dualisms without end (or until the world ends); it takes irony for granted . . . (222)

II. Cherríe Moraga in *Loving in the War Years* explores the themes of identity when one never possessed the original language, never told the original story, never resided in the harmony of legitimate heterosexuality in the garden of culture, and so cannot base identity on a myth or a fall from innocence and right to natural names, mother's or father's. (217)

I. Writing is preeminently the technology of cyborgs, etched surfaces of the late twentieth century. Cyborg politics is the struggle for language and the struggle against perfect communication, against the one code that translates all meaning perfectly, the central dogma of phallogocentrism. (218)

II. Figuratively and literally, language politics pervade the struggles of women of color, and stories about language have a special power in the rich contemporary writing by U.S. women of color. . . . Moraga's writing, her superb literacy, is presented in her poetry as the same kind of violation as Malinche's mastery of the conqueror's language—a violation, an illegitimate production, that allows survival. (217–18)

Haraway claims that "women of color" can be understood as a "cyborg identity, a potent subjectivity synthesized from fusions of outsider identities" (217). She bases her claim, in part, on her appropriation and misreading of the Mexicano/Chicano myth of Malinche—a misreading that allows her to celebrate the symbolic birth of a new "bastard" race and the death of the founding myth of original wholeness:

> For example, retellings of the story of the indigenous woman Malinche, mother of the mestizo "bastard" race of the new world, master of languages, and mistress of Cortés, carry special meaning for Chicana constructions of identity. . . . Sister Outsider hints at the possibility of world survival not because of her innocence, but because of her ability to live on the boundaries, to write without the founding myth of original wholeness. . . . Malinche was mother here, not Eve before eating the forbidden fruit. Writing affirms Sister Outsider, not the Woman-before-the-Fall-into-Writing needed by the phallogocentric Family of Man. (217–18)[3]

3. The name "Sister Outsider" derives from Audre Lorde's book of the same name. Haraway's easy substitution of the name "Sister Outsider" for that of "Malinche" and her conflation of Chicana with Malinche with Sister Outsider signal her inattention to the differences (temporal, historical, and material) that exist between the three distinct constructions of identity.

La Malinche, also referred to as Doña Marina or Malintzín Tenepal, was the Indian woman who served as translator for Hernán Cortés during the decisive period of the fall of the Aztec empire. According to the memoirs of Bernal Díaz del Castillo, who participated in and chronicled the conquest of the Aztec empire, Malintzín was born the daughter of *caciques* (Aztec nobility) (85). After the death of her father, and while she was still a young girl, her mother and stepfather sold her into captivity, ostensibly to leave the succession to the position of *cacique* free for her younger half brother. According to Díaz, she was sold to Indians from Xicalango who then gave or sold her to the Indians of Tabasco (85).

After the battle of Cintla, which took place shortly after Cortés landed at Cozumel, Malintzín was given to Cortés by the Tabascan Indians along with nineteen other women as a part of the spoils of war. From the Tabascans she learned to speak Chontal Maya, and it was her bilingualism that made her invaluable to Cortés. Cortés was able to speak Spanish to the Spaniard Aguilar (who had spent several years as a slave to the Maya Indians), who then spoke Chontal Maya to Doña Marina, who translated into Nahuatl for Moctezuma and his numerous vassals (Díaz del Castillo 86–87). It was in this manner that Cortés effected the communication that was so critical to his conquest of Mexico.

Today, La Malinche lives on as a symbol of enormous cultural significance for Mexicanas and Chicanas. As the mother of Cortés's son, she is figured as the symbolic mother of *mestizaje,* the mixing of Spanish and Indian blood. As the "dark" mother, the "fucked one," the "betrayer of her race," she is the figure against which women of Mexican descent have had to define themselves.[4] As the whore of the virgin/whore dichotomy in a culture that reveres la Virgen, she has been despised and reviled.

From the 1970s on, Mexicana and Chicana feminists have addressed the myth of Malinche, and several have attempted to recuperate and revalue her as a figure of empowering or empowered womanhood.[5] Such recuperations are generally problematic, inasmuch as attempts to absolve or empower the historical figure can result in reductive interpretations of

4. See Octavio Paz's influential essay, "The Sons of La Malinche," which in the process of describing has served to confirm Malinche's position as the "Mexican Eve."

5. Norma Alarcón, in her two essays "Traddutora, traditora" and "Chicana's Feminist Literature," provides a useful analysis of some of these attempts, as does Moraga in "A Long Line of Vendidas" in *Loving.* See also Adelaida R. del Castillo, "Malintzín Tenepal"; Cordelia Candelaria, "La Malinche, Feminist Prototype"; Sylvia Gonzales, "La Chicana"; and Rachel Phillips, "Marina/Malinche."

what is a very complex situation. Cherríe Moraga's treatment of Malinche is neither naive nor reductive; she confronts the myth and examines its implications for the sexual and social situation of Chicanas today. In her essay "A Long Line of Vendidas," she looks carefully at "this myth of the inherent unreliability of women, our natural propensity for treachery, which has been carved into the very bone of Mexican/Chicano collective psychology" (*Loving* 101), and addresses the continuing painful effects of the Malinche myth.

> The potential accusation of "traitor" or "vendida" is what hangs above the heads and beats in the hearts of most Chicanas seeking to develop our own autonomous sense of ourselves, particularly through sex and sexuality. Even if a Chicana knew no Mexican history, the concept of betraying one's race through sex and sexual politics is as common as corn. As cultural myths reflect the economics, mores, and social structures of a society, every Chicana suffers from their effects. (*Loving* 103)

Haraway's reading of the Malinche myth ignores the complexity of the situation. She concludes her discussion of Malinche by claiming, "Stripped of identity, the bastard race teaches about the power of the margins and the importance of a mother like Malinche. Women of color have transformed her from the evil mother of masculinist fear into the originally literate mother who teaches survival" (218–19). With this statement, Haraway conceals the painful legacy of the Malinche myth and overinvests the figure of Malinche with a questionable agency. Moreover, Haraway uncritically affirms a positionality (the margins) and a mode of existence (survival) that actual Chicanas have found to be rather less (instead of more) affirming. I do not mean to suggest that marginality and survival are not important and valuable. Certainly survival is valuable wherever the alternative is extinction. And, as I will argue, the experience and the theorizing of marginalized or oppressed people is important for arriving at a more objective understanding of the world. But I would suggest that neither marginality nor survival is a sufficient goal for a feminist project and that no theoretical account of feminist identity can be based exclusively on such goals.

My point is that Haraway's conflation of cyborgs with women of color raises serious theoretical and political issues, because she conceives the social identities of women of color in overly idealized terms. As previously noted, Haraway's conception of a cyborg is that of a creature who transcends or destroys boundaries. It is "the illegitimate offspring of militarism and patriarchal capitalism," "a kind of disassembled and reassembled, postmodern collective and personal self," a being "committed to partiality, irony, intimacy and perversity," who is "not afraid of permanently partial identities and contradictory standpoints," and who is "related [to other cyborgs] not by blood but by *choice*" (193, 205, 192, 196; emphasis added). The porosity and polysemy of the category "cyborg," in effect, leaves no criteria to determine who might *not* be a cyborg. Furthermore, since Haraway sees a lack of any essential criterion for determining who is a woman of color, anyone can be a woman of color. Thus all cyborgs can be women of color and all women of color can be cyborgs. By sheer force of will (by "choice" as Haraway puts it) and by committing oneself (or refusing to commit oneself) to "permanently partial identities and contradictory standpoints," anyone can be either one or the other—or neither.[6]

The key theoretical problem here is Haraway's understanding of identity as a willful construction, as independent of the limiting effects of social location. Lacking an analysis of how the social categories that make up our social locations are causally relevant for the experiences we have, as well as of how those experiences inform our cultural identities, Haraway cannot conceive of a way to ground identities without essentializing them. Although she correctly ascertains that people are not uniformly determined by any one social category, she wrongly concludes that social categories (such as gender or race) can be irrelevant to the identities we choose. Haraway's refusal to grant women of color grounded identities has the effect of rendering all claims to a woman of color identity equally valid. This theoretical stance allows Haraway to make the political move of assuming the position of the authoritative speaking subject with respect to women of color.

> From the perspective of cyborgs, freed of the need to ground politics in "our" privileged position of the oppression that incorporates all other dominations, the innocence of the merely violated, the ground of those closer to nature, we can see powerful possibilities. . . . With no available original dream of a common language or original symbiosis promising protection from hostile "masculine" separation, but written into the play of a text that has no finally priv-

6. Linda Alcoff has suggested to me that Haraway might not intend to imply that "all cyborgs can be women of color"—that she meant only that "women of color" is one particular kind of cyborg identity. If so, we are left with "women of color cyborgs" and "white women cyborgs" (and perhaps other kinds of male cyborgs as well). In that case, of what use is a cyborg identity? Unless a cyborg identity can effectively dismantle "difference" (and the effect difference has on our experiences of the world), it is at best innocuous and at worst quite dangerous. We must acknowledge that a cyborg identity has the potential to become simply another veil to hide behind in order not to have to examine the differences that both constitute and challenge our self-conceptions.

ileged reading or salvation history, to recognize "oneself" as fully implicated
in the world, frees us of the need to root politics in identification, vanguard
parties, purity, and mothering. Stripped of identity, the bastard race teaches
about the power of the margins and the importance of a mother like Malinche. Women of color have transformed her from the evil mother of masculinist fear into the originally literate mother who teaches survival. (219)

By freeing herself of the obligation to ground identity in social location, Haraway is able to arrogate the meaning of the term "woman of
color." With this misappropriation, Haraway authorizes herself to
speak for actual women of color, to dismiss our own interpretations of
our experiences of oppression, our "need to root politics in identification," and even our identities. Furthermore, she employs several
rhetorical strategies designed to undermine "identity" as a concept and
"identity politics" as a practice. First, she (incorrectly) implies that play-
ers of identity politics necessarily claim the "privileged position of the
oppression that incorporates all other dominations"; she then impov-
erishes the discussion by linking identity politics to naive forms of essentialism that base themselves in "vanguard parties, purity, and mothering." The fact that most women of color (including Moraga) continue
to organize and theorize on the basis of their identities as women of
color—and that their identities as women of color are intimately tied to
the social categories (race, gender, etc.) that make up their individual
social locations—completely drops from sight in Haraway's representation of their work. It is worth noting that even within the terms of
Haraway's cyborgian myth, the "bastard race" is not "stripped of identity" inasmuch as "bastard race" is itself a term of identification.

    Although far more cursory, Judith Butler's treatment of Moraga's
writings is also a highly questionable attempt to enlist women of color
for a postmodernist agenda. In her often-cited work, *Gender Trouble,*
Butler extracts one sentence from Moraga, buries it in a footnote, and
then misreads it in order to justify her own inability to account for the
complex interrelations that structure various forms of human identity
(see 153 n. 24). She reads Moraga's statement "the danger lies in ranking the oppressions" to mean that we have no way of adjudicating among
different kinds of oppressions—that any attempt to relate causally or
hierarchize the varieties of oppressions people suffer constitutes an imperializing, colonizing, or totalizing gesture that renders the effort invalid.
This misreading of Moraga follows on the heels of Butler's dismissal of
Luce Irigaray's notion of phallogocentrism (as globalizing and exclusionary) and clears the way for her to do away with the category

"women" altogether. Thus, although Butler at first appears to have understood the critiques of women (primarily of color) who have been historically precluded from occupying the position of the "subject" of feminism, it becomes clear that their voices have been merely instrumental to her. She writes,

> The opening discussion in this chapter argues that this globalizing gesture [to find universally shared structures of oppression along an axis of sexual difference] has spawned a number of criticisms from women who claim that the category of "women" is normative and exclusionary and is invoked with the unmarked dimensions of class and racial privilege intact. In other words, the insistence upon the coherence and unity of the category of women has effectively refused the multiplicity of cultural, social and political intersections in which the concrete array of "women" are constructed. (14)

Butler's response to this critique is not to rethink her understanding of the category "women" but rather to radically undermine it as a valid political or analytic category. Underlying her logic are the assumptions that because the varieties of oppressions cannot be "summarily" ranked, they cannot be ranked at all; because epistemological projects have been totalizing and imperializing, they are always and necessarily so; and unless a given category (such as "women") is transhistorical, transcultural, stable, and uncontestable, it is not a valid analytic and political category.

It should be emphasized that the passage in Moraga that Butler cites provides no actual support for Butler's argument. To read Moraga the way Butler reads her is to ignore the italicized statement that immediately follows the caution against ranking oppressions, namely, "*The danger lies in failing to acknowledge the specificity of the oppression,*" as well as to ignore the statement that immediately follows that one, "The danger lies in attempting to deal with oppression purely from a theoretical base" (Moraga and Anzaldúa, *Bridge* 52; henceforth referred to as *Bridge*). When Moraga talks about ranking the oppressions in the context from which this sentence is extracted, she is referring to the necessity of theorizing the connections between (and not simply ranking) the different kinds of oppressions people suffer.[7] More specifically, she is referring to the situation in which militant women of color with feminist convictions often find themselves. Militant men of color claim their first loyalty on the basis of race and disparage their involvement with femi-

---

7. See "A Long Line of Vendidas" in which Moraga talks about the necessity of theorizing the "simultaneity of oppression," by which she means taking "race, ethnicity and class into account in determining where women are at sexually," and in which she clearly acknowledges that some people "suffer more" than others (*Loving* 128).

nism, which is, the men insist, a "white women" thing. Meanwhile, their
white feminist sisters claim their first loyalty on the basis of gender, urging women of color to see the way in which they are being exploited by
their own fathers, husbands, and brothers.[8] When Moraga writes that
the "danger lies in ranking the oppressions," she is warning against the
reductive theoretical tendency (whether it be Marxist, feminist, or cultural nationalist) to posit one kind of oppression as primary for all time
and in all places. She is not advocating an admission of defeat in the
project of trying to figure out how the varieties of oppressions suffered
by the woman of color intersect with, or are determined by, each other.

Common to both Haraway's and Butler's accounts of identity is the
assumption of a postmodern "subject" of feminism whose identity is unstable, shifting, and contradictory: "she" can claim no grounded tie to
any aspect of "her" identit(ies) because "her" anti-imperialist, shifting,
and contradictory politics have no cognitive basis in *experience*. Ironically, although both Haraway and Butler lay claim to an anti-imperialist project, their strategies of resistance to oppression lack efficacy in a
material world. Their attempts to disrupt gender categories (Butler) or
to conjure away identity politics (Haraway) make it difficult to figure
out who is "us" and who is "them," who is the "oppressed" and who
is the "oppressor," who shares our interests and whose interests are opposed to ours.[9] Distinctions dissolve as all beings (human, plant, animal,
and machine) are granted citizenship in the radically fragmented, unstable
society of the postmodern world. "Difference" is magically subverted,
and we find out that we really are all the same after all!

The key theoretical issue turns on Haraway's and Butler's disavowal
of the link between identity (with its experiential and cognitive components) and social location (the particular nexus of gender, race, class, and

---

8. For a more developed explanation of this phenomenon, see the section "Who Are
My People," in Gloria Anzaldúa's essay "La Prieta" published in *This Bridge Called My
Back*. Anzaldúa writes of those who insist on viewing the different parts of her in isolation: "They would chop me up into little fragments and tag each piece with a label." She
then goes on to affirm her oneness: "Only your labels split me" (205). Rather than give
way to fragmentation, she insists on holding it all together: "The mixture of bloods and
affinities, rather than confusing or unbalancing me, has forced me to achieve a kind of
equilibrium. . . . I walk the tightrope with ease and grace. I span abysses. . . . I walk the
rope—an acrobat in equipoise, expert at the Balancing Act" (209).

9. As long as our world is hierarchically organized along relations of domination, categories such as "us" and "them" or "oppressed" and "oppressor" will retain their explanatory function. This is not because any one group belongs, in an essential way, to a
particular category but rather because the terms describe positions within prevailing social and economic relations.

sexuality in which a given individual exists in the world). Haraway and Butler err in the assumption that because there is no one-to-one correspondence between social location and identity or knowledge, there is simply no connection between social location and identity or knowledge. I agree that in theory boundaries are infinitely permeable and power may be amorphous. The difficulty is that people do not live in an entirely abstract or discursive realm. They live as biologically and temporally limited, as well as socially situated, human beings. Furthermore, although the "postmodern" moment does represent a time of rapid social, political, economic, and discursive shifts, it does not represent a radical break with systems, structures, and meanings of the past. Power is not amorphous since oppression is systematic and structural. A politics of discourse that does not provide for some sort of bodily or concrete action outside the realm of the academic text will forever be inadequate to change the difficult "reality" of our lives. Only by acknowledging the specificity and "simultaneity of oppression," and the fact that some people are more oppressed than others, can we begin to understand the systems and structures that perpetuate oppression and thereby place ourselves in a position to contest and change them (Moraga, *Loving* 128).

Until we do so, Cherríe Moraga, together with other women of color, will find herself leaving from Guatemala only to arrive at Guatepeor.[10] She will find herself caught in the dilemma of being reduced to her Chicana lesbian body, or having to deny her social location (for which her body is a compelling metaphor) as the principal place from which she derives her insights. Moraga's dilemma appears as a contradiction to the theorist who recognizes a choice only between essentialist and postmodernist accounts of identity and knowledge. On the one hand, Moraga is articulating a "theory in the flesh," derived from "the physical realities of [women of colors'] lives—[their] skin color, the land or concrete [they] grew up on, [their] sexual longings" (*Bridge* 23); on the other hand, she reminds us that "sex and race do not define a person's politics" (*Last Generation* 149). How can a theory be derived from the "physical realities of [women of color's] lives" if "sex and race do not define a person's politics"? When we examine this paradox from a "postpositivist realist" perspective, the contradiction will be dissolved. Theory, knowledge, and understanding can be linked to "our skin color, the land

---

10. The Spanish-language proverb "Salir de Guatemala para entrar en Guatepeor" plays with the word fragment "mala" in "Guatemala" to suggest the dilemma of a person caught between a bad (*mala*) and a worse (*peor*) situation. The proverb roughly approximates the English-language proverb "To go from the frying pan into the fire."

or concrete we grew up on, our sexual longings," without being uniformly
determined by them. Rather, those "physical realities of our lives" will
profoundly *inform* the contours and the context of both our theories and
our knowledge.[11] The effects that the "physical realities of our lives" have
on us, then, are what need to be addressed—not dismissed or dispersed—
by theorists of social identity.

TOWARD A REALIST THEORY OF CHICANA IDENTITY

In this section I draw on Satya Mohanty's important book, *Literary Theory
and the Claims of History,* to articulate a postpositivist realist account of
Chicana identity that theorizes the linkages among social location, experience, epistemic privilege, and cultural identity. I must emphasize that this
project is not an attempt to rehabilitate an essentialist view of identity.
The critiques of essentialism are numerous; the aporias of an essentialist
notion of identity have been well documented.[12] The mistake lies in assuming that our options for theorizing identities are inscribed within the
postmodernism/essentialism binary—that we are either completely fixed
and unitary or unstable and fragmented selves. The advantage of a realist theory of identity is that it allows for an acknowledgment of how the
social categories of race, class, gender, and sexuality function in individual lives without *reducing* individuals to those social determinants.

I begin by clarifying my claims and defining some terms. "Epistemic
privilege," as I use it in this chapter, refers to a special advantage with
respect to possessing or acquiring knowledge about how fundamental

---

11. At the risk of stating what should be obvious, this is as true for the white heterosexual politically conservative antifeminist as it is for the radical feminist lesbian of color.
And yet it is primarily women who address gender issues and primarily people of color
who address racial issues (both inside the academy and outside). The unspoken assumption is that only women have gender and only people of color are racialized beings. This
assumption reflects itself in the work of many male academics who talk about gender only
when they are referring to women and in the work of many white academics who talk
about race only when they are referring to people of color. A manifestation of this phenomenon can be found in Judith Butler's book *Bodies That Matter,* where she only theorizes race in the two chapters in which she discusses artistic productions by or about people
of color.

12. In my use of "essentialism," I am referring to the notion that individuals or groups
have an immutable and discoverable "essence"—a basic, unvariable, and presocial nature.
As a theoretical concept, essentialism expresses itself through the tendency to see one social category (class, gender, race, sexuality, etc.) as determinate in the last instance for the
cultural identity of the individual or group in question. As a political strategy, essentialism has had both liberatory and reactionary effects. For one poststructuralist critique of
essentialism that does not quite escape the postmodernist tendency I am critiquing in this
work, see Diana Fuss's *Essentially Speaking.*

aspects of our society (such as race, class, gender, and sexuality) operate to sustain matrices of power. Although I will claim that oppressed groups may have epistemic privilege, I am not implying that social locations have epistemic or political meanings in a self-evident way. The simple fact of having been born a person of color in the United States or of having suffered the effects of heterosexism or of economic deprivation does not, in and of itself, give someone a better understanding or knowledge of the structure of our society. The key to claiming epistemic privilege for people who have been oppressed in a particular way stems from an acknowledgment that they have experiences—experiences that people who are not oppressed in the same way usually lack—that *can* provide them with information we all need to understand how hierarchies of race, class, gender, and sexuality operate to uphold existing regimes of power in our society. Thus what is being claimed is not any a priori link between social location or identity and knowledge but a link that is historically variable and mediated through the interpretation of experience.

"Experience" here refers to the fact of personally observing, encountering, or undergoing a particular event or situation. By this definition, experience is admittedly subjective. Experiences are not wholly external events; they do not just happen. Experiences happen to us, and it is our theoretically mediated interpretation of an event that makes it an "experience." The meanings we give our experiences are inescapably conditioned by the ideologies and "theories" through which we view the world. But the crucial claim in my argument is not that experience is theoretically mediated but rather that experience *in its mediated form* contains a "cognitive component" through which we can gain access to knowledge of the world (Mohanty, *Literary Theory* 205). It is this contention, that it is "precisely in this *mediated* way that [personal experience] yields knowledge," that signals a theoretical departure from the opposed camps of essentialism and postmodernism (206; emphasis added).

The first claim of a postpositivist realist theory of identity is that the different social categories (such as gender, race, class, and sexuality) that together constitute an individual's social location are causally related to the experiences she will have. Thus a person who is racially coded as "white" in our society will usually face situations and have experiences that are significantly different from those of a person who is racially coded as "black."[13] Similarly, a person who is racially coded as "black" and who

---

13. This can happen even if both individuals in the example are born into an African American community and consider themselves "black." It should be clear that I am not

has ample financial resources at her disposal will usually face situations and have experiences that are significantly different from those of a person who is racially coded as "black" and lacks those resources. The examples can proliferate and become increasingly complex, but the basic point is this: the experiences a person is likely to have will be largely determined by her social location in a given society.[14] To appreciate the structural causality of the experiences of any given individual, we must take into account the mutual interaction of *all* the relevant social categories that constitute her social location and situate them within the particular social, cultural, and historical matrix in which she exists.

The second basic claim of a postpositivist realist theory of identity is that an individual's experiences will influence, but not entirely determine, the formation of her cultural identity. Thus, while I am suggesting that members of a group may share experiences as a result of their (voluntary or involuntary) membership in that group, I am not suggesting that they all come to the same conclusions about those experiences.[15] Because the theories through which humans interpret their experiences vary from individual to individual, from time to time, and from situation to situation, it follows that different people's interpretations of the same kind of event will differ. For example, one woman may interpret her jealous husband's monitoring of her interaction with other men as a sign that "he really loves her," while another may interpret it in terms of the social relations of gender domination, in which a man may be socialized to see himself as both responsible for and in control of his wife's behavior. The kinds of identities these women construct for themselves will both condition and be conditioned by the kinds of interpretations they give to the experiences they have. The first woman may see herself as a treasured wife, while the second sees herself as the victim in a hierar-

---

talking about race as a biological category. I am talking about people who, for one reason or another, appear to others as "white" or "black." As I demonstrate in my discussion of Moraga's work, this is an important distinction for theorizing the link between experience and cultural identity for people with real, but not visible, biological or cultural connections to minority communities.

14. For an illuminating discussion of the way in which the social category of gender has structured the experiences of at least one woman, and has profoundly informed the formation of her cultural identity, see Mohanty's *Literary Theory and the Claims of History* esp. 206–16.

15. It is not even necessary that they recognize themselves as members of that group. For example, a dark-skinned migrant from Puerto Rico who refuses identification with African Americans may nevertheless suffer racist experiences arising from the history of black/white race relations in the United States due to mainland U.S. citizens' inability to distinguish between the two distinct cultural groups.

chically organized society in which, by virtue of her gender, she exists in a subordinate position.

The third claim of a postpositivist realist theory of identity is that there is a cognitive component to identity that allows for the possibility of error and of accuracy in interpreting the things that happen to us. It is a feature of theoretically mediated experience that one person's understanding of the same situation may undergo revision over the course of time, thus rendering her subsequent interpretations of that situation more or less accurate. I have as an example my own experience of the fact that the other women in my freshman dorm at Yale treated me differently than they treated each other. My initial interpretation of the situation led me to conclude that they just did not like me—the individual, the particular package of hopes, dreams, habits, and mannerisms that I was. Never having had much trouble making friends, I found this experience both troubling and humbling. As a "Spanish" girl from New Mexico, I did not consider race or racism as social realities relevant to me. I might have wondered (but I did not) why I ended up spending my first semester at Yale with the other brown-skinned, Spanish-surnamed woman in my residential college. It was only after I moved to Texas, where prejudice against Mexicans is much more overt, that I realized that regardless of how I saw myself, other people saw me as "Mexican." Reflecting back, I came to understand that while I had not seen the other women in my dorm as being particularly different from me, the reverse was not the case. Simultaneous with that understanding came the suspicion that my claim to a Spanish identity might be both factually and ideologically suspect. A little digging proved my suspicion correct.[16] In Texas, then, I became belatedly and unceremoniously Mexican American. All this to illustrate the point that identities both condition and are conditioned by the kinds of interpretations people give to the experiences they have. As Mohanty says, "identities are ways of making sense of our experiences." They are "theoretical constructions that enable us to read the world in specific ways" (*Literary Theory* 216).

The fourth claim of a postpositivist realist theory of identity is that some identities, because they can more adequately account for the social categories constituting an individual's social location, have greater epis-

---

16. For an explanation of the historical origins of the myth that Spanish-surnamed residents of New Mexico are direct descendants of Spanish conquistadors, see Rodolfo Acuña, *Occupied America* 55–60; Nancie González, *The Spanish-Americans of New Mexico* 78–83; John Chávez, *The Lost Land* 85–106.

temic value than some others that the same individual might claim. If, as in the case of my Spanish identity, I am forced to ignore certain salient aspects of my social location in order to maintain my self-conception, we can fairly conclude that my identity is epistemically distorted. While my Spanish identity may have a measure of epistemic validity (mine is a Spanish surname; I undoubtedly have some "Spanish blood"), we can consider it less valid than an alternative identity that takes into consideration the ignored social aspects (my "Indian blood"; my Mexican cultural heritage) together with all the other social categories that are causally relevant for the experiences I might have. Identities have more or less epistemic validity to the extent that they "refer" outward to the world, that they accurately describe and explain the complex interactions between the multiple determinants of an individual's social location.[17] According to the realist theory of identity, identities are not self-evident, unchanging, and uncontestable, nor are they absolutely fragmented, contradictory, and unstable. Rather, identities are subject to multiple determinations and to a continual process of verification that takes place over the course of an individual's life through her interaction with the society she lives in. It is in this process of verification that identities can be (and often are) contested and that they can (and often do) change.

I want to consider now the possibility that my identity as a "Chicana" can grant me a knowledge about the world that is "truer," and more "objective," than an alternative identity I might claim as either a "Mexican American," a "Hispanic," or an "American" (who happens to be of Mexican descent). When I refer to a Mexican American, I am referring to a person of Mexican heritage born and/or raised in the United States whose nationality is U.S. American. The term for me is descriptive rather than political. The term "Hispanic" is generally used to refer to a person of Spanish, Mexican, Puerto Rican, Dominican, Cuban, Chilean, Peruvian, and so on, heritage who may or may not have a Spanish surname, who may or may not speak Spanish, who can be of any racial extraction, and who resides in the United States. As it is currently deployed, the term is so general as to be virtually useless as a descriptive or analytical tool. Moreover, the term has been shunned by progressive intellectuals for its overt privileging of the "Spanish" part of what for many of the people it

---

17. Identities can be evaluated, according to Mohanty, "using the same complex epistemic criteria we use to evaluate 'theories.'" He explains, "Since different experiences and identities refer to different aspects of one world, one complex causal structure that we call 'social reality,' the realist theory of identity implies that we can evaluate them comparatively by considering how adequately they explain this structure" (*Literary Theory* 230–31).

claims to describe is a racially and culturally mixed heritage. A Chicana, according to the usage of women who identify that way, is a politically aware woman of Mexican heritage who is at least partially descended from the indigenous people of Mesoamerica and who was born and/or raised in the United States. What distinguishes a Chicana from a Mexican American, a Hispanic, or an American of Mexican descent is her political awareness; her recognition of her disadvantaged position in a hierarchically organized society arranged according to categories of class, race, gender, and sexuality; and her propensity to engage in political struggle aimed at subverting and changing those structures.[18]

The fifth claim of a postpositivist realist theory of identity is that our ability to understand fundamental aspects of our world will depend on our ability to acknowledge and understand the social, political, economic, and epistemic consequences of our own social location. If we can agree that our *one* social world is, as Mohanty asserts, "constitutively defined by relations of domination" (*Literary Theory* 232), then we can begin to see how my cultural identity as a Chicana, which takes into account an acknowledgment and understanding of those relations, may be more epistemically valid than an alternative identity I might claim as a Mexican American, a Hispanic, or an American. While a description of myself as a Mexican American is not technically incorrect, it implies a structural equivalence with other ethnic Americans (Italian Americans, German Americans, African Americans, etc.) that erases the differential social, political, and economic relations that obtain for different groups. This erasure is even more marked in the cultural identity of the Hispanic or American (of Mexican descent), whose self-conception often depends on the idea that she is a member of one more assimilable ethnic group in what is simply a nation of immigrants.[19]

18. Historically, the term "Chicano" was a pejorative name applied to lower-class Mexican Americans. Like the term "black," it was consciously appropriated and revalued by (primarily) students during the Chicano movement of the 1960s. According to "El Plan de Santa Bárbara" (see n. 21), the term specifically implies a politics of resistance to Anglo-American domination.

19. An example of the assimilationist "Hispanic" is Linda Chavez whose book, *Out of the Barrio,* suggests that Hispanics, like "previous" white ethnic groups, are rapidly assimilating into the mainstream of U.S. culture and society (2). Not only does Chavez play fast and loose with sociological and historical evidence, but her thesis cannot account for the social fact of race. She does not mention race as being causally relevant for the experiences of Hispanics, and she repeatedly refers to "non-Hispanic whites," a grammatical formulation that assumes that all Hispanics are white. She accounts for Puerto Ricans and Dominicans by considering them "dysfunctional" "exceptions" to the white-Hispanic rule (139–59).

Factors of race, gender, and class get obscured in these identities, while a normative heterosexuality is simply presumed. We find that, to maintain her identity, the Hispanic or American (of Mexican descent) may have to repress or misinterpret her own or others' experiences of oppression. Moreover, she will most likely view her material situation (her "success" or "failure") as entirely a result of her individual merit and dismiss structural relations of domination as irrelevant to her personal situation. Thus my claim that social locations have epistemic consequences is not the same as claiming that a particular kind of knowledge inheres in a particular social location. An individual's understanding of herself and the world will be mediated, more or less accurately, through her cultural identity.

The sixth and final claim of a postpositivist realist theory of identity is that oppositional struggle is fundamental to our ability to understand the world more accurately. Mohanty, drawing on the work of Sandra Harding and Richard Boyd, explains this Marxian idea in this way:

> In the case of social phenomena like sexism and racism, whose distorted representation benefits the powerful and the established groups and institutions, an attempt at an objective explanation is necessarily continuous with oppositional political struggles. Objective knowledge of such social phenomena is in fact often dependent on the theoretical knowledge that activism creates. For without these alternative constructions and accounts our capacity to interpret and understand the dominant ideologies and institutions is limited to those created or sanctioned by these very ideologies and institutions. (*Literary Theory* 213)

The "alternative constructions and accounts" generated through oppositional struggle provide new ways of looking at our world that always complicate and often challenge dominant conceptions of what is "right," "true," and "beautiful." They call to account the distorted representations of peoples, ideas, and practices whose subjugation is fundamental to the colonial, neocolonial, imperial, or capitalist project. Furthermore, because the well-being (and sometimes even survival) of the groups or individuals who engage in oppositional struggle depends on their ability to refute or dismantle dominant ideologies and institutions, their vision is usually more critical, their efforts more diligent, and their arguments more comprehensive than those of individuals or groups whose well-being is predicated on the maintenance of the status quo. Oppressed groups and individuals have a stake in knowing "what it would take to change [our world and in] . . . identifying the central relations of power and privilege that sustain it and make the world what it is" (Mohanty,

Literary Theory 214). This is why "granting the possibility of epistemic privilege to the oppressed might be more than a sentimental gesture; in many cases in fact it is the only way to push us toward greater social objectivity" (232–33). Thus a realist theory of identity demands oppositional struggle as a necessary (although not sufficient) step toward the achievement of an epistemically privileged position.

A postpositivist realist theory of identity, in contrast to a postmodernist one, thus insists that we acknowledge and interrogate the consequences—social, political, economic, and epistemic—of social location. To do this, we must first acknowledge the reality of those social categories (race, class, gender, and sexuality) that together make up an individual's social location. We do not need to see these categories as uncontestable or absolutely fixed to acknowledge their ontological status. We do, however, need to recognize that they have real material effects and that their effects are systematic rather than accidental. A realist theory of identity understands that while identities are not fixed, neither are they random. There is a nonarbitrary limit to the range of identities we can plausibly "construct" or "choose" for any individual in a given society.

"THEORY IN THE FLESH": CHERRÍE MORAGA'S REALIST FEMINISM

Yvonne Yarbro-Bejarano, in her essay "Gloria Anzaldúa's *Borderlands/La frontera*," captures the exasperation and frustration of many Chicana/o academics who have been witness to the way Anzaldúa's work has been used and abused in the service of a postmodern celebration-cum-deconstruction of "difference." Yarbro-Bejarano's concern is that postmodernists have appropriated Anzaldúa's powerful image of the "border" and her theory of "mestiza consciousness" without attending to the social, cultural, and historical conditions that produced her thought. In the article, Yarbro-Bejarano elaborates what she identifies as "the isolation of this text from its conceptual community and the pitfalls in universalizing the theory of mestiza or border consciousness, which the text painstakingly grounds in specific historical and cultural experiences" (7). Taking Yarbro-Bejarano's cue, my goal in this section is twofold: to resituate Moraga's work within the conceptual community from which it emerges by regrounding it in her specific historical and cultural experiences; and to demonstrate that Moraga's theoretical framework is consistent with a realist theory of identity.

Partly as an outgrowth of ongoing struggles (from 1845) of resistance to American domination, and partly in conjunction with civil rights and other left liberation movements taking place during the 1960s, the Chicano movement, as a distinct historical and political phenomenon, was born. Some of the most visible manifestions of the Chicano movement were the New Mexico–based La Alianza Federal de Mercedes led by Reies Lopez Tijerina, the California-based United Farm Workers' (UFW's) movement headed by César Chávez and Dolores Huerta, the university-based Chicano Student Youth Movement, the Colorado-based Crusade for Justice led by Rodolfo "Corky" Gonzales, and, later, the founding of La Raza Unida party headed in Colorado by Gonzales and in South Texas by Jose Angel Gutierrez.[20]

Within a larger framework of resistance to Anglo-American hegemony, the groups that formed the Chicano movement employed distinct strategies and worked toward different goals. La Alianza and the UFW were primarily class- or labor-based movements working toward the economic improvement of the communities they represented. La Raza Unida emphasized electoral politics and working within existing democratic structures and institutions. The Chicano Student Youth Movement focused on Chicanos' lack of access to education and the problems associated with racial and cultural discrimination. Participants in the Youth Movement worked to establish Chicano Studies programs within existing institutions of higher education and to increase cultural consciousness and pride.[21]

The Chicano movement in general and the Chicano student youth movement in particular fostered the development of a cultural nationalist discourse that emphasized the importance of the family in the project of cultural survival. The sociologist Alma Garcia explains, "Historically, as well as during the 1960s and 1970s, the Chicano family represented a source of cultural and political resistance to the various types of discrimination experienced in American society. At the cultural level, the Chicano movement emphasized the need to safeguard the value of family loyalty. At the political level, the Chicano movement used the family as a strategic organizational tool for protest activities" (219). The Chicano nationalist emphasis on the importance of family loyalty assigned

20. For histories of the Chicano movement, see Acuña, *Occupied America;* Carlos Muñoz, *Youth, Identity, Power;* Sonia López, "The Role of the Chicana within the Student Movement"; Alma Garcia, "The Development of Chicana Feminist Discourse, 1970–1980"; and Ramón Gutiérrez, "Community, Patriarchy and Individualism."

21. "El Plan de Santa Bárbara," written in spring 1969 at a California statewide conference in Santa Barbara, California, founded MEChA (Movimiento Estudiantil Chicano de Aztlán) and is probably the definitive position paper of the Chicano Student Youth Movement. The "Plan" is published as an appendix in Muñoz 191–202.

Chicanas a subordinate and circumscribed role within the movement. They were often relegated to traditional female roles and denied decision-making power. Moreover, although Chicanas were active at every stage and at every level of the Chicano movement, their participation was rarely acknowledged or recorded.

The cultural nationalist emphasis on cultural survival in an Anglo-dominated society further instituted strict controls on the sexual autonomy of Chicanas. Chicanas who dated or married white men were often criticized as *vendidas* and *malinchistas* responsible for perpetuating the legacy of rape handed down to the Chicano community from the conquest of Mexico. This same standard did not apply to males, whose relations with white women were often seen as rectifying an unjust legacy of emasculation at the hands of the white man. Chicana lesbians were viewed as the greatest threat to the cultural integrity of the Chicano community. By engaging in sexual practices that render the male irrelevant, and by refusing to inhabit the culturally mandated subject position of the good wife and mother, Chicana lesbians create the possibility for a resistant Chicana subjectivity that exists outside the boundaries of culturally inscribed notions of Chicana womanhood.[22]

Chicano cultural nationalism found its most eloquent expression within the Chicano student youth movement, and it is from within that segment of the movement that what is frequently recognized as Chicana feminism emerged.[23] The Chicana feminist response to the kind of treatment they received from their Chicano brothers was to point out the contradictions inherent in maintaining one form of oppression in the service of abolishing another. Those who were explicit about their feminist convictions found themselves charged with "selling out" to white women's liberation. They were urged by their *compañeros* to drop their "divisive ideology" and to attend to the "primary" oppression facing all Chicanos—that is, racism. Chicanos often viewed an analysis of sexism within the Chicano movement or community as a threat not only to the movement but to the culture itself.

22. For more information on how both heterosexual and lesbian Chicanas fared within the Chicano movement, see the articles referred to above by López, Gutiérrez, and Garcia, as well as Carla Trujillo, "Chicana Lesbians," and Moraga, *Loving* 105–11.

23. This is not to say that Chicanas outside the university were not asserting themselves and coming to consciousness about their disadvantaged positions—just that the most consistently documented and published expressions of Chicana feminism have emerged from within the academy. For documentation of this claim, see the articles referred to above by Garcia, Gutiérrez, López, and Moraga, as well as Beatriz Pesquera and Denise Segura, "There Is No Going Back."

Some Chicana feminists, disillusioned with Chicano cultural nationalism, began to work within white women's liberation movements in the 1970s. Long-term coalitions never developed, owing to the inability of most white women to recognize the class and race biases inherent in the structures of their own organizations. Furthermore, white feminists often replicated, in another realm, the same kind of privileging of one kind of oppression over another that had bothered Chicanas in relation to Chicanos. Insisting on the primacy of gender oppression, white feminists disregarded the class- and race-based oppression suffered by most Chicanas. This resulted, in the 1980s, in Chicana feminists, together with feminists of other nonwhite racial groups, turning to their own experience as a ground for theorizing their multiple forms of oppression.

Moraga presents an interesting case because she did not participate in the Chicano movement but has been at the forefront of the Chicana feminist response to both Chicano cultural nationalism and Anglo-American feminism.[24] Her position in the forefront can be explained both by the strength of her writings and by the fact that she was initially published and distributed through white feminist presses. Moraga is an important figure for Chicana feminists in the academy today because she is one of two Chicanas (the other being Gloria Anzaldúa) whose work is more than occasionally taken up outside the field of Chicana/o studies. Thus she is one of the few Chicanas called on to "represent" Chicanas in women's studies and feminist theory courses throughout the United States. How she is read, then, is crucial for how we understand the position of the Chicana in U.S. society.

Moraga's Third World feminist political project takes as its starting point the transformation of the experience of women of color. This transformation can be accomplished, Moraga argues, only when women of color understand how their experiences are shaped by the relations of domination within which they live. Thus, while Moraga does not take the acquisition of knowledge as her goal, she sees the acquisition of

---

24. Moraga explains, "During the late 60s and early 70s, I was not an active part of la causa. I never managed to get myself to walk in the marches in East Los Angeles (I merely watched from the sidelines); I never went to one meeting of MECHA on campus. No soy tonta. I would have been murdered in El Movimiento—light-skinned, unable to speak Spanish well enough to hang; miserably attracted to women and fighting it; and constantly questioning all authority, including men's. I felt I did not belong there. Maybe I had really come to believe that 'Chicanos' were 'different,' not 'like us,' as my mother would say. But I fully knew that there was a part of me that was a part of that movement, but it seemed that part would have to go unexpressed until the time I could be a Chicano and the woman I had to be, too" (Loving 113).

knowledge—about women of color and their place in the world—as fundamental to her theoretical project. To that end, Moraga does not advocate turning away from, but toward, the bodies of women of color to develop what she calls a "theory in the flesh."

Moraga's theoretical project, which is consonant with her interest in building a movement of/for radical women of color, involves a heartfelt examination and analysis of the sources of her oppression and her pain. Haraway is correct when she says that Moraga never claims the "innocence of the merely violated." What Moraga does claim is a knowledge that derives from an interpretation of that violation. In a 1986 interview with Norma Alarcón, Moraga described the contours of her theoretical framework:

> I began to see that, in fact, [*Loving in the War Years*] is very much a love story about my family because they made me the lover I am. And also the belief in political change is similar because it can't be theoretical. It's got to be from your heart. They all seem related to me, and I feel that what happened since *Bridge* came out is that I got closer to my own dilemma and struggle—being both Chicana and lesbian. I really feel that all along that's been the heart of the book. I could see that this book was about trying to make some sense of what is supposed to be a contradiction, but you know it ain't cause it lives in your body. (Alarcón; "Interview" 129)

Condensed in this short passage are five concepts central to Moraga's theoretical approach: (1) the family as the primary instrument of socialization ("My family . . . made me the lover I am"); (2) the need for theory to be grounded in emotional investment ("Political change . . . can't be theoretical. It's got to be from your heart"); (3) the link between social location and experience (Moraga represents being Chicana and lesbian in her society as a "dilemma"); (4) the body as a source of knowledge ("You know it ain't cause it lives in your body"); and (5) the centrality of struggle to the formation of her political consciousness. Both in this interview and throughout her writings, Moraga makes clear that it was through her struggles—to deny her *chicanidad* and then to reclaim it; to repress her lesbianism and then to express it; to escape sexism and heterosexism within a Chicano/a cultural context and then to combat racism and classism within an Anglo-American feminist movement—that she comes to understand the necessity for a nonessentialist feminist theory that can explain the political and theoretical salience of social location.

According to Moraga, a "theory in the flesh means one where the physical realities of our lives—our skin color, the land or concrete we grew up on, our sexual longings—all fuse to create a politic born out of necessity" (*Bridge* 23). It attempts to describe "the ways in which Third World women derive a feminist political theory specifically from [their] racial/cultural background and experience" (*Bridge* xxiv). Implicit in these formulations are the realist insights that the different social categories of a woman's existence are relevant for the experiences she will have and that those experiences will inform her understanding of the world and the development of her politics. Moraga's contribution to the practice she names has been to recognize it and describe it as *theoretically mediated*. Unlike some other feminists of color whose writings seem to imply a self-evident relationship among social location, knowledge, and identity, Moraga explicitly posits that relationship as theoretically mediated through the interpretation of experience in the ways I have outlined.

As we have seen, Moraga's refusal to assume a self-evident or one-to-one correspondence between social location and knowledge opens her work to co-optation by postmodernist feminist critiques of identity. But what postmodernist interpretations of Moraga's writings fail to take into account is her emphasis on bodies and her insistence on the necessity of theorizing from the "flesh and blood experiences of the woman of color" (*Bridge* 23). In her own articulation of a theory in the flesh, Moraga emphasizes the materiality of the body by conceptualizing "flesh" as the site on or within which the woman of color experiences the painful material effects of living in her particular social location (*Bridge* xviii). Her focus on women of color's vulnerability to pain starkly emphasizes the way they experience themselves as embodied beings. Over the course of their lives, women of color face situations and have experiences that arise as a result of how other people misrecognize them. Others routinely react to women of color with preconceived ideas about the meanings their bodies convey. These misrecognitions can be amusing; often they are painful. Moreover, the way others misrecognize women of color can affect the kind of jobs they will "qualify" for, or where they might be able to live. The material effects these misrecognitions have are why postmodernist theories of identity that do not account for the causal connection between social location and experience have no real liberatory potential for women of color or other multiply oppressed individuals.

Moraga's personal example illustrates that a woman of color's response to her socially disadvantaged position is not uniform and can change over time. Moraga's initial prereflective and visceral response to being Chicana and lesbian was to deny her chicanidad and repress her lesbianism. This response represented an attempt on Moraga's part to claim access to the privilege that whiteness and heterosexuality are accorded in U.S.

society. In her essay "La Güera," Moraga talks about how the fact of her white skin facilitated her early denial of her Mexican cultural heritage: "I was educated, and wore it with a keen sense of pride and satisfaction, my head propped up with the knowledge, from my mother, that my life would be easier than hers. I was educated; but more than this, I was "la güera": fair-skinned. Born with the features of my Chicana mother, but the skin of my Anglo father, I had it made" (*Bridge* 28).[25]

As a young girl, Moraga shared her mother's concern that she be in a position to transcend the barriers faced by individuals in U.S. society who are situated as "poor, uneducated, and Chicana." The best way she and her mother could see for Moraga to accomplish this goal was for her to leave behind her Mexican cultural heritage—the presumed "cause" of her poverty and powerlessness. Their unstated goal was for Moraga to become "anglocized," a condition that, they assumed, would give her access to power and privilege. In the conceptual universe within which they were working, Moraga's white skin, her Anglo surname, and her education would be her tickets to the promised land.

Moraga's "anglocization" was at first encouraged by her growing awareness of her lesbian sexuality. The product of a strict Mexican and Catholic upbringing, Moraga concluded at the age of twelve that her strong emotional attachments to women, which she had started to identify as sexual, must be "impure" and "sinful" (*Loving* 119). Her response to this conclusion was to beat a terrified retreat into the region of religion, thus abandoning the body that was beginning to betray her biological femaleness. In the article she wrote with Amber Hollibaugh, "What We're Rollin Around in Bed With," Moraga reveals her alarm at the changes her body went through during puberty: "I didn't really think of myself as female, or male. I thought of myself as this hybrid or something. I just kinda thought of myself as this free agent until I got tits. Then I thought, '*oh, oh, some problem has occurred here*'" (Hollibaugh and Moraga 60). Moraga's growing awareness of her own biological femaleness, and the inability to act she associated with that femaleness, caused her to feel "crucially and critically alone and powerless" (*Loving* 120). This awareness, combined with the realization that her sexual feelings for women were inappropriate according to the standards of the

25. The fact of Moraga's "whiteness" is central to an accurate mapping of her social location and crucial to an understanding of the formation of her cultural identity. That her "whiteness" has been systematically overlooked by postmodernist readings of Moraga's work is symptomatic of the failure of postmodernist theories of identity to take account of the complex interactions among the multiple determinants of human identity.

society in which she lived, prompted Moraga to disavow her racialized and sexualized body. She writes that "in order to not embody the *chingada,* nor the femalized, and therefore perverse, version of the *chingón,* I became pure spirit—bodiless" (*Loving* 120).[26]

For years Moraga lived in a state of what she describes as "an absent inarticulate terror" (*Loving* 121). Her feelings for women, which she had tried so hard to suppress, did not fully reawaken until she became sexually active with men. Even then, Moraga could not face her lesbiansim. She explains, "The sheer prospect of being a lesbian was too great to bear, fully believing that giving into such desires would find me shot-up with bullets or drugs in a gutter somewhere" (*Loving* 122). She began to be revisited by "feelings of outsiderhood"; she saw herself as "half-animal/half-human, hairy-rumped and cloven-hoofed, como el diablo" (*Loving* 124). It took a series of breakdowns before Moraga could begin the process of learning to live with her sexual desire for women. In that process, she became further alienated from her Chicana/o community. Because Moraga experienced her sexuality as contrary to the social mores of a Chicana/o community, it was that particular community she needed to leave in order to, in the words of Anzaldúa, "come out as the person [she] really was" (*Loving* 116). Moraga explains, "I became anglocized because I thought it was the only option available to me toward gaining autonomy as a person without being sexually stigmatized. . . . I instinctively made choices which I thought would allow me greater freedom of movement in the future" (*Loving* 99).

Given the urgency of her need to come to terms with her sexual identity, Moraga became, as if by default, "white." As the light-skinned daughter of a dark-skinned Mexican-origin woman, Moraga had a choice, of sorts, as to which "race" she would identify with. According to the logic of what the anthropologist Marvin Harris calls hypo-descent, Moraga is Mexican and therefore nonwhite (56). The empirical fact that there is no "Mexican" race, that "Mexican" denotes a nationality and not a race, and that some Mexicans are phenotypically "white" seems to have little bearing on the ethnic/racial classification of Mexican-origin people in the United States. Practically speaking, the "racial" classification into which any given individual is placed in the United States today is pred-

---

26. The Spanish verb *chingar* is stronger than the English verb *to fuck.* A highly gendered word, it carries within it connotations of the English verb *to rape.* Thus *chingón* refers to the (active) male rapist/fucker and *chingada* refers to the (passive) female who is raped/fucked.

icated much more on how they look, speak, act, walk, think, and identify than on the word or words on their birth certificates. Thus Moraga can be seen as "white" by those who do not know her well and as a "woman of color" by those who do.

Moraga's identification as "white" was at least partially motivated by two underlying assumptions at work in the conceptual universe from which she emerged. The first assumption is that homosexuality belongs, in an essential way, to white people. Moraga explains that homosexuality is seen by many Chicana/os as "his [the white man's] disease with which he sinisterly infects Third World people, men and women alike" (*Loving* 114). The second assumption, which follows from the first, is that a woman cannot be a Chicana and a lesbian at the same time. These two assumptions, combined with the fact that Moraga was still clinging to the privilege (here figured as "freedom of movement") that the color of her skin might afford her, precluded any understanding of what it meant for her to be a *Chicana* lesbian. As long as Moraga avoided examining how the various social categories that constituted her social location intersected with, and were determined by, each other, she could conceive of her sexuality in isolation from her race. Moraga had not yet acknowledged how her Chicano "family . . . made [her] the lover [she is]" (*Loving* 129).

Moraga's eventual coming to terms with her Chicana cultural identity was facilitated by her experience of marginalization within the women's movement.[27] However "white" she might have felt in relation to a Chicano community, she felt a sense of cultural dislocation when other women of color were not present in the feminist organizations in which she was active. However accepting of lesbianism the feminist movement tried to be, it did not deal adequately with the ways in which race and class have shaped women's sexuality.[28]

27. Although I use the term "women's movement" in the singular, I am aware that the various feminisms are diverse and multidimensional. If I am vague, it is because Moraga does not specify which feminist group(s) she involved herself with. Throughout most of her writings, Moraga equates the "women's movement" or "feminism" with an unspecified and predominantly middle-class white women's movement. She does, at one point, specifically critique "Radical Feminism" (*Loving* 125–30).

28. See Amber Hollibaugh and Cherríe Moraga, "What We're Rollin Around in Bed With." In this conversation, Moraga and Hollibaugh address the failure of feminist theory and rhetoric to deal adequately with women's lived experiences of sexuality. They accuse the feminist movement of desexualizing women's sexuality by confusing sexuality with sexual oppression. They suggest that the refusal to acknowledge butch/femme roles in lesbian relationships and the failure to understand how those sexual identities influence and condition sexual behavior have led to (1) a delegitimization of sexual desire and (2) bad

Moraga realized that a feminist movement with an exclusive focus on gender oppression could not provide the home she was looking for (*Loving* 125). In 1981, partly as a result of the alienation each had suffered within the women's movement, Moraga and Anzaldúa published *This Bridge Called My Back*. Although the collection was originally conceived as an anthology to be written by women of color and addressed to white women for the purpose of exposing the race and class biases inherent in many feminist organizations and theories, it evolved into "a positive affirmation of the commitment of women of color to [their] own feminism" (xxiii). The project was transformative, especially for the women involved in its inception and execution. For Moraga, at least, an examination of the racism, classism, and heterosexism she saw in the society around her entailed an examination of the racism, classism, and homophobia she had internalized from that society. Following Audre Lorde's suggestion that "each one of us . . . reach down into that deep place of knowledge inside herself and touch that terror and loathing of difference that lives there," Moraga turned her attention to the sources of her own oppression and pain (*Bridge* xvi). It was this self-reflexive examination that allowed Moraga finally to make the connections between the sexual and the racial aspects of her cultural identity. By examining her own experience with oppression, Moraga was able to come to an empathetic understanding of the (different yet similar) experience of oppression suffered by her mother (*Bridge* 28–30). Moraga's understanding and empathy thus worked to free her from the internalized racism and classism that had kept her from claiming a Chicana identity.

Moraga's example illustrates the possibility of coming to understand someone else's experience of oppression through empathetic connection— what Moraga, following Emma Goldman, calls "entering into the lives of others" (*Bridge* 27). Her example also illustrates the point that however dependent empathetic understanding is on personal experience, the simple fact of experiencing oppression is not sufficient for understanding someone else's oppressive situation. Moraga's initial (and largely unexamined) reaction to her own experiences of oppression at first prevented her from empathizing with her mother's plight. It was not until she reinterpreted her experiences according to a different and more accurate theoretical framework that she was able to empathize with and

---

theory. They contend that a woman's sexual identity, which is necessarily influenced by her race and class background, can tell us something fundamental about the way she constitutes herself/is constituted as a woman.

understand her mother's position. In other words, "experience is epistemically indispensable but never epistemically sufficient" for arriving at a more objective understanding of a situation (Alcoff 6). How objectively it is understood will depend on how adequate is the "theory" that explains the intersecting social, economic, and political relations that constitute the subject and object of knowledge. What this suggests is that, in order to evaluate how accurately we understand a particular event or happening, we must first examine our interpretation of that event. Rather than argue, as postmodernist feminists do, that the theoretically mediated nature of experience renders it epistemically unreliable, we should address ourselves to the adequacy of the theoretical mediations that inform the different interpretations we give to our knowledge-generating experiences.

When, in her writings, Moraga talks about the need for people to "deal with the primary source of [their] own oppression . . . [and] to emotionally come to terms with what it feels like to be a victim," she is not advocating the kind of narcissistic navel gazing that equates victimhood with innocence (*Bridge* 30). As Haraway rightly suggests, Moraga does not claim the "privileged position of the oppression that incorporates all other dominations," or the self-righteous "innocence of the merely violated." Central to Moraga's understanding of oppression is that it is a physical, material, psychological, and/or rhetorical manifestation of the intersecting relations of domination that constitute our shared world. To the extent that individuals are differentially situated within those relations, they may be simultaneously constituted as both oppressor and oppressed. So, an upper-class white woman can be oppressed by patriarchy at the same time that she oppresses others (such as poor men of color) through the privilege afforded to her by her race and class. Moraga would further argue that relinquishing the notion that there is a "privileged position of the oppression that incorporates all other dominations" does not free us of the need to relate causally the intersecting relations of domination that condition our experiences of oppression. And since the exercise of oppression is systematic and relations of domination are structural, Moraga understands that an examination of oppression is simultaneously an examination of fundamental aspects of a world that is hierarchically organized according to categories of class, race, gender, and sexuality. Thus Moraga's call for women of color to examine their own lives is ultimately a call for women of color to understand the oppressive systems and structures within which they live as part of their larger project to "change the world" (*Bridge,* foreword to 2d ed.).

Moraga is aware that what she is asking for will not be easy. She understands why we are often afraid to examine how we are implicated in relations of domination: *"the sources of oppression form not only our radicalism, but also our pain.* Therefore, they are often the places we feel we must protect unexamined at all costs" (*Loving* 134; original emphasis). To do the kind of self-reflexive examination Moraga calls for can mean having to admit "how deeply 'the man's' words have been ingrained in us" (*Bridge* 32). The project of examining our own location within the relations of domination becomes even riskier when we realize that doing so might mean giving up "whatever privileges we have managed to squeeze out of this society by virtue of our gender, race, class or sexuality" (*Bridge* 30). We are afraid to admit that we have benefited from the oppression of others. "[We fear] the immobilization threatened by [our] own incipient guilt." We fear we might have to "change [our lives] once [we] have seen [ourselves] in the bodies of the people [we have] called different. [We fear] the hatred, anger, and vengeance of those [we have] hurt" (*Loving* 56–57).

Moraga's self-interrogation involved acknowledging how she has been guilty of working her own privilege, "ignorantly, at the expense of others" (*Bridge* 34). Moraga *now*, unlike many other white-skinned "Hispanics," has come to understand—through making connections between her experience as a woman in a male world and a lesbian in a heterosexual world—how what functions as the privilege of looking "white" in U.S. society has significantly shaped her experience of the world. The consequences, for Moraga, have been both positive and negative. On the one hand, she credits her light skin and Anglo surname with pushing her into the college prep "A" group in high school and with making her and her siblings *"the* success stories of the family," and, on the other, she has had to "push up against a wall of resistance from [her] own people" in her attempts to claim a Chicana/o identity (*Loving* 96–97; *Bridge* 33–34).

What should be clear from my analysis of Moraga's work is that her "theory in the flesh" is derived from, although not uniformly determined by, "the physical realities" of her life, her "social location." I have shown that the social categories that make up her particular social location are causally relevant for the experiences she has had, and demonstrated that Moraga's cultural identity both conditions and is conditioned by her interpretations of those experiences. I have also shown how and why Moraga's interpretations of her experiences have changed over time. Moraga's understanding of the world—her knowledge—has been mediated through her cultural identity, which is indissolubly linked, through her experiences, to the various social categories of her particular material existence.

A realist theory of identity thus provides women of color with a nonessentialist way to ground their identities. It gives us a way of knowing and acting from within our own social location or "flesh." Like Moraga, we will no longer have to aspire to a bodiless, genderless, raceless, and sexless existence (an existence that has traditionally been conceptualized in terms of the unmarked but nevertheless privileged heterosexual white male) to claim justifiable knowledge of the world around us. A realist theory of identity gives women of color a way to establish that we *do* possess knowledge—knowledge important not only for ourselves but also for all who wish to more accurately understand the world— and that we possess it partly as a result of the fact that we *are* women of color.

WORKS CITED

Acuña, Rodolfo. *Occupied America: A History of Chicanos*. 3d ed. New York: HarperCollins, 1988.

Alarcón, Norma. "Chicana's Feminist Literature: A Re-vision through Malintzin/or Malintzin: Putting Flesh Back on the Object." *This Bridge Called My Back: Writings by Radical Women of Color*. Ed. Gloria Anzaldúa and Cherríe Moraga. 2d ed. New York: Kitchen Table: Women of Color Press, 1983. 182–90.

———. "Interview with Cherríe Moraga." *Third Woman* 3.1–2 (1986): 127–34.

———. "Traddutora, traditora: A Paradigmatic Figure of Chicana Feminism." *Cultural Critique* 13 (Fall 1989): 57–87.

Alcoff, Linda Martín. "The Elimination of Experience in Feminist Theory." Paper presented at Women's Studies Symposium, Cornell University, February 23, 1995.

Butler, Judith. *Bodies That Matter: On the Discursive Limits of "Sex."* New York: Routledge, 1993.

———. *Gender Trouble: Feminism and the Subversion of Identity*. New York: Routledge, 1990.

Butler, Judith, and Joan Scott. Introduction. *Feminists Theorize the Political*. Ed. Judith Butler and Joan Scott. New York: Routledge, 1992.

Candelaria, Cordelia. "La Malinche, Feminist Prototype." *Frontiers: A Journal of Women's Studies* 2 (1980): 1–6.

Chávez, John R. *The Lost Land: The Chicano Image of the Southwest*. Albuquerque: University of New Mexico Press, 1984.

Chavez, Linda. *Out of the Barrio: Toward a New Politics of Hispanic Assimilation*. New York: Basic Books, 1991.

Del Castillo, Adelaida R. "Malintzin Tenepal: A Preliminary Look into a New

Perspective." *Essays on La Mujer.* Ed. Rosaura Sanchez and Rosa Martinez Cruz. Los Angeles: Chicano Studies Publications, UCLA, 1977. 124–49.

Díaz del Castillo, Bernal. *The Conquest of New Spain.* Trans. J. M. Cohen. Aylesbury, U.K.: Penguin, 1963.

Fuss, Diana. *Essentially Speaking: Feminism, Nature & Difference.* New York: Routledge, 1989.

Garcia, Alma M. "The Development of Chicana Feminist Discourse, 1970–1980." *Gender & Society* 3.2 (1989): 217–38.

Gonzales, Sylvia. "La Chicana: Guadalupe or Malinche." *Comparative Perspectives on Third World Women, the Impact of Race, Sex, and Class.* Ed. Beverly Lindsay. New York: Praeger, 1980.

González, Nancie L. *The Spanish-Americans of New Mexico: A Heritage of Pride.* Albuquerque: University of New Mexico Press, 1967.

Gutiérrez, Ramón A. "Community, Patriarchy and Individualism: The Politics of Chicano History and the Dream of Equality." *American Quarterly* 45.1 (1993): 44–72.

Haraway, Donna. "A Manifesto for Cyborgs: Science, Technology, and Socialist Feminism in the 1980s." *Feminism/Postmodernism.* Ed. Linda J. Nicholson. New York: Routledge, 1990. 190–233.

Harris, Marvin. *Patterns of Race in the Americas.* New York: Norton, 1964.

Hollibaugh, Amber, and Cherríe Moraga. "What We're Rollin Around in Bed With: Sexual Silences in Feminism, a Conversation Toward Ending Them." *Heresies* 12 (Spring 1981): 58–62.

López, Sonia. "The Role of the Chicana within the Student Movement." *Essays on La Mujer.* Ed. Rosaura Sanchez and Rosa Martinez Cruz. Los Angeles: University of California Press, 1977.

Lorde, Audre. *Sister Outsider.* Freedom, CA: Crossing Press, 1984.

Mohanty, Satya P. "Colonial Legacies, Multicultural Futures: Relativism, Objectivity, and the Challenge of Otherness." *PMLA* 110.1 (1995): 108–18.

———. *Literary Theory and the Claims of History: Postmodernism, Objectivity, Multicultural Politics.* Ithaca: Cornell University Press, 1997.

Moraga, Cherríe. *The Last Generation.* Boston: South End Press, 1993.

———. *Loving in the War Years: Lo que nunca pasó por sus labios.* Boston: South End Press, 1983.

Moraga, Cherríe, and Gloria Anzaldúa, eds. *This Bridge Called My Back: Writings by Radical Women of Color.* 2d ed. New York: Kitchen Table: Women of Color Press, 1983.

Muñoz, Carlos, Jr. *Youth, Identity, Power: The Chicano Movement.* London: Verso, 1989.

Paz, Octavio. "The Sons of La Malinche." Trans. Lysander Kemp. *The Labyrinth of Solitude.* New York: Grove Press, 1985. 65–88.

Pesquera, Beatriz M., and Denise M. Segura. "There Is No Going Back: Chicanas and Feminism." *Chicana Critical Issues.* Ed. Norma Alarcón, Rafaela Castro, Emma Pérez, Beatriz Pesquera, Adaljiza Sosa Riddell, and Patricia Zavella. Berkeley: Third Woman Press, 1993. 95–115.

Phillips, Rachel. "Marina/Malinche: Masks and Shadows." *Women in Hispanic*

Literature. Ed. Beth Miller. Berkeley: University of California Press, 1983. 97–114.

Singer, Linda. "Feminism and Postmodernism." *Feminists Theorize the Political.* Ed. Judith Butler and Joan Scott. New York: Routledge, 1992. 464–75.

Trujillo, Carla. "Chicana Lesbians: Fear and Loathing in the Chicano Community." *Chicana Lesbians: The Girls Our Mothers Warned Us About.* Ed. Carla Trujillo. Berkeley: Third Woman Press, 1991. 186–94.

Yarbro-Bejarano, Yvonne. "Gloria Anzaldúa's *Borderlands/La frontera*: Cultural Studies, 'Difference,' and the Non-Unitary Subject." *Cultural Critique* 28 (Fall 1994): 5–28.

CHAPTER 3

"Who Are Our Own People?"

Challenges for a Theory of Social Identity

Michael R. Hames-García

In this chapter I argue two points. First, I demonstrate that a postpositivist realist theory of identity can account for the role of multiplicity (of, for example, race, gender, class, and sexuality as determinants of identity) in an enabling way. This is because it offers the most adequate response to the challenge posed by multiplicity to restricted (i.e., reified, nonmultiple) ways of understanding identity. As I discuss below, this "challenge" is one of the most prominent features of literature by women of color and gay men of color. Second, I look at the question of ethical issues in U.S. multiethnic literatures and argue that these literatures have much to contribute to debates about community, justice, and freedom. Many works by racial and ethnic minorities develop ethical concepts out of particular contexts and experiences and present them for transcultural evaluation and application. In other words, literature by racial and ethnic minorities can offer something to members of other cultural groups. These insights are not simply "relative" to a particular social location but rather can be binding on those of other social groups. I address postpositivist realism, among other strategies (e.g., positivism and post-

Thank you to Satya Mohanty, Linda Alcoff, Biodun Jeyifo, Ben Olguín, Bill Wilkerson, Paula Moya, Jeff Paris, Patricia Huntington, Dana Luciano, Eduardo Mendieta, Ernesto Martínez, and others who commented on various parts and drafts of this project, including audiences at Morgan State University, the University of San Francisco, the University of Rhode Island, and Cornell University.

structuralism), as an attempt to respond to the need for a sophisticated theory of social identity.

MULTIPLICITY

Photographs can portray endless shapes and variations of hue and contrast. While one album may contain hundreds of photographs, no two even remotely alike, all of the photographs contain combinations of three primary colors: red, yellow, and blue. Each of the photographs may contain yellow, yet the yellow may be present in different densities and shapes and combine with red and blue in different densities and shapes. Thus no two photographs contain yellow in the same way. In some photographs, the yellow may not be visible; there may only be some green, or orange. What the yellow looks like depends not only on its own shape and density but also on the shape and density of the red and the blue and their position in relation both to the yellow and to each other. Thus yellow next to red looks different from yellow next to blue.[1]

One of the premises of this chapter is that the self is similar to this conception of a photograph. Memberships in various social groups combine with and mutually constitute one another. Membership in one group (e.g., "femaleness") thus means something different in the context of some simultaneous group memberships (e.g., "blackness") than in others (e.g., "motherhood"). The totality of these relations in their mutual constitution comprises the self. One important consequence of this fact is that one cannot understand a self as the sum of so many discrete parts, that is, femaleness + blackness + motherhood. The whole self is constituted by the mutual interaction and relation of its parts to one another. Politically salient aspects of the self, such as race, ethnicity, sexuality, gender, and class, link and imbricate themselves in fundamental ways.[2] These various categories of social identity do not, therefore, comprise essentially separate "axes" that occasionally "intersect." They do not simply intersect but blend, constantly and differently, like the colors of a photograph. They expand one another and mutually constitute each other's meanings. In other words, the subjective experience of any social group

1. Cf. "Our perception [of colors] is animated by a logic which assigns to each object its determinate features in virtue of those of the rest" (Merleau-Ponty 313).
2. Works that make this point particularly well include the following: Almaguer 86–90; Jordan 155–61, 181–87; Lorde 110–23; Moraga 52–55, 132–42; Spelman 114–32.

membership depends fundamentally on relations to memberships in other social groups.

RESTRICTION

Unfortunately, this multiplicity of the self becomes obscured through the logic of domination to which the self becomes subjected. According to the fracturing logic of domination inhering in capitalist cultures, this multiplicity of the self becomes restricted so that any one person's "identity" is reduced to and understood exclusively in terms of that aspect of her or his self with the most political salience. What does it mean to be understood exclusively in terms of one's race, gender, or sexuality? It means that one is understood in terms of the most dominant construction of that identity. Those whose interests conform largely to such dominant constructions of their identity might be said to have "transparent" interests. By contrast, there are those who, possibly by virtue of membership in multiple politically salient groups, often find themselves and their interests distorted by restricted definitions and understandings; their interests, rather than transparent, are "opaque."[3] I call the process by which such individuals come to be misrepresented and misunderstood "restriction." Thus a heterosexual, middle-class, white woman's interests as a woman would be transparent insofar as her interests as a woman are typically taken to represent those of women as a group. Black women, gay Chicanos, and Asian American lesbians are examples of people who have memberships in multiple politically subordinated groups in the United States. Their political interests thus often appear opaque insofar as they differ from those of the hegemonic members of the politically salient social groups to which they belong. Since restriction is fundamentally an issue of misknowing and being misknown, I will consider it and resistance to it in primarily epistemological terms. I will propose shortly that one viable approach to gaining a more adequate epistemological framework for evaluating these issues lies in the postpositivist realism recently proposed by Satya Mohanty and others. My discussion should not, however, be interpreted as making the claim that an academic inquiry into epistemology alone can counter what are also thoroughly political and material (ontological) issues.

I want to further illustrate the concepts of multiplicity and restriction

3. The distinction between transparent and opaque interests is adapted from Lugones's similar distinction between "transparent" and "thick" group members (474).

with a brief example from Michael Nava's 1992 mystery novel, *The Hidden Law*. The main character of the book is a gay Chicano lawyer named Henry Rios. In the novel, a prominent Chicano California state senator is shot and killed and the prime suspect is a troubled Chicano teenager. Convinced that the boy is innocent, Henry takes the case. A subplot in the book deals with the deteriorating relationship between Henry and his white, HIV positive lover, Josh. What interests me here is an aspect of the book that is a common theme in many writings by women of color and gays and lesbians of color. Throughout the novel Henry comes into contact with prominent Chicano academics and politicians. In all his interactions with these other Chicanos, there is a layer of hostility directed toward him because of his sexuality. Because the case receives a great deal of publicity, however, this hostility is veiled (however thinly). This projects an image of unity in the public eye. The effect of such experiences for the main character is to make him feel like an outsider in the Chicano community, a community that claims to include him. At the same time, Henry feels *solidarity* and *connection* with the homophobic Chicano characters (based on their shared position as members of an embattled U.S. minority group).[4] So, the question I want to answer is this: How can a critical epistemological realism account for such complexities and contradictions and also explain (and facilitate) the *expansion* of solidarity and group interests in a way that can help to overcome restriction and separation? Calls for the expansion of solidarity and understanding are common to many works by women of color and gay men of color, from Toni Morrison's *Beloved* to Marlon Riggs's *Tongues Untied*. Such calls demand that individuals see their own interests, their own people, their own familia, as extending beyond narrow conceptualizations of themselves, beyond their own experiences, beyond their immediate group identifications.

What does it mean for both Henry and the Chicano politicians who disdain him because of his sexuality to identify themselves as "Chicano"? Certainly, they do not belong to the group "Chicano" in an identical manner. For Henry, to be Chicano is to be a victim of homophobia within a community that claims to hold him as a member and to represent his interests. It is this as much as it is anything else. One might object that I am here confusing the specific features of "gay" and "Chicano," that I should separate "gay" and "Chicano" conceptually in order to under-

---

4. For other excellent discussions of the problem of fragmentation of opaque interests, see Moraga 112–17; Crenshaw 411–16, 419–27.

stand Henry's situation. Once I understand that Henry is subjected to *homophobia* in this instance, then I can understand that it has to do with "his gay identity" and not with "his Chicano identity." This objection, however, presupposes a preracialized (nonracial) sexual identity or essence that then intersects a presexualized (nonsexual) racial identity or essence. If one assumes that sexual meanings are brought to bear on (what can only then be nonsexual) racial identities, one posits *in advance* a separation between these identities. The crucial error here comes from asking how two *separate* identities come to "intersect," instead of starting from the presumption of mutual constitution.[5] This is like assuming that one can have pure essences of blue and yellow and that green is nothing more than the combination of the properties of each. Besides the question of whether green might be something more than this, it begs the question of how to determine which yellow (or blue) represents the true yellow (or blue). Yellow (or blue) against a white background, or a black one? Brightly lit, or dimly? Henry's membership and his experience in the group of Chicano men are not identical to those of a straight Chicano man because his sexuality is a central aspect of his Chicano identity. Similarly, because part of what it means for him to be gay, unlike his white lover, Josh, has to do with what it means for him to be Chicano, his membership and his experience in the group of gay men are not identical to those of a white gay man. For Henry, *to be gay* means, in part, to deal with homophobia in a community (the Chicano community) to which he feels a tremendous degree of personal commitment. Conversely, another salient difference between Henry and Josh proves to be HIV status. Their conflicts over this difference result in the disintegration of their relationship by the book's conclusion, because Josh, being HIV positive, has a fundamentally different understanding of *what it means to be gay* than does Henry.

Thus what a theory of social identity must be able to account for is multiplicity, the mutual imbrication of politically salient categories, such as race, ethnicity, sexuality, gender, and class. I want to repeat that these cannot be seen as essentially separate axes that sometimes intersect. Group memberships do not simply intersect; they blend, constantly and differently, expanding one another and mutually constituting one another's meanings. It is no coincidence that works by Cherríe Moraga, Gloria Anzaldúa, James Baldwin, Audre Lorde, and Octavia Butler are

---

5. Elizabeth Spelman makes this point rather well in *Inessential Woman* (133–37, esp. 135).

consistently interpreted as challenging "unitary," "monolithic," "mono-logic," or "essentialist" notions of identity. Often the portraits of mul-tiplicity these writers provide us with are painful and heartrending. Re-jection, homelessness, and suicide are not simply "metaphors" for the consequences of a misunderstood and persecuted multiplicity; they are lived realities.

The challenges posed by multiplicity in response to restrictive theories of identity might seem to invalidate the category of identity completely. Accordingly, one might conclude that any claim to an identity or to mem-bership in a group with substantively common interests and any nor-mative claim made on the basis of the experience of an identity or group membership must be "strategic" or "pragmatic." Such a conclusion con-tends that such claims can never find strong epistemological justification. I want to resist this kind of claim by turning to a postpositivist realist al-ternative to both naive positivism and relativism.

REALISM

Some kind of sophisticated epistemological and/or ontological realism has recently been proposed by many feminist, antiracist, and anticolo-nial theorists to talk about identity and agency. These theorists include Karen Barad (a theoretical physicist and feminist philosopher of science who draws from Niels Bohr and uses the term "agential realism" to de-scribe her work), Leslie Roman (who has written on the importance of a "critical realism" in education), and Satya Mohanty and Paula Moya (both literary theorists who have applied a postpositivist realist theory of identity to African American, Chicana/o, and postcolonial studies). In addition, Linda Martín Alcoff, a feminist epistemologist, has recently written on the resurgence of coherence theories of truth that could enable realist discussions to move beyond the entanglements of early-twentieth-century positivism's dependence on correspondence theories. Many of these theorists, in turn, have drawn (sometimes with a critical eye) from three decades of contributions to analytic epistemology and the philos-ophy of science by writers such as Hilary Putnam, W. V. O. Quine, Don-ald Davidson, and Richard Boyd.

Postpositivist realism differs from positivism or empiricism in that it does not seek to find bedrock foundations for knowledge. Foundation-alism in philosophy is the attempt to find foundations for knowledge that can guarantee absolute certainty. It exists predominantly in two forms: inferential and premise. Inferential foundationalism seeks rules of inference that can guarantee certainty for all knowledge. Premise foundationalism seeks the discovery of foundational premises that can form the bedrock justification for all claims deduced from them. The will-o'-the-wisp for all kinds of foundationalism is absolute, error- and presupposition-free certainty of knowledge (justified, true belief).

Twentieth-century positivism (also called logical empiricism) sought to further its foundationalist project by discounting talk of anything "metaphysical" or "theoretical," that is, not empirically verifiable. Its approach, like other positivist projects (e.g., the transcendental phenomenology of Husserl so rightly critiqued by Derrida and others), was to search for immediate experience, that is, experience of the world that is in no way mediated by theory or presupposition. In contrast to a foundationalist approach, postpositivist realism puts us in the world with nothing but our theories to make sense of things. There is thus an element of contingency and uncertainty in a postpositivist realist approach. However, unlike the conceptual-scheme relativism that characterizes some other reactions to positivism, postpositivist realism considers a theory-independent reality to exist and assumes that our theories of the (social) world can help us to understand it and are, to some extent, dependent on it.

Instead of giving up on reference to reality, this kind of realism seeks to replace the quest for immediacy entailed by correspondence theories with the mediated knowledge of a causal theory of reference. For example, if I have a theory that water boils at 100 degrees Celsius, I attempt an experiment to verify that theory. If the water does not boil, something independent of my theory (e.g., altitude) has acted on my experiment. I therefore revise my theory to take altitude into account. If altitude were not a theory-independent *causal* feature of the world, I could not be forced to revise my theory to improve its accuracy. This is a simplified example of what postpositivist realism means by "gaining epistemic access to reality." Using this kind of causal theory of reference, realism avoids the pitfalls of correspondence or representationalist theories.[6] Whereas a correspondence theorist might claim that the

6. In bridging the split between so-called continental philosophy and so-called analytic philosophy, it is important to remember that most "analytic" postpositivists recognize that the question of water boiling is as much a metaphysical issue as that of "identity." One of the theses of postpositivist realism is in fact that the distinction (held by many analysts and continentalists alike) between empirical and metaphysical questions (and between epistemic and ontological questions) is to some degree arbitrary, a position with supporters and detractors among both analysts and continentalists.

term "T" corresponds to kind "K" "out there in the world," a causal theorist would claim that the causal powers of "K" "out there in the world" *condition the social use of "T."* This social use is therefore at least partly conventional and must continually be interrogated, as alternative usages are debated and evaluated within a social framework laden with power relations.

Thus postpositivist realism does not claim that one can have unmediated knowledge. Instead, it claims that, through interpretation and theory mediation of the world, one can more or less accurately grasp the complexity of the social processes and multiple conditioning that make up the "truth" of experience. At issue in realism's understanding of social identity are the coherence and accuracy with which theories about groups account for the real social features of the systems of exploitation that give those social groups their political salience. Applying a realist analysis to social identity in a passage on feminist standpoint epistemology, Mohanty writes,

> The theoretical notion "women's lives" refers not just to the experiences of women, but also to a particular social arrangement of gender relations and hierarchies that can be analyzed and evaluated. The standpoint of women in this society . . . is based in "women's lives" to the extent that it articulates their material and epistemological interests. Such interests are discovered by an explanatory empirical account of the nature of gender-stratification, the ways in which it is reproduced and regulated, and the particular social groups and values it serves to legitimate. ("Epistemic Status" 51)

This kind of realism entails a recognition of the causally significant factors of the social world in which group memberships are experienced (69). What distinguishes this realism from "naive" realist philosophical positions (like positivism) is its recognition that all knowledge is theory dependent, that is, dependent on our theories of the world. This marks it as postpositivist and nonfoundational. Postpositivist realism sees that there are different ways that knowledge can be constructed and seeks a dialectical mediation of experience with the understanding that "theory-laden and socially constructed experiences can lead to a knowledge that is accurate and reliable" (48). It contends that an adequate account of causal features of the social world (e.g., colonialism, racism, sexism, or homophobia) can yield an accurate, reliable, and *revisable* understanding of the reality of experience and its construction, instead of taking reified constructs as "given." This distinguishes it from cultural relativism.

Key to the process of obtaining this more or less "accurate and reliable" knowledge is realism's understanding of error. Rather than fear it as an obstacle to certainty, realism views it as an instructive presence. For example, it has only been through an acknowledgment of error that feminists have been able to increasingly question the role of difference and multiplicity within the category "women." Related to this point, one should note that, in responding to domination and exploitation, the objective knowledge on which realism bases its claims often arises out of oppositional political practice. As Mohanty notes, without "alternative constructions and accounts our capacity to interpret and understand the dominant ideologies and institutions is limited to those created or sanctioned by these very ideologies and institutions" ("Epistemic Status" 52). In contrast to an epistemologically impoverished cultural relativism, realism is able to more easily account for the need for revision of theoretical constructions (e.g., of identity) in response to challenges from competing theoretical or cultural claims.[7]

A restricted understanding of group membership fails to correspond accurately to the social features of the world, and its failure has something to tell us about the reality of that world's organization. Realism sees that apparently "separate" identities result from real relations of oppression and exploitation that structure our society. They are not *merely* illusions, nor are they "really" separate simply because those relations attempt to make them appear so. The social processes of domination and exploitation become obscured by the reified appearance social groups take within an essentialist framework. Domination benefits from the naturalization of social identities, which is also therefore the naturalization of domination. Resistance to domination must recognize that immediacy is always already mediated by the conditions of existence in which experience is comprehended. Far from yielding the truth of experience, immediacy is thus untruth naturalized by domination.[8] By contrast, an adequately dialectical analysis acknowledges and incorporates the causal features of these social relations into any account of the identities resulting from them.

MULTIPLICITY REVISITED

Given this account of the realist project, what does a realist theory of multiplicity look like? Realism is able to account for the role of multiplicity by viewing social identity as a relationship between things that,

---

7. On error, see Mohanty, "Epistemic Status" 55; Caroline Hau's essay, this volume.
8. For an early Hegelian-Marxist statement of this view, see Lukács 14.

instead of having one aspect in common, bear various different kinds of commonalities and resemblances. These commonalities and resemblances create what Ludwig Wittgenstein called a family resemblance: "a complicated network of similarities overlapping and criss-crossing: sometimes overall similarities, sometimes similarities of detail" (Wittgenstein I, §66). Wittgenstein comes to this concept after trying to find necessary and sufficient conditions for the definition of "game." Some games have one player, others many; some have rules, some do not. Yet one does have a sense that these many disparate things that hold "no one thing in common" do comprise a body of sufficiently similar qualities that lead one to call them all "games." Such a concept is sometimes referred to in the analytic philosophical tradition as a "homeostatic property cluster." One of the classic examples of a homeostatic property cluster is a biological species. The Darwinian theory of speciation requires that necessary and sufficient conditions for defining the set of properties for a species *cannot exist*. This is because new species come into being through processes of variation and transformation. The theory of speciation therefore predicts indeterminacy in species definition so as to accommodate the process of evolution. This necessary and constitutive indeterminacy, however, does not prevent scientists from their unavoidable task of classification according to the kinds of overlapping and crisscrossing similarities noted by Wittgenstein.

Thus when I use the terms "social identity" and "group membership," I do not mean to imply absolute sameness or constancy. According to the Latina feminist philosopher María Lugones, "We have to constantly consider and reconsider the question: Who are our own people?" (477). Realism similarly calls for a constant process of verification and revision with regard to the status of identities.[9] To account for multiplicity, social identities can never be viewed as static entities sutured at all ends. However, despite this emphasis on revision and transformation, claims and references to these identities can be justified because the causal features of the social world that give rise to them and that give them their political salience are not arbitrary. Forces of exploitation and oppression are discoverable and can be accounted for in a theory of social identity even if their *exact* contours must remain indeterminate, like those of a

---

9. Cf. the Chicana feminist Paula Moya's postpositivist realist account of personal identities that are "subject to . . . a continual process of verification which takes place over the course of an individual's life through her interaction with the society she lives in." "It is in this process of verification that identities can be (and often are) contested, and that they can (and often do) change" (139).

family resemblance. Verifiable accounts of such discoverable causal features enable these kinds of claims to be more and less justified rather than always merely "strategic."

Realism gives us criteria for justification other than absolute certainty without requiring normative claims to be made "strategically" or "tactically." A claim to moral truth can be evaluated in terms of the adequacy and coherence of the theory of society on which it is based. For example, the claim that slavery is morally wrong advances our understanding of the concept of freedom. It is a more accurate moral statement than the claim that slavery is not morally wrong. How does one determine this? By looking at the theory of society on which both claims are based. The claim that slavery is not morally wrong entails, for example, a view of what it means to be human that does not include freedom, self-ownership, and the capacity for self-realization (or it defines slaves as nonhuman). It does not account for the demonstrable fact that a person whose freedom rests on the enslavement of others limits that very freedom (through fear of uprisings, mistrust of others, the necessary cultivation of cruelty or callousness, etc.).[10] The theory of society that claims slavery is morally wrong, however, gives us a fuller picture of what it means to be human, for example, that it includes freedom and self-ownership. It presents the premise that the freedom of one is connected to the freedom of all as a more adequate normative principle than the premise that one individual's freedom can be realized even if it rests on the enslavement of others. Such a theory more adequately accounts for the causal social features of the world and entails a more coherent and less contradictory conception of freedom. Although I do not have adequate space here to give this discussion the attention it deserves, this brief sketch provides an indication of how normative claims might be justified without reference to absolute certainty or foundational beliefs. As long as the theory of society on which they are based remains available to analysis, such claims remain open to verification, evaluation, and revision. This verification, evaluation, and revision would necessitate a critical conception of objectivity such as that developed by Sandra Harding in her work on feminist standpoint epistemology and "strong objectivity."[11] According to Harding, acknowledgment of how knowledges are situated

10. Descriptions of the detrimental effects of slavery on slave owners abound in literature by former slaves (see, e.g., Douglass 47–48; Jacobs 35–36, 51–52).
11. On postpositivist realism and objective knowledge, see Mohanty, "Colonial Legacies" 110–12, 113–17.

enables strong objectivity rather than hinders it, whereas the false objectivity rightly criticized by feminists and others results from taking partial perspectives as universal and not interrogating the causes and results of their partiality (49–82).

To return to my example from Nava's *The Hidden Law,* Henry Rios's insistence on being part of a Chicano community, his demand for inclusion, is not "strategic." It is a strong normative claim based on a moral sense of his "right" to participate in a Chicano community on the basis of his cultural upbringing and experience of racialization. His claim is further supported by a conception of gays and lesbians, not as detriments to community coherence and viability, but rather as assets. The novel argues for the accuracy of this conception through Henry's successful solving of the case of Senator Peña's murder. Despite Nava's retention of notions of ethical truth and justification, however, there does exist a sense in which moral truth is not absolute. The detective novel typically presents justice as an absolute value that can be known with certainty. For example, in *The Maltese Falcon,* Sam Spade's integrity brings him to pursue the cause of justice whatever his personal feelings; there can be no compromise, and there is no doubt about what is right. Although he hated his partner, he brings his partner's murderer to justice; although he loves the femme fatale, he turns her in; although he could have gotten away with a large sum of money, he hands it over to the police. Another standard feature of the genre is the way moral corruption is revealed in corporeal terms: Cairo's body in *The Maltese Falcon* is both racially and sexual ambiguous, "the fat man" is both corrupt and obese, and so on. One of the interesting things about *The Hidden Law* and other novels by Nava is that they present the nonwhite, nonheterosexual as the enforcer of justice in a world in which moral corruption is rampant among heterosexuals and white, middle-class communities. However, instead of merely reversing value hierarchies, Nava presents the issue of moral culpability as more dispersed throughout society, so that no one can really claim innocence in a corrupt world. In the world of *The Hidden Law,* this fact manifests itself in illness and addiction. Without exception, every major character, including Henry Rios and his lover, Josh, is either an alcoholic, or a drug addict, or HIV positive, or otherwise ill. At the same time, they all share guilt for the moral sickness of a violent society. This fact forces the main character, Henry, to retire from legal and detective work at the end of the novel. Rather than simply offer a strategic inversion of moral hierarchies or a quasi-relativist proposal for "alternative" values, Nava's work demands that we (all of us) take seriously the moral implications of Henry's experiences. It demands an acknowledgment of complicity in an unjust and immoral society. Furthermore, it demands that we consider Henry's claim to a multiply constructed identity as having consequences not only for himself and others like him but also for others who are straight and/or not Chicano. The recognition that Nava asks of the reader is not a one-way recognition that "grants" something to Henry but rather a two-way act of reconceptualization that leaves the presumed unity of the gazer forever altered.

POSTSTRUCTURALISM AND MULTIPLICITY: A CRITICAL EXCURSUS

Without dwelling too much on the topic, I wish to suggest that this postpositivist realist framework has much to recommend it over other (sometimes explicit, sometimes implicit) theoretical claims that have tended to dominate discussions of identity and multiplicity. I will loosely characterize the epistemological aspects of such claims as "poststructuralist," although my intention is not to argue that the ideas of the theorists cited in this discussion can be reduced to a single, unified "poststructuralist" theory or that the theorists themselves operate within a theoretical consensus. Poststructuralist epistemologies have proved attractive to those working on issues of multiplicity and social identity. This is partly because the recognition of processes of restriction calls for a theoretical framework that understands social identities and the self as social, historical, multiple, and evolving and views them within the context of power relations. In poststructuralist theories of identity, we find such a framework.[12] They reject experience as an unmediated foundation for knowledge and adopt an extreme skepticism toward the ability to know interests and needs definitively. Whereas restriction portrays group memberships as static and discrete "identities," poststructuralism dismantles both identities and the subjects assumed to reside within them. It thus seeks to make possible the recognition of experiential multiplicity. Poststructuralist epistemologies radically challenge the ability to know any-

12. I see poststructuralist theory as characterized by (although not limited to) a strong antifoundationalism, a strong epistemological skepticism, and a general suspicion of (and at times even hostility toward) all normative and/or universalist claims. It arose originally as a critique of the determinism and absolutism of French structuralism and Husserlian phenomenology. In focusing on explicit and implicit epistemological claims, I reject the notion that poststructuralism is a coherent intellectual "movement"; however, certain premises in the arguments of many dominant figures in contemporary feminist, anticolonial, antiracist, and queer theory can be characterized as "poststructuralist."

thing directly and absolutely. They see truth claims as always subjectively mediated by discourse, power, and desire.

Poststructuralism does not seek to escape from the discourses and powers that oppress us or to adopt essentialist identities as exterior sites of resistance, for "resistance is never in a position of exteriority in relation to power" (Foucault, *History* 95). Mediation through discourse, power, and desire means that the subject in search of liberation "turns out to be discursively constituted by the very political system that is supposed to facilitate its emancipation" (Butler, *Gender Trouble* 2).[13] Poststructuralism claims that, because of the mediated nature of knowledge and experience, normative judgments are always subjective and contingent, if not arbitrary. For this reason, they can never form a reliable justification for political action (Butler, "For a Careful Reading" 127–43; Spivak, *In Other Worlds* 201).[14]

Claims to critically evaluate oppressive conditions and discourses either from outside them or in their entirety forget that they are themselves produced by that very discourse. The only possibility poststructuralism offers for resistance is one from within. Resistance must arise from either critical appropriation or subversion of the terms of exclusion. This resistance cannot hope to liberate subjects. It can only either reverse the flow of power or dismantle subjects so that something new (which one cannot normatively specify in advance) might take their place (Foucault, *History* 156–59; Butler, *Gender Trouble* 148–49). In this way, poststructuralism promises not to foreclose liberatory possibilities in advance. No claims for freedom will be denied, because no other claims can be given priority over them. It hopes not to repeat the mistakes of exclusion and domination that it associates with the modern quest for "Truth." In fact, poststructuralism's most successful accomplishment is its descriptive project of clearly identifying the role of power and desire in such supposedly value-neutral quests for "Truth" and "Objectivity."

However, poststructuralism's antifoundationalism implicitly relies on the positivist vision of justification and suspicion of "metaphysics" for its claims. It assumes the same criteria for truth as foundationalism (un-

---

13. Although Foucault's emphasis is not always on "discourse," the principle of discursive constitution is often combined with his "panoptic" juridical model of power (see *Discipline* 216, 221–22; *History* 94–98).

14. The poststructuralist rejection of normative claims is most often implicit, frequently surfacing as a deep *suspicion* of normative claims as such (e.g., Spivak, *In Other Worlds* 201). For an excellent discussion of the rejection of normative standards in Foucault, see Fraser, *Unruly Practices* 17–34. See also Taylor, esp. 90–99, on the relation between this rejection and the relativist implications of Foucault's work.

mediated, error- and supposition-free) and hence adopts the same rigid dichotomy between certainty and error. Ernesto Laclau and Chantal Mouffe, writing on the existence of multiple subject positions within the proletariat, provide an instructive example of the poststructuralist retention of a positivist dichotomy between truth and error:

> The alternative is clear: *either* one has a theory of history according to which this contradictory plurality will be eliminated and an absolutely united working class will become transparent to itself . . . in which case its "objective interests" can be determined from the very beginning; *or else,* one abandons that theory and, with it, *any basis* for privileging certain subject positions over others in the determination of the "objective" interests of the agent as a whole— in which case this latter notion becomes meaningless. (84; emphasis added)[15]

Because they discover that positivism's "immediate" knowledge of experience is thoroughly mediated and subjective, poststructuralist epistemologies abandon the quest for objective knowledge and for truth. They see these things as always entailing a posture of domination and mystification.[16] Poststructuralism correctly discovers that all knowledge is socially mediated and linguistically constructed; no experience exists or can be understood apart from prior theoretical commitments. It concludes from this discovery that knowledge (of experience, interests, identities, etc.) is subjective and indeterminate and that claims to knowledge and truth should be viewed with suspicion. Thus alternative accounts of history or identity that claim to offer fuller explanations of social phenomena by including analyses of imperialism, for example, should not be normatively valued as better accounts (Spivak, "Can the Subaltern" 281). According to poststructuralism, to call such accounts more accurate or more coherent would be to offer a new "totalizing" and totalitarian vision of society.[17]

Because they want to enable political action, many feminist, anticolonial, and antiracist theorists remain ambivalent to postmodernism and poststructuralism and admit the necessity of normative judgments. The justification for these, however, is often viewed as strategic, tactical, or contingent. At times, these assertions amount to a relativizing of various approaches to knowledge and resistance, such that they may be picked up and discarded "tactically" (Sandoval 14–15). Some theorists even assert that an essentialist identity politics is an acceptable course of

15. See also Fuss 114.
16. A similar argument about poststructuralism's reliance on a positivist framework is made by Mohanty ("Epistemic Status" 48).
17. See Fraser's comments on Butler ("False Antitheses" 68–69; "Pragmatism" 162, 169 n. 6). See also Taylor.

action given the proper "political necessity" (Fuss 95, 98–99, 118; see also Spivak, *In Other Worlds* 203–7). How to determine when strategies or tactics are justified or whose political necessity warrants the legitimate use of essentialism, however, is a question that postmodernism's denial of objectivity and truth prevents it from answering. Acknowledgment of this dilemma forms the source for many poststructuralist theorists' reluctance to commit themselves wholeheartedly to postmodernism. Judith Butler, for example, has admitted that "it is crucial . . . to develop a way of adjudicating political norms without forgetting that such an adjudication will also always be a struggle of power" (Butler, "For a Careful Reading" 141).[18]

By refusing to distinguish between the fictional and the "merely" mediated, however, most poststructuralist theorists fail to make the crucial distinction between false claims to immediate knowledge and more or less accurate (fallible), mediated descriptions of the world. Spivak provides a useful example of this position in her claim about history and fiction: "That history deals with real events and literature with imagined ones may now be seen as a difference in degree rather than in kind. . . . This difference can never be exhaustively systematized" (*In Other Worlds* 243).[19] Poststructuralist epistemologies fail to adequately articulate a conception of truth that can transcend oppositions between an "exhaustively systematized" and "absolutely united" totality, on the one hand, and the abandonment of accuracy, coherency, and objectivity, on the other. In their fear of error, they relinquish the epistemological project of understanding error in the interest of fuller and more accurate accounts of the social world. They thus renounce the criteria for evaluating between enabling and restrictive discourses. Poststructuralism as a political theory thus fails, despite its intentions, to adequately acknowledge the legitimacy and reality of the concrete and historical existence of multiplicity in the words and traditions of oppressed peoples.[20]

18. In the same vein, see Fuss 118; Butler and Scott 37. As with Butler's account of why one should prefer subjects not predicated on abjection of others ("For a Careful Reading" 139–40), these attempts to bridge the gap between realism and relativism merely remove the normative concerns to a prior moment of evaluation, adjudication, or negotiation.

19. Cf. "The incomplete character of every totality necessarily leads us to abandon . . . the concept of *'society'* as a sutured and self-defined totality. [Therefore(?)] 'Society' is not a valid object of discourse" (Laclau and Mouffe 111).

20. Cf. "Juridical structures of language and politics constitute the contemporary field of power; hence, *there is no position outside this field.* . . . [T]he task is to formulate *within this constituted frame* a critique of the categories of identity that contemporary juridical structures engender, naturalize, and immobilize" (Butler, *Gender Trouble* 5; emphasis added).

Because poststructuralism's opponent is always epistemological foundationalism, whether that of Husserl, Moore, or a feminist essentialism, it always emphasizes fragmentation and disunity, deconstruction and negation. As a result, poststructuralist political theory can never account for the successful formation of coalitions, for the expansion of interests, and for the growth of moral knowledge. It can only account for the failure of coalitions and the fragmentation of interests. This is evident in poststructuralist social theory's preference for the local over the global, the particular over the universal, and fragmentation over unified multiplicity. At its worst, poststructuralism can constitute half a dialectic: negation without transcendence. It refuses to propose anything to replace that which it has negated, because it refuses to justify its normative truth claims.

To sum up briefly, poststructuralism seeks to avoid the totalizing and normalizing effects of restriction. It recognizes as a fiction the idea that experience and identity can form unmediated foundations for knowledge and political action. Instead, it grafts a relativist and skeptical approach to epistemological certainty and norms onto a progressive politics of liberation. This move makes visible the importance of multiplicity and the role of power in the pursuit for truth. The dilemma it faces is with the normative character of progressive politics. Realization of this dilemma leads to the conclusion that norms are unavoidable but can only be strategic, arbitrary, or accidental rather than more and less accurate, more and less epistemologically justified, and more and less objective.

I have not lingered on poststructuralist epistemological claims without reason. Such claims have resulted in many unfortunate consequences for readings of U.S. multiethnic literature, in particular those concerned with sexuality and multiplicity. One can easily imagine a reading of *The Hidden Law* that would seek to demonstrate how multiplicity proves identity to be an unstable fiction, for instance. Such a reading, however, would overlook Henry's desire for inclusion in a Chicano community. It would also have to blind itself to the novel's eventual demonstration of Henry's contributions to his community and to the attainment of justice. The novel's project is predicated on a commitment to the preservation of identity categories, albeit in an expanded form. Thus whatever critique of identity is present in the novel must be seen as one step in a positive reconstruction of a better vision of identity. Readings of such works that proceed from postmodern epistemological premises tend to belittle or ignore the substantive ethical and moral concerns that frequently constitute their dominant themes.

WHO OUR OWN PEOPLE ARE: EXPANSION AND SOLIDARITY

Instead of fearing all exclusion-through-definition as domination, realism recognizes that analysis and categorization are necessary to all attempts to understand the world, including those that seek to avoid exclusion and restriction.[21] Consider Linda Alcoff's discussion of "identity" as a position that can be taken as a political point of departure: "This, in fact, is what is happening when women who are not feminists downplay their identity as women and who, on becoming feminists, then begin making an issue of their femaleness. It is the claiming of their identity as women as a political point of departure that makes it possible to see, for instance, gender-biased language that in the absence of that departure point women often do not even notice" ("Cultural Feminism" 432). In other words, gender-biased language exists whether or not it is noticed. Certain conceptions of social group membership can help us to understand things such as gender-biased language more accurately in our struggles against domination. Alcoff's position is thus in keeping with a realist framework. She goes on to describe a kind of politics in which "being a 'woman' is to take up a position within a moving historical context and to be able to choose what we make of this position and how we alter this context" (435). Rather than avoid the necessary categorization entailed by theoretical abstractions, this kind of political theory self-consciously uses linguistic (and theoretical) mediation to come to a truer, revisable understanding of nonreified multiplicity and its wider social context.[22]

Instead of equating exclusion with domination, realism seeks to recognize the excluded (not-woman), the affirmed (woman), the context for exclusion and affirmation, and the historical character and social function of each. It views these together as a whole whose greater or lesser truth is ascertainable; realism seeks to make increasingly fuller contexts cohere within increasingly more accurate explanations. In this sense, its conception of truth is coherentist rather than foundationalist or relativist. Realism retains both essentialism's objective of affirming the political salience of identity and poststructuralism's objective of viewing group membership as socially conditioned. It avoids essentialism's desire to know identity and experience immediately and rejects poststruc-

21. Karen Barad makes this point in her discussion of "agential realism": "Boundaries are not our enemies; they are necessary for making meanings, but this does not make them innocent. Boundaries have real material consequences" (187).

22. Leslie Roman articulates a similar point (see 83).

turalism's extreme skepticism toward the reliability of knowledge and the subject's ability to transcend discourses of domination. This process need not entail a claim to discovery of absolute totalities. Quite the contrary, as I argued previously, it is entirely compatible with an account of radical indeterminacy.

Realism, echoing Lugones's essay "Purity, Impurity, and Separation," enables the expansion of possibilities for solidarity across difference. The realist notion of multiplicity can be understood by viewing it in relation to Lugones's ideas, from which I have already drawn substantially (although Lugones herself has not explicitly identified her ideas as "realist"). She portrays the act of separating something into pure parts as an act of domination (460). By contrast, she views "impurity" as a way of resisting the social forces of reification. Lugones's paradigmatic example of impurity ("curdling") is mestizaje, or racial mixing, which asserts its impure (undivided) multiplicity and rejects separation into pure, discrete parts (460). Separate and fragmented become ways of seeing others and oneself that facilitate domination and exploitation. The logic of *purity* views group members with opaque interests (whom she calls "thick" members) as split and fragmented rather than as whole and multiple. The reality of their experiences, interests, and needs becomes obscured because "the interlocking of memberships in oppressed groups is not seen as changing one's needs, interests, and ways qualitatively in any group but, rather, one's needs, interests, and ways are understood as the addition of those of the transparent members" (474).

The miscomprehension of the reality of multiple group membership by discrete, essentialist categories is what poststructuralism seeks to remedy and to avoid. Rather than provide a solution to the distress of "walking from one of one's groups to another," however, poststructuralism increases the sense of homelessness for members with opaque interests. It removes the epistemological ground on which one can claim that one "belongs" in a group (or that someone else does not) and of making normative demands for inclusion, acknowledgment, and legitimacy. In her emphasis on the reality of multiplicity's resistance to domination, Lugones's analysis is compatible with a postpositivist realist framework. For Lugones, the problem with pure separation is that a person's opaque "interests, needs, ways of seeing and valuing things, persons, and relations" are assumed to be those of the dominant members of the groups to which she or he belongs (474). Although such needs and interests are conditioned socially, they are not produced or determined solely by hegemonic discourses.[23] The objective of a realist theory of multiplicity and social identity must be to account for the experiences that generate opaque interests (without, of course, claiming to represent them "transparently") in order to justify the normative claims these interests make against dominating social relations.

Lugones's essay is in part an attempt to reconceptualize group membership, to go beyond, to resist, and to transform the very ways in which identities are imagined as separate and fragmented. As she points out, writing about lesbian separatism and being a Latina lesbian, "if we are to struggle against 'our' oppression, Latina Lesbian cannot be the name for a fragmented being. Our style cannot be outside the meaning of Latina and cannot be outside the meaning of Lesbian. *So, our struggle, the struggle of lesbians, goes beyond lesbians as a group*" (476; emphasis added). Emancipatory struggle can only be successful when straight people of color and white lesbians and gay men come to see the interests of queer people of color as *their own*. They must come to expand their sense of what their own interests are and who their own people are. Coalitions must cease to be coalitions of people with "different" interests, and the fragmentation within them must be healed. For this to happen, opaque interests must be acknowledged and reconceptualized as interests shared by all members of both groups. In other words, fighting racism and homophobia must be seen as a primary interest of all feminists and fighting sexism and homophobia must be seen as a primary interest of all people of color. Dominant group members must expand their sense of their own interests by attending to opaque interests.[24] As noted above, Lugones urges us "to constantly consider and reconsider the question: Who are our own people?" (477). In other words, resisting domination and taking into account the experiences of group members with opaque interests both require that we think beyond notions of group interests as tied simply to hegemonic group members. Lugones writes, "I don't think we can consider 'our own' only those who reject the same dichotomies

23. While I recognize that humans are socialized through discourse, it seems to me that discourse is as conditioned by us as we are by it. Discourse is neither just a "medium" through which we gain access to reality nor merely a social matrix or tool by or with which reality is constructed. It is a set of related practices that aid the organizing of a social world. These practices, in fact, are a part of that social world, as is the self. Only by viewing the self and discourse as mutually conditioned parts of a social process larger than the extent of either can the false dichotomy between positivism and skepticism be transcended.

24. Mohanty discusses something like this in his discussion of Paul D's "growth" in Morrison's novel *Beloved* ("Epistemic Status" 67–69).

we do"; instead, "we find our people as we make the threat [to domination] good, day to day, attentive to our company in our groups, across groups" (477).

Another example of resistance to restriction and affirmation of multiplicity through the expansion of group interests is the work of the New York City–based video collective House of Color. House of Color included Robert Garcia, Wellington Love, Robert Mignott, Jeff Nunokawa, Pamela Sneed, Jocelyn Taylor, and Julie Tolentino. The collective's members were bisexual, lesbian, and gay, and American Indian, Asian American, black, and Latino. Its first video project was the short subject, *I Object,* and was followed by the collective's only other video, *Probe* (Garcia Papers, V-129).[25] These projects, like Nava's *The Hidden Law,* attempt to give voice to the reality of multiple interests, needs, and ways of being that have been obscured by forces of restriction and domination.

I Object begins with a fast-paced, beat-driven pastiche of various images of white beauty, fashion, and erotica. These are periodically interrupted by members of House of Color speaking out against the lack of images of people of color. Next the video presents a succession of stylized, exotic, and/or "white-washed" images of people of color. One thing is clear. Despite Pamela Sneed's demand in the video, "Mirror, mirror, answer me!" the House of Color members who appear and speak amid and against the pastiche of images resemble none of the idealized and fetishized images. Each member speaks her or his critique of the portrayals of people of color in the media and in art (e.g., the photographs of Robert Mapplethorpe). Wellington Love: "We just don't exist"; Julie Tolentino: "I feel that this is something about exposing this big lie." Robert Garcia asks, "What is it that determines it to be beautiful?" and answers himself that it is the penetration of white ideologies of beauty and exoticism. As the video makes clear, this penetration amounts to being "shafted."

What House of Color uncovers in *I Object* is the reality of opaque interests. In an interview with House of Color, Pamela Sneed described the motivations behind the video this way: "While we wanted to give the world the message that we do exist, that we are not going to be spoken for by the white gay community, that we are going to take our own images into our own hands . . . we also wanted to pay attention to the fact that we are all individuals. We are Blacks, Latinos, Asians, who need to start a dialogue among ourselves" (Bowen 109). Developing this dialogue,

---

25. For another discussion of House of Color, see Saalfield.

the second part of the video features all the members of House of Color in a kitchen. They interact with one another, first in friendly conversation and then in a more erotic series of images. Yet, in contrast to the earlier images, produced by—and presumably for—white people, these are not highly stylized or idealized. Rather, they feature people of color as the subjects of their own desire, as intersubjective agents. They are also, as the voice-over states at one point, "the objects of [their] own desire." They are equal and reciprocal (although not symmetrical), respectful and respected. Instead of the intersubjective life-and-death struggle Hegel claims must result in the formation of unequal subjects, this video argues for a model of nondominating intersubjective self-recognition.

Through the ambivalence of the title and the presence of all members of the collective both in front of and behind the camera, something important comes into being. As Sneed says, the images of people of color are reappropriated by people of color. The members of House of Color are able to be objects, but to be their own objects, as well as their own subjects. In one sense of the title, "I, Object," we see them speaking from the position of objects, as objectified individuals. The images in the video contest, while demonstrating, the ways in which cultural depictions of people of color have objectified blacks, Latinos, and Asians. At the same time, however, we can detect the immense power of taking ownership of the objectified images of themselves: "I object." The forcefulness of the verb is arresting, stopping the proceedings of business as usual. The video signals an end to images of queer people of color being made only by heterosexuals or by, in Sneed's words, "the white gay community." Indeed, the video attempts to destroy a tradition of such images being excluded from representation altogether. House of Color developed a model for communication and solidarity across difference—through an appreciation of difference.

It did not, however, seek merely to present "unmediated" images or to present any new images whatsoever. Instead, its task was to come up with a process of mediation that allowed for the presentation of more accurate and more enabling images (i.e., better ones). This project therefore had a strong normative component. In a transcript of a conversation among several members of House of Color, which took place at the time they were planning *I Object,* Jocelyn Taylor described a need "to re-think our whole way of identifying beauty" (Garcia Papers). This is, in part, what the video does. Not only in the banal sense of portraying images of people who, because they are not white, do not conform to a Eurocentric standard of beauty. The images here are being labeled as beautiful by people of color. In objecting to the traditional subject/object relationship in which people of color are objects and whites are subjects, *I Object* speaks on behalf of the objectified person of color telling herself that she is beautiful. It is not merely a question of *redefining* beauty by changing the role models who give definition to aesthetic standards. It is a matter of rethinking our whole way of *identifying* beauty. The subject/object relationship that grants agency to call oneself or another beautiful is transformed.

Consider, by contrast, if a national toothpaste manufacturer were to begin producing television commercials that featured two women of color with minty-fresh breath kissing one another. Granted, this may be a positive and well-intentioned portrayal. In formulating an explanatory account for understanding the position of the women in this commercial, however, a realist would want to interrogate the mechanisms of production, ownership, and marketing that brought the commercial into being. With what theory of society is the manufacturer operating? How well does that theory explain the structure of our society? Has the traditional conception of the subject been altered or challenged significantly if the toothpaste is produced by exploited workers in an unsafe workplace in a polluted county in North Carolina? If the toothpaste company is controlled by a wealthy group of international shareholders? The women in the commercial may not become subjects in the eyes of the company or many viewers. The subjectivity of these women will most likely not be understood in a nonreified way, because their interests, needs, and ways will not have been acknowledged as "real," for and in themselves. Instead, they will only exist *for others,* for the owners of the company as objects for the maximization of surplus profit, for the viewers as objects of eroticization, identification, or abjection. As "objects," they would have only the reality posited by a knowing "subject."

Even more important to the topic at hand, therefore, is the formation of House of Color itself. Writing in 1983, the Chicana lesbian feminist Cherríe Moraga noted, "[We Latinas] have not been allowed to express ourselves in specifically female and Latina ways or even to explore what those ways are. As long as that is held in check, so much of the rest of our potential power is as well" (137). The project of House of Color had importance for precisely this reason. It was trying to establish from scratch a way of being specifically queer and of color. The dialogue among queer Asians, blacks, Latinos, and American Indians was one that had never taken place before. Furthermore, House of Color was a tremendous source of personal power. As Robert Garcia noted, "Each time I speak as an individual . . . there is nothing. What fucks us up is that we wait for straight society to give us the models, the modalities for our existence, and we buy into it" (Garcia Papers).

There is not the sense in their videos of an unmediated access to reality. The act of what Garcia called "creating new modalities for existence" belies the claim that such modalities are given and immediate. Instead, House of Color, in its second video, *Probe,* used the concrete lived experience of lesbian, gay, and bisexual people of color to elaborate commonalities and differences. This elaboration enabled a mediated, fuller understanding of the forces of domination that act on their lives. *Probe* intersperses short, experimental segments with longer, documentary-style interviews with lesbian, gay, and bisexual people of color. These interviews capture experiences both painful and liberating, while the other segments provide a social-theoretical context in which one can understand the importance of these experiences as insights into the nature of multiplicity.

Writers, artists, and activists such as the members of House of Color and Michael Nava do not, then, take a racially uncoded sexuality and add to it considerations of race and ethnicity, understood separately but as intersecting. (Or vice versa.) Their project is much more profound. They seek to describe the experiences of multiplicity that characterize the existence of gay and lesbian people of color. They thus want to transcend the "complex set of fictions" that have attempted to separate women, men, lesbians, gay men, Asians, Latinos, blacks, and American Indians into "pure," separate, and reified parts. In the process, *The Hidden Law, I Object,* and *Probe* assert the multiplicity of queer people of color, expanding notions of group membership and group interests through the exploration of intra- and intergroup differences. This expansion, in turn, creates the possibility for solidarity across differences.

CONCLUSION: USING TOOLS OTHER THAN THE MASTER'S

In closing, I would like to offer an example from some of my experiences with coalition organizing to further illustrate the point regarding the expansion of interests beyond reified notions of identity. Many years ago I attended for the first time a meeting of an organization composed entirely of gay, bisexual, and lesbian people of color. Through my experiences as a member, and later co-chair, of that organization, I came to understand my interests as more than just resistance to anti-Chicano racism and to homophobia and heterosexism. Once I came to understand "my own people" as black, Asian, Puerto Rican, male, female, and transgendered, I was able to see the struggles against, for example, sexism and anti-Asian racism as my struggles. This is not to say that I came to see myself as sharing the experience of Asian women or as being able to identify as Asian or female. Instead, as I came to think of myself as a queer person of color, I came to see myself as being part of a group that included Asian women and others. Although our experience was certainly not identical, there were similarities and commonalities according to which I was able to see them as my people. Thus whatever forces of domination and exploitation they faced, they faced as my people. My interests came to expand beyond my own experience and beyond either Chicanos, gay men, or Chicano gay men as discrete groups.

This kind of resistance is one through which the self grows, transforms, and expands. It counters restriction with expansion, fragmentation with multiplicity, separation with solidarity, and exploitation with transformation. Thus a realist understanding of group membership that takes into account the social structures underlying domination must conceptualize group membership beyond the limits imposed by restriction. In this sense, it must reject "the master's tools," the tools of purity and separation, and make connections between, among, and across groups. Expansion of the self can only take place once we allow that groups truly *constitute* one another, constitute one another in such a way that their constitution is forever altered, enriched, and expanded. In other words, once "gay experience" can be understood in such a way as to include "Chicano experience." Only then can we expand the horizons of political action. This will not represent an end to identity politics but an expansion of it and a growth of the self.[26]

Postpositivist realism's dialectical approach to social identity and the self thus echoes Audre Lorde's account of the role of difference in forging political resistance:

> Advocating the mere tolerance of difference between women is the grossest reformism. It is a total denial of the creative function of difference in our lives.

---

26. I have many times been pressed to draw conclusions from my argument for how people located in dominant positions can come to expand their sense of their own people. I consider this question to be beyond the scope of this chapter, although an investigation into such issues is certainly a necessary complement to my work here. Certainly one step would be to draw from one's own sources of pain and victimization to make connections with others, but the process of a white upper-class male finding solidarity with the oppressed in the United States in a useful and substantive way is more complex than simply generalizing from the examples I have given of solidarity work among members of different oppressed groups. Anzaldúa is suggestive on this point (83–85). See also Henze's essay in this volume.

Difference must be not merely tolerated, but seen as a fund of necessary polarities between which our creativity can spark like a dialectic. Only then does
the necessity for interdependency become unthreatening. Only within that interdependency of different strengths, acknowledged and equal, can the power
to seek new ways of being in the world generate, as well as the courage and
sustenance to act where there are no charters. (111)

Lorde's words are a call to use the resource of differences among women—
intragroup, *experiential* differences—to create new ways of understanding the connections between women. These new ways of understanding
must adequately accommodate the multiple ways of experiencing membership in the group "women." Hers is a call, not to discard "reality"
or "identity politics," but to recognize the reality of different women's
experiences. This recognition can help to create more accurate ways of
accounting for the transparent and opaque interests of all women. Understood in the context of a postpositivist realist theory of identity, this
is a difficult, long-term, and transformational project. It is one predicated
on the belief that differences among women (and among Chicanos or
gay men, for that matter) are not incommensurable. It argues, therefore,
for the possibility and necessity of transcultural understanding and evaluation. In turn, it entails a theory of how group interests can expand. It
acknowledges the possibility of more and less objective knowledge of universal human needs and interests, like the need for self-determination and
freedom from gender, racial, and economic slavery, or the interest in being a whole and multiple self.

WORKS CITED

Alcoff, Linda [Martín]. "Cultural Feminism versus Post-Structuralism: The Iden-
tity Crisis in Feminist Theory." Signs 13.3 (1988): 405–36.
———. *Real Knowing: New Versions of the Coherence Theory.* Ithaca: Cornell
University Press, 1996.
Almaguer, Tomás. "Chicano Men: A Cartography of Homosexual Identity and
Behavior." *differences* 3.2 (Summer 1991): 75–100.
Anzaldúa, Gloria. *Borderlands/La Frontera: The New Mestiza.* San Francisco:
Spinsters/Aunt Lute, 1987.
Barad, Karen. "Meeting the Universe Halfway: Realism and Social Construc-
tivism without Contradiction." *Feminism, Science, and the Philosophy of Sci-
ence.* Ed. Lynn Hankinson Nelson and Jack Nelson. Dordrecht: Kluwer, 1996.
161–94.
Bowen, Peter. "Collect Yourself." *Outweek* 52 (27 June 1990): 108–9.
Boyd, Richard N. "How to Be a Moral Realist." *Essays on Moral Realism.* Ed.
Geoffrey Sayre-McCord. Ithaca: Cornell University Press, 1988. 181–228.

Butler, Judith. *Bodies That Matter: On the Discursive Limits of "Sex."* New York: Routledge, 1993.

————. "For a Careful Reading." *Feminist Contentions: A Philosophical Exchange.* New York: Routledge, 1995. 127–43.

————. *Gender Trouble: Feminism and the Subversion of Identity.* New York: Routledge, 1990.

Butler, Judith, and Joan Scott, eds. *Feminists Theorize the Political.* New York: Routledge, 1992.

Crenshaw, Kimberlé. "Whose Story Is It, Anyway? Feminist and Antiracist Appropriations of Anita Hill." *Race-Ing Justice, En-Gendering Power: Essays on Anita Hill, Clarence Thomas, and the Construction of Social Reality.* Ed. Toni Morrison. New York: Pantheon, 1992. 402–40.

Douglass, Frederick. *Narrative of the Life of Frederick Douglass. The Oxford Frederick Douglass Reader.* Ed. William L. Andrews. New York: Oxford University Press, 1996.

Foucault, Michel. *Discipline and Punish: The Birth of the Prison.* Trans. Alan Sheridan. New York: Vintage, 1979.

————. *The History of Sexuality. Volume I: An Introduction.* Trans. Robert Hurley. New York: Vintage, 1980.

Fraser, Nancy. "False Antitheses: A Response to Seyla Benhabib and Judith Butler." *Feminist Contentions: A Philosophical Exchange.* New York: Routledge, 1995. 59–74.

————. "Pragmatism, Feminism, and the Linguistic Turn." *Feminist Contentions: A Philosophical Exchange.* New York: Routledge, 1995. 157–71.

————. *Unruly Practices: Power, Discourse and Gender in Contemporary Social Theory.* Minneapolis: University of Minnesota Press, 1989.

Fuss, Diana. *Essentially Speaking: Feminism, Nature & Difference.* New York: Routledge, 1989.

Garcia Papers. Rare and Manuscript Collection #7574. Carl A. Kroch Library, Cornell University.

Harding, Sandra. "Rethinking Standpoint Epistemology: 'What Is Strong Objectivity'?" *Feminist Epistemologies.* Ed. Linda Alcoff and Elizabeth Potter. New York: Routledge, 1993. 49–82.

Jacobs, Harriet A. *Incidents in the Life of a Slave Girl.* Ed. Jean Fagan Yellin. Cambridge, MA: Harvard University Press, 1987.

Jordan, June. *Technical Difficulties: Selected Political Essays.* London: Virago, 1993.

Laclau, Ernesto, and Chantal Mouffe. *Hegemony & Socialist Strategy: Towards a Radical Democratic Politics.* London: Verso, 1985.

Lorde, Audre. *Sister Outsider: Essays & Speeches.* Freedom, CA: Crossing Press, 1984.

Lugones, María C. "Purity, Impurity, and Separation." *Signs* 19.21 (1994): 458–79.

Lukács, Georg. *History and Class Consciousness: Studies in Marxist Dialectics.* Trans. Rodney Livingstone. Boston: MIT Press, 1985.

Merleau-Ponty, Maurice. *The Phenomenology of Perception.* Trans. Colin Smith. London: Routledge, 1978.

Mohanty, Satya P. "Colonial Legacies, Multicultural Futures: Relativism, Objectivity, and the Challenge of Otherness." *PMLA* 110.1 (1995): 108–18.

———. "The Epistemic Status of Cultural Identity: On *Beloved* and the Postcolonial Condition." *Cultural Critique* 24 (Spring 1993): 41–80. [Reprinted as chapter 1 in this volume.]

Moraga, Cherríe. *Loving in the War Years: Lo que nunca pasó por sus labios.* Boston: South End Press, 1983.

Moya, Paula M. L. "Postmodernism, 'Realism,' and the Politics of Identity: Cherríe Moraga and Chicana Feminism." *Feminist Genealogies, Colonial Legacies, Democratic Futures.* Ed. M. Jacqui Alexander and Chandra Talpade Mohanty. New York: Routledge, 1997. 125–50. [Reprinted as chapter 2 in this volume.]

Quine, W. V. O. *Pursuit of Truth.* Cambridge, MA: Harvard University Press, 1990.

Roman, Leslie G. "White Is a Color! White Defensiveness, Postmodernism, and Anti-racist Pedagogy." *Race, Identity, and Representation in Education.* Ed. Cameron McCarthy and Warren Crichlow. New York: Routledge, 1993. 71–88.

Saalfield, Catherine. "On the Make: Activist Video Collectives." *Queer Looks: Perspectives on Lesbian and Gay Film and Video.* Ed. Martha Gever, John Greyson, and Pratibha Parmar. New York: Routledge, 1993. 21–37.

Sandoval, Chela. "U.S. Third World Feminism: The Theory and Method of Oppositional Consciousness in the Postmodern World." *Genders* 10 (Spring 1991): 1–24.

Spelman, Elizabeth V. *Inessential Woman: Problems of Exclusion in Feminist Thought.* Boston: Beacon, 1988.

Spivak, Gayatri Chakravorty. "Can the Subaltern Speak?" *Marxism and the Interpretation of Culture.* Ed. Cary Nelson and Lawrence Grossberg. Urbana: University of Illinois Press, 1988. 271–313.

———. *In Other Worlds: Essays in Cultural Politics.* New York: Routledge, 1988.

Taylor, Charles. "Foucault on Freedom and Truth." *Foucault: A Critical Reader.* Ed. David Couzens Hoy. Cambridge: Blackwell, 1986. 69–102.

Wittgenstein, Ludwig. *Philosophical Investigations.* Trans. G. E. M. Anscombe. New York: Macmillan, 1967.

POSTPOSITIVIST OBJECTIVITY:

USES OF ERROR, VALUES, AND IDENTITY

On Representing Others

Intellectuals, Pedagogy, and the Uses of Error

Caroline S. Hau

"The liberation struggles of the Third World still are the best schools of good sense," wrote Regis Debray in his *Modeste contribution aux discours et cérémonies officielles du dixième anniversaire* (86; cited in Brown 192). The enthusiasm with which Debray holds up the struggle for national liberation in the Third World as the paradigmatic arena that puts the intellectual's skills to good use (Brown 192) is equaled only by the cursoriness of critical consideration that he accords such an issue. For while Debray went on to write about the French intellectual class with great insight and wit,[1] he seemed to have adopted a curiously uncritical stance toward the phenomenon of decolonization and to the role played by the intellectuals in these struggles (193).

Although theoretical inquiry into the role of intellectuals in political struggles has not been lacking, most notably within the Marxist tradition,[2] this inquiry has focused primarily on Europe and America. And

---

1. See his *Le pouvoir intellectuel en France.*
2. For a brief discussion of the historical emergence of the concepts "intelligentsia" and "intellectuals," see Tibor Huszar, "Changes in the Concept of Intellectuals"; and Lewis S. Feuer, "What Is an Intellectual?" For a brief overview of the theoretical contributions to the issue of the political role of the intellectual, see Carl Boggs's *Intellectuals and the Crisis of Modernity*, esp. 11–62. Among the publications since the 1970s that discuss and problematize the relationship between intellectuals and politics are Alvin W. Gouldner, *The Future of Intellectuals and the Rise of the New Class* and *Against Fragmentation*; George Konrad and Istvan Szelenyi, *Intellectuals on the Road to Class Power*; Pat Walker, ed., *Between Labor and Capital*; Stanley Aronowitz and Henry Giroux, *Education under Siege*; Allan Bloom, *The Closing of the American Mind*; Bruce Robbins, ed., *Intellectuals, Aes-*

yet the political role of intellectuals has been a persistent theme in key
theoretical texts on decolonization in the non-Western countries.[3] The
question of the role of the intellectual-writer in the struggle for social
and political change is often posed as a problem of the *authority* of the
intellectual, a function not only of a perceived divide between intellectual and manual labor (i.e., the intellectual's assumed separation from
her object of study—"the people") but also of the artist's obligation to
speak for others, to express through the work of art the hopes, aspirations, and experiences of "the people" (i.e., to represent the people both
politically and semiotically). This position emphasizes the potential contribution that the intellectual can make as one whose epistemic access to
and articulations of the experiences of others are crucial in generalizing—
broadening or, in the context of anticolonial struggle, "nationalizing"—
popular consciousness.[4] To generalize popular consciousness is to effectively move from local to collective concerns, from the particular to the
universal. Generalizing popular consciousness is a necessary goal of any
program of struggle for social and political change, since exclusive emphasis on localized struggle by the people cannot properly or successfully combat hegemonic power (Lazarus 199). The forging of popular
consciousness into what Neil Lazarus has called the "nationalitarian"
force thus functions to mobilize "the people" by actively registering and
articulating their aspirations (199), and by doing it accurately and reli-
ably. Political struggles, therefore, implicitly commit themselves to the
idea of the epistemic reliability of intellectual praxis, to the possibility
of obtaining *accurate* and *reliable* accounts of the world (or of a particular society) that can help to demystify existing institutions and their systems of oppression. In other words, to the extent that it is about forging
epistemically reliable accounts of the people's hopes, visions, and expe-

---

thetics, Politics, Academics; Charles C. Lemert, ed., *Intellectuals and Politics;* and Ian
Maclean, Alan Montefiore and Peter Winch, eds., *The Political Responsibility of Intellectuals.* Paul Thomas's *Marx and the Anarchists* and Alvin Gouldner's *The Two Marxisms*
address the issue of intellectualism in the Marxist tradition.

3. I am using the term "non-Western" to refer to countries in Asia, Africa, and Latin
America, with no intention of implying homogeneity of cultures or social structures and
unchanging economic positions of these countries vis-à-vis the "advanced," "developed,"
or "core" capitalist countries.

4. These issues have often been cast in the form of debates on the generalizing and dis-
ciplining of popular consciousness by a core organizational structure like the political party.
Within Marxist discourse, significant theoretical contributions include V. I. Lenin's "What
Is to Be Done?" and Rosa Luxemburg's "Organizational Questions of Russian Social
Democracy." Antonio Gramsci attempted to move beyond the Vanguardist-Spontaneist
debate; see Quintin Hoare and Geoffrey Nowell Smith, eds., *Selections from the Prison
Notebooks of Antonio Gramsci.* See Boggs 41–60.

riences, sound intellectual praxis is a necessary component of sound political praxis.

But the valorization of intellectual praxis is also often strongly inflected
by an ambivalence toward the intellectual. Understandably enough, this
ambivalence is an ambivalence about the status of error in intellectualism—
about epistemic failure. The ambivalence, in other words, is about the
intellectual's ability to *successfully* articulate the conditions and aspirations of the people. How, in fact, does the intellectual go about identifying and articulating, creating and communicating knowledge and experiences adequately? By tracing a clear trajectory from Mao Zedong's
work to Frantz Fanon and Amilcar Cabral's work on the intellectuals[5]
in the first section of this chapter, I hope to provide a nuanced rendering of this specific problem and of the prospects of the discourse on intellectualism as it is deployed in classical accounts of decolonization. I
am concerned with the ways in which Mao, Fanon, and Cabral deal with
the role played by intellectual work and pedagogy in political struggle.
I argue that the role they assign to the intellectual in the liberation struggle is informed by varying assumptions, sometimes expressed as ambivalence, about the possibility of error that is the ineradicable risk of
intellectual activity. Laying out and clarifying these assumptions will help
us to see what is at stake in the debates about the specific task of the intellectual and to find a way out of the theoretical impasse reached by
these debates.

The problematization of the authority of intellectuals in the discourse
on decolonization thus opens out onto broader issues concerning objectivity and relativism that constitute some of the basic concerns of what
has loosely been called "poststructuralist" and "postmodern" theory in
American academia.[6] In telling us that all knowledge is informed by "back-

5. I am cognizant of the fact that the writings of Mao, Fanon, and Cabral do not provide an extended and systematic exposition on intellectualism. Most of Cabral's writings,
for example, were culled from speeches and short articles. My decision to treat each of
these intellectuals' work as a corpus is necessarily heuristic.

6. Philip Lewis's "The Post-structuralist Condition" draws on the work of Derrida and
Lyotard to provide a nuanced discussion of structuralism and poststructuralism. Lewis's
characterization allows us to distinguish between valid accounts of the poststructuralist
condition and the muddled appropriations of these claims in contemporary critical discourse that pass themselves off as "poststructuralist" or "postmodernist" theory. In the
field of literary studies, Jonathan Culler's *On Deconstruction* is an influential formulation
of some of the key claims of "poststructuralist" theory. In political theory, see Chantal
Mouffe and Ernesto Laclau, *Hegemony and Socialist Strategy.*

Feminist discourse has also proven to be a fertile ground for debates on the status of
reason, and on the related issues of objectivity and intellectual skepticism, in light of philosophical developments that have brought the "rational" subject of modernity into ques-

ground beliefs" that are socially situated,[7] recent critiques of knowledge necessarily complicate the question of error and mystification by their insistence on the constructedness of truth. Given such an antifoundationalist stance, should the concept of error and mystification be retained at all?

Since it is precisely the *epistemic* authority invested in the intellectual that has come under attack in a number of these formulations, I devote the second section of this chapter to a reading of an influential essay from the "canon" of postcolonial studies, Gayatri Chakravorty Spivak's "Can the Subaltern Speak?" Spivak's cogent defense of the need to think through—rather than simply abjure—the concepts of representation and ideology is undermined by her adoption of an uncritical stance toward the very idea that the act of "speaking for 'others'" is necessarily authoritarian and suspect. I argue that this kind of position actually vitiates any serious consideration of the very issue of ideology to which Spivak's essay so persuasively draws our attention.

Keeping the valid theoretical points of Spivak's essay in mind and drawing on a body of recent scholarship, I proceed to argue in the third section that a "realist" account that seeks to forge a postfoundationalist account of experience by upholding the theory dependence of objectivity and error[8] provides one way of resolving some of the problems opened up by the related issues of representation and the politics of social change. It is precisely because the "experience" of others (and of the intellectual herself) is not self-evidently transparent that I argue in favor of the importance of providing theories of error and mystification in representing others. In so doing, I use the realist notion of theory-dependent knowledge to deepen the insights that we have gained from Mao, Fanon, and Cabral, and from the poststructuralist and postmodern cri-

---

tion. While feminism has unquestionably played an important role in foregrounding the need to reappraise "rationalist values," it is divided over the issue of "just how much continuity there can be between pre-feminist and feminist intellectual expressions" (Lovibond 73). Critiques on the viability of "rationality" range from Judith Butler's *Gender Trouble*, Donna Haraway's "Situated Knowledges," and Rosa Braidotti's *Patterns of Dissonance* to Sandra Harding's *Whose Science? Whose Knowledge?* Susan Babbitt's "Feminism and Objective Interests" and Michelle LeDoeuff's "Woman, Reason, etc."

See Martin Hollis and Steven Lukes, eds., *Rationality and Relativism;* Michael Krausz and Jack Meiland, eds., *Relativism: Cognitive and Moral;* and especially Satya P. Mohanty, "'Us and Them'" for contributions to the debate about objectivity and relativism.

7. See W. V. O. Quine, "Two Dogmas of Empiricism"; Phillip Kitcher, "The Naturalists Return."

8. I am especially indebted to the following essays for their cogent framing and discussion of the notion of theory-dependent objectivity: Satya P. Mohanty, "The Epistemic Status of Cultural Identity"; Richard N. Boyd, "How to Be a Moral Realist." See also Boyd's "Metaphor and Theory Change."

tiques, by arguing that the realist notion of theory-dependent knowledge upholds the necessity of retaining the concept of error but goes farther than the above critiques in refining it. I argue that the realist account strengthens the claims of the classical accounts concerning the specificity of the intellectual's role in the struggle for social change by *revaluing* the issues of error and mystification. That is, it shifts the debate about the epistemic authority of the intellectual away from an exclusive emphasis on error per se and instead transforms error into a mode of explicating the precise nature of theory mediation and an important component of the evaluation of theory-dependent knowledges.

I

The importance that Mao Zedong assigns to the work of theory in accounting for and responding to the irreducible contradictions of Chinese society in revolution is indissociable from the central place that he accords the notion of practice in his epistemology.[9] The way in which Mao articulates this notion is itself informed by the contradictions that inhere in a society that, as Arif Dirlik observes, "stands at the intersection of two histories: a global history that, beginning in the late nineteenth century, intruded with increasing forcefulness on Chinese thinking and provided a new frame of reference for thinking about the past, present and future of Chinese society; and a Chinese history, the autonomy of which appeared as an issue as the new world impressed itself on Chinese consciousness" (119).[10]

Mao's efforts to rethink the relationship between theory and practice recognizes the defining influence in real terms of the division of labor. In his "Talks at the Yenan Forum on Literature and Art," Mao blames the disjuncture of intellectual and political work on the "reactionaries" who had "cut them off from each other" (2). The question of the intellectual's contribution to the practice of revolution must, therefore, take into account the social location of the intellectual, a location induced from a combination of material and historical forces obtaining in Chinese society. The

9. For accounts of the evolution, content, and context of Mao Zedong's political thought, see Stuart S. Schram, *The Political Thought of Mao Tse-tung*; Fredric Wakeman, Jr., *History and Will*; and Raymond F. Wylie, *The Emergence of Maoism*. For discussions of the impact of Mao Zedong's thought on global Marxism, see Arif Dirlik, Paul Healy, and Nick Knight, eds., *Critical Perspectives on Mao Zedong's Thought* pt. 3.

10. Dirlik's essay also provides an account of the "vernacularization of Marxism" by Mao Zedong as well as Mao's epistemology (see esp. 137–38).

problem, for Mao, has its premise in the intellectual's alienation (because of her social location) from the liberation struggle: the danger always exists that the "petty bourgeois" writer, however sympathetic to political and social change and to the cause of the people, may, in practice, end up writing only about the concerns of people from her own class (12–13).

And yet Mao's elaboration of the concept of contradiction[11] in his analysis of Chinese society also stresses the contingency of social locations, which can generate different practices and perceptions of the world. Thus Mao also considers the contribution that the *sympathetic* intellectual can make to radical politics:

> Although man's social life is the only source of literature and art and is incomparably richer and livelier in content, people are not satisfied with life alone, but demand literature and art as well. Why? Because while both are beautiful, life as reflected in works of art can and ought to be on a higher plane, more intense, more concentrated, more typical, nearer the ideal and therefore more universal than actual everyday life. Revolutionary literature and art should create a variety of characters out of real life and help the masses to propel history forward. (19)

Implicit in Mao's analysis is a line of reasoning that not only sees the intellectual's contribution as dependent on the accuracy of the intellectual's representation of the life of "the people"[12] but also defines this contribution as something that involves more than simply accurate representation. The work of art putatively transforms the "life" material by moving from local to general concerns. Indeed, it is this ability to transform our specific visions into something that can be shared by others, the ability to transcend narrow particularism, that makes the work revolutionary.[13] What is held to be revolutionary about literature, then, is that it both *imagines* and *actualizes* the principle of unifying the ranks in the struggle for social change.

But it is precisely the discontinuousness of these closely related moves of invocation and performance (which allow for the movement from lo-

---

11. Mao's "On Contradiction," "On Practice," and "Lecture Notes on Dialectical Materialism" (1936–37) contain his influential discussions of the concept.

12. As should be obvious from the account that follows, the translations of Mao's, Fanon's, and Cabral's work use the terms "the people" and "the masses" interchangeably. This interchangeability can create some problems for readers unfamiliar with Marxist discourse, because of the differences in popular connotations attached to each term (with "the masses," for example, often carrying negative associations).

13. For Mao, revolution already implies a kind of self-transformation of "the masses": "The masses have remoulded themselves in struggle or are doing so, and our literature and art should depict this process" (4).

cal to general that characterizes the revolutionary moment of political struggle) that defines the two main concerns of the Yenan forum: a popular consciousness that is capable of pushing the struggle beyond its localized form needs to be both educated (thereby justifying the work of the party) and transformed or distilled into a "general," universalizable form (thereby justifying the work of the intellectual); hence Mao's assertion that the "liberation of the Chinese people" requires training both military and cultural armies (1).

The issue of pedagogy is thus inscribed in the logic of the liberation struggle. But because *real* (not just formal) unity among the people is the hallmark as well as the basis of political struggle, revolutionary pedagogy cannot operate on the assumed hierarchy of knowledge that has hitherto kept the student-pupil relation in place. At the same time, this pedagogy cannot operate without any hierarchizing since the gap between imagining and actualizing unity among the people cannot be wished away without a program of struggle. Mao provides the quintessential solution to this dilemma: "No revolutionary writer or artist can do any meaningful work unless he is closely linked with the masses, gives expression to their thoughts and feelings and serves them as loyal spokesman. Only by speaking for the masses can he educate them and only by being their pupil can he be their teacher" (23).

Putting the intellectual and "the masses" in such a reciprocal relation allows Mao to posit the idea of a *critical* distance between the intellectual and her object of study while emphasizing the importance of the interaction between them. This critical distance assumes that the intellectuals and "the masses" are not connected in any natural sense; it is, in fact, precisely this lack of an assumed connection that allows one to become a potential *medium* for the other. At the same time, in Mao's analysis, this critical distance must be continually posed in the face of the vicissitudes of the interaction between the two, because there can be no interaction that leaves the two untouched.

Mao has no problem essaying the education of the intellectual. In some instances, he stresses the fact that the transformation that the intellectual herself goes through when she comes in contact with her object of study—change in feelings is also a "change from one class to another" (7)—makes her one of "the masses." The intellectual, by speaking of her experience, also speaks for others. In other instances, Mao sees the transformation of the intellectual as the basis for forging a mode of address proper to her object of study: "If you want the masses to understand you, you must make up your mind to undergo the long and even painful process of tempering" (6). The intellectual, by speaking of the experience of others, also speaks for herself.

But what about the education of "the masses"? There is considerable ambiguity in Mao's elucidation of the "others." He implicitly links the revolutionary situation to the transformation of "the masses": "The masses have remoulded themselves in struggle or are doing so, and our literature and art should depict this process" (4). But because this *self-*remolding is in process and is therefore open-ended, clearly the unknown and the unforeseeable term in the agenda, Mao does not always conquer the urge to settle the question in favor of a simplistic rendering of the task of the intellectual—the "life of the masses" is a "crude" material that awaits "concentration" into an ideological form by the intellectual (18). This rendering of "the masses" along the lines of an active/passive split, I think, arises from *Mao's failure to specify the nature of revolutionary pedagogy itself.* Just what is involved in the (self-)remolding of "the masses"? What are "the masses" remolding themselves into? Are there material and symbolic constraints on the ways in which "the masses" can remold themselves?

Because Mao treats "the masses" as a sociological referent—"the masses" are workers, peasants, and soldiers—his position leaves little room for interrogating the objectifying logic that sees these workers, peasants, and soldiers as "the masses" in the first place. Neither does his position allow for the possibility that revolutionary pedagogy can provide the theoretical tools for interrogating the objectifying logic. If the task of the writers and artists is to "concentrate . . . everyday phenomena, typify the contradictions and struggles within them, and produce works which awaken the masses, fire them with enthusiasm, and impel them to unite and struggle to transform their environment" (19), this task hinges on a rigorous theorizing of "the masses." In a situation in which "the masses" and the intellectuals "come to know each other well" (40) through revolutionary pedagogy, the transformation of both groups actually enriches the theorizing of both terms.

Mao, in fact, tends to emphasize political work over intellectual work (25), since he can never trust the intellectuals to do a decent job of representing the masses, or the masses to do a decent job of representing themselves.[14] This is because by "masses" he means both the term of ad-

---

14. To some extent, the work of the scholars cited above have sought to reformulate Mao's epistemology in light of the nuances of his notion of practice as an indispensable component of the process of cognition. See, for example, Dirlik's argument concerning

dress that denotes the revolutionized "popular" consciousness (not local but general) and the aggregate of individuals whose interests have yet
to be radicalized. Because he does not always account for the theoretical grounds of the interplay between these two denotations of "the
masses," an interplay that is an important component of revolutionary
pedagogy, Mao remains ambivalent not only about the intellectual's ability to achieve the necessary critical distance (both from her old ways of
thought and being and from the as yet unradicalized interests of the individuals around her) but also about the pedagogical task of the "truly
revolutionary" intellectual.

These ambivalences stem from a more fundamental ambivalence
about the status of error in intellectual activity. The necessity of accounting for error is tarred by the fear of committing error, which politics putatively absorbs and neutralizes. Accordingly, Mao valorizes politics for its ability to deal with the risk of error by rendering it a pragmatic
rather than an intellectual concern. This move truncates a serious exploration of the specificity and complexity of intellectual praxis and, more
important to Mao's concerns at hand, the exigencies of training "cultural armies."

Like Mao, Frantz Fanon believes that the anticolonial struggle not only
grounds popular consciousness but also enables the intellectual to come
in touch with her people (46–47) and carry out the program of generalizing popular consciousness.[15] Like Mao, Fanon is aware of the potential failure of intellectual service—which happens when the national party
leaders "do not put their theoretical knowledge to the service of the

---

the openness of Mao's notion of cognition to "reconstruction" ("Mao Zedong and 'Chinese Marxism'" 138). My discussion of Mao, Fanon, and Cabral acknowledges the fact
that their writings, especially Mao's and Cabral's, were often tactical and practical inter-
ventions that deployed a variety of rhetorical and explanatory strategies that would seem
to give rise to contradictory statements. Thus my comment on Fanon's romanticization of
"the masses" must be qualified by the fact that he also spoke of the necessity for what the
Fanon scholar Ato Sekyi-Otu calls "the political education of spontaneity" (5). Similarly,
Cabral's ideas about political education must be read alongside his tactical appeals to a
romanticized notion of "the people." I subscribe to Sekyi-Otu's proposal that "an utterance or a representation or a practice we encounter in a text is to be considered not as a
discrete and conclusive event, but rather as a strategic and self-revising act set in motion
by changing circumstances and perspectives, increasingly intricate configurations of experience" (5). The account that I give of these Third World theorists' ambivalence about error aims to elucidate a recurring instance in Mao's, Fanon's, and Cabral's configurations
of revolutionary consciousness and practice.

    15. For book-length critical studies on Fanon, see Ato Sekyi-Otu, *Fanon's Dialectic of
Experience;* Lewis R. Gordon, *Fanon and the Crisis of European Man;* Irene L. Gendzier,
Frantz Fanon; Adele Jinadu, *Fanon;* Emmanuel Hansen, *Frantz Fanon;* and Renate Zahar,
Frantz Fanon.

people; they only try to erect a framework around the people which follows an a priori schedule" (113). Alienation is thus a *precondition* of the intellectual, and can only be overcome if the intellectual participates in the struggle. The intellectual's work is legitimized only if it is linked to decolonization. In the same vein, "the people" are a product of decolonization, because they were hitherto only colonized "thing[s]" before they undertook the process of freeing themselves (37).[16]

Fanon makes it clear that the work of theorizing does not precede the transformative experiences of both the intellectual and the people, since there can be no a priori framework into which the intellectuals and the nationalist leaders can fit "the people." Yet for Fanon, the intellectual's work in decolonization is fundamental to the way in which decolonization itself influences and transforms people, creates "a new language and a new humanity" (36). Fanon's idea of decolonization is of one that explicitly *supersedes* the heterogeneity created by the colonial order: decolonization "unifies people [erstwhile dichotomized by the colonial situation] by its radical decision to remove from it its heterogeneity and by unifying it on a national, sometimes racial, basis" (46). In decolonization, Fanon assigns the party the task of making itself the "direct expression" of the masses, the "energetic spokesman and incorruptible defender of the masses"—an epistemic task that must come to terms with the fact that the masses are "perfectly capable of governing themselves" (187–88). To this effect, Fanon advocates a decentralized administrative network that allows for free exchange of ideas and consultations with the people on all levels of decision making.

Yet Fanon's awareness of the multifarious ways in which class and other differences among the colonized people can inform the epistemic project of forging a "national culture" leads him to advocate political education, which will be instrumental in getting the masses to understand that certain fractions of the population have particular interests and that they do not always coincide with the national interest. "The people will then come to understand that national independence sheds light upon facts which are sometimes divergent and antagonist. Such a taking stock of the situation at this precise moment of the struggle is decisive, for it allows the people to pass from total, indiscriminatory nationalism to social and economic awareness" (144). The intellectual's pedagogical task is to get the "mass of the people interested in the ordering of public affairs" (180), because national identity is not ready-made but is forged in revolutionary praxis.

16. In this sense, Fanon claims that all decolonization is successful (37).

At the same time, however, Fanon invokes a romanticized notion of the people, a people invested with more than epistemic privilege—the space of the people, the "zone of occult instability where the people dwell" (227), is what allows the intellectual to access the truth about the people. The intellectual learns to address her own people (245), but her task is mainly supplementary, since it is the people who speak thus: "If the leader drives me on, I want him to realize that at the same time I show him the way; the nation ought not to be something bossed by a Grand Panjandrum" (184). Political leaders and intellectuals "give a name to the nation," which the people then *realize* when they identify with the name and fight for the demands that are given shape by their leaders (68).[17]

Because Fanon romanticizes the masses (by projecting "unity and co-ordinated political will" on to them) (Lazarus 200) and invests the term with self-identificatory presence ("the masses" know), he expresses a deep ambivalence about the intellectual. The intellectual, because she is a mediating term, is haunted by her role in the transmission of the wishes and desires of the masses: "The danger that will haunt him continually is that of becoming an uncritical mouthpiece of the masses; he becomes a kind of yes-man who nods assent at every word coming from the people, which he interprets as considered judgments" (Fanon 49). For Fanon, "the masses" represent pure *unmediated* truth—"Now the fellah, the unemployed man, the starving native do not lay claim to the truth; they do not *say* that they represent the truth, for they are the truth" (49; original emphasis). The problem of representation is therefore inseparable from the *problem that is* the intellectual, since it is the masses who can rightly embody history (140) by giving content to the empty form supplied by the intellectual (Cheah, "Modelling the Nation" 2). Fanon's intellectual is at once passive[18] and active,[19] because, like Mao, Fanon ignores the provenance and theoretical consequences of the objectifying logic that constitutes "the masses" in the first place.

One articulation of the need to provide adequate political analysis that

17. I am grateful to Pheng Cheah's unpublished essay, "Modelling the Nation" (1995), for its insightful reading of Fanon's *Wretched of the Earth,* particularly its discussion of the "modular and objectifying logic" that informs the very concept of "the masses" that Fanon invokes in his work (7).

18. "Revolution's greatest service to the intellectuals is to place them in contact with the people, to have placed them in contact with the people, to have allowed them to see the extreme, ineffable poverty of the people, at the same time allowing them to watch the awakening of the people's intelligence and the onward progress of their consciousness" (188).

19. The party and the intellectuals as leaders "armed with revolutionary principles" are able to defeat the "useless and harmful middle class" (175).

can be consistently applied across the spectrum of political struggles can
be found in the writings of Amilcar Cabral (Davidson xv–xvi).[20] Like
Mao and Fanon, Cabral thinks that the intellectual comes to identify with
the "culture" and hopes of "the masses" through struggle. While Cabral
shared Fanon's concern with the need to consider alienation a factor in
distinguishing between the situation of "the masses" and "those social
groups that are assimilated to colonial culture or partially so" (61), he
had to address this question from the perspective of his involvement in
the formulation of party policies in both the institutional and the grass-
roots context of the national liberation movement in Guinea-Bissau.
Cabral grounds his analysis of the mediating function performed by the
intellectual in the anticolonial struggle in a consideration of the actual
and potential ramifications of the epistemic task in day-to-day decisions.
For while Cabral shares Fanon's implicit faith in the transformative character of political struggle for both the intellectual and the people (see,
e.g., Cabral, *National Liberation and Culture* 7), he differs from Fanon
in the emphasis that he gives to the program of political analysis involved
in the struggle. In some cases, Cabral's position echoes Fanon's in that
he locates political analysis in "the masses" themselves: "The leaders realize, not without a certain astonishment, the richness of spirit, the capacity for reasoned discussions and clear disposition of ideas, the facil-
ity for understanding and assimilating concepts on the part of popular
groups who yesterday were forgotten, considered incompetent by colonizers and even by some nationalists" (13). But by investing "the people"
not only with epistemic privilege but also with epistemic *skills,* Cabral
advocates a definition of "the people," not only in Fanonian terms of
people as embodiment of history but of people "seen in light of their own
history" (*Unity and Struggle* 89). Here "the people" are not only defined
existentially by anticolonial struggle, but theoretically by the desire for
"what corresponds to the fundamental necessity of the history of our
land." In other words, for Cabral, to talk about "the people" is to *theorize* history;[21] "the people," then, do not exist prior to the theorizing

20. For a discussion of Cabral's social and political thought, see Patrick Chabal, *Amilcar Cabral;* Ronald H. Chilcote, *Amilcar Cabral's Revolutionary Theory and Practice* esp.
26–88. Chilcote's book also contains an invaluable annotated bibliography of writings by
and about Cabral.
21. In this sense, Cabral is right to say that "the people have no need to assert or reassert their identity" (*Unity and Struggle* 67). To do so is superfluous, given that this notion of "the people" is not an empty form that is then filled by a sociological referent;
rather, it already carries within it a complex theory of identity that names (constitutes) the
referent and theorizes its causal relevance to an analysis of the society in revolution.

of "their" history. Cabral writes that "the people" are defined "in terms of the mainstream of history, in terms of the highest interests of the majority of that society" (90). *"The people" are the truth, not in the sense of nonderivative, self-posited truth, but in the sense of truth that is always already mediated by theory and representation.*[22]

Cabral's foregrounding of theory-mediatedness in his discussion not only of the politics of transformation but also of knowledge leads to a nuanced reading of the epistemic task of political analysis that is shared by "the people" and "the intellectual" alike. The pedagogic function of the intellectuals and "the masses" can only be understood if it is seen as both a practical and a theoretical undertaking. Cabral assigns to the intellectual the task of aiding in the transformation of the levels of culture of different social groups into a "national" culture, which is based on a "political and moral unity" that represents, *on a theoretical level,* "the complexity of cultural problems raised in all its dimensions" (*National Liberation and Culture* 12).

By granting some specificity to theoretical work in revolutionary praxis, Cabral is able to resolve one of the thornier problems that a reading of Fanon's work raises. This is the issue of the contribution made by the colonial state to the development of national consciousness. Fanon did not address the question of the link between the colonial state and national consciousness, preferring to concentrate on the transformative moment that characterizes the liberation of that consciousness (Cheah, "Modelling the Nation" 3–4). Fanon sees decolonization as superseding the dichotomy colonizer/colonized that was created by the colonial order. The main weakness of Fanon's position, however, is that it fails to consider the provenance of the "homogeneity" created by decolonization.

As Cabral notes, the daily "practice of imperialist rule demanded a more or less *accurate* knowledge of the society it was supposed to rule and of the historical reality (both economic, social and cultural) in the middle of which it exists" (*Unity and Struggle* 58; my emphasis). This knowledge, argues Cabral, has contributed to the "general enrichment of human and social knowledge in spite of the fact that it was one-sided, subjective and very often unjust" (58). Cabral suggests that we cannot

---

22. For Cabral, "the people" cannot be mistaken for "the population" because "it must be clearly defined who are the people at *every moment* of the life of a population" (*Unity and Struggle* 89; my emphasis). Such a notion entails an analysis of the differences in social location generated even within "the people" and the potential contribution of different sections of the lumpenproletariat to the liberation movement. See Cabral, *Revolution in Guinea,* esp. 48–51.

begin to understand the "political and moral unity" achieved by revolutionary struggle unless we take into account the fact that the knowledge that grounds this unity may have been partly derived from knowledge that was deployed to forge a *prior* "unity" ("Guine" itself)[23]
imposed by colonial rule.

Cabral does not take this implication further,[24] but his reliance on
the concept of the cumulative nature of knowledge allows him to justify his belief in the gradual identification and elimination of error:
"Sufficient number of experiences have already been accumulated to enable us to define the general line of thought and action in order to eliminate ideological deficiency" (*Unity and Struggle* 122–23). Given that
Cabral's definition of "the people" necessarily commits him to the idea
of the theory-mediatedness of revolutionary struggle, Cabral's positing
of the necessity of obtaining reliable accounts through progressive
identification of the sources of error of "the people," "their" history,
and the national liberation struggle stresses the openness of intellectual
work not just to interpretation but also to reinterpretation and revision.
For Cabral, culture, as a "creation of society and synthesis of balances
and solutions which society engenders to resolve conflicts which characterize every phase of its history" (*National Liberation and Culture* 9),
can be both a source of material, epistemic, *and* moral support and a
source of obstacles and difficulties, of "erroneous conceptions about reality, deviation in the carrying out of duty, limits of the tempo and
efficiency of struggle" (13).

We may read Cabral's writings in light of Mao's and Fanon's ideas as
providing the parameters, however sketchy and incomplete, for a further accounting and theoretical justification of political education. Speaking of the success of the Cuban Revolution, Cabral argues that the vanguard "kept the people permanently informed about national and
international questions, which affect their life; it makes them take an active part in answering these questions. The vanguard, which soon understood that the dynamic existence of a strong and united Party was indispensable, has been able not only to interpret correctly the objective

23. Cabral had a sense of how much "Guine" owed its boundedness as a territorial
unit to the Portuguese colonial machine. He had, in fact, worked on and published an agri-
cultural consensus of Guinea in 1953 (see Cabral, *Unity and Struggle* 4–16).

24. To do so would have meant arguing that national consciousness owed something
of its provenance to colonial rule, because the colonial state contributed substantially to
the discursive and institutional construction of the "other" as native, a necessary project
given the colonial state's drive for greater efficiency in extracting surplus from the colony
(cf. Cheah).

conditions and specific demands of the environment, but also to forge
the most powerful of weapons for defence, security and guarantee of continuity for the Revolution: the revolutionary consciousness of the masses
of the people. *The latter, as we know, is not and never was spontaneous
in any part of the world"* (*Unity and Struggle* 120; my emphasis). The
vanguard itself, of course, would have to become "revolutionary" before it can have the consciousness, ab initio, of the distinction between
"genuine" national independence and "fictitious" political independence
(132). Because Cabral is sensitive to the specificity of theoretical *work*,
he is able to justify his claim that the vanguard's success in mobilizing
"the people" is in part a function of its ability to register and articulate
their aspirations. Cabral's contribution to the theorizing of national liberation, as I see it, lies in the fact that he helped to define the space cleared
by Mao, Fanon, and other Third World theorist-activists for a serious
consideration of the complexity of theoretical work that is involved in
forging the unity of "the people" in decolonization.

II

Having discussed three pathbreaking texts from the Third World on the
problem of the intellectual and "speaking for the masses," let me now
turn to a more recent text that addresses the issue within the conjunc-
ture of discourses on poststructuralism, postmodernism, and postcolonialism in the American academy.[25] Here I shall concentrate on Spivak's
"Can the Subaltern Speak?" which addresses the problem of representation and the role of the intellectual through a reading of Michel Foucault and Gilles Deleuze.[26] I argue that although Spivak's essay offers an
important and insightful rendering of the problem of representation (here
understood in both its political and its semiotic sense), it also *performs*
what it sets out to criticize when it tackles the problem of the intellectual. I argue that her dismissal of the intellectual's task of "speaking for
the masses" may in part be due to the fact that she does not quite spell
out the cognitive component of ideology.

25. There exists a growing body of theoretical contributions that interrogate the link
between postcolonialism and postmodernism. See Kwame Anthony Appiah, *In My Father's
House* and "Is the Post- in Postmodernism the Post- in Postcolonial?"; Kumkum Sangari,
"The Politics of the Possible"; Ian Adam and Helen Tiffin, eds., *Past the Last Post;* Arun
P. Mukherjee, "Whose Post-colonialism and Whose Post-modernism?"; Simon During,
"Postmodernism or Post-colonialism Today" and "Postmodernism or Postcolonialism?"
   26. R. Radhakrishnan has used Spivak's criticism of the Foucault-Deleuze interview
in "Toward an Effective Intellectual."

Spivak begins her essay with an extended discussion of the passages in "Intellectuals and Power: A Conversation between Michel Foucault and Gilles Deleuze," noting that the very form of the exchange "undoes the opposition between authoritative theoretical production and the unguarded practice of conversation, enabling one to glimpse the track of ideology" (272). The "track of ideology" evinces itself in what Spivak sees as the contribution of French poststructuralism: its emphasis on the heterogeneity of power (Foucault) and desire (Deleuze) and its disavowal of the role of the intellectual in "knowing" and "disclosing" the discourse of the other. Spivak correctly argues that because of their failure to undertake a serious interrogation of the relationship among desire, power, and subjectivity, and therefore their failure to articulate a theory of interests when they discuss revolutionary practice, Foucault and Deleuze end up ignoring the question of ideology and obscuring their own implication in the intellectual and economic history of late capitalism (272–73). Foucault and Deleuze's distrust of ideology manifests itself in the theoretical opposition that they establish between interest and desire; this opposition, argues Spivak, merely replicates the work of "bourgeois sociologists" who equate ideology (as "false" ideas) with culture. This kind of opposition has an important impact on Foucault and Deleuze's take on "the masses," since it is "the masses" that Foucault and Deleuze invest with the revolutionary force of resistance. Foucault and Deleuze valorize "the oppressed" as *subject*[27] and in so doing circumvent the *difficulty* of the task of "counterhegemonic ideological production" by adopting a "positivist empiricism—the justifying foundation of advanced capitalist neocolonialism—" that uncritically uses terms like "concrete experience" and "what actually happens" (274). In other words, Foucault and Deleuze play down the role of the intellectual, but in the process of disavowing the intellectual, they end up *performing* anyway the (disavowed intellectual's) task of diagnosing concrete experience, thus playing into the international division of labor.

This kind of slippage, according to Spivak, stems from Foucault and Deleuze's conflation of the two meanings of representation—representation as "speaking for" (politics) and representation as "to re-present" (art and philosophy) (275). This conflation, in turn, has its roots in what is held, commonsensically, to be the proper role of the intellectual and "the

---

27. Foucault: "The masses *know* perfectly well, clearly"—are "undeceived"—and "know far better than [the intellectuals] and they certainly say it very well" (cited in Spivak 274; Foucault's emphasis).

masses": "Because theory is also only 'action,' the theoretician does not represent (speak for) the oppressed group. Indeed, the subject is not seen as a representative consciousness (one re-presenting reality adequately)" (275). The two meanings of representation are related but discontinuous; the danger of conflating the two is that one risks privileging a version of intellectualism that one wants to question in the first place, an intellectualism that sees the intellectual as acting *and* speaking while "the masses" only act *and* struggle. Foucault and Deleuze's account not only leaves out the possibility of what Spivak calls the "critique of ideological subject-constitution," but forgoes any serious attempts to think about the "active theoretical practice of the 'transformation of consciousness'" (275). According to Spivak, any unquestioning valorization of the practical politics of the subjects "speaking for themselves" incurs the danger of reinstalling the idea of a "sovereign subject" within a radical theory that seeks to criticize it in the first place (278). Only a theory of ideology, says Spivak, can account for the "micrological texture of power" (279) that works through interests.

Spivak argues that the poststructuralist suspicion of representation as a theoretical activity and the collapsing of theory into practice conveniently neglects the theoretical problems that need to be worked out. She correctly states that Foucault and Deleuze's disavowal of the institutional power that they wield as intellectuals puts them in the position of "merely reporting on a non-represented subject and analyzing (without really doing so) the workings of (the unnamed subject irreducibly presupposed by) power and desire" (279). Spivak sees the task of the intellectual as that of "read[ing] and writ[ing] so that the impossibility of such interested individualistic refusals of the institutional privileges of power bestowed on the subject is taken seriously" (280).[28]

Spivak is right to argue against an uncritical celebration of the "masses" as "speaking for themselves," as though the consciousness of the masses exists in a pure form awaiting retrieval (280). For Spivak, foregrounding the question of ideology lends credence to the problem that "the masses" may not necessarily speak their interests and transform their consciousness accordingly. But while Spivak argues for the specificity of

28. Spivak's essay on the native-as-subaltern is not concerned to theorize native agency; rather, it seeks to examine the way in which the disenfranchised elements of the "native" population are represented in the colonial and nationalist discourses. Spivak's weakest point, however, is her deferral of a detailed presentation of the mass politics of the colonized: "Spivak does not write out the 'evidence' of native agency, but much of the time, it is *as though she did*" (Lazarus 206; original emphasis).

the intellectual's task, she appears too wary of the intellectual's contribution to the ideological critique of the oppressed people. In one passage, she portrays the confrontation between the intellectuals and "the masses" as leading to self-questioning on the part of the intellectuals: "Here are subsistence farmers, unorganized peasant labor, the tribals and the communities of zero workers on the streets or in the countryside. To confront them is not to represent (*vertreten*) them, but to learn to represent (*darstellen*) ourselves" (289). Further, she writes: "In seeking to speak to (rather than listen to or speak for) the historically muted subject of the subaltern woman, the postcolonial intellectual systematically 'unlearns' female privilege" (295).

While I grant the general validity of Spivak's point, I also think that she gives too little credit to the complexity of intellectual work.[29] Her circumscription of the role of the intellectual springs from her failure to consider the epistemological component of the theory of ideology.[30] The only error the intellectual seems to see is her own. Spivak sets up a narcissistic view of intellectualism. In the passages where Spivak brings up the intellectual, she highlights only the self-re/presentation of the intellectual. Who else is the intellectual speaking "to" when she speaks "to" the "historically muted subject" but herself?

While Spivak is able to write with great insight about the colonial and poststructuralist desire for the other, she is unable to fully justify her argument that the neocolonial order does, in fact, put the intellectual and the oppressed people in a relation of existential proximity (*"Here,"* she writes, "are subsistence farmers . . ."). Unlike Mao, Fanon, and Cabral, for whom the problem has been that of how the struggle for social change can sanction and supersede the heterogeneity of intellectuals, subsistence farmers, urban workers, tribals, and so on,[31] Spivak seems to hold that the development of a theory of ideology (as a mediating term) performs no other function except to illuminate the compromised position of the

29. Lazarus argues that Spivak "claims too little for the work of intellectuals" (208).
30. Marx did not have a systematic explication of social ideologies, but it would be too simplistic to argue from this that Marx was indifferent to epistemological considerations and that functionalist interpretations of ideology were his sole concerns. "If anything, epistemological considerations of ideology were extremely important to [Marx] because in his view false and illusory social views were practically disadvantageous for both oppressed groups and society as a whole" (Pines 160). See Christopher Pines's *Ideology and False Consciousness* for an extended critique of the functionalist interpretations of ideology.
31. Put another way, the problem that I think Mao, Fanon, and Cabral tried to deal with is that the intellectual stands in for the problem of the *mediating* term that both sanctions and supersedes the heterogeneity of Revolution itself.

intellectual and to circumscribe the *political* task of the intellectual.[32] Given that she is silent about the epistemological component of the theory of ideology, she cannot justify speaking *for* the intellectual in these terms either.

If Foucault and Deleuze are guilty of conflating the *darstellen* (represent through art and philosophy) and *vertreten* (political representation) senses of representation, Spivak's problem seems to be that she sees *only* the discontinuity between the two, rather than also take their relatedness into account. In so doing, she elides the socially transformative capabilities of intellectualism, part of which inheres in the intellectual's ability to accurately represent the aspirations of the "historically muted subjects." For Mao, Fanon, and Cabral, the failure of the postcolonial national bourgeoisie to speak for the nation consisted of their failure to unify the domains of elite and popular politics on the national level. This failure is also a failure to win the consent of "the people," whose interests, to quote Lazarus, the national bourgeoisie "failed to recognize, let alone represent." While Mao, Fanon, and Cabral remain committed to the possibility of a movement or party speaking for the nation, Spivak draws back from this. She analyzes quite astutely the problems that inhere in the assumption of a self-identifying, self-present re-presentation of "the people" but leaves off considering the contribution of theoretical work to the "transformation of consciousness" (both the intellectual's and "the masses'"). Spivak highlights the "situatedness" of the intellectual, only to cut the intellectual off from social practice, even though she admits her ideological solidarity with those who engage in this practice.

Although it would be unwise to think that we can wish away the division of intellectual and manual labor without transforming society, it would be equally unwise (if not more so) to buy in to the ideology that secures this division. Spivak sees the intellectual as both powerful and powerless, but because she does not seriously consider the possibility of the intellectual's theoretical contribution to transformative politics (i.e., to political education), she cannot see the intellectual's contribution to political struggle (as activist *and* theoretician) as contributing to the even-

32. One implication of this point is a somewhat individualistic view of the political tasks of intellectuals and of the struggles of oppressed groups. The problem of forging collective political struggle does not get much of a hearing from this kind of perspective, since one is not encouraged to look for ways of connecting the struggles of the subsistence farmer with that of the unorganized peasant labor and that of the tribals, communities of zero workers on the streets, and so on.

tual dissolution of this opposition. To do so would have meant acknowledging that the intellectual can contribute to enriching the knowledge of social relations *other than her own,* a knowledge that, Spivak agrees, is crucial to the transformation of consciousness (285–86). The task of re-presenting "the oppressed," in order for it to be a valid undertaking at all, can only be justified as an *epistemic* task that involves a complex interaction between the intellectuals and "the masses" and a serious consideration of the sources of error and mystification. Only when we think about the theoretical component of revolutionary praxis can we begin to understand what learning and unlearning (i.e., political education) involves.

III

I argued above that classical accounts of the role played by the intellectual in the struggle for social change acknowledged the intellectual's contribution to political struggle but failed to spell out the precise nature of the theoretical component of revolutionary praxis. I argued that the lack of specificity accorded the issue of intellectualism in these accounts sprang from their ambivalence about the intellectual's ability to accurately register and articulate the visions and experiences of "the people," an ambivalence, essentially, about the status of error in intellectual work. I also argued that in the case of certain critiques that uphold the necessity of theorizing rather than abjuring representation (in both its political and semiotic senses), this ambivalence may actually vitiate the cogency of political claims regarding the demystifying function of the concepts of ideology and mystification.

Here I look into the problem of the epistemic reliability of intellectual work in order to specify the theoretical component of revolutionary praxis. The extent to which we can justify making claims about the possibility and validity of "learning from the masses" and, concomitantly, the transformation of consciousness is determined by our ability to argue in favor of the epistemic character of representation (in the semiotic sense). I draw on "realist" contributions to the theorization of knowledge to work out Mao's, Fanon's, and Cabral's notions of political pedagogy, which assumes that "experience" (say, the experience of oppression) is not only linked to ideology, but it is also linked to the acquisition of knowledge about social relations. Drawing on "realist" accounts of (transformative) experience, I argue that the theory-mediatedness of knowledge, far from inhibiting our understanding of social relations, allows us to evaluate such knowledge in terms of its epistemic reliability. Only by taking this point seriously can we effectively rework the idea of "speaking for the masses" in a way that avoids the romantic essentialist objectification of "the masses" (Fanon) and the radical constructionist (most "postmodern" theories) disavowals of the epistemic character of the experience of "the masses," while granting specificity to intellectual praxis and pedagogical work in the broader context of political struggle.

I begin by tackling head-on the more controversial claims of realist theories of experience. In his "Epistemic Status of Cultural Identity," Satya P. Mohanty frames the issue succinctly by arguing in favor of a "postpositivist realist" account of identity that treats experiences as claims to knowledge, which involves the complex processing of information (including adjudication between competing background theories) and which is open to evaluation and revision. Mohanty premises the cognitive aspect of experience on the fact that identities are both constructed and *real*.[33] Identities are constructed because they are based on interpreted experience and on theories that explain the social world (Mohanty, "Epistemic Status" 54). They are also real because they "refer outward to causally significant features of the social world" (69).

One can see how such an argument would immediately run aground in the shoals of certain "postmodernist" axioms in cultural theory because postulating that identities are theory mediated is held to be incompatible with claiming "true" (justified) knowledge. The realist position, however, differs from postmodernist accounts in that it does *not* presume an opposition between constructedness and realness. This refusal to oppose constructedness to realness appears contradictory in the eyes of those for whom a generalized attitude of skepticism toward intellectual work has acquired the status of a truism. Before elaborating on the realist reformulation of the real/construct debate, let me, therefore, provide a brief sketch of the intellectual context in which contemporary realism took shape as a philosophical mode of inquiry. R. J. Hirst provides the following basic definition of realism in *The Encyclopedia of Philosophy*:

> In the early history of philosophy, particularly in medieval thought, the term "realism" was used, in opposition to nominalism, for the doctrine that uni-

33. Satya P. Mohanty, "The Epistemic Status of Cultural Identity." The arguments are elaborated as part of an extended treatise on and contextualization of realism in Satya P. Mohanty, *Literary Theory and the Claims of History*, esp. 202–34.

versals have a real, objective existence. In modern philosophy, however, it is used for the view that material objects exist externally to us and independently of our sense experience. Realism is thus opposed to idealism, which holds that no such material objects or external realities exist apart from our knowledge or consciousness of them, the whole universe thus being dependent on the mind or in some sense mental. (77)

Hirst's definition of realism highlights the fact that modern realism, in upholding the view that the world exists "objectively" (i.e., independently of our mental apprehension, experience, and knowledge of "it"), concerned itself primarily with ontological questions regarding the nature of reality, about "what there is and what it is like," rather than with epistemic issues regarding the nature of thought and language (Devitt, *Realism and Truth* 40, 43). Arguments about the *knowability* of the mind-independent world, about our ability to refer to these existents, for example, were held to apply to our attempts to theorize only one part of the reality—the part where we theorize ourselves and our language.

That the realist quickly went from arguing that the world has an objective existence to defending the knowability of this mind-independent world—a move that conflated metaphysical and epistemic issues—owes its existence to the fact that criticism against realism usually took off from epistemological concerns. The conflation of metaphysical issues with semantic and epistemic issues also owed something to the growing interest in and dominance of the philosophy of language in England and America.[34] Developments in linguistics have called attention to the constitutive role played by language in our social lives and in our own attempts to study the relationship between language and the world (Devitt, *Realism and Truth* 103, 105, 226). Epistemology came to be "naturalized" in philosophy because the linguistic concerns of such a philosphy often entailed accounting for the "truth" not just on the level of description but on the level of justification as well. To say that something is true also raises the question of whether and how one can determine that something is true.

34. A short account is provided by Michael Devitt and Kim Sterelny, *Language and Reality* 3–4, 229–35. For a summary of realist works, see William H. Werkmeister, *A History of Philosophical Ideas in America;* John Passmore, *A Hundred Years of Philosophy;* Rudolf Metz, *A Hundred Years of British Philosophy.* For an exposition of the main ideas of new realism, see E. B. Holt et al., *The New Realism,* which is strongly influenced by William James, *Essays in Radical Empiricism,* esp. "Does Consciousness Exist?" (1–38) and "A World of Pure Experience" (39–91), which date from 1904. See also Roderick M. Chisolm, *Realism and the Background of Phenomenology.* See R. B. Perry's "The Egocentric Predicament"; Bertrand Russell's "On the Nature of Truth"; and G. E. Moore's "The Refutation of Idealism" in his *Philosophical Studies.* For an influential example of language-based philosophy, see Ludwig Wittgenstein, *Philosophical Investigations.*

Not surprisingly, the constant sliding from metaphysical to semantic and epistemic issues that characterizes the reception of realism has meant that questions of meaning and truth conditions take center stage at the expense of a finer elaboration of ontological issues. Influential antirealists like Thomas Kuhn and Paul Feyerabend, it turns out, do not actually disagree with the core realist position on mind-independent "reality"; what they would argue is that this "real" world, and the constraints it exerts on our theories, cannot in principle be known.[35] This position subscribes to something like a Kantian noumenal world of the thing-in-itself that is separate from the phenomenal world of appearances that are "constructed" by our concepts.[36] Both constructivist and realist positions assume that a gap exists between the world as we know it and the world as it is, but whereas the realist believes that the "truth" about the entities that we posit comes out of the interaction between ideas and nonideas, the constructivist locks the truth solely within the realm of the phenomenal world.

The constructivist position may be seen, on the one hand, as coming out of the critique of the dominant conception of correspondence theory of truth that advocated a naive "mirrorlike" or "picturelike" relationship between language and reality, a relationship based on the presumed identity of linguistic and objective structures. The critique of the classical notion of the correspondence theory of truth rightly emphasizes the need to give up our commonsensical notions of an immediate, transparent, nonmediated reality.

What the realist would disagree with, on the other hand, is not the claim concerning the theory-mediatedness of reality but rather the implications regarding observation that can be drawn from this claim. For the constructivist, the claim to theory-mediatedness often leads to the view that since our observations of the world "out there" are determined solely by the theory from which our statements about the world are derived, the truth value of our statements cannot itself be determined. The realist, however, would claim that our evaluation of the truth value of an observation may in part depend on the various theories to which we subscribe, theories that can be right or wrong (Devitt, *Realism and Truth*

---

35. See, e.g., Thomas Kuhn, *The Structure of Scientific Revolutions* 206; "Logic of Discovery or Psychology of Research," esp. 16, 20; and "Reflections on My Critics," esp. 235, 263, 267. See also Paul Feyerabend, "Reply to Critics," esp. 242, 246; "Problems of Empiricism, Part II," esp. 303; "Consolations for the Specialist," esp. 227; and *Science in a Free Society.*

36. For a discussion of constructivism, see Devitt, *Realism and Truth* 157.

168). Arguing that our knowledge of the world is theory mediated does not automatically lead to the conclusion that this world is unknowable. Rather, the epistemic relations between human beings and the world become not only an object of inquiry and study but an empirical question as well. What makes our opinions and observations "knowledge"? What is the process by which we acquire knowledge?

It is precisely this refusal to oppose constructedness to realness that provides the main justification for Mohanty's argument that knowledge is theory dependent. For one thing, the notion of theory dependence can be extended to cover aspects of human practice, including experiences such as emotions, which are traditionally held to belong not only in a separate realm from public/social meaning but also in a category distinct from the cognitive and, therefore, from questions of epistemology. Furthermore, in arguing that experience and identity—and not merely the theories about them—are "bits of social and political theory themselves, and are to be evaluated as such" (Mohanty, "Epistemic Status" 71), Mohanty in effect is asking us to take seriously the idea that epistemology is a *social* process that involves the production, justification, and regulation of knowledge.

In other words, experience is constructed insofar as it is defined and elaborated within a social context and the theories of the world that one finds or holds there. While experience cannot be assumed to be self-evident and always reliable, such that no a priori principles can guarantee in advance the reliability of experience as a source of knowledge, it would be wrong to argue that experience is always "epistemologically suspect." One way of conceptualizing experience in cognitive terms is to look at it as involving a range of processes of organizing information, processes that, like all cognitive activities, involve constant reinterpretation, reevaluation, and adjudication. These processes do not have to be consciously or even fully elaborated—since, as in a battered woman's case (to use an example that Mohanty adopts from Naomi Scheman's essay "Anger and the Politics of Naming"), the woman's confused feelings can be a process whereby the woman "weighs one vaguely felt hunch against another, reinterprets and re-evaluates the information she considers relevant to her feelings and her situation and thus redefines the 'contours' of her world" (Mohanty, "Epistemic Status" 49).

As we know only too well from the discussion of constructivism above, the emphasis on the theory-mediatedness of identity, on its inscription within presuppositions, does not necessarily lead to a realist account. What makes Mohanty's theory of identity realist is his more controversial point that, in highlighting the cognitive aspect of experience, we do and can learn or discover something about the reality that shapes our experience. In other words, a realist position would entail holding the view that theory dependence actually contributes to rather than detracts from the reliability of knowledge; furthermore, knowledge is reliable to the extent that the theory that mediates it approximates the truth. The idea that actual, material features in the world play a part in regulating theories (they impose limits on the ways in which we make sense of the world), such that these theories can be evaluated in terms of their reliability in approximating the truth (i.e., in terms of the accuracy of their reference to "real" features of the world), is something that a realist like Mohanty stresses.[37] Only when this statement is taken seriously can we begin to try to explain the way in which theory-dependent procedures of processing information actually contribute to the growth of accurate knowledge. For the battered woman, the social fact of gender, based on empirical evidence that refers outward to causally significant features of the world (wife-beating, low wages, sexist remarks, pink slips), provides the causal explanations that are relevant to her experience and the possibilities and choices that are open to her.

In this account, then, experience does not have self-evident meanings but is dependent on social narratives, paradigms, and ideologies. Indeed, the very fact that it is a theoretical affair allows for the possibility that it can be analyzed and evaluated. Theories are evaluated using epistemological criteria that examine such things as the choices that guide our inquiry—our basic perception of facts (what we consider relevant or irrelevant), how we organize and process the information, the basic assumptions about our selves and our world that we bring to interpretation and decision making, the coherence and adequacy of these assumptions (or paradigms) in accounting for our experience and location (48–50). These theories "do not only organize the 'pregiven' facts about the world; they also make it possible to detect new ones . . . by guiding us to new patterns of salience and relevance, teaching us what to take seriously and what to reinterpret" (70). (An obvious example is the growing body of knowledge about women's lives and writings in the light of reinterpretive efforts among feminists, especially feminists of color.)

What makes the above ideas different from the constructivist approach

37. This point is developed in Boyd, "How to Be a Moral Realist," esp. 188–95. Mohanty is adapting Boyd's general points to the more specific discussion of experience, identity, and politics.

of postmodern relativism? Certain postmodernist formulations posit the constructedness of experiences, but their notion that the constructedness of experience therefore makes experience questionable as a potential source of objective knowledge actually operates on the basis of the positivist assumption that they claim to critique, that is, the assumption that objectivity and knowledge must be presupposition-free, error-free, and unmediated by theory. This kind of assumption actually presupposes idealized conditions of knowledge that do not require the (equally idealized rational) agent to engage with other people and the world. Moreover, such an idealized rational agency defines itself primarily in terms of transcendence from "the messy contingencies of the human condition" (Antony, "Quine as Feminist" 195). Adopting this kind of positivist assumption leads to the rather disingenuous and dubious assertion that either we have direct knowledge of reality or we do not bother with objectivity at all, since everything is constructed. Mohanty's realist account suggests that we need not let ourselves be caught in such an untenable (closet idealist) impasse, since the constructedness of knowledge is not necessarily opposed to its ability to refer to features of the world.

Moreover, the important point about a realist account of theory-dependent knowledge is that it need not be debilitated by positivist assumptions about certainty and unrevisability (about an a priori epistemology that offers only one true and complete description of the world) that inform the skepticist's doubts about the accuracy of representation. A realist account does not preclude the openness of theory-dependent knowledge to analysis, evaluation, and revision. The question of accuracy and adequacy of the theory in explaining social relations and other features of the world is always a real problem. The same attention that we accord the complex evaluation of theories must therefore be accorded experience too. Mohanty, for example, states that questions about the legitimacy of emotion are answered by looking at the features of the subject in her world; an accurate picture of these features is possible through the right theory (or narrative description) and the relevant information that we can potentially examine or share. The assessment of justifiability or legitimacy of emotion (e.g., the battered woman's anger vis-à-vis her husband's) is therefore based on the examination of the underlying political and moral views of the subject about the society (the idea of social location and interests) and the information she draws on to support these views. What information/evidence do the woman and her husband draw on or ignore to support their views? Can their respective theories adequately account for the material features of the world?

To stress the cognitive aspect of experience is to argue that it can be susceptible to varying degrees of socially constructed truth and error, that it can be a source of objective knowledge but also social mystification. The realist position attaches importance as much to error as to truth. What makes identity "real" is the fact that it "refers outward to causally significant features of the world" (Mohanty, "Epistemic Status" 69). Reference is determined in part by the causal interactions[38] that obtain between us and the mind-independent world. As such, our referential relations are determinate and therefore open to analysis, just like any other relations, even if our interpretations of these relations are not automatically correct.[39] Because this theory-mediated reference does imply a connection to causally relevant material features of the world, some evaluations—whether vague or fully articulated theories of right and wrong—can enable and facilitate greater accuracy in representing social reality, providing better ways of organizing the relevant and salient facts.[40]

What does it mean to take *both* accuracy and error into account when we consider theories? The complex processing and evaluation of information invites a closer examination of the notion of fallibility. The criteria for evaluating theories are twofold: how well does the theory explain the features of the world, and how well does it accommodate new and specific information (processed, for example, as experience), opening itself to revision and reinterpretation? Fallibility may be the ineluctable risk of any intellectual inquiry, but being wrong does not necessarily mean that we give up on obtaining accurate and reliable theories. "Error is not opposed to certainty" and "the possibility of error does not sanction skepticism about the possibility of knowledge" (Mohanty, "Epistemic Status" 54). The realist account argues that theory-dependent objectivity is

38. For excellent discussions of the relation between causation and causal explanation, see Helen Steward, *The Ontology of Mind,* esp. 135–202, 205–31; Mohanty, *Literary Theory and the Claims of History,* esp. 149–97. Both Mohanty and Steward argue that causality needs to be seen not as a "natural" relation but as a general categorical notion that we use to explain particular events or circumstances and discover the mechanisms of effects. This means that causation must also be treated as a theoretical affair in which the questions of reference and empirical investigation play key roles.

39. One of the contradictory aspects of constructivist accounts is that they are often perfectly willing to treat social relations that inform scientific knowledge as accessible to intellectual inquiry, but they balk at treating epistemic and semantic issues (such as the epistemic relations between humans and the world) in the same terms.

40. One implication of theory-mediated reference is that we do not theorize from scratch but draw on the cumulative knowledge and methodologies supplied by scientific and social inquiries, inquiries that are themselves subject to empirical investigation.

based on our complex and growing understanding of the various causes of distortion and mystification. The notion of fallibility, then, can best be elaborated by taking error seriously as an object of inquiry. The realist account foregrounds the question of error and mystification and highlights the potential contribution of our understanding of error to the revision and reinterpretation of knowledge. In other words, the extent to which a theory can be revised and improved on the basis of new information depends in large part on our ability to acquire a precise understanding of the nature and sources of error and mystification.

Taking error seriously implies that when we reposition the issue of error and mystification within the framework of theory-mediated knowledge, we necessarily shift the debate about the status of error away from a consideration of error per se (which often bogs down into an examination of the injurious consequences of false beliefs and bad analysis) to a consideration of the *uses* of error. This move conceives of error as having two components: a descriptive one, whereby we examine how error arises; and a normative one, whereby we determine procedures that will help us to identify error.[41]

Questions of error and mystification bring into clearer focus the necessity of adjudicating between competing theories, a necessity implicit in any viable theory of ideology, since we cannot assume that all knowledges are equally valid. The seemingly commonsensical argument that all knowledges are equally valid because they are all theory dependent is as dubious as the assumption that the ideas of constructedness and realness are mutually exclusive.

Being wrong even in the most important way does not necessarily mean that one's judgment cannot in other cases be relatively reliable in referring to facts about the world. (The battered woman's husband is wrong about blaming the consciousness-raising group, but his chauvinist understanding of women would not have been so deeply believed, or, for that matter, deeply contested, if it did not meet the minimum objective requirement of referring outward, in however erroneous a way, to certain material needs or psychological features.) If the question of accuracy is built into contexts with epistemic connections to their referents, any analysis or evaluation must then be carried out not only on the basis of empirical information about social situation but also on the basis

---

41. See, e.g., D. Kahneman and A. Tversky's "On the Psychology of Predictions" for a discussion of procedures that allow us to identify and predict certain forms of belief formation.

of theoretical accounts of current social and political arrangements. These analyses and evaluations demand that critical attention be given to the ways in which social locations can facilitate or inhibit knowledge by predisposing us to register and interpret information in certain ways. The realist theory of identity implies that we can evaluate different experiences comparatively (since they provide knowledge of different aspects of one world) by considering how adequately they can explain the complex causal structure that we call "social reality." As Mohanty notes, "This comparison is often a complex and difficult negotiation (since it involves competing interpretations and only partially overlapping information), but it is facilitated by making buried explanations explicit, by examining social and political views that are involved in what seems like purely personal choices and predilections" ("Epistemic Status" 71).

Finally, objective knowledge is not a product of disinterested inquiry but a form of social practice. Attempts at objective explanation are necessarily continuous with oppositional political struggles. Activism strives to create conditions for better knowledge and, as a form of experience, can itself be a repository of knowledge, and can contribute to refining the alternative accounts and constructions that allow us to understand and interpret and struggle against the dominant ideologies and institutions. "The possibility of interpreting our world accurately depends fundamentally on our coming to know what it would take to change it, on our identifying the central relations of power and privilege that sustain it and make it what it is" (Mohanty, "Epistemic Status" 53). As social practice, knowledge is necessarily political. Objectivity is "something we struggle for." "Through knowledge, we define and reshape values and commitments and give texture and form to collective futures" (Mohanty "Epistemic Status" 53). By encouraging us to think through the issue of fallibility and its epistemic implications, the realist position cements rather than severs or collapses the link between intellectual work and political struggle. In so doing, it resolves some of the major problems that Mao encountered in dealing with the training of political and cultural armies. As I argued above, Mao began by addressing the issue of intellectual praxis and ended up by subordinating intellectual work to political work. The realist position suggests that the relationship between intellectual and political work does not have to be couched in either/or terms, nor does it need to be posed as a problem of hierarchy. By ascribing some complexity and specificity to theoretical work, the realist position emphasizes the indissoluble link between theory and practice, between learning and teaching.

Political education thus comes out of political struggle, which *in part consists of* the complex task of adjudication between competing theories. But how does the transformation of consciousness figure in political education? Mao, Fanon, and Cabral saw it as one of the aims of political education.[42] To "speak for the masses" thus implies not only being able to accurately express "their" hopes and aspirations, but to actively register "their" transformation in the course of the struggle for liberation. We have seen, through a discussion of the feminist case, the possible interaction between experience and theory. Although we can see the task of the intellectual as that of contributing to the refining of theory by crafting the re-presentation of "the masses," by rendering the "experience" of "the masses" in meaningful terms, we can also see how the committed intellectual's and "the people's" exposure to and adjudication of competing theories (including their own theories) can also bring about the testing of these theories.

But how, in fact, does change of consciousness come about? One answer to this lies in the possibilities opened up by interpersonal communication, or the act of going into the midst of "the masses." In his essay "How to Be a Moral Realist," Richard Boyd puts it succinctly:

> It is extremely plausible that for human beings the capacity to access human goods and harms—the capacity to *recognize* the extent to which others are well or poorly off with respect to the homeostatic cluster of moral goods and the capacity to *anticipate correctly* the probable effect on others' well-being of various contrafactual circumstances—depends on their capacity to imagine themselves in the situation of others or to find themselves involuntarily doing so in cases in which others are especially well or badly off. (215; original emphasis)

Boyd's discussion of "sympathy" underscores the emotional contribution to epistemic accessing and, following Hume, to motivation to act on our judgment.[43]

42. Paulo Freire's *Pedagogy of the Oppressed* is one example of the attempts to develop an explicit pedagogy that will be empowering for those who are oppressed.

43. Since emotions, along with "nonrational" beliefs and desires, are held to play a crucial role in motivation, they become an issue (and a controversial one) when they are linked to the Marxist (and realist) proposition that interests are factual (and therefore capable of yielding "objective" knowledge). For a credible account of this connection, see Denise Meyerson's *False Consciousness*. Meyerson argues that beliefs about interests have a motivational force (80). One's motivation to act on the basis of one's desires can part ways with one's interest (defined as that which allows one to access human good and welfare). It is thus necessary to have a theory of ideology that can properly account for the existence of "false" desires. The Marxist argument for the facticity of interests allows for the possibility that misperceptions, then, can be explained by the interests they serve. If

How will "the people" be won over? The difficult task of persuasion is a matter not only of ascertaining the right re-presentation, but of bringing about the conditions under which the "right" information can have an impact on the individual. Again, a look at the feminist theorizing of the transformation of consciousness is instructive. Susan Babbitt's "Feminism and Objective Interests" reiterates the point I made earlier about the link between adequate understanding (both personal and political) and the actual bringing about of alternative social relations and political structures (245). According to Babbitt, feminist theorizing of the epistemic status of personal experience contributes to the reconception of objective, rational interests; indeed, personal experiences can advance the possibility of "objective justification" for claims about social and political realities (246). Babbitt argues for expanding the issue of interests and motives beyond the psychological processing of information to include the complex interaction between the individual and the social world. The "liberal" perspective defines objective interest by positing a self that chooses under idealized conditions (i.e., this is what she would have chosen if the conditions were right).[44] Because the determination of objective interest is based on the initial perspective that the self possesses, it cannot account for the impact that the transformation of self can have on the ability of that self to identify her interest and act on her motives (250). Using Alice Walker's Celie in *The Color Purple* as an example, Babbitt argues that "being in a particular, personal state and relation to society sometimes constitutes a kind of understanding of that society that could not be obtained through an examination of the expressible truths about that society" (253). The nonpropositional content of what counts as adequate understanding can constitute the "interpretative situation" that makes "a more adequate,

---

transformation of consciousness implies a relationship between valuation and action, it is possible to explain the gap between valuation and action by using factual interests as a criterion. Are interests based on want? But there are cases in which what we want may not be in our interest (e.g., continuing to use the faulty bridge in our barrio), either because of deficiency in knowledge (we were not informed that the bridge could collapse anytime) or reasoning (since we have been using the bridge for hundreds of years, it can be used a hundred years more). There are also cases in which we do not want what is in our interests (e.g., smoking despite all health warnings). If interests are not based on wants, but are factual, we can turn the interest-want upside down: it is not interests that are based on wants but wants that are interest-based. If something is not good for us and we still want it, our beliefs must be false. The issue of mystification, then, raises the issue of relating historically situated knowledge to maximal objectivity.

44. See Babbitt's discussion of John Rawls's *A Theory of Justice* (247–53). See her footnote on Rawls (263) for bibliographic leads on the "liberal" approach to rational choice.

expressed experience possible" (255). One's understanding of one's situation "depends importantly upon the bringing about of social relations in terms of which she can properly interpret her personal perception" (255). This explains why no accurate account of identity ("the masses") can do without a viable theory of ideology, program of political struggle, and political education.

One can then see that "speaking for the masses" has a theoretical and practical agenda, in fact brings these two agenda together in an intimate but not conflative relation. The realist position is compatible with the argument that the claims we make about things are not all and fully controlled by us. But unlike constructivist accounts, which hold that we cannot in principle know anything about the mind-independent world (let alone the ways in which this world exercises constraints on us and our knowledge),[45] the realist account actually takes the idea of causal interactions between humans and the world seriously without discounting either our dependence as finite beings on the world or our own causal interference in it. In fact, rather than close off an account of our material imbrication, a realist account holds that background theories provide explanations of the influences and constraints posed by the world on our judgments. It operates not on the presumption of idealized knowledge conditions and agents but on the givenness of our finitude as creatures possessed of minimal rationality.[46] Moreover, it argues that such causal relations are open to empirical investigations that are part of our social practices. Our social practices are part of a material transformation that is theory mediated (at least on the human level), because embarking on political struggle is indissolubly linked to the process of maximizing objectivity, of formulating and articulating epistemically reliable accounts of collective interests, experiences, and visions. It is, in fact, the intimate interaction of matter and idea in the human world, with its constraining and enabling forces, that allows us to pose the question, not of whether we can "reach" (or not reach) the real, but of whether we can have a more or less effective significative

45. In fact, the constructivists' inadequate treatment of the constraints posed by the material world often shades into the tendency to misconstrue the distinction between the world and the theories of the world, leading to pronouncements concerning our "literal" making or construction of the world that deny our dependence on the world and smack of a Kantian notion of freedom as transcendence from the given. See Cheah's critique of the nature/culture divide in "Mattering."

46. For a discussion of the concept of minimal rationality, which presupposes that epistemic agents (whether human or animal) have fixed limits on their cognitive resources (such as time and memory), see Christopher Cherniak, *Minimal Rationality,* esp. 3–71.

mediation/knowledge of the world, with its attendant questions of particular error or correctness.

Realist accounts see error as *constitutive* of the condition of possibility, indeed the necessity, of truth. To argue this is, in some ways, to argue for the materiality of intellectual inquiry, a materiality that enables but also constrains inquiry. This is a way of saying that the intellectual's ability to effectively represent "the people" is often contingent on the transformation of the intellectual and "the people" in the field of struggle. That is, the intellectual's task is partly testimonial in character, because it attests to a transformation (perhaps not even necessarily on the human level) already in progress, a transformation that it seeks to intensify to bring about the much-needed changes in society.

One of the implications of a realist account is that it allows us to reformulate the relationship between truth and error not in terms of a relation of pure opposition but one of ineluctable intimacy. The question of error is an important factor in making considerations and specifications of context relevant and imperative. The risk of error inherent in political struggle impels rather than suspends or terminates the theoretical task of the intellectual,[47] because we learn about ourselves and about the world *in the course* of our social practices in and our active theorizing about the world. The intellectual's task of refining the interests and knowledge, even the experiences, of others must ceaselessly contribute to her goal of generalizing popular consciousness because her ability to forge a collective vision out of local concerns, to situate the struggle for change within the movement between the particular and the universal, not only affirms but also *makes the most of,* in effect helps to maximize or intensify, the transformation at hand in order to help propel the struggle for social change. Far from rendering intellectual work useless, the possibility of error demands and impels the ordeal and responsibility of the intellectual task, in the same way that it demands that we do something about the situation we find ourselves in. It is, in one sense, the condition of possibility of truth, of any form of political inquiry and struggle, of history itself. Liberation struggles are, indeed, "the best schools of good sense" because they deepen our understanding not only of what is involved in the fight for radical change but also of what is involved in the principled study of reality.

47. For a thorough and nuanced discussion of the dynamism of finite bodies and its implications for accounts of ethical transformative agency, see Cheah, "Mattering," esp. 129–35.

WORKS CITED

Adam, Ian, and Helen Tiffin, eds. *Past the Last Post: Theorizing Post-colonialism and Post-modernism.* Hemel Hempstead: Harvester Wheatsheaf, 1991.

Antony, Louise M. "Quine as Feminist: The Radical Import of Naturalized Epistemology." *A Mind of One's Own: Feminist Essays on Reason and Objectivity.* Ed. Louise M. Antony and Charlotte Witt. Boulder, CO: Westview Press, 1993. 185–225.

Appiah, Kwame Anthony. *In My Father's House: Africa in the Philosophy of Culture.* London: Methuen, 1992.

———. "Is the Post- in Postmodernism the Post- in Postcolonial?" *Critical Inquiry* 17.2 (Winter 1991): 336–57.

Aronowitz, Stanley, and Henry Giroux. *Education under Siege.* South Hadley, MA: Bergin and Garvey, 1985.

Babbitt, Susan. "Feminism and Objective Interests: The Role of Transformation Experiences in Rational Deliberation." *Feminist Epistemologies.* Ed. Linda Alcoff and Elizabeth Potter. New York: Routledge, 1993. 245–64.

Bloom, Allan. *The Closing of the American Mind.* New York: Simon and Schuster, 1987.

Boggs, Carl. *Intellectuals and the Crisis of Modernity.* Albany: State University of New York Press, 1993.

Boyd, Richard. "How to Be a Moral Realist." *Essays on Moral Realism.* Ed. Geoffrey Sayre-McCord. Ithaca: Cornell University Press, 1988. 181–228.

———. "Metaphor and Theory Change: What Is 'Metaphor' a Metaphor For?" *Metaphor and Thought.* Ed. Andrew Ortony. New York: Cambridge University Press, 1979. 356–408.

Braidotti, Rosi. *Patterns of Dissonance: A Study of Women in Contemporary Philosophy.* Cambridge: Cambridge University Press, 1991.

Brown, Bernard E. *Intellectuals and Other Traitors.* New York: Ark House, 1980.

Butler, Judith. *Gender Trouble: Feminism and the Subversion of Identity.* New York: Routledge, 1990.

Cabral, Amilcar. *National Liberation and Culture.* 1970 Eduardo Mondlane Memorial Lecture. Trans. Maureen Webster. Syracuse: Program of Eastern African Studies of the Maxwell School of Citizenship and Public Affairs, 1970.

———. *Revolution in Guinea.* London: Stage 1, 1969.

———. *Unity and Struggle.* Trans. Michael Wolfers. New York: Monthly Review Press, 1979.

Chabal, Patrick. *Amilcar Cabral: Revolutionary Leadership and People's War.* Cambridge: Cambridge University Press, 1983.

Cheah, Pheng. "Mattering." *Diacritics* 26.1 (Spring 1998): 108–39.

———. "Modelling the Nation—[Frantz] Fanon and [Timothy] Mitchell." Unpublished paper, 1995.

Cherniak, Christopher. *Minimal Rationality.* Cambridge, MA: MIT Press, 1986.

Chilcote, Ronald H. *Amilcar Cabral's Revolutionary Theory and Practice: A Critical Guide.* Boulder, CO: Lynne Rienner, 1991.

Chisolm, Roderick M., ed. *Realism and the Background of Phenomenology.* Glencoe, IL: Free Press, 1960.

Culler, Jonathan. *On Deconstruction.* Ithaca: Cornell University Press, 1982.

Davidson, Basil. Introduction. Amilcar Cabral, *Unity and Struggle.* New York: Monthly Review Press, 1979.

Debray, Regis. *Modeste contribution aux discours et cérémonies officielles du dixième anniversaire.* Paris: Maspero, 1978.

———. *Le pouvoir intellectuel en France.* Paris: Editions Ramsay, 1979.

Devitt, Michael. *Realism and Truth.* 2d ed. Oxford: Blackwell, 1991.

Devitt, Michael, and Kim Sterelny. *Language and Reality: An Introduction to the Philosophy of Language.* Cambridge, MA: MIT Press, 1987.

Dirlik, Arif. "Mao Zedong and 'Chinese Marxism.'" *Marxism Beyond Marxism.* Ed. Saree Makdisi, Cesare Casarino, and Rebecca E. Karl. New York: Routledge, 1996.

Dirlik, Arif, Paul Healy, and Nick Knight, eds. *Critical Perspectives on Mao Zedong's Thought.* Atlantic Highlands, NJ: Humanities Press, 1997. 119–48.

During, Simon. "Postmodernism or Postcolonialism?" *Landfall* 39.3 (1985): 366–80.

———. "Post-modernism or Post-colonialism Today." *Textual Practice* 1.1 (1987): 32–47.

Fanon, Frantz. *The Wretched of the Earth.* Trans. Constance Farrington. New York: Grove Press, 1968.

Feuer, Lewis S. "What Is an Intellectual?" *The Intelligentsia and the Intellectuals: Theory, Method and Case Study.* Ed. Aleksander Gella. Beverly Hills, CA: Sage, 1976. 47–58.

Feyerabend, Paul. "Consolations for the Specialist." *Criticism and the Growth of Knowledge.* Ed. Imre Lakatos and Alan Musgrave. Cambridge: Cambridge University Press, 1970. 197–230.

———. "Problems of Empiricism, Part II." *The Nature and Function of Scientific Theory.* Ed. R. G. Colodny. Pittsburgh: University of Pittsburgh Press, 1969. 275–353.

———. "Reply to Critics." *Boston Studies in the Philosophy of Science.* Ed. R. S. Cohen and M. Wartofsky. Vol. 2. New York: Humanities Press, 1965. 223–57.

———. *Science in a Free Society.* London: New Left Books, 1978.

Freire, Paulo. *Pedagogy of the Oppressed.* New York: Herder and Herder, 1970.

Gella, Aleksander, ed. *The Intelligentsia and the Intellectuals: Theory, Method and Case Study.* Beverly Hills, CA: Sage, 1976.

Gendzier, Irene L. *Frantz Fanon: A Critical Study.* Rev. ed. New York: Grove Press, 1985.

Gordon, Lewis R. *Fanon and the Crisis of European Man: An Essay on Philosophy and the Human Sciences.* New York: Routledge, 1995.

Gouldner, Alvin W. *Against Fragmentation: The Origins of Marxism and the Sociology of Intellectuals.* New York: Oxford University Press, 1979.

———. *The Future of Intellectuals and the Rise of the New Class.* London: Macmillan, 1979.

———. *The Two Marxisms.* New York: Seabury Press, 1980.

Gramsci, Antonio. *Selections from the Prison Notebooks of Antonio Gramsci.* Ed. Quintin Hoare and Geoffrey Nowell Smith. New York: International Publishers, 1971.

Hansen, Emmanuel. *Frantz Fanon: Social and Political Thought*. Columbus: Ohio State University Press, 1977.

Haraway, Donna J. "Situated Knowledges: The Science Question in Feminism and the Privilege of Partial Perspective." *Simians, Cyborgs and Women*. New York: Routledge, 1991.

Harding, Sandra. *Whose Science? Whose Knowledge? Thinking from Women's Lives*. Ithaca: Cornell University Press, 1991.

Hirst, R. J. "Realism." *The Encyclopedia of Philosophy*. Vol. 7. Ed. Paul Edwards. New York: Macmillan; Free Press, 1967.

Hoare, Quintin, and Geoffrey Nowell Smith, eds. *Selections from the Prison Notebooks of Antonio Gramsci*. New York: International Publishers, 1971.

Hollis, Martin, and Steven Lukes, eds. *Rationality and Relativism*. Cambridge, MA: MIT Press, 1982.

Holt, Edwin B., et al. *The New Realism*. New York: Macmillan, 1912.

Huszar, Tibor. "Changes in the Concept of Intellectuals." *The Intelligentsia and the Intellectuals: Theory, Method and Case Study*. Ed. Aleksander Gella. Beverly Hills, CA: Sage, 1976. 79–110.

James, William. *Essays in Radical Empiricism: A Pluralistic Universe*. New York: Longmans, Green, 1912.

Jinadu, Adele. *Fanon: In Search of the African Revolution*. Enugu, Nigeria: Fourth Dimension, 1980.

Kahneman, D., and A. Tversky. "On the Psychology of Predictions." *Psychological Review* 80 (1973): 237–51.

Kitcher, Phillip. "The Naturalists Return." *Philosophy in Review: Essays on Contemporary Philosophy*. Special issue. *Philosophical Review* 101.1 (1992): 53–114.

Konrad, George, and Istvan Szelenyi. *Intellectuals on the Road to Class Power*. New York: Harcourt Brace Jovanovich, 1979.

Krausz, Michael, and Jack Meiland, eds. *Relativism: Cognitive and Moral*. Notre Dame, IN: Notre Dame University Press, 1982.

Kuhn, Thomas. "Logic of Discovery or Psychology of Research." *Criticism and the Growth of Knowledge*. Ed. Imre Lakatos and Alan Musgrave. Cambridge: Cambridge University Press, 1970. 1–23.

———. "Reflections on My Critics." *Criticism and the Growth of Knowledge*. Ed. Imre Lakatos and Alan Musgrave. Cambridge: Cambridge University Press, 1970. 231–78.

———. *The Structure of Scientific Revolutions*. 2d ed. Chicago: University of Chicago Press, 1970.

Lazarus, Neil. "National Consciousness and the Specificity of (Post)Colonial Intellectualism." *Colonial Discourse/Postcolonial Theory*. Ed. Francis Barker, Peter Hulme, and Margaret Iversen. Manchester: University of Manchester Press, 1994.

LeDoeuff, Michelle. "Women, Reason, etc." *differences* 2.3 (1990): 1–13.

Lemert, Charles, ed. *Intellectuals and Politics*. Newbury Park, CA: Sage, 1991.

Lenin, V. I. "What Is to Be Done?" *The Lenin Anthology*. Ed. Robert C. Tucker. New York: Norton, 1975.

Lewis, Philip. "The Post-structuralist Condition." *Diacritics* 12.1 (Spring 1982): 2–24.

Lovibond, Sabina. "Feminism and the 'Crisis of Rationality.'" *New Left Review* (September–October 1994): 72–86.

Luxemburg, Rosa. "Organizational Questions of Russian Social Democracy." *Selected Political Writings of Rosa Luxemburg*. Ed. Dick Howard. New York: Monthly Review Press, 1971.

Maclean, Ian, Alan Montefiore, and Peter Winch, eds. *The Political Responsibility of Intellectuals*. Cambridge: Cambridge University Press, 1990.

Mao Zedong. "Talks at the Yenan Forum on Literature and Art." *On Literature and Art*. Beijing: Foreign Languages Press, 1967.

Metz, Rudolf. *A Hundred Years of British Philosophy*. Trans J. W. Harvey, T. E. Jessop, and Henry Sturt. Ed. J. H. Muirhead. London: G. Allen and Unwin; New York: Macmillan, 1938.

Meyerson, Denise. *False Consciousness*. Oxford: Clarendon Press, 1991.

Mohanty, Satya P. "The Epistemic Status of Cultural Identity: On *Beloved* and the Postcolonial Condition." *Cultural Critique* 24 (Spring 1993): 41–80. [Reprinted as chapter 1 in this volume.]

———. *Literary Theory and the Claims of History: Postmodernism, Objectivity, Multicultural Politics*. Ithaca: Cornell University Press, 1997.

———. "'Us and Them': On the Philosophical Bases of Political Criticism." *Yale Journal of Criticism* 2.2 (1989): 1–31.

Moore, G. E. *Philosophical Studies*. London: Routledge and Kegan Paul, 1922.

Mouffe, Chantal, and Ernesto Laclau. *Hegemony and Socialist Strategy: Towards a Radical Democratic Politics*. Trans. Winston Moore and Paul Cammack. London: Verso, 1985.

Mukherjee, Arun P. "Whose Post-colonialism and Whose Post-modernism?" *World Literature Written in English* 30.2 (1990): 1–9.

Passmore, John. *A Hundred Years of Philosophy*. London: Duckworth, 1957.

Perry, R. B. "The Ego-centric Predicament." *Journal of Philosophy* 7.1 (1910): 5–14.

Pines, Christopher L. *Ideology and False Consciousness: Marx and His Historical Progenitors*. Albany: State University of New York Press, 1993.

Quine, W. V. O. "Two Dogmas of Empiricism." *Philosophical Review* 60 (1951): 20–44.

Radhakrishnan, R. "Toward an Effective Intellectual." *Intellectuals, Aesthetics, Politics, Academics*. Ed. Bruce Robbins. Minneapolis: University of Minnesota Press, 1990. 66–74.

Rawls, John. *A Theory of Justice*. Cambridge, MA: Harvard University Press, 1971.

Robbins, Bruce, ed. *Intellectuals, Aesthetics, Politics, Academics*. Minneapolis: University of Minnesota Press, 1990.

Russell, Bertrand. "On the Nature of Truth." *PAS* 7 (1906–7): 28–49.

Sangari, Kumkum. "The Politics of the Possible." *Cultural Critique* 7 (1987): 157–86.

Scheman, Naomi. "Anger and the Politics of Naming." *Women and Language in Literature and Society*. New York: Praeger, 1980.

Schram, Stuart S. *The Political Thought of Mao Tse-tung*. Rev. and enlarged ed. New York: Praeger, 1971.

Sekyi-Otu, Ato. *Fanon's Dialectic of Experience*. Cambridge, MA: Harvard University Press, 1996.

Spivak, Gayatri. "Can the Subaltern Speak?" *Marxism and the Interpretation of Culture*. Ed. Cary Nelson and Lawrence Grossberg. Urbana: University of Illinois Press, 1988.

Steward, Helen. *The Ontology of Mind: Events, Processes and States*. Oxford: Clarendon Press, 1997.

Thomas, Paul. *Marx and the Anarchists*. London: Routledge and Kegan Paul, 1981.

Wakeman, Frederic, Jr. *History and Will: Philosophical Perspectives of Mao Tse-tung's Thought*. Berkeley: University of California Press, 1973.

Walker, Pat, ed. *Between Labor and Capital*. Boston: South End Press, 1978.

Werkmeister, William H. *A History of Philosophical Ideas in America*. New York: Ronald Press, 1949.

Wittgenstein, Ludwig. *Philosophical Investigations*. Trans. G. E. M. Anscombe. Oxford: Blackwell, 1963.

Wylie, Raymond F. *The Emergence of Maoism: Mao Tse-tung, Ch'en Po-ta, and the Search for Chinese Theory, 1935–1945*. Stanford: Stanford University Press, 1980.

Zahar, Renate. *Frantz Fanon: Colonialism and Alienation*. New York: Monthly Review Press, 1974.

CHAPTER 5

"It Matters to Get the Facts Straight"

Joy Kogawa, Realism, and Objectivity of Values

Minh T. Nguyen

There are clear signs that Asian American studies—specifically, Asian American literary studies—has been affected by the current postmodern turn. As postmodernist ideas and theory filter through the traditional disciplines in the humanities and social sciences, scholars in Asian American studies find themselves grappling in different ways with various postmodernist claims and arguments. In their introduction to the special issue of *Amerasia Journal*, "Thinking Theory in Asian American Studies," the editors, Michael Omi and Dana Takagi, comment on the increasing interest in critical theory—particularly postmodernist theory—within the field, noting how this theoretical engagement has left its mark on the ways in which scholars now conceptualize identity, community, and politics (xiv). They go on to point out, however, that the broadening of the domain of theory has influenced the disciplines in Asian American studies in unequal ways: the humanities, especially literary studies, and not the social sciences mostly define the range and tone of theoretical discussions in Asian American studies. This phenomenon is not surprising, given that the prominence of postmodernism in literary studies is being replicated in the area of Asian American literary criticism, and postmodernist readings of Asian American literature have proliferated in the past decade. Here it might be useful for me to define what I mean by "postmodernism," since it is a highly contested and variable term, as many have pointed out. For the purposes of my argument, I define postmodernism as an intellectual position characterized by an epistemology of radical skepticism that takes truth and objectivity to be always socially and discursively constructed, mediated by power, discourse, and desire.[1]

Postmodernist theory has indeed made possible new and different readings of Asian American texts, helping to move Asian American literature, as one literary critic has observed, from "the margins to the center" (Palumbo-Liu, "The Ethnic" 162). This shift has been registered, however, by a number of concerned scholars who caution and critique the application of postmodernist theory to Asian American literary studies. David Palumbo-Liu, for example, warns of the material and historical elisions that take place in the uncritical move to embrace postmodernist interpretations of Asian American texts and to privilege the ethnic as the postmodern par excellence ("The Ethnic" 161–68). He contends that ethnic literature is not simply another postcolonial or postmodern effect, as these theoretical categories, as currently formulated, are unable to sufficiently account for the social and historical specificities of ethnicity and race and their relation to cultural production. Palumbo-Liu's critique of the "postmodernization" of Asian American literature is opportune and relevant; other insightful critiques have similarly called attention to the important weaknesses in the postmodernist framework by pointing out the intellectual and political limitations of importing such a framework wholesale to the ethnic and racial context.[2]

Although useful in contextualizing postmodernism and delineating the historical and cultural specificities of Asian American cultural production, these critiques have not yet adequately carried out the necessary task of examining the deeper underlying epistemological claims of postmodernism and evaluating the ethical and political implications these claims have for Asian American literary criticism. In particular, there is an underanalysis in this scholarship of the implicit and explicit epistemic claims to objectivity—objectivity of knowledge, of social interests, and of values—posed by Asian American literature. The crux of the problem

---

1. Jane Flax uses a similar definition of postmodernism, noting that "postmodernist discourses . . . seek to distance us from and make us skeptical about beliefs concerning truth, knowledge, power, the self, and language that are often taken for granted within and serve as legitimation for contemporary Western culture" (41). I, however, do not share Flax's belief in the intellectual promise of postmodernism.

2. Cautionary warnings against the uncritical application of postmodernist theory have been advanced by a number of Asian Americanists. See, e.g., E. San Juan, Jr., *Racial Formations/Critical Transformations;* and his *Hegemony and Strategies of Transgression,* esp. 193–218; Sau-ling C. Wong, "Denationalization Reconsidered"; David Palumbo-Liu, "Theory and the Subject of Asian American Studies"; Gordon Chang, "History and Postmodernism."

seems to lie in the growing implicit acceptance in Asian American literary criticism of the postmodernist denial of objectivity, especially since postmodernism encourages readings that take a radically skeptical stance toward the status of experience and cultural identity. A close examination shows that some of these skeptical premises and antirealist conclusions are intellectually underjustified and that the literary interpretations deriving from them are inadequate and, in a number of crucial instances, unwarranted. I demonstrate here, through an analysis of the specific case of Joy Kogawa and the literary criticism of her work, how the terms of the literary debates—experience, values, and objective knowledge—have circulated in an underspecified and confused manner in the eagerness of many critics to overthrow the positivist conception of objectivity. I do agree that the foundationalist account of objectivity, which naively demands that knowledge and knowledge acquisition be neutral and impartial, free of subjective bias and social and political interests, should rightfully be critiqued; I maintain, however, that the concept of objectivity should not be abandoned. Instead, we need to revise the positivist understanding of objectivity to productively recuperate what is epistemically valuable in the concept. My position is greatly informed by the postpositivist realist conception of objectivity, which understands objectivity to be essentially theory dependent and socially and theoretically situated.[3] In fact, within the postpositivist realist framework, objective knowledge is gained not by rejecting all forms of bias (which is the positivist take) but rather by examining and taking into account the epistemic consequences of biases.[4] Thus, whereas the postmodernist skeptical stance regarding the epistemic status of experience is mainly a reaction to positivist accounts of objectivity, it is in postpositivist realism that we find a more nuanced discussion of how one can glean objective knowledge from personal experience, as my reading of Kogawa's *Obasan* and *Itsuka* will demonstrate. In the second half of this chapter, I extend my realist discussion of personal experience and objective knowledge to show how Kogawa's understanding of the epistemic status of emotions and values actually points to a strong case for the objectivity

3. Based on an antifoundationalist-naturalist approach to language and knowledge, postpositivist realism acknowledges the mediated nature of language and reference, but it also argues that we can still come to know something about the world, to distinguish truth from error and fact from fiction. For a general introduction to realism and its importance for literary studies, see Paisley Livingston, *Literary Knowledge*.

4. For a discussion of the epistemic consequences of biases and their significance to objectivity, see Louise M. Antony, "Quine as Feminist."

of values, especially of our social values. Importantly, the possibility of objectivity, of social knowledge and of values, suggests that we might need once again to reconsider how we conceptualize identity, community, and politics in Asian American literary criticism and Asian American studies.

READING KOGAWA WITHIN
A REALIST THEORY OF IDENTITY

Kogawa's *Obasan* has a secure place in the Asian American literary canon.[5] In addition, the political dimension of Kogawa's work is readily acknowledged and analyzed in numerous critical essays. Recent critical interpretations, however, have sought to situate this political dimension within a postmodernist framework by arguing that *Obasan* highlights the indeterminacy of truth and the impossibility of gleaning objective knowledge from history and experience.[6] This is the conclusion reached, for instance, by the literary critic Donald C. Goellnicht in his essay, "Minority History as Metafiction." Goellnicht reads Kogawa through a postmodernist lens, viewing the traditional mimetic and humanistic approaches to her work, and to ethnic literature in general, as seriously limited.[7] He argues that Kogawa has replaced humanistic realism with a complex work of historiographic metafiction that shows historical reality to be relative (302). Historiographic metafiction, according to Linda Hutcheon, reveals language as constituting reality rather than merely reflecting it; history and historical writing cannot present an objective record of past events but can only give us a form of fiction making (*Narcissistic* xii). Importing this postmodernist premise to his reading of *Obasan,* Goellnicht argues that the novel "thematiz[es] the concept of the partial, perhaps solipsistic, nature of truth based on differences in perception" (291). Goellnicht's acceptance of the postmodernist view of truth as partial and relative leads him to interpret statements made by the narrator and focalizing charac-

---

5. I realize that the term "Asian American literature" has been used in some cases to refer exclusively to literature produced in the context of the United States. I use the term "Asian American" here to refer to the broader North American context. I also realize that the term "Asian American canon" has been called into question and contested; however, for the purposes of my argument in this chapter I will retain the rubric.

6. Examples of readings of Kogawa that are underwritten by postmodernist premises are A. Lynne Magnusson, "Language and Longing in Joy Kogawa's *Obasan*"; Linda Hutcheon, *The Canadian Postmodern;* Manina Jones, "The Avenues of Speech and Silence."

7. For a summary of Goellnicht's main postmodernist points on *Obasan,* and on other Asian American texts, see his "Blurring Boundaries," esp. 351–55.

ter Naomi Nakane (e.g., "The truth for me is more murky, shadowy and gray")[8] as indirect contestations to the claim voiced by the character Aunt Emily that it is possible to know the past by gathering the facts and separating right from wrong (293). For Goellnicht, objective knowledge, in *Obasan* and in general, is an unattainable goal. Our memories, experiences, and identities, moreover, are partial and "fluid" (300), epistemically unreliable and suspect. The abiding strength of Naomi and, by extension, of Kogawa lies in their ability to maintain "the self-consciousness to recognize the uncertainties in epistemology" (294).

King-Kok Cheung's analysis of *Obasan* is underwritten by similar postmodernist presuppositions about the nature of language and truth.[9] Drawing on feminist and post-Saussurean theories of language and subjectivity, Cheung maintains, along with Goellnicht, that Kogawa "dramatize[s] the elusiveness of 'truth' as linguistically transmitted" (11) and "question[s] the possibility of restoring an authoritative minority history" (13). According to Cheung, language, prone to manipulation and biases, can only convey partial and subjective realities (137). While I would agree with Cheung (and Goellnicht) that we need to call into question the notion of a transparent language and a transparent past, it seems to me that the theory-mediated nature of language and history does not necessarily have to "signify the instability of 'truth' and 'history'" (Cheung 15). In what follows, I argue that Cheung's acceptance of certain postmodernist premises limits her reading of the text and weakens some of the crucial points she makes, particularly with regard to the category of experience. I do so to suggest that Cheung's ability to assert the link between the characters' experience and their understanding of their subject position would be better served by a postpositivist realist approach that acknowledges the cognitive components of experience and identity. In the process, I introduce the realist theory of identity and give my own realist reading of *Obasan* and *Itsuka*, explaining how these two novels theorize the epistemic significance of personal experience and cultural identity. I end by examining Kogawa's theoretical insights, as articulated in her essay "Is There a Just Cause?" to show how her writings present a strong case for the causal link between emotions and objectivity of knowledge and between objectivity of knowledge and objectivity of values. But at this point I would like to return to Cheung's argument.

8. Kogawa, *Obasan* 32.
9. King-Kok Cheung, *Articulate Silences,* esp. 126–67.

In her analysis of *Obasan,* Cheung maintains that certain experiences
in the novel are "beyond words" (137), straining enunciation, while other
experiences and memories are lost or distorted over time due to the equivocal nature of language (138). If this is indeed the case, and if we take
Cheung's constructivist premise to its logical endpoint, we would have
to conclude that experience is not epistemically accessible or authoritative because of the constructed and indeterminate nature of language and
signification—a conclusion that I think Cheung herself would not accept,
and one that is not supported by other points that she makes in her reading of *Obasan.* For instance, in sketching and evaluating the complex
cognitive implications of silence in specific cultural contexts, Cheung
refers to the experiences of the characters (Naomi, Obasan, Uncle Isamu,
and others) and analyzes their experiences to distill knowledge about the
cultural identity of Japanese Canadians and their historical and social
reality (140–45). In so doing, Cheung draws on a cognitivist understanding of experience, taking experience as a legitimate basis for gleaning historical understanding and knowledge. As Cheung later states,
"Even as Naomi contradicts the printed facts, she provides an alternative 'telling' that makes for a *truer* picture of the enforced relocation"
(154; emphasis added). That is, Naomi's experience, her "personal memorial" as Cheung rightly calls it, functions as an oppositional testimony
to social memory and official facts (154); and it is, more crucially, a reliable source for deriving a "truer," more accurate account of what happened to the Japanese Canadians.[10]

Cheung's contradictory view regarding the cognitive status of experience is not unusual, however; it points to a wider, more serious impasse
in contemporary literary criticism and cultural studies, where theorization of experience and cultural identity has oscillated between a foundationalist essentialism that asserts the transparent nature and self-evident
authority of experience and an extreme radical constructivism that discredits experience as mystifying and subjective. This oscillation has resulted in a stalled understanding of cultural identity and identity politics. Recently, however, a strong theoretical account of experience that

10. An epistemic and ethical contradiction seems to underlie Goellnicht's and Cheung's position: both support the postmodernist claim that narratives and history are partial, subjective constructs, forms of fiction making; yet, at the same time, they also want
to privilege Kogawa's text as a source of a better and more accurate analysis of what happened to the Japanese Canadians during and after World War II. For instance, Goellnicht
maintains that Kogawa's text "attempts not simply to reflect, but to influence" (300), by
"reveal[ing] an unintended truth: the pervasive racism that forms an integral part of the
social context and that we as Canadians have tried so long to deny" (294).

moves beyond the stalemate of essentialism versus antiessentialism has been proffered by the realist theory of identity. This theory, as outlined by Satya P. Mohanty and other contributors to this volume, gives us a useful understanding of language, experience, and cultural identity while providing us with an explanatory account of the causal linkages among these categories.[11] According to the realist theory of identity, our cultural identities are both constructed and "real": on the one hand, identities are constructed because they are based on the subjective theoretical constructs and values that we bring to our interpretation of our personal experience; on the other, identities are also real because they refer outward to causally salient features of the social world, features that can accurately describe and explain the complex interactions among the multiple determinants of a person's experience.[12] This "reality" factor of cultural identity suggests that we need to take the epistemic status of experience seriously.

One of the key theses of the realist theory of identity is that the experience of social subjects has a cognitive component. That is, our experience, properly interpreted, can provide reliable and accurate knowledge, of ourselves and of social reality. Importantly, this realist-cognitivist account of experience is neither essentialist nor skeptical. While the realist view does not deny the socially and linguistically constructed nature of experience, it rejects the postmodernist claim that experience is therefore always epistemically unstable and unreliable.[13] According to realists, it is precisely the theory-dependent nature of experience that makes it cognitively valuable. In addition, realists would maintain that our personal experience refers outward to the social world we inhabit, to causally significant aspects of this world (Mohanty, *Literary Theory* 230). That is, our experience can index the world, providing us with knowledge of

11. See Mohanty's essay in this volume. Mohanty provides a detailed sketch of the realist theory of identity in *Literary Theory* 202–34. See also Moya, "Postmodernism, 'Realism,' and the Politics of Identity." Drawing and elaborating on the realist theory of identity, Moya shows how our understanding of our identity changes over time as a result of our theory-mediated experiences; and how the social facts that make up our social location are causally relevant for the experiences that we have.

12. For a defense of the realist claim that experience and identity are both constructed and "real," see Mohanty, *Literary Theory* 202–16.

13. Postmodernist criticism posits the linguistically and socially constructed nature of experience (and hence identity) and, from this account, concludes that this constructedness makes experience and identity unstable and unreliable sources of objective knowledge. One influential postmodernist account of experience is provided by Joan Scott in her essay "'Experience.'" A realist, however, would argue that there are different kinds and degrees of theory dependence, maintaining that theory-laden and socially constructed experiences can lead to knowledge that is accurate and reliable (Mohanty, *Literary Theory* 209).

how the world is structured and where we stand in relation to it (e.g., racial discrimination against Japanese Canadians during World War II, loss of property, dissolution of the family unit, etc.). Therefore, our experience can reveal to us some of the salient determining features of our social reality, providing us with epistemic access to this reality.

In light of the realist alternative, particularly the realist account of experience and identity, it might be more fruitful—and more accurate—to situate Kogawa's novels within an epistemological framework of post-positivist realism rather than postmodernist skepticism.[14] Let me show how experience, historical knowledge, and cultural identity are presented in realist terms in *Obasan* and *Itsuka*.[15] These two novels suggest that the truth value of our statements and our memories of our experiences might be "murky" and "gray," indicating the necessarily messy and complicated task of sorting and interpreting their meanings. However, objective knowledge of our historical past and our identities can be gleaned from this process of sorting out and interpreting our experiences and memories, a crucial lesson that Naomi learns. Indeed, the two novels point up the necessary act of interpreting and adjudicating between various truth claims and competing accounts of the world; they caution against the retreat into a noncognitivist relativism that avoids all responsibility for hermeneutical and normative adjudication. Importantly, Kogawa's work upholds the character Aunt Emily's belief that "it matters to get the facts straight" (*Obasan* 219). To gain an adequate understanding of the past, we must try to gather all the facts. In the process, we might find that some accounts of the past will be partial and even contradictory, but we must subject what we find to evaluation and adjudication, in order to get the facts straight.

For Kogawa, one's personal experience can serve as a valuable resource for getting the facts straight, an insight she shares with the realist position. Within the realist framework, experience does not have to be con-

14. Kogawa does employ innovative narrative techniques in *Obasan* and, to a lesser extent, in *Itsuka*. However, this feature does not necessarily signify that Kogawa has a postmodernist aesthetics, or, more crucially, a postmodernist epistemology. Innovative formal techniques, such as nonlinearity and multiple narratorial perspectives, are compatible with a realist epistemology.

15. *Itsuka* is the sequel to *Obasan;* it traces Naomi Nakane's political involvement in the Japanese Canadian redress movement in the late 1970s and throughout the 1980s. Naomi, in her early forties, is now living in Toronto. Along with her Aunt Emily and other Nisei and Sansei, she participates in the fight to get government compensation for the thousands of Japanese Canadians who were interned during World War II. In the process, she and others learn the intellectual, social, and emotional value of asserting a cultural-political identity, on both individual and collective levels.

ceived as either immediate or epistemically unreliable—the construct-edness of experience does not have to rule out the possibility that it can also provide a reliable register of past events. Unfortunately, the hasty and underjustified belief in the mutually exclusive nature of experience leads some critics to read Naomi's assertion, "All our ordinary stories are changed in time, altered as much by the present as the present is shaped by the past" (*Obasan* 30), as evidence not only of the fallibility of memory but also of the subjective, indeterminate nature of our expe-rience and of history.[16] They read textual moments such as this as lend-ing support to the postmodernist claim that all personal experience is contingent and unreliable, and thus cannot serve as a source of objec-tive knowledge. Can we, however, read this statement not as a sign of postmodernist skepticism but as a change in Naomi's understanding of her experiences, so that she comes to reinterpret her experiences, her "or-dinary stories," according to a different, and more accurate, theoretical framework?[17] In other words, can it be that Naomi learns from her ex-periences and, as a result, grows morally and politically?

Interestingly, critics who hold a postmodernist reading of the state-ment quoted above seem to have overlooked the context in which it appears—a richly intricate passage where Obasan, accompanied by Naomi, is searching through the attic for an item that she thinks is there. As Naomi helps her aunt around the attic, she comes across various fam-ily items that lead her to reflect about the past and about the "potent and pervasive" (*Obasan* 30) nature of memories and dreams. She begins to realize that there are different ways to conceive of the past and of one's relationship with the past. As Arnold Davidson perceptively points out in his reading of this scene, Naomi's "attic philosophy" admits of four basic possibilities: one can shut oneself up in the past as Obasan has done; one can flee the past, as Naomi's brother has done; one can use it as a convenient junk room where anything and everything can be consigned; or one can view it as a repository that allows and even requires order-

---

16. Although critical of postmodernism and postmodernist readings of Kogawa, Rachelle Kanefsky nevertheless takes this statement as an indication of Naomi's initial relativist stance, concluding thus: "It is the fallibility of memory, then, that renders the past, and Aunt Emily's truth, questionable. . . . Thus, it is not possible, according to Naomi, to know history with any certainty, because past experiences are lost or distorted with time" (19).

17. No doubt rigorous skepticism is healthy; but we need to be wary about skepticism as a general attitude and approach to challenging the possibility of making knowledge claims, since it leads us to a situation of debilitating relativism, as I show in my analysis of Kogawa's work.

ing and sorting of information and experiences ("Writing against" 36). These possibilities demand adjudication, and it is the fourth possibility that Naomi very soon finds herself inclined toward and which the novel explores. The choice of this particular view of the past is underscored by the images of spider webs and patchwork quilt that embroider the description of this scene and associatively link it to other moments in the narrative where we find images of quilt, blanket, cloth, and weaving. These intricate images, in turn, are connected to the narrative's overall discussion of the past, of the difficult but necessary process of sorting and weaving together the past out of fragments to create a "whole" picture.[18] Moreover, the crucial point, I would argue, is not that our memories are fallible (for indeed they are); rather, what is important to keep in mind is that there are certain empirical cognitive constraints that have to be acknowledged and taken into account in our reading of this novel and in our understanding of the historical past in general. Let me go back to the narrative to explain what I mean.

On the morning following the attic search, Obasan hands Naomi the package from Aunt Emily that Obasan had been searching for in the attic and that she thought was lost and forgotten. Inside Naomi finds documents, old newspaper clippings, and Aunt Emily's private journals. In reading Aunt Emily's journal entries as an adult, Naomi is forced to return to specific moments in the past but this time with new salient observations and facts that help her to reinterpret her memories of these moments, and consequently change her relationship to the past: "I feel like a burglar as I read, breaking into a private house only to discover it's my childhood house filled with corners and rooms I've never seen. Aunt Emily's Christmas 1941 is not the Christmas I remember" (*Obasan* 95). Here we see the partiality of Naomi's memory of her childhood, and it is partial not just because her memory is fallible but also because this adult memory had been based on a child's cognitive perspective and understanding at that particular point in her life (e.g., Naomi as a five-year-old child). It is important to keep in mind the fact that Naomi's memory was limited by certain empirical constraints. For instance, even though Naomi was present during the Christmas gathering in 1941, there were things that she did not see or know about because her family shielded her from certain sights and kept information from her. In addition, what-

18. I am indebted to Paola Loreto's formalist examination of the poetic structure of *Obasan*, particularly her perceptive reading of this rich passage. See Loreto, "The Poetic Texture of Joy Kogawa's *Obasan*," esp. 181.

ever information Naomi did come across or whatever events she did witness were processed through her understanding of the world at that young age. Her mental development at five years old very likely would have precluded her from registering certain observations and facts as salient. In the present time of the narrative, however, Naomi's act of remembering, of sifting through her memories, is now filled in and made fuller many years later by the perspective provided by her aunt's documents, allowing her to see corners and rooms she had not remembered and, in some cases, never seen before. In acquiring new facts and information from Aunt Emily, Naomi begins to see how Aunt Emily can have a different experience of those wartime events and how her own understanding of her experience is slowly changing in light of the new information she now gains from her aunt.

In the case of Aunt Emily, it is on the basis of her own experience and her research into the experiences of other Japanese Canadians that she makes her claims about what *really* happened to people of Japanese ancestry during and after World War II in Canada. For more than thirty years Aunt Emily has collected government documents and compiled her own personal records of the relocation and internment experience. Her research draws on the personal experiences and history of the Issei and Nisei to form an alternative body of historical knowledge that she then uses to counter the "official" account disseminated by the government and the media. It should be noted, though, that Aunt Emily's version of the past is not entirely "subjective," nor is it uniperspectival. She takes her own subjective experience, sets it beside the accounts of other Japanese Canadians as well as beside the government documents, and, through the process of interpretation and evaluation, attempts to present a fuller and more accurate picture than what the "official" account provides. It is only by undergoing this complex cognitive process of examining her experience and adjudicating between different accounts of the past "to get the facts straight" that Aunt Emily then makes the assertion that the policies and actions of the Canadian government have been racist and unjust. Aunt Emily extends this responsibility of adjudication to Naomi, symbolically calling her niece to the witness stand to "write the vision and make it plain" (*Obasan* 38). Naomi, however, finds that she is not able to do so at this point, since "the truth for [her] is more murky, shadowy and gray" (*Obasan* 38).

But Naomi's admission is not an indication of epistemological skepticism, as Goellnicht, Cheung, and others claim. The truth is unknown to Naomi at this time; at this point in her life, she does not yet have the necessary relevant information (e.g., her mother's tragic death, the details surrounding the fate of many Issei and Nisei who were dispersed and relocated), the right theoretical tools, or the proper social and emotional environment to more accurately interpret her past experiences. It is only later in the narrative and in Naomi's psychological development that she undergoes the process of remembering and reinterpreting her past and present experiences, so that she gains a more accurate understanding of what happened to her in the past and of her current relationship to the world around her. Naomi's understanding of her experiences is in keeping with the second key thesis of the realist theory of identity: that experience has a cognitive component means that we can consider and take into account the question of error as well as accuracy in interpreting experience. That is, because experience is theory mediated a person's understanding of a given situation may undergo revision over the course of time, thus rendering her subsequent interpretations of her experience in and of that situation more (or less) accurate.[19] This process of revising and reinterpreting experience is epistemic; it is what Naomi goes through in each novel and between the span of the two novels.[20] From the realist perspective, our knowledge claims and accounts of our present world and of our historical past are certainly changeable and revisable, as we come across new facts, consider additional information and hypotheses, and build on and improve our knowledge-gathering procedures.

The "revisability" of knowledge is highlighted in the two novels, which stage and explore Naomi's process of piecing together the fragments of memories and the dispersed bits of information and coming to a better and more accurate understanding of what happened during those wartime years. This understanding is achieved through a complex series of flashbacks and the meditative surfacing of repressed memories and emotions triggered by documents, letters, personal items, and interpersonal relationships. Naomi and the reader find out at the end of the novel that certain information and facts were deliberately kept from her by members of her own family because they wanted to protect her and to honor her

19. For a discussion of this realist thesis of experience, see Moya, "Postmodernism, 'Realism,' and the Politics of Identity" 138.

20. I realize that each novel is autonomous and self-contained in its literary execution. My attempt to trace the epistemic and political growth of the character of Naomi Nakane in the two novels should not be read as a disavowal of each novel's formal integrity. Rather, I wish to draw attention to the epistemological continuity and coherence underlying Kogawa's fiction.

mother's dying wish that Naomi not be told about her mother's tragic fate in the bombing of Nagasaki. *Kodomo no tame,* "for the sake of the children," is what Naomi grows up hearing from Obasan and Uncle Isamu (*Obasan* 26), but she doesn't understand the real significance of this phrase until the information about her mother's whereabouts and fate is finally disclosed to her at the age of thirty-six. Ironically, this strategy not only did not protect Naomi, but in fact contributed to her wounding. As a five-year-old child who was very close to her mother, she was left with permanent emotional and psychological scars as a result of her separation from her mother, a separation that she experienced as complete abandonment. Not surprisingly, then, her mother's absence and unknown fate haunts Naomi throughout her childhood and is one of the major sources of her emotional and epistemic confusion and uncertainty.[21] Moreover, it is at the time of her mother's departure that Naomi is sexually molested by her white neighbor, Old Man Gower. Because she is not able to understand the significance of this violation done to her, Naomi internalizes her shame over the years, seeing herself not as a victim of sexual abuse but as an accomplice. As a result of her feeling of shame, the two events, the molestation and her mother's disappearance, become causally linked in Naomi's mind. These two pivotal incidents, combined with the dispossession and dissolution of her family and community, lead Naomi to withdraw inside herself, to shut herself off from the world. Her emotional wounds remain open, leaving her numb and frozen throughout her childhood and early adult years. Consequently, as an adult she does not see how she can possibly become living flesh: "My abominable abdomen. Something vast as childhood lies hidden in the belly's wars. There's a rage whose name has been forgotten" (*Itsuka* 134). We see, then, that she cannot even identify and name her pain; she does not have the vocabulary to do so.

Naomi's psychological numbness is further crystallized by her family's and community's insistence on dignified passivity and stoic silence. Her ability to speak out and name her pain and anger has been curbed by her upbringing in the protective and undemanding silence of Obasan, Uncle Isamu, and the other Issei. She cannot become whole again until the intuited knowledge that is accrued in childhood and the "real" information that she discovers in Aunt Emily's documents, letters, and jour-

---

21. Naomi Nakane's epistemic uncertainty (about her historical past and about her cultural identity) in *Obasan* is causally connected to her emotional uncertainty, to the emotional wounds that have yet to find resolution and healing.

nals come together and become a part of her. It is only later that Naomi begins to understand and adopt Aunt Emily's indignant position: "Over the years I have learned to understand some of Aunt Emily's sources of anger. And back in Granton and Cecil, in the years following Uncle's death, I was discovering my own capacity for that unpleasant emotion" (*Itsuka* 69). This feeling of anger is something that was not allowed before, not for Naomi or for the Issei. The Issei were denied the personal and social contexts to express and acknowledge their emotions (of anger and bitterness), a denial sustained by both their own community's cultural practices and the dominant society's racist policies. "It is significant," the philosopher Naomi Scheman observes in her discussion of women's anger and the role that feminist consciousness-raising groups play, "that a denial that one is angry often takes the form of a denial that one would be justified in being angry. Thus one's discovery of anger can often occur not from focusing on one's feelings but from a political redescription of one's situation" (25). The important point to which Scheman calls our attention is that emotions, such as anger, can have different epistemic salience and significance in different interpretive contexts, depending on the epistemic legitimacy or illegitimacy of the interpretive context. In other words, a person could feel anger and express this anger, but this individual's affective experience and affective expression might not be accurately recognized and acknowledged as anger by others in a certain interpretive context. For instance, the failure by a community of interpreters to recognize and acknowledge an individual's emotion of anger could stem from various factors, such as a genuine misreading of the affective expression (e.g., labeling it instead as guilt and depression) or a disavowal of the affective experience and expression (e.g., seeing the anger as unjustified or invalid for the individual and/or for the context). We can suppose that these two factors are operative in the case of Naomi and the Japanese Canadians, who did not have available, at a certain point in their lives, the proper supportive context (both social and emotional) that would facilitate a "political redescription of [their] situation" and allow them to publicly express anger about what they had been through.

Naomi eventually does undergo this process of political redescription of her situation. As she encounters more racist attacks and situations of disempowerment in her work in the redress movement, she begins to interpret these experiences, to identify causal connections between them, and to allow herself to feel the anger and bitterness, rather than suppress these emotions and submit to self-deprecation and self-blame. Naomi's new awareness of her emotions, her newfound ability to feel and name her emotions more fully, is in keeping with the realist-cognitivist view that emotions are not blind, reflexlike impulses or sensations; rather, emotions are ways of construing the world, intimately connected to our beliefs and judgments about ourselves and about the world.[22] Thus we see that what has been changed is not just Naomi's understanding of her emotions (e.g., she now knows that she does feel anger and pain) but also her understanding of her personhood and identity. Whereas before she did not see herself as someone who has been wronged and thus has a right to feel and express anger, she now holds different beliefs about her self and about her relationship to the world around her. She now sees herself as a person who has been oppressed, and who is entitled to a range of emotional, moral, and political claims and needs. Her new fuller and more accurate perspective is mutually enabled by her growing awareness of the wider injustice committed against her family and community. "We all know we are a people who were wronged. It's time to stand up. It's time," Naomi proclaims (*Itsuka* 242). As Naomi gains more information and reinterprets her emotions and experiences in this process of political self-redescription, her beliefs and judgment of the situation of other members of her community also undergo a redescription. For instance, the adult Naomi learns from reading Aunt Emily's journals and other writings that there were feelings of confusion, anger, and fear among the Japanese Canadians throughout the wartime years. She learns that the Issei also felt the pain and anger that she did, but they did not express these emotions in the overt manner that Aunt Emily or other more vocal Japanese Canadians would have liked them to. The Issei were consequently perceived by the Canadian government and media, as well as to some extent by Aunt Emily and the younger Nisei, as being passive and compliant.

My discussion of the particular affective experiences that Naomi and the Issei underwent, and the failure of others around them to recognize and acknowledge these emotions in certain interpretive contexts, points

22. Inquiries into the nature of emotions have been vast and extensive, carried out in such domains as philosophy of the mind, cultural and cognitive anthropology, and cognitive psychology. For an excellent selection of readings that introduce the rich history of theories and debates about emotions, see Cheshire Calhoun and Robert Solomon, eds., *What Is an Emotion?* For a well-argued cognitivist account of emotions, see Ronald de Sousa, *The Rationality of Emotion.* For a positive critique of cognitive theories of emotions, see Patricia S. Greenspan, *Emotions and Reasons.* For an anthropological examination of the epistemic status of emotions, see Robert I. Levy, "Emotion, Knowing, and Culture."

to the fact that emotions are theory laden. As I have mentioned, from the realist perspective, our emotions are intimately connected to our beliefs and judgments. In the case of the Issei and of Naomi, it is thus relevant to consider Scheman's claim that "the patterns we pick out when we name the emotions have to do with the needs of social life: seeing people as angry is connected with a complex set of expectations of them, and their not seeing themselves in the same way affects the validity of those expectations" (27). Elaborating on Scheman's discussion of anger, Mohanty underscores the following important point.

> This anger . . . should not be seen as a fully formed emotion that was waiting to be released or expressed in the context of the group. Rather, the emotion becomes what it is through the mediation of the social and emotional environment that the consciousness-raising group provides. Part of what constitutes this environment is an alternative narrative or account of the individual's relationship with the world, and these alternative accounts are unavoidably theoretical. (*Literary Theory* 207)

The recognition that adequate understanding, both personal and political, often depends on the availability of, and access to, alternative social relations and political structures is one of the important insights of feminist theory. Kogawa's novels extend this insight by pointing to the crucial role that the mediation of the social and emotional environment plays in providing alternative accounts that would permit us to organize our emotions and experiences and to give them coherence and clarity.

Naomi is able to get these alternative accounts of her relationship with the world and an alternative narrative of her cultural identity as a Japanese Canadian first through Aunt Emily, who sends her the necessary documents and letters from which she begins piecing together and making sense of her past. But this stirring of her emotional and political consciousness is not compelling enough to pull Naomi out of her state of inertia; she also needs the right supportive context in which to get drawn into the political struggle. In *Itsuka* she finds that emotional and social support among the people involved in the redress movement, people who provide her with a safe emotional environment and a consciousness-raising context to begin reevaluating her feelings and experiences. The people in the redress movement, along with Aunt Emily, provide Naomi with alternative accounts of her experiences and social location, helping her to organize her inchoate and confused feelings to produce the emotions of pain and anger that then get experienced more directly and fully. Consequently, it is only after an extended period that she can meaningfully understand and take heed of Aunt Emily's earlier exhortation: "Don't deny the past. Remember everything. If you're bitter, be bitter. Cry it out! Scream! Denial is gangrene!" (*Obasan* 60). Naomi gradually learns to "scream" in her adult years, to feel more fully the bitterness and pain, and, in the process, to remember her past.

It is Naomi's indirect recognition of the cognitive implications of her emotions and experiences that enables her to finally come to understand how she has shut herself off from the world mainly because of her severance from her mother.

> All my waiting life I kept my heart turned toward her and away from the tiny choices of love offered in the inch-high rooms of possibilities. I sought her and only her, tumbling downstream, back and back till I reached her grave and I sought her in dream beyond the grave, in the stream that circles forever and in the song that does not vanish. Love, it seems to me, must be at the end of the journey without end. (*Itsuka* 104–5)

For most of her childhood and young adult life, Naomi has been yearning for her mother, yearning for the love that she identifies with the figure of her mother. Her complete focus on her real need for maternal love contributes, however, to her emotional numbness because it prevents her from bringing to the surface of her consciousness the great pain and anger she feels deep down as a result of her mother's unexplained absence. She was not able to recognize until now how her great desire for her mother's love has prevented her from discerning "the tiny choices of love offered in the inch-high rooms of possibilities." This newly gained insight about her past and her relationship with her absent mother directs Naomi to the realization that she needed something more than Aunt Emily's facts and statistics to accurately organize and interpret her experiences, to gain objectivity; she needed to feel again, to let the emotions surface in order to acknowledge them and allow them to connect her with another human being. Accordingly, it is precisely Naomi's intuitive need for something more than Aunt Emily's facts and statistics, rather than a postmodernist "los[s] of faith in linguistic signs" (Goellnicht, "Minority History" 295), that leads her to declare, "All of Aunt Emily's words, all her papers, the telegrams and petitions, are like scratchings in the barnyard, the evidence of much activity, scaly claws hard at work. But what good they do, I do not know—those little black typewritten words— words, cloud droppings. They do not touch us where we are planted here in Alberta. . . . The words are not made flesh. . . . All my prayers disappear into space" (*Obasan* 189). The words do need to be "made flesh" before Naomi can embrace their meaning. Concomitantly, in order for some situations to be adequately understood and for certain kinds of knowledge of one's social and cultural identity to be gained, it is not just new conceptions and information that need to be provided; new social relations and arrangements also need to be explored and introduced.

Naomi's recognition of her emotional needs and her exploration of them in new social relations and a different political framework take place explicitly in *Itsuka*. This sequel charts Naomi's emotional and political awakening, as she opens up and responds to the loving support of her community and to Father Cedric, an unorthodox priest who joins the redress cause. It is Father Cedric who plays a key role in helping Naomi to work through her suppressed emotions by offering her genuine friendship and, most of all, love. Nurtured by his love and support, Naomi finds herself emerging from her emotional numbness as she begins the process of healing.

> [Cedric] sighs and he is weary but he is here and he is whispering to me. See? Up there? Love is watching us through the branches of the tree. Love watches the spaces between people, while they are absent from each other. He says that in all our hands are many wounds, and in the wounds Love toils and strives with us. And I am striving now, within my body, that I may be free. I am burrowing into the coils within, challenging the old rage, the fears and the old griefs, the old old sadness, the envy, the loneliness and other still militant demons that ravage my flesh and encase it in disease. (*Itsuka* 298)

In place of a distant, impenetrable love, one that induces feelings of alienation, numbness, and abandonment, Cedric draws Naomi's attention to another kind of love. This love is tangibly present, "watching through the branches of the trees" and protectively sustaining the affective links between people amid absence; it is salving, "toil[ing] and striv[ing] with us" in our emotional journey toward healing and freedom. Guided by this alternative conception of love, Naomi begins to examine the layers of repressed feelings and buried knowledge, feelings and knowledge she had consciously and unconsciously wanted to deny due to her childhood traumas and her deep sense of self-hatred fostered by living in a racist society. She learns to face her fears, grief, and sadness and to articulate and share them with Cedric. In trusting Cedric and seeing herself through his eyes, Naomi uses his view of her as a theoretical prism through which she comes to resee herself in a more accurate light; she comes to see herself as a person who is capable of love and of being loved, whose feelings of anger and pain are real and legitimate. Importantly, this new self-perception and self-love is made possible by Naomi's and the novels'

crucial recognition of the epistemic significance of experience, particularly affective experience, to understanding one's identity and one's relationship to the world.

The epistemic value of experience is a key lesson not only in Kogawa's
novels; Asian American literary criticism and, more generally, Asian American studies can be better served by a theoretical rehabilitation of experience. Indeed, one of the core categories and organizing principles in Asian
American studies since its inception has been the personal experience of
its constituents. However, the category of experience currently faces the
danger of being attenuated by ethnic studies scholars who too quickly accept the postmodernist critique of experience, seeing experience as an unreliable source of knowledge. These scholars have called for a shift in the
focus of Asian American studies, from the project of deriving knowledge
about the world through the examination of the ethnic and racialized experience to that of what the historian Joan Scott calls the "analysis of the
production of knowledge" (37).[23] But this postmodernist approach to the
question of experience and knowledge is inadequate, with debilitating intellectual and political consequences, because it mistakenly rejects the idea
that we can gain accurate and reliable knowledge from our experience.
In fact, my realist discussion of Kogawa's novels shows that knowledge
about one's self and one's past can and does derive from an examination
of one's personal experience and emotions. Below I elaborate on the postpositivist realist conception of objectivity, extending my discussion of objective knowledge derived from experience and emotions to consider how
objectivity of knowledge is inextricably tied to objectivity of values. I do
so by drawing out the epistemic link between our emotions and our values; and I show how this connection is based on a strong defense of objectivity, the kind that postpositivist realism provides.

23. This shift, from the aim of unearthing a "buried past" to that of problematizing
knowledge, seems to be the contentious point motivating K. Scott Wong's comment, "We
tend to study HOW to study history rather than history itself," a comment that Omi and
Takagi note in their introduction to the "Thinking Theory" issue of *Amerasia Journal* (xiv).
Interestingly, the project of the "analysis of the production of knowledge" seems to be at
the heart of Dana Y. Takagi's plea that Asian American studies and ethnic studies position
themselves in the center of theoretical debates rather than sit on the margins. While ab-
staining from directly advocating a postmodernist theoretical approach to Asian American studies and ethnic studies, Takagi believes that one of the areas of postmodernist discussion that scholars in these fields need to be engaged in is the category of experience.
She calls for a problematizing of "experience": "The major critics, and feminists have I
think taken the lead on this matter, have suggested that experience represents a new 'foundationalism.' . . . The real question, according to Scott, . . . is not experience itself but why
the discursive telling of experience became possible at any given historical moment" ("Postmodernism from the Edge" 42).

EMOTIONS, OBJECTIVITY OF VALUES,
AND ASIAN AMERICAN STUDIES

Concomitant with a theoretical rehabilitation of experience, a postpositivist realist approach to Asian American literary criticism and Asian American studies would reintroduce the discussion of social and moral values in the field, demonstrating why such a discussion needs to be taken seriously, particularly within leftist and progressive circles. A serious examination of values will show that many social activists and progressive writers of color have been intensely engaged in the project of theorizing human values, such as the values of solidarity and human equality. But their contributions to the discussion of values are not informed by an additive or compensatory model of social change. By this I mean that they do not seek to reform the current social structure by adding on or modifying a few variables of the social equation. Rather, I would argue that their insights on values, drawn from their personal experiences, are tied to larger explanatory visions and theories of social justice. That is, their perspectives of the world should not be taken as only resistant or counterhegemonic contestations; they should also be seen as constituting normative theories of social relationships and arrangements. My claim, put otherwise, is that the personal experiences of people of color are theoretically mediated by visions and values that are deeply social and political in nature and which refer outward, beyond their specific racial and ethnic contexts, to the general features of the one social world we all inhabit. I need to emphasize that this is not a novel claim; this insight constituted the original impetus behind the founding of Asian American studies and ethnic studies.

But in recasting this claim in a realist discussion of emotions, values, and objectivity, I hope to strengthen it by suggesting that the experiences and visions of people of color are to be taken as significant social and moral theories.[24] That is, out of their personal experiences and partial perspectives people of color have elaborated normative accounts of social reality and human values. For example, from her experiences in social activism, the revolutionist-activist-theorist Grace Lee Boggs came to see the crucial role that theorization of human and moral values plays in struggles for social change.[25] Human values and moral choices are the

---

24. The radical claim for the epistemic implications of cultural experience and identity, implications that point to the need to reconceptualize experience and identity as bits of social and political theories, is made by Mohanty in his essay in this volume.
25. See Grace Lee Boggs, *Living for Change*, esp. 149–57.

key terms in Boggs's distinction between rebellion and revolution. Boggs notes, "A rebellion disrupts the society but it does not provide what is necessary to make a revolution and establish a new social order. To make a revolution, people must not only struggle against existing institutions. They must make a philosophical/spiritual leap and become more human human beings. In order to change/transform the world, they must change/transform themselves" (153). But to transform ourselves, to become more human human beings, we need to know what it would take to be more human, to change ourselves. And such an inquiry into what it would take to be more human requires coming up with normative conceptions of human needs and values. Consequently, in developing their theory of "dialectical humanism," Boggs and her husband, James Boggs, came to realize that progressive political struggles crucially require tackling, rather than deferring, complex questions of basic human needs and human values.[26] Many other social activists and writers have also pointed out the importance of grappling with these questions of human needs and human values and the necessity of formulating normative moral and social theories, and Joy Kogawa is one such activist-writer-theorist.[27]

It is the normative dimension of Kogawa's writings that I now turn to and examine, beginning with her theorization of values and focusing on her understanding of uncertainty, which she sees as an enabling element of epistemic inquiry and human agency rather than as a catalyst of debilitating skepticism. Kogawa's theorization of human and social values constitutes a central contribution to the realist project, which conceives of values not as purely conventional and solely context-specific

26. Boggs makes the following points:

If, however, those who need to make a revolution also need to transform themselves into more socially responsible, more self-critical human beings, then our role as revolutionists is to involve them in activities that are both self-transforming and structure-transforming, exploring and trying to resolve in theory and practice fundamental questions of human life more complex than anything Marx could possibly have dreamed of. What kind of an economy, what kind of technology would serve both human and economic needs? What kind of transformation do we need in our values, institutions, and behavior to reconnect us with the rhythms and processes of nature? Should we do something just because we can do it? What is the difference between needs and wants? How do we meet people's psychic hungers? What does it mean to care? (156)

27. Kogawa's project is not at all different from other contemporary writers, activists, and critics who are also engaged in human inquiry with a strong belief in the possibility of objective knowledge and objective values. Of course, this claim does not exclude the possibility that there are other writers who are not engaged in this kind of realist project. Kogawa addresses many of the main concerns of postmodernist writers and theorists—the status of experience, the nature of cultural identity, the issue of human needs and values—but she does not reach the same conclusions.

but as having an epistemic content that can be examined and tested, within both particular and cross-cultural frameworks.[28] For a moral realist, our values are more than just personal and subjective beliefs; they are crucial theoretical "prisms," or interpretive frameworks, through which people view the world and make sense of their experiences and social location. Our values are often based on our conscious beliefs and explicit visions, but they also arise out of our nonpropositional knowledge—our hunches, intuitions, and often inchoate emotions. Intuitions, hunches, and emotions, however, have traditionally been viewed in Western philosophy as being unreliable and "irrational"; and they have been assigned to the realm of the epistemically uncertain. But this foundationalist strict demarcation between certainty and uncertainty has been recently challenged and revised by feminist critiques of epistemology, critiques that demonstrate the epistemic credibility of women's and others' modes of knowing and show how these alternative epistemological frameworks come out of women's and less privileged groups' experiences and perspectives.[29] It seems to me that Kogawa's exploration of the epistemic value of uncertainty engages with, and contributes to, this epistemological critique.

On Kogawa's view, uncertainty does not inevitably lead us to the position of antifoundationalist skepticism. Uncertainty can have its own affirmative cognitive implications and epistemic authority, and this acknowledgment is compatible with the realist framework. In fact, Kogawa's view on uncertainty resonates with and extends the realist understanding of fallibility and error. For the realist, error and bias are not obstacles to avoid at all cost but instead are instructive, even necessary, elements of inquiry. From this perspective, the dialectic is then between error and objectivity; error is opposed not to certainty but rather to objectivity as a theory-dependent, socially realizable goal.[30] The possibility of error, then, does not sanction radical skepticism about the possibility of knowledge. Rather, the realist approach entails a striving for precision

28. For an engaging realist-cognitivist argument for seeing moral inquiry as an interpretive enterprise that is capable of transcending the boundaries of culture and history through scrupulous attention to the complex and difficult contexts and particulars of moral experiences, see Michelle Moody-Adams, *Fieldwork in Familiar Places*, esp. 147–221. For other realist-cognitivist approaches to moral inquiry, see Boyd, "How to Be a Moral Realist"; and Mohanty, *Literary Theory* 240–51.

29. Examples of feminist critiques of epistemology are Linda Alcoff and Elizabeth Potter, eds., *Feminist Epistemologies;* Louise M. Antony and Charlotte Witt, eds., *A Mind of One's Own;* Ann Garry and Marilyn Pearsall, eds., *Women, Knowledge, and Reality;* and Lorraine Code, *Rhetorical Spaces.*

30. Mohanty, *Literary Theory* 215.

and depth in understanding the sources of error, for such inquiry will help us define the nature of objectivity. In other words, a consideration of the role of error brings us closer to the actualization of objectivity in knowledge and human inquiry, since we can identify and specify, through research and experimentation, the causes of error and distortion.[31]

In her examination in this volume of the essential role that error plays in objective inquiry, Caroline S. Hau notes that "taking error seriously implies that when we reposition the issue of error and mystification within the framework of theory-mediated knowledge, we necessarily shift the debate about the status of error way from a consideration of error per se . . . to a consideration of the uses of error." Hau's realist elaboration of error can be productively extended to the question of uncertainty, so that we can make a case for the epistemic uses of uncertainty.

Kogawa's understanding of uncertainty postulates the inclusion of uncertainty in the dialectic between error and objectivity and makes the epistemic connection among the three terms. As she has eloquently stated in her essay "Is There a Just Cause?": "Life is a series of making and unmaking plans along a continuum of uncertainty. . . . Perhaps we will never be fully adequate to see the whole picture of which the causes we uphold are a part. But inadequacy is not an excuse for inaction. . . . Inadequacy is a universal experience and we are all broken and incomplete like jig saw puzzle pieces. Our wholeness comes from joining and from sharing our brokenness" (20–24). On Kogawa's view, we live within a "continuum of uncertainty," and we often do not know the full picture (i.e., have complete certainty or complete mastery). In this sense, we might be the fragmented and split subject, but this does not mean that we are doomed to a state of radical subjectivism and skepticism, or that we have to give up the responsibility to exercise our agency and to act. "Inadequacy," Kogawa asserts, "is not an excuse for inaction." On the contrary, it is precisely because we are "broken and incomplete" that we are called on to act; for it is in acting that we can join and share our individual perspectives (the "fragments of fragments" [*Obasan* 64]) to construct the larger picture, to establish our collectivity, and to achieve our "wholeness."

31. Mohanty, *Literary Theory* 209. Interestingly, the realist account of error points up the implicit foundationalism embedded in the postmodernist formulation of the constructedness of knowledge. The postmodernist position rejects all attempts to seek objectivity of knowledge because it sees such a project as futile. Knowledge, according to the postmodernist, must be untainted by presuppositions, errors, and biases, and since we can never have this condition of purity in inquiry, we should give up the quest for objectivity of knowledge. Yet ironically, this idealist assumption that objectivity must be fully in the realm of certainty and unmediated by theory is also what underwrites (foundationalist) positivism.

Indeed, this brokenness, this inadequacy, this fragmented state is what leads us, Kogawa would argue, to a condition of psychological, moral, and political "wholeness," of trust, love, and solidarity.[32] She does acknowledge that this imagery of inadequacy and brokenness might be seen as inappropriate and disempowering for women and minority groups, since it does not seem to provide us with the kind of transforming strength that is needed ("Just Cause" 20). But the alternative is not to adopt the position of the unified, dislocated and disinterested observer of traditional Cartesian philosophy. Kogawa makes, instead, the following appeal:

> Rather than abandoning the way of brokenness, I believe we need to remember the paradoxical power in mutual vulnerability. Where there is doubt, the authority of certainty is put aside, but the capacity to hear is heightened. . . . In our limping we may discover that we walk with others who also limp and that even our enemies know pain. . . . If we cannot have such moments, if we cannot risk ever being weak, if we are unable to seek to understand an opposing position, we must admit our blindness to that other's reality. And a cause born in such blindness cannot presume to be just. ("Just Cause" 20)

In the face of the temptation to forgo the way of brokenness in search of that illusive state of foundationalist certainty and autonomy, or, at the other extreme, to reify the brokenness and celebrate the incompleteness, Kogawa urges us to embrace "the paradoxical power in mutual vulnerability." She does not view vulnerability as a weakness; for her, it is a source of strength because it lays the groundwork for establishing trust and empathy with others. It does so because our experience of our own vulnerability will more likely guide us to self-reflection and self-examination, to an opening and deepening of our perception of our self.[33] This process of opening up allows us to more sensitively and more accurately perceive our physical, emotional, and psychological states, an achievement that, in turn, places us in a better position to gain self-knowledge and self-understanding. And this self-knowledge will direct us to trust our emotions and rational capacity, to trust ourselves.

It is not surprising, then, that trust is an essential cornerstone of Kogawa's moral and political vision. In the face of inadequacy and uncertainty, she asserts the importance of self-trust in her life and her work: "So, you know, most of the time I stumble here and there. Then, I say,

---

32. Kogawa's understanding of the human need for "wholeness" derives from her commitment to the values of solidarity and connectiveness. In her interview with Ruth Y. Hsu, Kogawa explicitly makes the following point: "I know that I value the connectiveness and I value the peace that comes from the alleviation of suffering" (213).

33. This is one of the basic principles of many forms of Buddhist meditation.

okay, I will trust that I am doing the right thing. If I go wrong, I will trust myself to the mercy and to the forgiveness that is there. You see, that somehow has to be good enough" (Hsu 213).[34] It is good enough because self-trust promotes a general condition of trust: once we have established self-trust and appreciate its epistemic worth, we are more inclined to trust others, to entrust our vulnerability to the "mercy and forgiveness" of others; and, in exchange, to honor the trust that we are safeguarded with by others.[35] This is admittedly a risky scenario; we are completely in the realm of the epistemically uncertain, exposing ourselves to the possibility of being hurt and betrayed. But we cannot afford not to trust. "In the midst of all the unknown," Naomi Nakane reminds herself and us, "it matters to trust. It matters in this time of not-yet sight that some skin cells seem sensitized to light . . . in those murky days before there were eyes" (*Itsuka* 2).[36] Kogawa's point is that not to trust closes us off from ourselves and from others, and limits our perception, while trust enables a fuller, more accurate perception of reality. This is one of the key lessons that Naomi learns in her relationship with Father Cedric: her learned ability to trust him over time leads to a more accurate understanding on her part of her past experiences and of her current emotional needs and hence gives rise to a fuller conception of her self and the world she inhabits.

At the same time, trusting our vulnerability to others puts us in an epistemic position to be more empathetically aware of the vulnerability of others; we can recognize the mutuality in our relationships with others because our perception of others is sharpened, improved, and rendered more accurate. "Where there is doubt," Kogawa notes, "the authority of certainty is put aside, but the capacity to hear is heightened"

34. The philosopher Keith Lehrer argues that the capacity for self-trust is a necessary first element in the life of reason (5). Lehrer proposes that what makes a person worthy of her own trust is her rational capacity to evaluate her beliefs and desires; and this is possible because of the uniquely human capacity for metamental ascent, the ability to consider and evaluate first-order mental states that arise naturally within us: "I trust myself in what I accept and prefer, and I consider myself worthy of my trust in what I accept or prefer. Acceptance and preference are, after all, my best efforts to obtain truth and merit, and if they are not worthy of my trust, then I am not worthy of my trust, and reason is impotent" (5). Lehrer goes on to demonstrate in his book how self-trust can lead to knowledge and rational autonomy.

35. See Annette Baier's perceptive meditation on trust in her *Moral Prejudices* esp. 95–202.

36. The appearance of the word *murky* here in the narrative, in the context of Naomi's reflection on the nature of knowing and trusting, resonates with another moment in *Obasan* ("The truth for me is more murky, shadowy, and gray" [38]). In both cases, the epistemic uncertainty that seems to be suggested by the word *murky* does not signal, in my view, postmodernist skepticism. This is one of my main points in this chapter.

("Just Cause" 20). In the context of doubt and confusion, of multiple competing explanations and truth claims, the authority of (foundational) certainty is put aside, replaced by a better, more applicable cognitive skill: an epistemic reorientation in the form of a finely tuned capacity to hear, to see, to feel. This reorientation is the paradoxical power of vulnerability that Kogawa insightfully pinpoints and to which her characters speak. As Aunt Emily, drawing on her experience in political activism, puts it, "What heals people is the transforming power of mutuality. Mutual vulnerability. Mutual strength" (*Itsuka* 220). Mutuality is the transforming strength; it enables us to expand beyond particular contingent interests to perspicuously recognize who our broader allies are; who, beyond our immediate group membership and identification, we share political interests and values with; who we can build coalitions with, for "in our limping we may discover that we walk with others who also limp" ("Just Cause" 20).[37] Our perception does not end with our allies, however; Kogawa reminds us that even our enemies—those most radically other from us (e.g., in terms of ideology, race, culture)—know pain. They are different from us, but they cannot be so different that they are radically incommensurable and unintelligible. We must be able to transcend our particularities by seeking to understand different, opposing positions. If we cannot take this step, then, "we must admit our blindness to that other's reality"; we must admit that we have closed ourselves off from the opportunity to perceive ourselves and our reality more completely and hence more accurately—and such a myopic view "cannot presume to be just" ("Just Cause" 20). Only by taking the step to "hear" the other can we more accurately discern where we are indeed different, and where, crucially, we share a common ground. It is only by taking such a risk that we may be able to glimpse, from an objective standpoint, the universality of our experiences and achieve our wholeness. In looking at the Japanese Canadian experience, Kogawa makes the following extrapolation: "The Japanese Canadian community is only one small pebble on the beach of human experience but there is a universal element in our struggling political endeavour" (Delbaere 462). It is this universal element, the universal import of the Japanese Canadian community's fight for redress, that constitutes a legitimate justification for arguing that the epistemic and moral insights that Kogawa and Japanese Canadians have

---

37. For a discussion of the political and moral significance of mutuality in theorizing social interests and group membership, see Michael R. Hames-García's "'Who Are Our Own People?'" in this volume.

distilled from their particular experiences are not merely context-specific, but that these insights have a normative dimension.

As I have mentioned earlier, the realist's commitment to the objectivity of knowledge takes into account the possibility of error and its epistemic significance. This understanding of error also informs the realist's metatheoretical commitment to the objectivity of values. The possibility that we might hold misguided or erroneous values (whether personal or social) does not mean that we can never examine our values beyond the local domain and criteria of personal preferences, individual attitudes, and subjective interests. On the contrary, a moral realist would argue that our values, like our emotions and experiences, are not just "private," individual affairs; they can also refer outward, beyond their personal and local meanings and contexts, to causally salient aspects of our reality.[38] For instance, I might hold the values of respect for others and cooperative human interaction. These values could just be particular to me, my own idiosyncratic predilection. But empirical research could also be carried out to find out the place and role of these values in the society and culture in which I live, as well as in other societies and realms of cultural practices. The results of the research might reveal that these values I hold constitute the core principles of the social structure of my society and that in fact the promotion of these values results in a higher level of well-being of my society and its individual members. From this empirical investigation I might discover causal connections between a particular set of values and how these values deeply inform certain forms of social organization and arrangement in my particular society and/or other societies. And the discovery of these causal connections can provide me with salient facts about the society in which I live.

But, like our knowledge claims and knowledge-gathering procedures, our social values and moral inquiry might necessarily be tentative, imprecise, and open-ended, subject to revision in light of new information and changes in social norms and practices. However, the revisability of values and moral inquiry means that we can deepen and refine our understanding of them, as we learn more about social relations and cultural practices, about the kinds of social organizations and interactions that will promote or limit certain values in a given society. Moreover, our values, as explanatory, interpretive lenses through which we view the world, are theory dependent, in the same way that our personal ex-

---

38. For a discussion of the epistemic status of values, see Mohanty, *Literary Theory* 243–45. See also Michelle Moody-Adams, *Fieldwork in Familiar Places*, esp. 150–86.

periences and emotions are; and thus they can be evaluated for their epistemic salience and legitimacy.[39] In fact, our values (which include our
beliefs and judgments about ourselves and the world) are causally connected to our experiences and emotions, informing the kinds of experiences and emotions that we might have and our interpretation and evaluation of these experiences and emotions, as I have shown in my
discussion of Kogawa's novels. The theory-laden nature of values means
that there can be an evaluative progress in mutuality and cooperation,
requiring that we identify and discern between true and false experiences
of mutual interaction and cooperation and seek, through theoretical and
empirical inquiry and social experimentation, better and more genuine
ways of developing cooperative relationships and solidarity.

In this conception of values and morality as fields of inquiry that can
be elaborated and specified through research and social practices, the
presence of doubt does not necessarily lead us to skepticism; rather, doubt
serves to fine tune our sensitivity; to expand our openness and responsiveness to the people and things around us; to hone our observations
and interpretations, thus making them more accurate and more objective. In other words, doubt puts us in a better epistemic position to see
and hear the opposing position and to take this opposing position into
account in our perception and evaluation. At the same time, Kogawa is
cognizant of the epistemic and political pitfalls of an uncritical reliance
on doubt, noting that "doubt and ambivalence can sometimes so immobilize us that in the end we serve to maintain oppressors in their positions of power" ("Just Cause" 20). But she goes on to underscore the
valuable implication of trusting our doubt: "healthy doubt is also that
which prevents us from succumbing to the demonic power of an un-
thinking trust" ("Just Cause" 20). Rather than act to immobilize us,
doubt and distrust are valuable epistemic tools that we can use to interpret and evaluate our theory-mediated experiences. This is especially true
in the case of marginalized and oppressed people. For instance, just as
Naomi learns to trust herself and others through her process of personal
and political awakening, she also comes to better understand her feelings of doubt and distrust of the Canadian government and their strategies to appease redress demands. She and other activists in the redress
movement think that they have reasons not to trust the Canadian government and its promises, and to believe that the government might be
bargaining in bad faith in the current redress campaign. Their feeling of

39. Mohanty, *Literary Theory* 240–43.

distrust in this context is not "irrational," for it is based on the knowledge they have gained from their experiences in dealing with the Canadian government and the ways in which the government has used and abused power.[40] In turn, this emotion of distrust will provide an epistemic framework in which the Japanese Canadian activists can situate new information and experiences, sorting and evaluating these through the lens of their legitimate feeling of distrust.

While we might find doubt and distrust to belong to the realm of uncertainty and of messy particularities, involving continual sorting and resorting of information and complex evaluation and reevaluation, these emotions are also subsumed under the larger universal context of human suffering. "Beyond our doubt and confusion," Kogawa maintains, "lies our capacity to recognize what suffering is and where health lies and to identify with both. I believe that it is the identification of and with suffering at every level, in every condition and in every person that magnetizes the compass of justice and points us to home" ("Just Cause" 21). We have the capacity to detect suffering in others, to recognize when someone is vulnerable and in pain. In a sense, suffering is the common denominator of what it means to be human and that which enables the recognition of our universally shared condition as vulnerable creatures with a minimum level of needs. This minimum level of human needs, however, cannot be determined a priori or in the abstract; we have to start with the acknowledgment of human suffering and vulnerability and go from there, using this basic recognition as a compass to guide us in our conception of social justice and human ethics.[41] It is by cultivating our ability to perceive with creative attention and fine details another person's suffering and vulnerability, to vividly picture ourselves in another person's place, that we can expand our moral imagination, making ourselves more likely to respond with the morally illuminating and therefore just sort of response.

It follows for Kogawa that because suffering and mutual vulnerability enlarge our moral imagination and deepen our ethical responsiveness, they open us up to the possibility of love: "Whether we err or fail in our causes,

40. The emotions of doubt and distrust in the context of redress and political activism are explored in the second half of *Itsuka*.

41. What constitutes this minimum level of human needs cannot be determined a priori. It requires working with the tentative hypotheses and bits of knowledge that we presently possess, as well as empirical studies that we can carry out in the future. Defining a minimum level of human needs also does not entail the imposition of homogeneity; rather, as an open-ended project, it leaves room for cultural differences and heterogeneity—it actually promotes genuine diversity, as Mohanty argues in *Literary Theory*.

we can abandon ourselves to the transforming and miraculous power of an utterly unlimited and terrifying love. We can limp triumphantly in the certitude that as we entrust ourselves to that love, we will be transformed, enemies will become friends and the just cause of love will yet be won" ("Just Cause" 21). This is Kogawa's belief. But at the same time, she also stresses that while she believes in this injunction to love and attend to the enemy, it is still an abstraction. Kogawa reminds us that what draws people together are not sermons but stories and storytelling, for it is stories that bring out our particularities: Who are you? Who am I? What is your cause? What is mine? From this perspective, Kogawa finds sermons and slogans of justice to be empty, noting that they rarely help us to achieve our progressive political goals. Our social and political theories, such as our theory of justice, need to be informed by our emotions—our empathy and love— and emotions, in turn, need to be concretized within the narrative ties of human relationships and human values.

This essential epistemic interdependence between our social theories and our emotions is underscored in the debates over redress that take place in *Itsuka*. After an extended period of involvement in the redress movement, Naomi finds herself faced with doubt and confusion regarding the just nature of redress claims, as internal and external criticisms of redress activities mount: "When I talk about these things to Marion, she says, 'Love is the answer, Naomi,' but I have no idea what that means. At church a man told Aunt Emily that she should love more and that redress was about vengeance, not love. Cedric was as impatient as I've ever seen him. 'Without justice, love is a mockery,' he said" (203). Without justice, love is indeed a mockery; but Kogawa would also remind Cedric that without love, justice is an empty, useless concept. In her interview with Magdalene Redekop, Kogawa tells us: "Documents and facts are intended to direct our prejudiced hearts but rarely provide direction by themselves. I have boxes and boxes of documents but what I need is vision and vision comes from relationship. Facts bereft of love direct us nowhere" (Redekop 15). Kogawa's moving assertion strengthens the realist claim that objectivity is inextricably tied to love and personal and social relationships; we attain objectivity not by disregarding or disavowing our emotions and values but by interrogating their epistemic character to assess the relevant insights they might provide. It is *interested* inquiry, then, that allows us to perceive and interpret our reality more accurately.[42]

---

42. This is one of Caroline Simon's main points in her book, *The Disciplined Heart*. In her discussion of the epistemic role of love, Simon posits: "Lack of love, with its con-

Since "interested inquiry," an inquiry informed by certain emotions (such as trust and love) and values (such as mutual cooperation and loving attention to vulnerability), is the enabling condition for achieving objectivity of knowledge, we can make the case that objectivity of knowledge is inextricably tied to objectivity of values. That is, having the right general values, the right visions/theories to guide us in our inquiry can ensure a more accurate perception and interpretation of reality. Kogawa's evaluative view of trust and love and her realist insights on how these emotions are causally connected to social values suggest deep metatheoretical commitments to the objectivity of values. Her knowledge of her experience, identity, and social reality is derived from her understanding of the transformative power of trust and love. Her writings call attention to the causal connections between forms of trust and love and our "humanness"; these emotions not only can tell us about our needs, capabilities, and possibilities, but they also mutually inform and are informed by our values. The fact of epistemic causality in emotions, values, and identities means that we can learn from ourselves and from each other; we can grow, morally and politically, from the insights distilled from our personal experiences; and we can chart and evaluate our learning and growth. The emotions of trust and love and the values of mutuality and solidarity thus function as evaluative concepts that we can use to gauge a society's moral health and political development. Indeed, our everyday lives, which include not only our "obvious" rational activities but also our not so obvious cognitive processes, such as our emotions and intuitions, have great epistemic worth. And it is because our everyday lives can, and often do, provide us with knowledge about our human condition that we can conduct theoretical and empirical inquiry to specify the kinds of social arrangements and human relationships that will nurture better modes of trusting and loving, modes that will bring about greater human connectedness and solidarity, and ultimately human equality. Not surprisingly, it is by taking their everyday lives—their emotions and personal experiences—seriously that Naomi and other Japanese Canadian redress activists come to fully and more accurately understand their social values and cultural identity, to articulate them,

---

comitant lack of justice and mercy, causes warped perceptions of others. In contrast, love, with its accompanying attention to reality, allows us to see others as they are; seeing them as they are, in turn, throws light on who we are. . . . [L]ove brings about an attentiveness to reality that results in self-knowledge" (65). See also Iris Murdoch, "Imagination," esp. 342–48, for an examination of the epistemological links between love and our creative and moral imagination.

and to develop social arrangements and political organizations that would embody their values and cultural identity.

It is along this line of trust, solidarity, and human equality that Kogawa's realist *perception* of historical knowledge, progressive social values, and objectivity is compatible with, and elaborates, the fundamental ideals and goals of Asian American studies and ethnic studies. Kogawa's work implicitly envisions Asian American literature, Asian American studies, and ethnic studies as both oppositional and normative political projects. On this conception, our racialized experiences, cultural practices, and perspectives signify more than just contestations of the dominant structure and ideology; they are undergirded by a rich and meaningful constellation of social values and theoretical assumptions about what it would take to be more human human beings and what constitutes a just society. In other words, our racialized experiences and perspectives contain a normative component; and, as such, this normative dimension points to the need for a strong defense of objectivity. A strong postpositivist conception of objectivity will allow us to reconfigure a viable notion of radical and progressive humanism, one that would attend to the particularity and heterogeneity of historical and cultural contexts while leaving room for a genuine moral universalism. It is to this wider context of moral universalism that I think Asian American literary criticism, Asian American studies, and ethnic studies speak, and within which we should be situated, especially in these times of neoconservative attacks on ethnic studies and other civil rights gains. And this is why, as a starting point of discussion, for both Kogawa and for our purposes in Asian American literary criticism and Asian American studies, it matters to get the facts straight.

WORKS CITED

Alcoff, Linda, and Elizabeth Potter, eds. *Feminist Epistemologies.* New York: Routledge, 1993.

Antony, Louise M. "Quine as Feminist: The Radical Import of Naturalized Epistemology." *A Mind of One's Own: Feminist Essays on Reason and Objectivity.* Ed. Louise M. Antony and Charlotte Witt. Boulder, CO: Westview Press, 1993. 185–225.

Antony, Louise M., and Charlotte Witt, eds. *A Mind of One's Own: Feminist Essays on Reason and Objectivity.* Boulder, CO: Westview Press, 1993.

Baier, Annette C. *Moral Prejudices: Essays on Ethics.* Cambridge, MA: Harvard University Press, 1994.

Boggs, Grace Lee. *Living for Change: An Autobiography*. Minneapolis: University of Minnesota Press, 1998.

Boyd, Richard. "How to Be a Moral Realist." *Essays in Moral Realism*. Ed. Geoffrey Sayre-McCord. Ithaca: Cornell University Press, 1988. 181–228.

Calhoun, Cheshire, and Robert Solomon, eds. *What Is an Emotion?* Cambridge: Cambridge University Press, 1983.

Chang, Gordon. "History and Postmodernism." *Amerasia Journal* 21.1–2 (1995): 89–93.

Cheung, King-Kok. *Articulate Silences: Hisaye Yamamoto, Maxine Hong Kingston, Joy Kogawa*. Ithaca: Cornell University Press, 1993.

Code, Lorraine. *Rhetorical Spaces: Essays on Gendered Locations*. New York: Routledge, 1995.

Davidson, Arnold. *Writing against the Silence: Joy Kogawa's* Obasan. Toronto: ECW Press, 1993.

Delbaere, Jeanne. "Joy Kogawa Interviewed by Jeanne Delbaere." *Kunapipi* 16.1 (1994): 461–63.

de Sousa, Ronald. *The Rationality of Emotion*. Cambridge, MA: MIT Press, 1987.

Flax, Jane. "Postmodernism and Gender Relations in Feminist Theory." *Feminism/Postmodernism*. Ed. Linda J. Nicholson. New York: Routledge, 1990. 39–62.

Garry, Ann, and Marilyn Pearsall, eds. *Women, Knowledge, and Reality: Explorations in Feminist Philosophy*. New York: Routledge, 1996.

Goellnicht, Donald C. "Blurring Boundaries: Asian American Literature as Theory." *An Interethnic Companion to Asian American Literature*. Ed. King-Kok Cheung. Cambridge: Cambridge University Press, 1997. 338–65.

———. "Minority History as Metafiction: Joy Kogawa's *Obasan*." *Tulsa Studies in Women's Literature* 8 (1989): 287–306.

Greenspan, Patricia S. *Emotions and Reasons: An Inquiry into Emotional Justification*. New York: Routledge, 1988.

Hsu, Ruth Y. "A Conversation with Joy Kogawa." *Amerasia Journal* 22.1 (1996): 199–216.

Hutcheon, Linda. *The Canadian Postmodern: A Study of Contemporary English-Canadian Fiction*. Toronto: Oxford University Press, 1988.

———. *Narcissistic Narrative: The Metafictional Paradox*. London: Methuen, 1984.

Jones, Manina. "The Avenues of Speech and Silence: Telling Difference in Joy Kogawa's *Obasan*." *Theory between the Disciplines: Authority/Vision/Politics*. Ed. Martin Kreiswirth and Mark A. Cheetham. Ann Arbor: University of Michigan Press, 1990. 213–29.

Kanefsky, Rachelle. "Debunking a Postmodern Conception of History: A Defence of Humanist Values in the Novels of Joy Kogawa." *Canadian Literature* 148 (Spring 1996): 11–36.

Kogawa, Joy. "Is There a Just Cause?" *Canadian Forum* (March 1984): 20–24.

———. *Itsuka*. New York: Anchor Books, 1994.

———. *Obasan*. New York: Anchor Books, 1992.

Lehrer, Keith. *Self-Trust: A Study of Reason, Knowledge, and Autonomy.* Oxford: Clarendon Press, 1997.

Levy, Robert I. "Emotion, Knowing, and Culture." *Culture Theory: Essays on Mind, Self, and Emotion.* Ed. Richard A. Shweder and Robert A. LeVine. Cambridge: Cambridge University Press, 1984. 214–37.

Livingston, Paisley. *Literary Knowledge: Humanistic Inquiry and the Philosophy of Science.* Ithaca: Cornell University Press, 1988.

Loreto, Paola. "The Poetic Texture of Joy Kogawa's *Obasan.*" *Canadian StudiesReview/Revue d'Etudes Canadiennes* 8 (1995): 177–86.

Magnusson, A. Lynne. "Language and Longing in Joy Kogawa's *Obasan.*" *Canadian Literature* 116 (1988): 58–66.

Mohanty, Satya P. *Literary Theory and the Claims of History: Postmodernism, Objectivity, Multicultural Politics.* Ithaca: Cornell University Press, 1997.

Moody-Adams, Michelle M. *Fieldwork in Familiar Places: Morality, Culture, and Philosophy.* Cambridge, MA: Harvard University Press, 1997.

Moya, Paula M. L. "Postmodernism, 'Realism,' and the Politics of Identity: Cherríe Moraga and Chicana Feminism." *Feminist Genealogies, Colonial Legacies, Democratic Futures.* Ed. M. Jacqui Alexander and Chandra Talpade Mohanty. New York: Routledge, 1997. 125–50. [Reprinted as chapter 2 in this volume.]

Murdoch, Iris. "Imagination." *Metaphysics as a Guide to Morals.* London: Penguin Books, 1992. 308–48.

Omi, Michael, and Dana Takagi. "Thinking Theory in Asian American Studies." *Amerasia Journal* 21.1–2 (1995): xi–xv.

Palumbo-Liu, David. "The Ethnic as 'Post-': Reading *Reading the Literatures of Asian America.*" *American Literary History* 7.1 (1995): 161–68.

———. "Theory and the Subject of Asian American Studies." *Amerasia Journal* 21.1–2 (1995): 55–65.

Redekop, Magdalene. "The Literary Politics of the Victim." *Canadian Forum* (November 1989): 14–17.

San Juan, E., Jr. *Hegemony and Strategies of Transgression: Essays in Cultural Studies and Comparative Literature.* Albany: State University of New York Press, 1995.

———. *Racial Formations/Critical Transformations.* Atlantic Highlands, NJ: Humanities Press, 1992.

Scheman, Naomi. "Anger and the Politics of Naming." *Engenderings: Constructions of Knowledge, Authority and Privilege.* New York: Routledge, 1993. 22–35.

Scott, Joan. "'Experience.'" *Feminists Theorize the Political.* Ed. Judith Butler and Joan Scott. New York: Routledge, 1992. 22–40.

Simon, Caroline. *The Disciplined Heart: Love, Destiny, and Imagination.* Grand Rapids, MI: William B. Eerdmans, 1997.

Takagi, Dana. "Postmodernism from the Edge." *Privileging Positions: The Sites of Asian American Studies.* Ed. Gary Y. Okihiro et al. Pullman: Washington State University Press, 1995. 37–45.

Wong, Sau-ling C. "Denationalization Reconsidered: Asian American Cultural Criticism at a Theoretical Crossroads." *Amerasia Journal* 21.1–2 (1995): 1–21.

CHAPTER 6

Racial Authenticity and White Separatism

The Future of Racial Program Housing on College Campuses

Amie A. Macdonald

Although most institutions of higher education have made substantial progress in establishing racial democracy in regard to educational opportunity, it is arguably the case that this goal has not been fully achieved. Students of color on our predominantly white campuses are routinely the targets of racial abuse and discrimination in both social and educational settings.[1] Systematic social exclusion (e.g., from fraternities and sorori-

---

1. Numerous reports from students, faculty, and administrators confirm that racial tensions and racist violence continue to plague American colleges and universities. The *New York Times* reports that colleges have found race to be a frequent cause of friction between roommates and that racism is typically veiled. For example, parents call housing directors and say that the roommate "listens to rap and [our] daughter doesn't like that"(August 10, 1997, A53). At the University of California at Irvine a student faced trial on federal civil rights charges alleging that he sent an e-mail message to sixty Asian American students, threatening to kill them if they did not leave campus (*Los Angeles Times,* May 13, 1997); at Boston College hundreds of students "expressed pain and anger in the wake of racist incidents on campus, and what they felt was an inadequate response by the administration. . . . [A] Black student told of being shunned by a college staff member when she sought to ask a question"(*Boston Globe,* April 30, 1997); the *Christian Science Monitor* reported that students at the University of North Texas, the University of Mississippi, and the University of North Carolina at Chapel Hill are all addressing racist incidents with conversation and negotiation, in contrast to the demonstrations typical in the 1960s and 1970s (November 21, 1996, 1); at Arizona State University an English professor gave her students racist and misogynist jokes to show students how words create action (*Arizona Republic,* February 22, 1996, A12); the Oscar-nominated director Frances Reid made a film entitled *Skin Deep* about racism among college students at the University of Massachusetts at Amherst, UC Berkeley, and Texas A&M (*San Francisco Chronicle,* January 15, 1996); Central Missouri State University experienced a "near riot" in the wake of the 1992

ties), presumptive queries regarding hair, clothing, personal anatomy, food, religion, and so on, and insidious institutional tendencies to discourage students from pursuing math and science are common experiences for many Latino, Native American, Asian American, and African American students.[2] Far less frequently, but still with alarming regularity, students of color are the victims of racial violence, in the form of either anonymous harassment (e.g., phone and mail abuse) or outright physical or verbal assaults. While students of color on historically white campuses are often seen as fully responsible for racial segregation there, a more careful analysis allows us to see that the significantly larger white student population is systematically engaged in separating itself from the activities of students of color.[3] This news should come as no surprise to those who acknowledge that college and university campuses are not miraculously immune to the patterns of racial violence, injustice, and white normativity that are entrenched in contemporary U.S. society.

In this political climate, the idea of race-based student housing, a practice of intentional racial segregation that would be categorically rejected

---

verdict exonerating white police officers in their brutal assault on Rodney King, and a racial separatist aroused awareness of racism on campus (*Kansas City Star,* April 25, 1996, 6); at Indiana University the predominantly Jewish ZBT fraternity "chose to have pledges pretend they were all Black men and sent them out looking for pornography, items resembling drug paraphernalia, and articles that offended student and faculty minority and women's groups (*Indianapolis Star,* October 27, 1997, B1); at Purdue University a report on race relations indicated that students of color reported discrimination, but university officials denied any racial bias (*Indianapolis Star,* September 10, 1997, B1); hate crimes against Asian American students campaigning against California's anti-affirmative action initiative included harassing phone calls and property vandalism (*Newsday,* September 10, 1997); as part of President Bill Clinton's initiatives on race, U.S. Secretary of Energy Federico Pena conducted a forum at San Diego State University where he heard that "despite growing diversity at SDSU students of color find it hard to feel part of the mainstream" (*San Diego Union Tribune,* December 6, 1997, B1).

2. Obviously, these examples vary significantly depending on racial identity; Asians and Asian Americans, for example, are not typically discouraged from studying math and science. However, racist myths about the "natural disposition" of Asians and Asian Americans to math and science can be equally destructive to the process of intellectual development. The *Pittsburgh Post-Gazette* reported that "Black students in advanced classes are subconsciously perceived by white classmates as out of place" and that University of Chicago professor Jawanza Kunjufu claims that white people's "perceptions and understanding of Black culture are so monolithic that they can't believe a Black would be in the math club" (February 22, 1998, A1).

3. Consider that whereas black, Latino, and Asian students routinely live in overwhelmingly white dormitories, sit at dining tables with all whites, play on white-dominated sports teams, attend parties that are mostly white, and so on, rarely do white students venture into predominantly black, Latino, or Asian spaces (dances and lectures sponsored by student racial solidarity organizations, dining tables of mostly black or Latino students, etc.). For further documentation, see Beverly Daniel Tatum's "*Why Are All the Black Kids Sitting Together in the Cafeteria?*"

as racist in society at large, has become one of the more controversial strategies adopted by historically white institutions attempting to create racial democracy. African American students living in Brown University's African American–identified Harambee House claim not only that the living environment "feels more like home" but also that living with other students who have experienced the violence of racism helps them to keep their focus on academic work.[4] There is strong evidence that African American students earn higher grades when they are living in African American dormitories.[5]

Moreover, program houses offer students of color the opportunity to empower themselves through the development of political identities.[6] A Chickasaw Indian student who lived in Cornell University's Akwe:kon House claimed that the program house helped her to recognize and survive the hegemony of whiteness at Cornell.[7] Students of color at Brown, Cornell, the University of Pennsylvania, Duke, Stanford, and the University of California at Berkeley have testified similarly. Finally, apart from issues of identity and politics, many college officials recognize that the inherent stresses of academic life are more severe for students of color attending institutions that are overwhelmingly white.[8]

Predictably, demands for program housing have been contentious.[9] Cornell's program houses have been the subject of numerous legal actions

4. See *Washington Post*, March 6, 1994, A1.

5. See *Washington Post*, March 6, 1994, A1.

6. When she was a senior at Cornell University living in the (African American) Ujaama House, Dana Miller argued that the administration's attempt to dismantle the program houses was actually an effort "to socialize students into a [racially] homogeneous group based upon the generic [white] Cornellian"(*New York Times*, May 6, 1996, B5).

7. *New York Times*, April 20, 1994, B13.

8. Cornell has increased its student of color population from 19 to 25 percent of the entire student body. Duke, UC Berkeley, Brown, and Middlebury have also successfully attracted more talented students of color through a variety of campus and curricular initiatives that include race- and ethnic-based dormitories.

Pointing out that black and Latino students have higher college dropout rates than whites, the president of the United Negro College Fund, William H. Gray III, has urged colleges and universities to do everything in their power to help students of color survive racially hostile campus communities; in response to criticism of race-based student housing he suggested that instead of asking why are "Black students separating from whites at white college campuses, we should be asking what is wrong with white America and its institutions that Blacks don't feel welcome" (*Washington Post*, March 6, 1994, A1).

9. In April 1969 black students at Cornell University occupied the Student Union in protest of various racist policies of the university administration. The first race-based dormitory at Cornell, Ujaama House, opened in 1971 as a result of that protest. In the ensuing twenty-seven-year existence of program houses at Cornell, twenty-three annual reports have been inconclusive on the overall benefits to the university community of program houses.

at both the state and the federal level, all contending that the dormitories violate civil rights statutes. While recent state and federal decisions have confirmed their legality,[10] the criticisms that such housing is a capitulation to racial separatists, that it is a facile attempt to buy racial peace, that it further segregates already racially polarized campuses, and that it defies the finding of *Brown v. Board of Education,* ought to lead us to question seriously the wisdom of lending our support to program housing.

Nonetheless, in this chapter I am interested in exploring how we can support the creation of residential communities that move beyond the persistently intractable antinomy of diversity versus community. In fact, I am going to argue that we should preserve racial program housing on our campuses and that we should work to establish such housing at our home institutions if it is not already available.[11] We teachers have the opportunity to stand in solidarity with our students, who call for program houses on the basis of politicized racial identities. Furthermore, I will suggest that by forging connections between our efforts to establish intellectual and cultural diversity, we can improve the learning environment for students of color and begin to confront white student separatism.

While the political components of racial identity are fundamental to this discussion, equally central is the epistemic status of racial identity. Thus I will argue that a realist theory of identity allows us to grasp that racially defined communities provide not only for the affective needs of the so-called target-group of students but also for the epistemic needs of a racially diverse university community. Indeed, advocating the creation and support of racial program housing requires that we strain our understanding of both diversity and community in order to hold out the possibility of creating the unlikely humanist alliances we seek in a residential academic community.

THE LOGIC OF RACISM: SELF-SEGREGATION, EPISTEMOLOGY, AND POLITICAL POWER

The strength of the opposition to racial program housing is formidable, in both the public intellectual sphere and in specialized academic dis-

10. In September 1996 the U.S. Department of Education ruled that Cornell University is not in violation of federal civil rights statutes by maintaining dormitories that attract mostly students of color. In 1995 the New York State Department of Education dismissed a similar complaint (*New York Times,* September 24, 1996, B2).

11. At some colleges and universities (e.g., Hamilton College and Harvard University) administrators have quietly changed student housing policies to either phase out or entirely do away with existing racial program houses.

course. Shelby Steele argues strenuously against institutional capitulation to black students' demands for program houses. He claims that the politics of difference is troubling because it grounds assertions of worth and power on difference alone. Steele maintains that the decision of (mostly white) college presidents, deans, and faculty to support black dorms, black fraternities, black yearbooks, and black student unions is not going to address the fact that "black students have the highest dropout rate and the lowest grade point average of any group in American universities" (181). Essentially, for Steele, race is an "unprincipled source of power" (182), and "when Blackness (and femaleness) become power, then white maleness is also sanctioned as power" (183). Moreover, he claims that "when difference is celebrated . . . people must think in terms of difference, they must find meaning in difference, and this meaning comes from an endless process of contrasting one's group with other groups" (183).

However, taking seriously the view that self-segregation of students of color re-creates racist social structures does not automatically entail rejecting all forms of self-segregation. Actions that appear to acquiesce in the logic of racism may also produce progressive outcomes. Of special interest here are the epistemic consequences of sustaining a diversity of racial communities of meaning, which may very well mitigate the apparent complicity of racial program housing with certain aspects of racist logic.

Without reverting to theoretically and politically troublesome versions of standpoint epistemology (whether Marxist, feminist, or something else), I would like to suggest that we consider the epistemic functions, and value, of racial identity. It is possible to chart identifiable relationships between cultural identity—in this case racial identity—and the production of knowledge. I want to be extremely clear that I am *not* suggesting that there is a determinate or one-to-one correspondence between any given racial identity and a given set of epistemic claims. Instead, I am operating on the view that racial identities can be sources of both objective knowledge and mystification. However, I am approaching this discussion with the view that cultural identities provide us with what Satya P. Mohanty calls "fields of moral inquiry" (*Literary Theory* 240). That is, cultural identities enable us to have a certain experience of the world, which, though invariably resistant to essentialist definition, is undeniably distinct from many other culturally based experiences of the world. For example, Cornel West has written extensively about an identifiably black cultural value of returning service to one's home community. Acknowledging that such a racially defined community value should be engaged critically, West points out that black colleges were "hegemonic among the Black elite" and that the "ethic of service" was reinforced for young black students every Sunday "with the important business of chapel" where congregants were encouraged to "give service to the race" (hooks and West, "Breaking Bread" 101). I am not arguing that this cultural value on service is unique to black communities, or universal among black people;[12] however, viewing this ethic of service as embedded in black histories of struggle demonstrates its specificity as a racially defined value.[13] Culturally, black traditions of returning the benefits gained as individuals to one's home community generate an ethical framework that might organize the approach a young student takes to her education and thus the use to which she puts that education.[14]

Therefore, the view I am defending is that cultural identities serve an invaluable epistemic function in the process of developing ethical judgments. The maintenance of racially defined communities is central to the continued presence of culturally specific fields of moral inquiry. On this view, various strategies of self-segregation become defensible not merely in political terms but also in epistemic and ethical terms. An honest assessment of the political and epistemic consequences of self-segregation in recent U.S. history demonstrates that many of the advances gained by people of color were accomplished through self-segregation. For example, the U.S. civil rights movement offers compelling evidence of the protection of racial identity through self-segregation, and of the attendant epistemic function of racial identity. The civil rights movement was never universally black, but the center of organizing remained decisively situated within black communities and institutions (i.e., churches,

12. Diaspora Jewish communities tend to place an enormously high value on education. Now, while this certainly does not mean that all Jews value education, or that only Jewish cultures value education so highly, this prioritizing of education above many other important goals toward which a family or community might dedicate itself does in many ways establish a field of moral inquiry that is identifiably Jewish. This Jewish Diaspora identity may very well be an intangible theoretical construction. But it does, nonetheless, enable people within that cultural framework to have a given experience of the world. Importantly, that culturally Jewish experience of the world can serve as an ethical framework from which individuals approach the social world. So, when faced with the necessity to make decisions about the allocation of finite resources, a Diaspora Jewish identity may establish the ethical priority of responsiveness to educational needs over other pressing social programs.

13. For further discussion, see West, *Prophetic Fragments,* esp. 3–13; and "Martin Luther King, Jr."

14. Incidentally, such a culturally specific attitude toward education may necessarily compete with another culturally specific attitude, typically associated with the children of ruling-class Americans who view the purpose of education in terms of legitimizing one's proper place in corporate leadership, preserving family fortunes (often to the exclusion of community wealth), and generating individual economic growth under capitalism.

schools, civic groups, etc.). Pivotal organizations such as the Niagara Movement, the National Association for the Advancement of Colored People (NAACP), the Southern Christian Leadership Conference (SCLC), the Student Non-Violent Coordinating Committee (SNCC), the Black Panther Party, and the United Negro College Fund all developed through purposeful and deliberate strategies of black self-segregation. The success of even the NAACP and the Southern Poverty Law Center, whose early leadership was dominated by white progressive lawyers, ultimately relied on the organizational structure of black churches in the South.[15] Highly organized black churches provided the organizational structure necessary to the creation and existence of both integrationist (e.g., NAACP, Southern Poverty Law Center) and separatist (e.g., SNCC, SCLC, Black Panther Party) civil rights groups. This historical evidence thereby demonstrates that Steele's categorical rejection of all forms of self-segregation as entirely "unprincipled source[s] of power" belies the positive aspects of self-segregation, and ultimately of racial specificity. To claim that there is no inherent worth in racial identity, that calling attention to racial markers can only facilitate discrimination, is to claim that there is no positive relation between the meaning of an individual's life and the racial group or groups to which she belongs. Moreover, to take such a stance is to reject wholesale the view that social locations have epistemic consequences.

Underlying this view is the assumption that for people of color, racial specificity is the occasion only for victimization.[16] If this were the case, then of course it would be unconscionable to advocate race-based dormitories on our already racially polarized campuses. Despite this opposition, it is my view that racial identity, racial specificity, and determined racial self-segregation all have the potential to effect positive outcomes, both political and epistemic. It is arguably the case that black people working in the civil rights movement, black people who were fully enmeshed in black communities of meaning, were able to generate analyses of racial oppression and strategies for achieving racial justice (in part) because of their social location.

I want to be careful here to emphasize that I am not asserting that experience of an oppressed racial identity generates any sort of automatic

15. Aldon D. Morris's extensive study, *The Origin of the Civil Rights Movement*, demonstrates convincingly that black churches proved to be the center of civil rights organizing.

16. Consider the racist white pride and white power militia movements in the United States.

epistemic privilege or guaranteed objectivity. Following Satya Mohanty (*Literary Theory*), Paula M. L. Moya ("Postmodernism, 'Realism'"), Linda Alcoff, and many other feminist and progressive theorists, I am maintaining the view that "experience is epistemically indispensable but never epistemically sufficient"(Alcoff, "Elimination of Experience") for producing what Sandra Harding terms "strong objectivity." At the same time, the understanding of political power does seem to be at least partially contingent on the experience of political struggle against oppression. Perhaps most famously asserted by Marx, people who are at one and the same time both *oppressed by* and *central to* the continued existence of an economic, social, or political system have a unique opportunity to understand and analyze that system. There are epistemic consequences to the experience of social subordination, and although these consequences are not universally progressive, it is nonetheless evident that an accurate account of social power remains incomplete without the inclusion of analyses from oppressed people. So, in academic terms, a comprehensive understanding of one's discipline is imperiled by a failure to consider the views, criticisms, and contributions of those who have been oppressed.[17] Thus, on a residential university campus where students and teachers are engaged in learning not only about their chosen field of study but also about how to live ethically, epistemic diversity is imperative.

Far too often, though, these concrete details of racial identity and racist history lead white people to conclude that Latina existence, for example, is nothing more than a litany of material privation, emotional distress, and social inferiority. Such a conclusion is further justification for the view that self-segregation by people of color is just as immoral as Jim Crow–style white separatism. I would like to suggest, however, that from the immorality of racist segregation, one need not conclude that mandated universal racial integration in all aspects of public life is a necessary condition for achieving racial justice. In fact, one of the enduring hallmarks of white supremacy in the United States is the legal or practical proscription of religious services, linguistic codes, schools, political parties, and social organizations that exclude white people by signifying

17. I take as a foregone conclusion that the racist oppression of black, Latino, Native American, and Asian people by white people in the United States (and by the United States acting in other nations) is sufficiently evidenced by the histories of genocide, race hatred, and land theft. While the contemporary conditions of racist oppression in the United States certainly differ dramatically from the civil rights era, people of color in general make less money, have fewer and inferior educational and employment opportunities, are imprisoned at a higher rate, and suffer more from environmental and occupational illnesses such as asthma and lead poisoning than their white counterparts.

nonwhite racial identity. Laws that barred enslaved black people from worshiping together without white sanction, that mandated compulsory education for Native American children in white-run residential schools, and that forbid Latino children to speak Spanish in public schools are evidence of this recent history. This racist legacy is given contemporary expression in a variety of social and legal practices. In June 1998 Californians passed a voter initiative banning all bilingual education in public schools. In both urban and suburban communities in the Northeast, any group of young black or Latino men in shopping malls, on street corners, or in cars is routinely subject to police harassment and arrest for suspicion of so-called gang or drug activity. In the rural South, the late 1990s have seen a dramatic resurgence in the racist crime of burning black churches.

So we see that while white supremacist politics have consistently attempted to prevent the *self*-segregation of people of color, in many cases it is this very *self*-segregation that has been at the center of resistance to oppression, and thus the creation of racial justice and racial democracy. The analysis of racial oppression and the formation of strategies for achieving political justice are contingent on communities of meaning that are racially identified. Thus anyone concerned with the long-range goal of securing broad-based freedom and autonomy should be committed to the continued existence of racially defined communities on the grounds that different racial identities provide people with different experiences of the world. If we are to have a hope of effectively interpreting the world we need to draw on all epistemic resources. The preservation of racially defined communities of meaning secures the continued diversity of interpretations of the social world, thereby providing a richer array of knowledges from which to construct social, political, aesthetic, spiritual, and scientific accounts of our experience. Given that the most general function of the university is to provide an arena in which people may search for the truth, nowhere is this epistemic diversity more necessary than on our university campuses.

Of course, it is crucial here to distinguish between *self*-segregation and *imposed* segregation, since of course the *imposed* segregation of people of color by whites (in housing, education, transportation, marriage, employment, military service, etc.) is and has been a primary strategy of racist legal, economic, and political practice. But the deliberate and purposeful self-segregation of people of color proceeds from a different motivation and has produced different outcomes. This racist practice of denying people of color the legitimate right to worship, learn, and associate with one another and without white interference should, at the very least, urge us to take pause as we examine one of the most recent manifestations of such denial: the widespread attack on racial program dormitories.

It is from this perspective that I object to the view that program houses are inherently suspect because they mistakenly and perniciously tend to construct racial identity as a source of power. Racial particularity is a source of political and epistemic power—and not simplistically a marker of difference from white racial identity. Moreover, the webs of meaning within which racial particularity exists are not delimited by the experiences of racism.[18] As Lucius Outlaw argues, "For many persons—and I place myself in this group—the continued existence of race and ethnic based communities of meaning is highly desirable *even if, in the very next instant, racism and perverted, invidious ethnocentrism in every form and manifestation would disappear forever"* (*On Race and Philosophy* 157; original emphasis).

ESSENTIALISM AND RACIAL IDENTITY

What, then, are the strategies residential colleges can adopt in the effort to support the continued existence of race-based communities of meaning? Far too many of academia's attempts to serve the needs of students of color are preoccupied with simplistic naming of racial specificity, without sustained attention to the challenge of supporting nonwhite race-based communities. And in the face of this, one can understand a serious objection to program houses: it allows institutions to look as though they are serving the needs of students of color, when actually the program houses divert attention from the more complex task of creating racial democracy on campus. I am arguing instead that when institutions

18. A cursory examination of recent autobiographical, fictional, and theoretical work by U.S. people of color confirms that nonwhite racial identities are experienced as meaning giving, life sustaining, and identity forming—apart from racial and racist politics. Consider the expansive depiction of Southern black family life, gay politics, and racial identity depicted in Marlon Riggs's documentary film *Black is . . . Black ain't.* In her most recent film, *The Watermelon Woman,* Cheryl Dunye explores images of black lesbians in the history of American cinema. Cornel West's *Prophetic Fragments* offers an analysis of contemporary U.S. politics from a specifically black vernacular framework. The contours of mestiza identity and Mexican American generational knowledge are central subjects in Cherríe Moraga's *Loving in the War Years.* Similarly, Leslie Marmon Silko's *Ceremony* contests the Eurocentric rejection of Native American approaches to change and loss as obsolete, irrational, and barbaric. Finally, Amy Tan's *The Kitchen God's Wife* documents the rich structure of Chinese rites, specifically as they are practiced in the United States. In each of these films or texts the meanings of racial specificity extend far beyond oppositional relation to white supremacy and racism.

endorse the creation of program housing, they support the processes whereby students of color legitimately struggle together for complex understandings of racial identity. And while Steele is likely correct in claiming that when people of color in the United States consolidate their power on the basis of racial identity white men (and white women for that matter) *feel* incited to seize on their difference *as power,* this is not a legitimate reason to reject or even avoid any expressions of racial identity. For white people are so incited to maintain their superior position not by people of color but by the history of white supremacy that asserts the legitimacy of white racial dominance.

But this is not to say that there are no serious objections, both theoretical and political, to the articulation of racial specificity. If we acknowledge that program housing has even the potential to solidify invidious forms of racial authenticity, then to defend it effectively requires establishing, first, that it will more likely produce complex articulations of racial identity; and second, that its potential to increase racial tensions is significantly outweighed by what we stand to gain in our efforts to achieve racial democracy. Kwame Anthony Appiah has raised the possibility that all assertions of racial group identity, especially those appealed to in the creation of program houses, are untenable because the notion of race on which they rely is theoretically incoherent.[19] Pointing out that there is no empirical evidence[20] to justify the division of human beings into racial categories (*In My Father's House* 38), Appiah recommends that we give up on the practice of appealing to race as a classification.[21] But Appiah's convincing argument denying the materiality of race says little about the current condition of racist politics on college campuses. His claim that modern genetics shows no underlying racial essence is cold comfort to those who do experience hateful racist stereotyping.[22] Such a position on the overall meaninglessness of race requires

19. Appiah contends that although Du Bois aims to distance himself from the nineteenth-century biological definition of race, that biologism is implicit in the sociohistorical conception of race underlying Du Bois's effort to "defend his belief in the connection between race and morally relevant properties" (*In My Father's House* 45).

20. Appiah explains that the most recent research demonstrates that there is little more genetic variation between individuals from different racial groups than there is between different individuals from the same racial group.

21. The existence of biracial, multiracial, and multiethnic individuals does present another significant challenge to the very idea of racial classification. Again, however, the theoretical difficulties with the concept of race say nothing about the existence, or lack thereof, of racism.

22. Appiah goes on to say that in the absence of such a racial essence "being told that someone is of African origin gives you little basis for supposing anything much about them" (*In My Father's House* 39).

a willful ignorance of both the history of racial significance in the United States and the contemporary conditions of U.S. people of color in comparison to U.S. whites.[23] As Paula Moya has argued, "The empirical fact that there is no 'Mexican' race, that 'Mexican' denotes a nationality and not a race, and that some Mexicans are phenotypically 'white' seems to have little bearing on the ethnic/racial classification of Mexican-origin people in the U.S." ("Postmodernism, 'Realism,'" 147). So Appiah's preoccupation with establishing the lack of empirical data to explain the existence of racial identity has little bearing on the very real social and epistemic consequences of racial identity.

Appiah's exposure of the conceptual emptiness of race, however, leads to a serious political objection to the articulation of racial identity; namely, that the attempt to articulate racial identity, in the case of Latinos for example, is both theoretically wrong and politically dangerous because doing so reifies a nonexistent essence, a "Latinoness," which is then used perniciously both by non-Latinos to stereotype Latino individuals (as in "All Latinos are illegal immigrants") and by Latinos themselves who appeal to the nonexistent racial essence in order to exclude from the community anyone they believe is not Latino enough (as in "Light-skinned Latinos are not really Latino"). This tendency to enforce invidious forms of racial authenticity is the basis of what I take to be the most serious objection to racial program houses.

On this view, program houses are objectionable because they rely conceptually on a nonexistent racial essence. On predominantly white campuses this unreal essence becomes the focal point for white supremacist attacks—both subtle and explicit. Moreover, within student of color com-

---

23. Several randomly selected statistics are relevant here:
· 33.1% of all African Americans, 30.6% of Latinos, and 18.8% of other nonwhites live in poverty, as compared to 9.9% of white Americans (Taeber 145).
· While 10.3% of Hispanic families were unemployed in 1996, 19.0% were underemployed (Bernstein 1–4).
· Among blacks aged 16 to 25, about 35% were underemployed in 1996 (Bernstein 1–4).
· Gaps in the academic performance of black and white students appear as early as age 9 and persist through age 17 (National Center for Educational Statistics 3).
· Hispanic children start elementary school with less preschool experience than white children, and this gap has widened over time (National Center for Educational Statistics 2).
· A June 1998 report from the National Cancer Institute found that two-thirds of HIV-infected young people in America are black or Latino, when blacks and Latinos make up only 27% of the population in these age groups (*New York Times,* June 17, 1998, A22).

munities, the apparent obligation to self-segregate in program houses encourages students of color to enforce on one another authentic adherence to the contours of this unreal, essentialist racial identity. In this sense, the call for program houses is racist.

One might answer this objection by claiming that program houses rely on an ethically permissible, though unreal, essentialism of defense.[24] I would like to suggest, however, that to defend program houses by employing even *strategic* essentialism requires us to reassert untenable notions of racial authenticity. Moreover, as Michael R. Hames-García argues, in this volume, the reliance on strategic essentialism requires us ultimately to concede that there is no "strong epistemological justification" for the assertion of racial group identity. Instead, the effective defense of program housing rests on a rejection of the view that it is impossible to instantiate racial identity without some version of essentialism. Critics argue that without any real basis for constituting racial identity, imagined communities of distinct races are allegedly based on naturalized fictions of homogeneous racial groups.[25] And thus program houses are criticized for their role in reinstantiating the mythic categorizations of racial identity and thereby enforcing increasingly invidious versions of racial authenticity.

POLITICAL IDENTITIES

Certainly, program housing cannot be defended unless there is some coherent way to conceive of racial groups. Thus I would like to propose that mythologizing fictions of universal racial identity are not the only tenable concepts on which to ground assertions of group identity. Many feminists have successfully outlined the contours of identity for "Third World women" without appealing to essentialist or ethnocentric frameworks. Chandra Talpade Mohanty explains that the category "Third World women," as a political definition, is based not on shared and falsely homogenized categories of race or gender but instead on a common context of struggle against sexist, racist, and imperialist structures ("Cartographies" 7). Melanie Kaye/Kantrowitz's volume, *The Is-*

24. Omi and Winant make this very argument.

25. As Appiah has claimed, "Group identity seems to work only—or, at least, to work best—when it is seen as natural, as 'real'" (*In My Father's House* 175). Importantly, though, for Appiah, this so-called natural organization of racial categories is based on unreal idealized notions of racial identity, leading him to conclude therefore that one "cannot build [racial] alliances without mystifications and mythologies" (175).

sue Is Power, illustrates the heterogeneity of Jewish identities by exploring secular, lesbian, working-class, and Sephardic Jewish realities. In so doing she undermines the mistaken essentialist versions of Jewish authenticity, as she offers a progressive structure for conceiving of Jews as a social group.[26] Similarly, Outlaw argues that we can interpret Du Bois's definition of race expressly as inessentialist, given that Du Bois understood race as a *"cluster* concept in which the elements are connected in an indefinitely long *dis*junctive definition" (155; original emphasis). In his most recent book, *Blackness Visible*, Charles Mills outlines a far more specific "metaphysics of race" (41) according to which the elements of racial identity[27] may conflict with one another in the overall determination of individual racial categorization. For example, someone who subjectively identifies as Latino may have the bodily appearance of a white person.

Following the lead of these philosophers, we can see how the articulation of racial identity can be based on a disjunctively joined series that might include shared histories, geographic origins, political identities, struggles for racial and economic justice, cultural manifestations, and religious practices. If we adopt Mills's constructivist view of racial identity, asserting that racial categories do have a social objectivity (*Blackness Visible* 48), we are not put off by a racial classification system that can categorize people lighter skinned than many whites as black and vice versa. Mills successfully demonstrates that coherent racial group identity does not depend, logically or practically, on all individuals of a given group sharing at least one essential characteristic. Exploding even the most foundational beliefs about racial identity, Mills shows that in theory and practice Americans have historically operated with inessentialist conceptions of racial identity. Dominant white normativity unproblematically classifies brown-skinned Jews as white, light-skinned Puerto Ricans as "Hispanic," and relatively darker-skinned foreign nationals or immigrants (Greeks, Italians, Spaniards, Indians, etc.) as white/Caucasian. Ironically, then, the American racial group "white" is one of the best examples of inessentialist conceptions of racial iden-

26. In scholarly, mainstream, religious, and secular discourse the categorization of the Jewish people as a religious group, a racial group, an ethnic group, a nationality, or a culture remains a contested issue. Without attempting to take up this issue in all of its complexity, it is worth recognizing that many Jews do consider themselves to be members of the Jewish "race." Melanie Kaye/Kantrowitz, for example, has written extensively on the structure of anti-Semitism as a variety of "race-hatred"(149).

27. Mills's criteria for racial identity include bodily appearance, ancestry, self-awareness of ancestry, public awareness of ancestry, culture, experience, and subjective identification.

tity, composed as it is of diverse nationalities, ethnicities, races, religions, and skin colors.[28]

However, it is the effortful practice of resisting the tendency to revert to essentialist conceptions of racial group membership that opens the conceptual space for articulating the actual heterogeneous racial identities in existence. I would like to emphasize here that on this understanding of racial identity, the meaning of racial specificity extends far beyond simple opposition to whiteness and even complex political struggles against racism and imperialism to include constitutive meanings, such as aesthetic traditions, spiritual practices, and philosophical webs of belief. Program houses that provide a safe social and intellectual space for students of color and white students to address themselves to these questions thereby foster the development of inessentialist racial identities. Students of color are empowered by such an opportunity because it gives them increased authority over decisions that affect their lives and life chances. The same holds true for white students, whose racial separatism is authentically challenged by the expression of inessentialist versions of racial identity. And it is this process of maintaining dynamic tension between racial diversity and human community that stands to advance us toward racial democracy.

It seems evident, therefore, that while the process of articulating racial identities, particularly in a context of white supremacy, has tended toward the impulse to falsely homogenize identity, it is both theoretically and practically possible to conceive of racial groups that are at one and the same time ultimately diverse.[29] Clearly, however, *intentional* disruption of the standard discourse on racial difference and identity is crucial if we are to be successful in the effort to support these political, inessentialist, realist versions of racial identity. Program housing offers us a remarkable opportunity to engage the unique structure of academic and social life we find on our residential campuses, and specifically, to intentionally interrupt the perpetuation of essentialist racial identities.

28. In fact, one could argue that the U.S. racial category "white" is also a political identity, which masks itself as natural and performs a central role in the maintenance of white hegemony.

29. In his *Literary Theory and the Claims of History* Satya Mohanty argues convincingly to show that the opposition between conceiving of racial identity according to essentialist definitions (that racial group membership is based on one or more characteristics—such as skin color—allegedly shared by all members of a racial group) or postmodern definitions (that racial groups cannot be defined as groups since every individual is so radically unique) is actually an antinomy. Alternatively, Mohanty asserts that racial groups can be defined based on a realist theory of identity, which acknowledges that our personal experiences as members of socially defined races yield knowledge that is theoretically mediated.

MULTICULTURALISM: CURRICULAR
REFORM AND RACIAL DEMOCRACY

In only the last twenty years the standard curricular offerings in American colleges and universities have changed dramatically. Not only have the traditional disciplines undergone significant modifications to represent more accurately the global creation of intellectual history, but the categories of inquiry themselves have also changed with the introduction of a variety of new disciplines. One of the primary aims of the insurgent disciplines—and here I mean women's studies, Africana studies, Latino studies, Asian studies, Native American studies, queer studies—has been to demonstrate the diversity of experience within various social groups, for example, differences among people who nonetheless identify themselves as members of the following groups: women, people of African descent, Latinos/as, Asians and Asian Americans, Native Americans, and gay/lesbian/bisexual/transgendered people. While these articulations of difference may very well challenge our received essentialist notions of racial/ethnic/gender identity, they do not preclude the assertion of realist political identities that are predicated on an understanding of difference within coherent groups. Let me suggest, then, that by forging connections between the efforts to diversify curricula and the attempt to create racial democracy, we can create the space for students of color to articulate racial identity that is not racist, ethnocentric, or essentialist.

Critics of curricular reform often argue that multiculturalism threatens the real work of academic inquiry, by substituting vacuous and banal celebrations of oppression for old-style intellectual rigor. For example, Steele claims that "when [racial or ethnic] difference is celebrated . . . people must . . . find meaning in difference, and this meaning comes from an endless process of contrasting one's group with other groups" (183). But these "taste of the world" and "oppression olympics" views of multicultural education are distortions. One of the chief goals of the insurgent disciplines is to undertake analysis of the diversity of individual experiences in marginalized communities. These projects are necessarily complex, given that they move beyond simple comparison and contend with the positive and political meanings of racial specificity.

For instance, even introductory courses in Latino history delineate the divergent and often contradictory experiences of Latinos with respect to economic development, political action, national origin, and racial identification. Teachers and students in these courses must contend with dismantling not only the most obviously mistaken racist assertions of essentialist nonwhite racial identity, for example, of black intellectual inferiority, Latino hypersexuality, Arab brutality, or Asian rejection of human individuality. These essentialist versions of racial identity are obviously factually erroneous, hateful, and antithetical to the development of legitimate political democracy. But the intellectual and political work of contesting essentialist versions of racial identity extends well beyond the criticism of racist essentialism. Strategically essentialist assertions of racial identity, many of which have their origin in the struggle against white supremacy, are also subject to critical analysis in the insurgent disciplines. Declarations of Asians' superhuman intelligence, black women's maternal love, and Latinos' emotional intensity are extremely complex. These views appear to valorize desirable human qualities that racist ideology defines as uncharacteristically Asian, black, or Latino. However, contemporary scholars from the insurgent disciplines have demonstrated the logic by which these essentialist claims actually advance covert racist agendas. For example, Elaine Kim, in "Home Is Where the Han Is," explains how the "model-minority" stereotype of Asian Americans has fueled racial tensions between African Americans and Asian Americans. In her book *Yearning*, bell hooks exposes how valorization of black women's capacity for maternal love, as an attempt to redress slave-era denial of black women's rights to mother their children, is distorted by racist sexist ideology into the view that black women "matriarchs" are responsible for unemployment among black men, gang violence among black boys, and teen pregnancy among black girls. Similarly, María Lugones, in "Hablando Cara a Cara," discusses the racist uses of viewing Latinos as stereotypically intense; the "Latin Lover" and the "Fiery Latina" are familiar and recurrent tropes in racist nationalist discourse.

From these examples and many others we can see that directing our attention to the project of creating racial program housing on predominantly white campuses is logically of a piece with the effort to diversify intellectual inquiry. While both program houses and insurgent intellectual work serve a variety of functions, the central purpose of racial program housing and insurgent academic disciplines is the same: to provide a legitimate place in academic communities for sustained critical inquiry into the histories, meanings, and expressions of racial difference and identity. In this shared goal is the strong epistemological justification for preserving racially defined communities of meaning. Additional benefits of racial program houses include higher grade point averages for students of color and the very real testimony from students of color that the houses are a significant aid in their efforts to meet social, emotional, and academic challenges in the predominantly white communities of colleges and universities. Furthermore, most program houses are not uniformly occupied by students from the designated racial group, and thus these residences provide the opportunity for racially and ethnically diverse groups of students to live and work together. Indeed, the successful proposal for the Cornell University Latino Living Center included extensive analysis and documentation of the benefits such a program house provides to the entire campus community, which is of course predominantly white. Finally, I think it is important to recognize that dormitories are only one of many student spaces on campus and that when given the option many students of color choose to live in program houses for only a fraction of their undergraduate residency, if they choose to live there at all.[30]

Finally, no matter how radically the curriculum changes in the academy, the basic mission of the university to pursue truth and produce knowledge about the social, political, scientific, and aesthetic worlds we encounter as humans remains the same. Satya Mohanty has asserted that once we recognize the "complexity of human nature and the deeply theoretical nature of moral and cultural practice, the realist will favor cultural diversity as the *best social condition* in which objective knowledge about human flourishing might be sought" (243; original emphasis). That is, once we acknowledge that pure objective knowledge about anything is neither possible nor desirable, we conclude that our ability to achieve the sort of "strong objectivity" (Harding) or "theory-mediated objectivity" (S. Mohanty) we can strive for will be considerably enhanced by contending as thinkers with a diversity of socially embedded knowledge claims. The slow, but undeniable, reform of university curricula to reflect this diversity of socially constructed knowledge is evidence that the academy acknowledges the intellectual and epistemic value of the insurgent disciplines. By forging the connections between the academic disciplines that take as their subject of study the histories, languages, literatures, and theories by and about people of color and the activities of the program houses, we create an institutional commitment to the possibility of heterogeneous race-based communities of meaning. In so doing, we contribute to the possibility of reconstructing these historically mar-

---

30. I wish to emphasize, though, that by instituting program houses, the progress white institutions stand to gain in terms of racial integration and racial democracy is far more expansive than increasing grade point averages and making students of color more comfortable.

ginalized categories of identity, we challenge white student separatism, and we promote racial democracy by supporting politically defined racial communities.

WORKS CITED

Alarcón, Norma. "The Theoretical Subject(s) of *This Bridge Called My Back* and Anglo-American Feminism." *Making Face, Making Soul/Haciendo Caras.* Ed. Gloria Anzaldúa. San Francisco: Aunt Lute Books, 1990. 356–70.

Alcoff, Linda Martín. "The Elimination of Experience in Feminist Theory." Paper presented at Women's Studies Symposium, Cornell University, February 23, 1995.

Anthony, Earl. *Picking Up the Guns: The Story of the Black Panthers.* New York: Dial Press, 1970.

Appiah, Kwame Anthony. *In My Father's House: Africa in the Philosophy of Culture.* New York: Oxford University Press, 1992.

———. "The Uncompleted Argument: Du Bois and the Illusion of Race." *Critical Inquiry* 12 (Autumn 1985): 21–27.

Bell, Derrick. "The Case for a Separate Black School System." *Black Education: A Quest for Equity and Excellence.* Ed. W. D. Smith and E. W. Chunn. New Brunswick, NJ: Transaction, 1989. 136–46.

Bernstein, Jared. "The Challenge of Moving from Welfare to Work: Depressed Labor Market Awaits Those Leaving the Rolls." Washington, D.C.: Economic Policy Institute, 1997. 1–4.

Boxill, Bernard R. "Separation or Assimilation?" *Campus Wars.* Ed. John Arthur and Amy Shapiro. Boulder, CO: Westview Press, 1995. 235–48.

Du Bois, W. E. B. "The Conservation of Races." *African-American Social and Political Thought.* Ed. Howard Brotz. New Brunswick, NJ: Transaction, 1992. 483–92.

———. "Races." *The Crisis: A Record of the Darker Races* 2.4 (August 1911): 157–59.

Dunye, Cheryl. *The Watermelon Woman* [film]. New York: First Run Features, 1996.

Franklin, John Hope, and Alfred A. Moss, Jr. *From Slavery to Freedom: A History of African-Americans.* 7th ed. New York: Knopf, 1994.

Harding, Sandra. "Rethinking Standpoint Epistemology: What Is Strong Objectivity?" *Feminist Epistemologies.* Ed. Linda Alcoff and Elizabeth Potter. New York: Routledge, 1993. 49–82.

hooks, bell. *Yearning: Race, Gender, and Cultural Politics.* Boston: South End Press, 1990.

hooks, bell, and Cornel West. "Breaking Bread." *Free Spirits: Feminist Philosophers on Culture.* Ed. Kate Mehuron and Gary Percesepe. Englewood Cliffs, NJ: Prentice-Hall, 1995. 96–105.

Kaye/Kantrowitz, Melanie. *The Issue Is Power: Essays on Women, Jews, Violence, and Resistance.* San Francisco: Aunt Lute Books, 1992.

Kim, Elaine. "Home Is Where the Han Is." *Free Spirits: Feminist Philosophers* on Culture. Ed. Kate Mehuron and Gary Percesepe. Englewood Cliffs, NJ: Prentice-Hall, 1995. 160–73.

Lowe, Lisa. "Heterogeneity, Hybridity, Multiplicity: Marking Asian American Differences." Diaspora l.l (Spring 1996): 24–44.

Lugones, María C. "Hablando Cara a Cara/Speaking Face to Face: An Exploration of Ethnocentric Racism." Making Face, Making Soul: Haciendo Caras. Ed. Gloria Anzaldúa. San Francisco: Aunt Lute Books, 1990. 46–54.

Mills, Charles W. Blackness Visible: Essays on Philosophy and Race. Ithaca: Cornell University Press, 1998.

——. The Racial Contract. Ithaca: Cornell University Press, 1997.

Mohanty, Chandra Talpade. "Cartographies of Struggle: Third World Women and the Politics of Feminism." Third World Women and the Politics of Feminism. Ed. Chandra Talpade Mohanty, Ann Russo, and Lourdes Torres. Bloomington: Indiana University Press, 1991. 1–47.

Mohanty, Satya P. Literary Theory and the Claims of History: Postmodernism, Objectivity, Multicultural Politics. Ithaca: Cornell University Press, 1997.

Moraga, Cherríe. Loving in the War Years: Lo que nunca pasó por sus labios. Boston: South End Press, 1983.

Morris, Aldon D. The Origins of the Civil Rights Movement: Black Communities Organizing for Change. New York: Free Press, 1984.

Moya, Paula M. L. "Postmodernism, 'Realism,' and the Politics of Identity: Cherríe Moraga and Chicana Feminism." Feminist Genealogies, Colonial Legacies, Democratic Futures. Ed. M. Jacqui Alexander and Chandra Talpade Mohanty. New York: Routledge, 1997. 125–50. [Reprinted as chapter 2 in this volume.]

Mullin, Amy. "Selves, Diverse and Divided: Can Feminists Have Diversity without Multiplicity?" Hypatia 10.4 (Fall 1995): 1–31.

Narayan, Uma. "The Project of Feminist Epistemology: Perspectives from a Nonwestern Feminist." Gender/Body/Language. Ed. Susan Bordo and Alison Jaggar. New Brunswick, NJ: Rutgers University Press, 1989. 256–69.

National Center for Educational Statistics. "The Educational Progress of Black Students." Washington, D.C.: National Center for Educational Statistics, 1995.

——. "The Educational Progress of Hispanic Students." Washington, D.C.: National Center for Educational Statistics, 1995.

Omi, Michael, and Howard Winant. Racial Formation in the United States: From the 1960s to the 1990s. 2d ed. New York: Routledge, 1994.

Outlaw, Lucius T. On Race and Philosophy. New York: Routledge, 1996.

——. "On W. E. B. Du Bois's 'The Conservation of Races.'" Lecture delivered at Hamilton College, November 1994.

Riggs, Marlon. Black is . . . Black ain't [film]. San Francisco: California Newsreel, 1995.

Silko, Leslie Marmon. Ceremony. New York: Viking Press, 1977.

Spivak, Gayatri Chakravorty. In Other Worlds: Essays in Cultural Politics. New York: Methuen, 1987.

Steele, Shelby. "The Recoloring of Campus Life." Campus Wars. Ed. John Arthur and Amy Shapiro. Boulder, CO: Westview Press, 1995. 176–87.

Taeber, Cynthia, ed. *The Statistical Handbook on Women in America.* 2d ed. Phoenix, AZ: Oryx Press, 1996.

Tan, Amy. *The Kitchen God's Wife.* New York: Putnam, 1991.

Tatum, Beverly Daniel. *"Why Are All the Black Kids Sitting Together in the Cafeteria?" and Other Conversations about Race.* New York: BasicBooks, 1997.

West, Cornel. *Prophetic Fragments.* Trenton, NJ: Africa World Press, 1988.

———. *Race Matters.* New York: Vintage Books, 1994.

REALIST CONCEPTIONS

OF AGENCY, EXPERIENCE,

AND IDENTITY

Who Says Who Says?

*The Epistemological Grounds for
Agency in Liberatory Political Projects*

Brent R. Henze

AGENCY IN EPISTEMIC PRIVILEGE

In this chapter I make an argument about some features of an effective liberatory project; largely, the claims I make are central principles for many in progressive politics but have not always been explicitly and systematically theorized. Many activists involved in liberatory political movements, many organizers of and participants in rallies and marches, many people who identify themselves as members of disenfranchised cultural and social groups, and a few academics take the positions developed below largely for granted, as the basis for the transformative political work they engage in.

The chief claim that I argue for below is this: the most potentially transformative politics of liberation must be in the hands of the people being liberated.[1] For people actively involved in battling the systematic oppressions confronting the communities in which they themselves claim membership, this is a widely held position. For practical reasons, the oppressed are the key agents in combating their own oppression because they are the people whose conditions necessitate this resistance. Others

---

1. Note that I am suggesting neither that political advocacy by others is ineffective nor that it is never called for. Clearly, when the conditions of someone's oppression make resistance impossible—for instance, in cases of physical imprisonment, or less material but equally constraining forms of bondage—outside action may be necessary. But in this chapter I am concerned with the effects of outside participation in the liberatory political projects of groups relatively able and willing to advocate for themselves.

for humanitarian reasons may "take up the cause," but those suffering from the oppression, as Cherríe Moraga writes, "have had it breathing down [their] necks" (62).[2]

In addition to the activists' conviction that the oppressed must theorize and enact their own liberatory political projects for practical reasons, some activists and theorists have supported versions of this claim on epistemological grounds; it is in this debate that I locate my arguments. In particular, while most would agree that for practical reasons (mentioned above) the oppressed who most need liberation will most assiduously fight for it, a curious silence surrounds the question of agency when it is considered in epistemological terms. Amid all the discussion of who possesses, or "should be given," epistemic privilege, the question of an individual's agency drops out of the debate. It is seen as a relatively autonomous question, one that seems to be tabled from the "epistemological" debate lest it confuse the question of epistemic privilege. My goal here is to reintroduce "agency" into the debate on epistemic privilege, as an issue that has the potential to shape rather than interfere with our understanding of epistemic privilege. In the arguments I offer below, individual agency—a person's socially acknowledged right to interpret and speak for herself—will serve as the grounds for the collective agency of identity groups; by virtue of individuals' processes of understanding their relationships to their social milieus, the groups they identify with become better able to represent their members in political struggles against oppression.

When the question of agency is discussed as a practical issue, sometimes locating agency in the oppressed carries with it the following two conclusions: first, that "others" can play no important role in these political projects; and second, that the reason is that the needs and experiences of the oppressed cannot be understood by those who do not share these experiences. These claims often lead to isolationist or essentialist projects, the main tenets of which I will argue against here. Following the lead of many theorists and activists—Paula M. L. Moya, Satya P. Mohanty, Cherríe Moraga, Gloria Anzaldúa, and others—I draw on an understanding of "theory-mediated" identity grounded in the experiences and the "flesh" of the oppressed, but not thereby opaque to others willing to work toward an understanding of it through a process of "empathy."

---

2. Except where otherwise noted, citations of Moraga are from *This Bridge Called My Back*. References to other writers in *Bridge* are so noted in the text.

In the first section I look at the approaches to agency and epistemic privilege taken by a range of epistemological projects: essentialism, "realist" theories of cultural identity, and, finally, Moraga's "theory in the flesh" (and, more broadly, the political project of Moraga and Anzaldúa's 1981 anthology, *This Bridge Called My Back*). The second section discusses this last project—*Bridge* and "theory in the flesh" together—as well as feminist consciousness-raising groups (discussed by Naomi Scheman in "Anger and the Politics of Naming") as projects that usefully theorize and demonstrate effective strategies for generating political, social, and individual change. I argue here that these projects succeed, among other reasons, because of the stance they take on the issue of agency.

AGENCY AND EPISTEMIC PRIVILEGE IN ESSENTIALISM, THE REALIST THEORY OF CULTURAL IDENTITY, AND "THEORY IN THE FLESH"

ESSENTIALISM

One approach to the question of epistemic privilege and agency, in which agency is granted to the possessors of epistemic privilege, is represented by a set of theories of "cultural identity" (or identity politics). Satya Mohanty, in "The Epistemic Status of Cultural Identity," outlines the debate over cultural identity, then proposes a stance that I will address later, a "realist" theory of cultural identity. Mohanty situates the standard debate over identity in terms of the opposition of "postmodernism" and "essentialism," arguing that the postmodernist argument against experience as a source of objective knowledge "can be best appreciated as part of a more general suspicion toward foundationalism in contemporary thought" (42–43).[3] The more practicable (and hence, for my purposes here, more relevant) essentialist stance assumes, at least, that one's experience can have cognitive value.

The essentialist view of identity is grounded in a fixed set of shared characteristics or experiences of members of an identity group. This view of group identity exists more often as an underlying principle in a larger interpretive framework, or as a premise adopted for pragmatic (political or cultural) purposes. Thus self-help texts such as John Gray's *Men Are from Mars, Women Are from Venus* propound essentialist views of

---

3. Pursuing the postmodernist stance further is beyond the range of this chapter; for relevant arguments, see Mohanty, esp. 43–45.

gender, emphasizing the differences between men and women to the relative exclusion of internal distinctions within either category. Similarly, many "identity group" political movements depend on the essential identity of group members; differences among members, whether or not they are acknowledged, are seen as less important than the fundamental identity on which the group is built.

In essentialist models of group identity, oppressed people are granted a form of agency to interpret their experiences, since their experiences or characteristics as individual agents undergird their membership in the group; but this agency is mitigated by the effects of the claim that, in the relevant ways, the members of the group are "the same" (or that they all possess some "essence" that characterizes the group). This prescribed sameness of experience means that an individual can interpret her experience, and can know something from it, but it also means that other members of the group have the same authority to interpret her experience. In addition, the experiences as well as the interpretations of her experience represent all the others in the group. Sharing an "identity" translates into sharing the interpretive framework that can be brought to bear on one's experience.[4] One's "individual" understanding of her experience is subject to the group's understanding, and only the common experiences of group members (and the interpretive framework arising out of these experiences) are privileged.

As I discuss in greater detail below, this limitation seriously compromises the capacity of the essentialist project to develop an effective interpretive framework; limited are both the range of available experiences contributing to this development and the possibility of dialectical change arising from competing individual and collective interpretations of experience.

MOHANTY'S "REALIST" THEORY OF CULTURAL IDENTITY

Satya Mohanty's "realist" view of identity resolves some of the limitations of essentialism by reconceiving "experience" as a source of knowledge. His objective is to argue that "experience, properly interpreted, can yield reliable and genuine knowledge, just as it can point up instances and sources of real mystification" (44). In his theory, experiences do not ground

---

4. This "interpretive framework" is generally a rather simple and unproblematic affair, consisting of the basic assumptions and organizing principles held to be self-evident by the group members.

knowledge "because of their self-evident authenticity but rather [they] provide some of the raw material with which we construct identities" (45).

Though Mohanty begins his article by marking a "practical problem" tied to identity—"Who can be trusted to represent the real interests of the group without fear of betrayal or misrepresentation?" (41)—the question of agency is not his primary concern, and he offers few remarks on the subject. Mohanty dedicates a section of his article to a discussion of Scheman's "anti-individualist" analysis of a feminist consciousness-raising group, and from this discussion we can draw some conclusions about Mohanty's stance on the question of agency. Working from Scheman's discussion of the formation of emotions, Mohanty asserts that an emotion "becomes what it is through the mediation of the social and emotional environment" of the consciousness-raising group: "In many important instances . . . alternative accounts and notions help organize inchoate or confused feelings to produce an emotion that is experienced more directly and fully. It follows then that this new emotion, say anger, and the ways it is experienced, is not a purely personal or individual matter. A necessary part of its form and structure is determined by the non-individual, social meanings that the theories and accounts supply" (45–46). According to this view, a person's interpretation of her experience—in this example, her experience of her feelings—is necessarily social; it draws on "accounts and notions" provided by one's social environment. In this respect, there is an important role for others to play: as with the consciousness-raising groups, others provide necessary ways of understanding experiences.

This mediation on the part of others is different in important ways from the roles played by others in other theories, such as essentialist identity politics. Others, here, play a role in one's process of interpreting one's own experience, but they do not have the ability to preempt one's own interpretation. At most, others can exert a great deal of persuasive pressure (including, at its most extreme, political, economic, and even physical forms of coercion) to convince a person to act in accordance with a certain view of the world. But even while subject to this type of pressure, an individual's understanding of her life is derived from the interpretive framework through which she sees her situation and experiences, more or less affected by the external persuasive forces but not altogether determined by them. So although "one's own interpretation" is socially and theoretically (in)formed—in some cases massively so— the actual interpretive act remains in the hands of the person whose experiences are being interpreted. Others play an essential and inevitable collaborative role in producing the interpretive framework through which one views one's life.

This articulation of a "collaborative" role for others in one's interpretive project is reinforced and extended in Mohanty's analysis of Toni Morrison's *Beloved*. Mohanty describes the creation of a "community of the oppressed," which is formed by a process of "rememory"— remembering the past and "recapitulating its events" (or reinterpreting them) (56). Mohanty points to the necessity of a supportive community for this painful process of "rememory": "Sethe's capacity to know herself is tied up with her capacity to feel with others. . . . Trusting enables remembering because it organizes and interprets crucial new information about one's life: it might be safe, now, to acknowledge one's feelings; one might be justified in counting on the relative safety of this environment. This safe environment is based on cooperation, the most basic form of social activity" (57). As with the Scheman example, others in the process of forming a community provide needed support for an individual's interpretive process; the authority to interpret experience remains with the individual. By the same token, in Mohanty's discussion of the "narrative braiding of perspectives" among Sethe, Denver, and Beloved, we see the sort of process of self-discovery Paul D must undergo in order to properly interpret Sethe's decisions, which he had earlier "too abstractly" condemned as inhuman—"You got two feet, Sethe, not four" (Morrison, cited in Mohanty 56). The epistemological claim is not that Paul, who comes to the house on Bluestone Road as a relative outsider to this community of women, is unable to participate in the "intersubjective knowing" of these women. Rather, he cannot apply a general law of humanity without first entering into this intersubjective knowing. It is through the work of constructing community—"a complex and ongoing process that involves both emotional and cognitive effort" (Mohanty 68) on Paul's part as well as Sethe's—that Paul becomes able to participate in the cognitive work of liberation taking place among them.

MOYA'S "REALIST ACCOUNT OF CHICANA IDENTITY" AND MORAGA'S "THEORY IN THE FLESH"

In her article "Postmodernism, 'Realism,' and the Politics of Identity," Paula Moya draws on the work of Satya Mohanty to articulate a "realist" account of Chicana identity in conjunction with Cherríe Moraga's "theory in the flesh," which, Moya demonstrates, "gestures toward a realist theory of identity" (128).

Moya introduces Moraga as a Chicana feminist "at the forefront of the Chicana feminist response to both Chicano cultural nationalism and Anglo-American feminism" (143). Moraga's project arises from her (and others') conflicting experiences as an individual caught between two movements—"the feminist movement" and "the Chicana/o movement"— which in many ways opposed each other by asserting the primacy of their own projects.

Moya begins by pointing out instances in which the postmodernist feminists Judith Butler and Donna Haraway misappropriate Moraga's work in order to "delegitimize any theoretical project that attends to the linkages between identity (with its experiential and cognitive components) and social location (the particular nexus of gender, race, class, and sexuality in which a given individual exists in the world)" (127). While Moraga's "theory in the flesh" problematizes the essentialist concept of "identity" in order to produce a well-theorized and politically effective understanding of "identities as relational and grounded in the historically produced social facts which constitute social locations" (127), Haraway in particular co-opts Moraga's work to support claims that have the opposite effect of "trap[ping Chicanas] . . . within a specific *signifying* location [that of the cyborg]" (Moya 129; original emphasis). By eliminating from Moraga's theory the cultural specificity of her portrayal of Chicanas as an identity group, Haraway ignores Moraga's key claim that such a group can produce real knowledge of the systemic workings of power in society because of its specific relations to history and the social world.

Moya moves on to articulate a "realist" theory of Chicana identity. She offers a definition of epistemic privilege that, significantly, marks the potential for possessing knowledge as one of its components: "'Epistemic privilege,' as I will use it in this essay, refers to a special advantage with respect to possessing or acquiring knowledge about how fundamental aspects of our society (such as race, class, gender, and sexuality) operate to sustain matrices of power" (136). Moya locates the potential for knowledge, and thus for agency in a theoretically informed liberatory project, in the "interpreted experiences," not simply the social locations, of the oppressed. Knowledge is not produced simply by understanding social relations, but by understanding experiences in terms of social relations.

The difference is evident when we try to understand who is (or can be) doing the thinking in either case. Social locations (or subject positions) are sites that people occupy; they can be studied in relation to systems of oppression or other such structures, but they themselves are not agents. For example, the subject position "Chicana" does not carry with it any particular knowledge until an actual social agent—a thinking and experiencing person—occupies that subject position. Social locations lead to particular knowledge only when a person experiences the effects of the social structures brought to bear on these social locations and actively interprets her experiences. Furthermore, as Moya is careful to point out, these experiences make objective knowledge possible but do not automatically lead to objective knowledge: the link between social location and knowledge is contingent on effective interpretation of experience.

In Moya's discussion of Moraga's theoretical project, it is clear that transformative political theory and action are united and that theorist/activists are to work with their experiences of the world in order best to produce needed political and social changes. "Moraga's theoretical project," says Moya, "which is consonant with her interest in building a movement of/for radical women of color, involves a heartfelt examination and analysis of the sources of her oppression and her pain. . . . What Moraga [claims] is a knowledge that can be grasped as a result of an interpretation of [her experiences of] violation" (Moya 144). On the question of individual agency, this passage makes a couple of important gestures. First, Moraga is building a movement whose constituents (including herself) are involved in their own liberation, whose needs and resources (epistemic and otherwise) are the grounds for political action. And second, Moraga deliberately claims the knowledge that arises out of her act of theorizing her experience. In this respect, Moraga's project resembles Mohanty's (in which Sethe undergoes a process of interpreting her experience for herself). Moraga maintains agency through the process of theorization and interpretation of her experience. As we will see in the next section, this agency is important not because others are not useful in liberation projects but because, as I will argue, agency is necessary for the transformative politics she is building.

We have now looked at two approaches to identity with regard to "agency." The "essentialist" version of identity politics seemed to offer considerable agency to members of oppressed groups. But it also placed constraints on the sorts of interpretation (or representation) of experience that an individual in one of these groups could produce, because such interpretations had to arise from and represent all members of a given identity group.

Mohanty's "realist" theory of cultural identity addressed this problem by reconceiving identity as arising from theory-mediated interpretations of experience. In Mohanty's theory, identity is quite real, but it is not self-evident or homogeneous; the processes of interpreting experiences ground identities. Agency, then, is socially mediated but no less available to oppressed people pursuing liberatory political or personal projects.

Finally, Moya's realist approach to Chicana identity and the reading of Moraga's "theory in the flesh" that Moya presents theorize full agency for individuals making sense of their experiences of oppression. For Moya and Moraga, the site of oppression is the body (or "the flesh"), where oppression is experienced and where (through a process of interpretation) it is theorized, understood, and eventually confronted.

THE NECESSITY OF AGENCY: MORAGA AND ANZALDÚA'S *THIS BRIDGE CALLED MY BACK* AND SCHEMAN'S "ALICE"

MORAGA'S "THEORY IN THE FLESH" AND *THIS BRIDGE CALLED MY BACK:* AGENCY IN THE FORMATION OF COLLECTIVITY

My discussion has dealt almost exclusively with how various projects address the issue of "individual agency"—that is, the opportunity (or the right) for an oppressed person to represent and act for herself, as opposed to simply providing the epistemic "grounds" for another to represent her and act on her behalf. I have alluded to "groups" acting together, but only very generally. But even the most effective individual political strategy would seem to be ineffective in combating the structural apparatuses and institutions holding oppression in place; if "individual agency" is so important, lest a supposed advocate misrepresent or misunderstand one's needs, then how do we avoid the trap we thought we had escaped by aligning ourselves with an antirelativist stance (the trap being, of course, the claim that "experience" can provide no basis for objective knowledge, and thus that "common identity" does not exist in any relevant sense)? We would seem again to be on the brink of paralyzing ourselves, this time not due to an epistemic issue but due to a conflict between our principles, which necessitate individual agency, and a practical concern, the need for solidarity.

I argue here that, far from conflicting with the formation of a true collectivity, individual agency facilitates the process; and the resultant collective has greater potential for liberatory political transformation. The reasons are not just practical but epistemological: agency is necessary for epistemological reasons because it provides a site for alternative interpretive frameworks to be exchanged and "tried on," tested against the experiences and in the lives of oppressed people. Agency, as we will see, enables a dialectical process of development to take place among members of a politically formed collective that would not exist in the terms I offer below were it not for the agency of the individuals in the group. So, paradoxically, only with individual agency can we have an effective political collective that truly works on behalf of its constituents.

Moraga's goal—to form a "movement," to serve other women of color as she combats her own oppression—necessitates the formation of collectivity. I will outline her method for achieving collectivity, working toward an understanding of how this collectivity operates politically. Throughout this discussion, I will be referring to *Bridge* not just as a site where Moraga tells us her "theory in the flesh" but also as a real demonstration of this theory in practice. *Bridge* is the result of the collective practices of "theory in the flesh" of the text's many contributors, speaking together as a political, expressive, and liberatory act. It *enacts* Moraga's theory.

I begin by making a case that will perhaps seem trivial: that ostensibly, all experiences, and hence all interpretive frameworks, are unique. This is not the same as the postmodernist claim that there can be no relevant similarities between experiences of different people; rather, it is related to Mohanty's argument that experience is "theory mediated": "Our experiences do not have self-evident meanings, for they are in part theoretical affairs; our access to our remotest personal feelings is dependent on social narratives, paradigms, and even ideologies" (47–48). Experiences themselves, then, do not contain some essential "meaning" that we need only to root out; rather, we interpret them through some "interpretive framework," which is itself constructed out of these social narratives and ideologies as well as our past attempts to understand and interpret our experiences and lives. Moya refers to experience as "the fact of personally observing, encountering, or undergoing a particular event or situation," suggesting that experiences depend not only on events themselves but also on our "theoretically mediated interpretation" of events (136). Moreover, because of the different sociohistorical conditions, characteristics, and sets of relations of different individuals, people having similar experiences will interpret them differently. That is, due to the complexity and the specificity of both a person's experiences and her "interpretive framework" for understanding them, we cannot unproblematically assume even that people in apparently similar "social locations" will experience and understand their lives similarly.

This is not to say that social location has no bearing on one's interpretation of experiences, only that the former does not altogether determine the latter. Due to the real effects of social location, there is likely to be a strong correlation between social location and experiences/interpretive frameworks. Moya notes,

> The different social facts (such as gender, race, class, and sexuality) that mutually constitute an individual's social location are causally relevant for the experiences she will have. . . . [T]he experiences a person is likely to have will be largely determined by her social location in a given society. In order to appreciate the structural causality of the experiences of any given individual, we must take into account the mutual interaction of all the different social facts which constitute her social location, and situate them within the particular social, cultural, and historical matrix in which she exists. (137)

That is, social location and experiences/interpretive frameworks are "problematically" (or complexly) related. It is critical to mark the gap between an unproblematical, a priori understanding of a person's experiences based on limited facts about her social location and the complex analysis Moya describes. For Moya's case to be accurate, we must (and she does) recognize the basic, though generally trivial, "uniqueness" or "difference" between any two experiences and any two individuals' sets of interpretive frameworks.

Experiences of oppression, like all experiences, are specific to the complex conditions and characteristics of individuals, and a key feature of Moraga's "theory in the flesh" is that we account for this specificity. "A theory in the flesh means one where the physical realities of our lives— our skin color, the land or concrete we grew up on, our sexual longings— all fuse to create a politic born out of necessity" (Moraga xviii–xix). The kind of "fusing," "welding," joining together that pervades *Bridge* presupposes the differences between experiences of different people. Moraga's project, then, is to turn that difference into a resource by explaining how in important ways there is common ground among these different experiences. The project is what Toni Cade Bambara, in her foreword to *Bridge,* calls "the possibility of several million women refuting the numbers game inherent in 'minority,' the possibility of denouncing the insulated/orchestrated conflict game of divide and conquer" (vi) that is the strategy of the oppressive institutions in the world to deploy "difference" as "division."

This is how Moraga's "theory in the flesh" works: a group of differently oppressed people all bring to bear on their oppression a couple of resources available to them individually. First, they bring their experiences of oppression as resources for their liberation. These are the experiences narrated to us by the writers of *Bridge:* experiences including "coming of age and coming to terms with community—race, group, class, gender, self—its expectations, supports, and lessons. And coming to grips with its perversions—racism, prejudice, elitism, misogyny, homophobia, and murder" (*Bridge* vii). As the "roots" of a radical politics, these experiences arising from "the flesh" and the lives of oppressed women are the individual raw materials for a transformative project that is not automatically collective but is *made* collective.

The second resource brought to bear on their oppression is an interpretive framework, a way of understanding their world and their experience. This, too, is demonstrated in the individual texts in *Bridge,* in which we witness how these writers understand and interpret their lives and experiences. As with the experiences themselves, while these interpretive frameworks arise in part from individuals' social locations, they are diverse strategies that attempt, with varying degrees of effectiveness, to understand diverse experiences.

Two political acts are then performed. First, these women relay their experience, interpreting it through their interpretive framework. The production of *Bridge* enacts this step. All these women had these experiences, and these interpretive frameworks, before the book came to exist. It is in offering up their interpretations of their experiences and lives— offerings Moraga and Anzaldúa describe as "non-rhetorical, highly personal chronicles that present a political analysis in everyday terms" (xxiv)—that they begin the political work leading to a liberatory movement. The texts are "chronicles," not just of events in the lives of the writers, but of "experiences," mediated by the theories—the interpretive frameworks; in this way the texts are also "political analyses," presented in the "everyday terms" of regular experience.

In the introduction to *Bridge,* Moraga and Anzaldúa describe their "major role as editors" as "encourag[ing] writers to delve even more deeply into their lives, to make some meaning out of it for themselves and their readers" (xxv). The political act of relaying their experiences and their interpretations, then, is performed for themselves (they are informing others of their conditions, their lives) and for their readers, a heterogeneous group that includes, among others, a good share of the people with whom they are aiming to form a liberatory political movement. What use for others—the readers, the other contributors—can these texts provide (beyond the most basic formation of solidarity)? The answer to this question can be found in the second political act, a process of individual interpretation, drawing on the resources brought together by the group as a whole, in which collectivity is produced.

This move is critical; it turns what would otherwise be a comparatively weak coalition into collectivity, empathy. All the individuals (in this case, individuals politically and personally motivated by a range of disparate concerns and experiences) mark as similar some of these diverse experiences they have offered to the group, sharing features of the multiple interpretive frameworks. Recall the earlier argument that we cannot claim unproblematically that any two experiences are (or will be understood as) the same between any two individuals. Here, however, individuals make the political decision to understand their experiences as like that of others; they reconstruct what they take to be the relevant features of their experience, rearticulate to themselves and others what they take the experience to mean, and so on.

Here is where true collectivity arises, and what is key is that it is a condition that could only be achieved, not prescribed. Think about what is necessary for this process to take place, paying particular attention to the points where individuals have to make a choice about what to do with their experiences. Then consider how such a situation would be different if agency were stripped from the people in question—if the theorizing and the "representing" were done by others. In this alternative, the experiences informing the researcher (or other external agent) may very well be interpreted as "the same," either unproblematically (as in essentialist theories of identity) or via some interpretive framework generated externally and brought to the set of experiences by the researcher. Unlike what is the case in *Bridge,* the multiple interpretive frameworks that have informed individual members of the oppressed community fail to influence the process of understanding these experiences. In addition, the interpretations of the experiences, which in Moraga's approach could be "tried on," and which could once again be entered into the collective pool of resources (leading to further interpretive work, further exchange, and so on), instead yields static and disembodied knowledge, suitable for little other than demonstrating that one's interpretive framework is capable of producing a stable set of facts of indeterminate accuracy.

But in Moraga's "theory in the flesh," and in its embodiment in *Bridge,* the results of this process of reflexive interpretation can be both tested (by determining empirically whether the framework succeeds in organizing the relevant facts of people's experience) and redirected back into the pool of collective resources. The cyclic process becomes a dialectical transformation of the interpretive frameworks relied on to understand the experiences of oppression. It is a fairly empirical, trial-and-error process of collectively and individually "trying on" the interpretive frameworks that have worked best for group members, and it leads to increasingly objective and useful understandings of experiences of oppression.

Once again, it should be clear why agency is necessary: the process of "trying on" frameworks must be "in the flesh," tested against the lives and experiences of the people actually dealing with experiences of oppression. Without agency—for instance, in situations in which an outside researcher performs all the cognitive and theoretical labor—this transformative dialectic does not progress past the first stage of interpretation based on a relatively disembodied interpretive framework.

SCHEMAN'S "ALICE" AND FEMINIST CONSCIOUSNESS-RAISING GROUPS: THE DIALECTICS OF COLLECTIVITY

In "Anger and the Politics of Naming," Naomi Scheman articulates the role of consciousness-raising groups in providing necessary ways of interpreting members' experiences. She acknowledges the political agendas of such groups, arguing that unlike the "hidden political framework[s]" in which people are often expected to make sense of their emotions, the political frameworks of consciousness-raising groups are both honest and explicit. Although Scheman focuses on the role of the group in making sense of an individual's experience, we can use her example to theorize collectivity building at the local, experiential level. Like Moraga's "theory in the flesh" and its exemplification in *Bridge,* Scheman's example of "Alice," a participant in a feminist consciousness-raising group, demonstrates the kind of transformative political project that meets the real needs of the oppressed. As I explain below, this example is important because it demonstrates not only the group's contribution to the welfare of its individual members but also the individual members' roles in shaping the interpretive framework of the group. Understanding Scheman's example in terms of individual agency, in fact, even more clearly demonstrates the differences between the deployment of a theory/practice in the hands of the oppressed and one that strips agency from those whose needs and experiences are at stake.

Scheman discusses the process of women's coming to recognize certain inarticulate feelings as "anger" in the supportive and politically conscious environment of a women's consciousness-raising group. Her primary example, Alice, engages in a process of interpretation and labeling of what began as conflicting feelings that could not be fully explained by her prior worldview.

When I first read Scheman's account of Alice, I was skeptical about the capacity of such a group to avoid two traps. I worried that, as with any organized institution, complete with a powerful ideological apparatus, the interpretive framework of the group would dominate, becoming the only acceptable framework for an individual participant to employ. This concern is precisely the concern Moraga and other feminists of color hold regarding the dominance of middle-class, white perspectives in the women's movement, which intends to serve the interests of all women but instead exerts a normalizing pressure and denies internal differences among members (xxiii). In the case of the consciousness-raising group, this pressure could have been exerted through the group's representing "its interpretation" of Alice's experiences as dogma, forcing Alice to accept the interpretation or be rejected from this social group.

Or alternately, I wondered how even a sincere and well-intentioned group could possibly deal with a truly unique case. The group already has constructed a viable interpretive framework; if Alice were to come into the group with an importantly different or unique experience, even one with which she has not come to terms fully, the application by the group of its interpretive framework might actually lead Alice away from a more objective interpretation of her experience. Even if the new interpretation doesn't "feel right" to Alice, she is likely to accept it because of social pressure from the group and the fact that she is simply moving from one confusing understanding of her situation to another, with little else to compare them to.[5]

But we can understand Alice's participation in the group more constructively if we consider not just the group's role in Alice's interpretive processes but also Alice's role in the group's processes. Whereas I had at first seen Alice as the "case" that provided the experiences that the group itself interpreted through the framework it had constructed (giving Al-

---

5. In an analysis of a similar case, Wahl discusses Freud's construction of the conscious/unconscious duality to secure the therapist's "interpretive duty" in interpreting the patient's experience: "The Relations between the conscious mind and body were obvious to the patient, but those were less important for fixing the machine than was the relationship between the unconscious mind and body. If this relationship was the arbiter of the body's functions and of the conscious mind, how could one go about fixing it? One couldn't; a therapist had to be called in for repair. The 'unconscious' drives were given over to the interpretation of the therapist" (7). Although the formulation of Freud's "interpretive framework" could be questioned, it is at least conceivable that it had been successful in uncovering repressed desires and so forth in some cases prior to Dora's. With Dora, Freud encountered a case that was extremely different from the cases in which his interpretation worked; it is the difference between Dora's case and other cases that Freud's framework failed to understand. For all Freud knew, Dora's case was precisely like other cases he had succeeded with, and his project became to force Dora to recognize this fact.

ice the power to "tell" her experiences, but the group the more critical authority to "represent" these experiences through its lens), it is more useful to see her as a still-autonomous participant in this interpretive process, motivated to bring both her experiences and her interpretive frameworks to the group setting. Since this autonomy is the key factor that makes Alice's relationship with the group dialogic and mutually transformative, it is worth considering in more detail.

As a self-described collective, the group possesses its own set of disparate experiences and interpretive frameworks that it can bring to bear on interpretations of experiences. But instead of simply co-opting Alice's agency, giving her an "authoritative" reading of her experiences through the group's framework, Alice is invited to perform the political (and also personal) act of naming her experience as similar in relevant ways to that of other group members. As with *Bridge,* Alice is free to identify features of her experiences that seem to her to match up with features of the experiences of other group members. In the process of doing so, the interpretive strategies that have served these others also become available for Alice.

One important feature of this process is that Alice has the opportunity to try on these interpretive frameworks, to conditionally understand herself in a certain way to see if it helps her to understand her overall experiences well. This is a largely empirical process, one that really could not be performed by anyone but Alice, whose "flesh" serves as the site of the experiences being interpreted. If the new framework helps Alice to understand her life more effectively, and if this leads her to become healthier, less "depressed" or "guilty," or otherwise psychically uncomfortable "without knowing why" (Scheman 176), she will have come to know something about herself and the social relations that contribute to her experiences. She will have come to this achievement, not because another person or group told her about herself, but because through a process of hearing others tell about themselves she recognized aspects of herself, making a connection with these others and their experiences. Out of these connections arises a sense of collective identity.

At the same time, her experience is now added to the set of relevantly similar experiences contributing to the formation of the collective interpretive framework. Alice enters into a position of agency with regard to the group as well as herself, because she can now draw on her relevantly similar experiences to provide part of the basis for developing and honing the collective interpretive framework. The grounds of the group's "common" experiences and interpretive frameworks, after all, are the lives and experiences (the bodies) of the individual women who make up the group; Alice's life adds to this collective pool of resources. The group framework becomes more effective as it is tested on an increasing range of experiences, leading it to become better able to help Alice to interpret her experiences; she understands better, she has more to offer back to the group, and so the cycle continues.

So two kinds of development occur here, each fundamentally shaping the other. Alice draws on the intellectual framework of the group to more effectively interpret her experiences, while the group draws on Alice's experiences and her insights into the effectiveness of the interpretive framework—what works, what doesn't, and where, and why—to develop the group's framework and to expand the pool of experiences that can provide connections with others.

CONCLUSION: WHAT ROLE CAN OTHERS PLAY IN THE POLITICS OF THE OPPRESSED?

The question has necessarily shaped my approach to the work I have presented above: since there is a history of "others," nonmembers in a given cultural community, appropriating the voices of the community, nullifying the progressive work engaged in by the group, and so forth, what role should others occupy with regard to oppressed groups?[6] For there is also a history of others participating productively in political struggle alongside the people most immediately affected by this struggle. The arguments I have offered above lead me to some tentative conclusions about the role for others in liberatory political movements. The first point I will develop is that outsiders must recognize their situatedness in oppressive systems of power even if they do not directly experience those systems as oppressive. Though differently related to such systems, outsiders must learn to participate responsibly in them; doing so calls for knowledge that can only be obtained in concert with those who are themselves oppressed, but it produces knowledge that elucidates the workings of power structures and relations for outsiders. Furthermore, the knowledge thus

---

6. I use the term "others" (as well as "outsiders," here used as a synonym) deliberately. "Others" is commonly used to refer to marginal or oppressed people rather than the mainstream or unoppressed; as many have observed (including Moraga and Anzaldúa; see their introduction to *Bridge*), typically these "others" must adapt themselves to the conceptual frameworks of the mainstream in order to participate in mainstream activities, movements, or cultures. In my use of these terms, I hope both to distinguish members from nonmembers of identity groups and to mark the need for these others to do comparable work.

produced may be valuable for members of oppressed groups who can use it to better understand their experiences of oppression as entailments of broader power structures. Finally, the nature of and possible uses for outsiders' knowledge suggests that effective alliances between group members and others must be grounded in imaginative, but not imaginary, forms of identification.

It is comparatively simple to see how the oppressed are related to certain oppressive structures; but it may be more difficult to see how (or even whether) that same power structure relates to others who do not experience it as oppressive. So, for instance, it may be apparent that the various power structures that enforce normative male heterosexuality oppress gay men (the effects of this oppression may be evident in many ways, even visible on the body), but less visible are the ways that these same structures relate to hetero men (or women)—and if they do produce visible effects, they are at least as likely to appear enabling as oppressive. To give another example, when I buy a T-shirt at the Gap, my immediate experience is positive, though the effect of my experience on garment workers in a Salvadoran free trade zone is quite the opposite. In other words, as an outsider, I lack the particular experiences of oppression (low wages, miserable working conditions, physical and psychological abuse) that potentially ground the laborer's knowledge of the workings of the structure in question. Such knowledge, hard to come by even for the worker herself, is essential for effective resistance to be enacted; but how can an outsider come to such knowledge, and what, in the end, is the object of such knowledge for someone who lacks the specific experiences of oppression?

Many theorists argue for "starting off thought" from the lives of the oppressed in order to produce maximally effective projects of resistance.[7] Though I argue against efforts to speak for those otherwise able to produce and enact liberatory agendas for themselves, "starting off thought" from the lives of the oppressed is useful for grounding the knowledge of outsiders seeking to understand their own complex relations to systems of oppression. Outsiders cannot simply investigate the effects of oppressive power structures in their own lives; on the contrary, their relationships to the oppressed require them to understand systems of oppression from the perspectives of the oppressed, producing a less partial

7. I am thinking particularly of proponents of "feminist standpoint epistemology," notably Sandra Harding and Nancy Hartsock. For a useful introduction to the topic, see Harding, "Rethinking Standpoint Epistemology."

awareness of matrices of power, as well as their specific relationships with those matrices (including the broader implications of their experiences of enablement). Only by becoming conscious of the experiences of the garment worker can I properly understand my contribution to the power structure that incongruously yields me a T-shirt and yields the laborer a penny on every dollar I spend. Without working to understand her perspective, my own partial perspective is ineffectual. But by supplementing my perspective with hers, I am enabled to make better-informed choices about my own actions—actions that resist or contribute to the oppression that I may only witness secondhand.

Hence the first result of this approach is a more suitable platform from which to understand and manage the effects of our own actions as they feed into and are shaped by systems of power that oppress others. Instead of seeing our activity simply as a kind of transaction between ourselves and a system of power (which we may manipulate to our benefit), we may become better able to understand the effects of our involvement in relation to the involvement of others. In other words, the standpoint of the oppressed is necessary to manage our own involvement with systems of oppression so as most effectively to combat oppression as a systemic yet particular effect of power.

This shift toward understanding one's own implication in oppressive structures suggests that our experiences (even as outsiders) can be understood in relation to the experiences of the oppressed, though not without a reconception of our experiences. Thus far, this reconception affects our own actions and perspectives, facilitating our resistance to structures of oppression in passive or active ways (e.g., by no longer choosing to buy Gap T-shirts, or by actively motivating others to take the same step). But knowledge gained from the outsider's perspective, thus situated, can also be put to work by members of oppressed groups themselves. For example, drawing on the perspectives of garment workers, my insights into the effects of buying Gap T-shirts generates important knowledge for me but may help to contextualize the experiences of the workers as well. International human rights workers report that most workers did not know the retail prices of their garments, or the wages and conditions of comparable laborers in the United States. These prices, wages, and conditions help to solidify the particular manifestations of power on the workers' experiences, explaining why companies prefer to produce goods in export-producing zones, why production quotas rise and fall, and even why industry codes of conduct are withheld from them. Without such information, workers lack an important context from which to make sense of their experiences. Thus an understanding of the outsider's perspective can be valuable to the oppressed, not because the oppressed need to be spoken for, but because they can understand their experiences most productively when the structures shaping them are visible.

The comments above detail two possible objectives for outsiders' understanding of their implication in structures of oppression. These comments focus on how outsiders and the oppressed might make independent use of this knowledge, setting aside the question of alliances between outsiders and oppressed groups. But the idea that we must reconceive our experience relationally, and that this reconception bears on the perspectives of both outsiders and members of oppressed groups, suggests the form that productive alliances between these two groups might take. Outsiders wishing to support the liberatory work of the oppressed must form responsible and imaginative alliances—alliances grounded in appropriate reconceptions of their experiences in relation to others. That is, we should not work toward *imaginary* identifications of ourselves with others, in which we make claims about our "sameness" without regard for the real differences in our experiences and lives; rather, we should work toward *imaginative* identifications of ourselves with others, in which we interrogate our own experience, seeking points where common ground or empathy might be actively constructed between us while remaining conscious of the real differences between our experiences and lives.

I call this type of identification "imaginative" because it calls for us to imagine how our experiences might be analogous to rather than equivalent to the experiences of others. Moraga suggests a similar process when she describes what is required for a gay male friend to "create an authentic alliance" with her: "He must deal with the primary source of his own sense of oppression. He must, first, emotionally come to terms with what it feels like to be a victim. If he—or anyone—were to truly do this, it would be impossible to discount the oppression of others, except by again forgetting how we have been hurt" (Moraga 30). Before he can support her cause, he must empathize with her by coming to terms with his own experiences of oppression. This empathy will not provide him with the actual experiences of her oppression, but it will give them a basis for relating their experiences.

This approach to forming responsible alliances with others resembles the process of identifying experiences as "relevantly similar" in order for members of a group to produce useful frameworks for understanding oppression collectively (as I discussed above). But in forming alliances between an oppressed group and outsiders, experiences themselves cannot be related; rather, the oppressive effects of the experience become the basis for common ground. Moraga's gay male friend cannot share her specific experiences of being a woman of color, but he may share an experience of certain effects of this oppression to the extent that the oppression of gay men and the oppression of women of color produce relevantly similar effects. By investigating his experience of these effects, he can better understand her experience without ever needing to claim that he has shared it.

One outcome of these approaches to participating in the politics of the oppressed is that our ways of thinking about oppression must be modified. Rather than treat oppression as a binary force either oppressive or unoppressive to ourselves (and, if unoppressive, also unrelated to ourselves), we must see it as complex and relational, linking us to others and at the same time making us responsible for how we participate in the matrices of power that sustain oppression.[8] The result of seeing oppression in this way is to enable more effective participation in these systems; by broadening our ways of knowing about the systems within which we operate, we at least potentially increase our ability to shape these systems in the long term. It enables us to participate in liberatory political projects more effectively, working in concert with rather than against or in place of those whose experiences of oppression both necessitate and ground this work.

WORKS CITED

Bordo, Susan. *Unbearable Weight: Feminism, Western Culture, and the Body.* Berkeley: University of California Press, 1993.

Gray, John. *Men Are from Mars, Women Are from Venus.* New York: HarperCollins, 1992.

Harding, Susan. "Rethinking Standpoint Epistemology: What is 'Strong Objectivity'?" *Feminist Epistemologies.* Ed. Linda Alcoff and Elizabeth Potter. New York: Routledge, 1993. 49–82.

Mohanty, Satya P. "The Epistemic Status of Cultural Identity: On *Beloved* and the Postcolonial Condition." *Cultural Critique* 24 (Spring 1993): 41–80. [Reprinted as chapter 1 in this volume.]

Moraga, Cherríe. "La Güera." *This Bridge Called My Back: Writings by Radi-*

8. Thus, in her discussion of the effects of participating in a diet program, Susan Bordo observes that she at once seemed to benefit from acting within the complex social structure that produces institutions like "national weight-loss programs" and "normative concepts of body weight" and to also potentially take away a "small but possibly important source of self-validation and encouragement" from some of her female students who are unable to maintain societally acceptable bodies (30–31).

cal Women of Color. Ed. Cherríe Moraga and Gloria Anzaldúa. New York: Kitchen Table: Women of Color Press, 1983. 27–34.

Moraga, Cherríe, and Gloria Anzaldúa, eds. *This Bridge Called My Back: Writings by Radical Women of Color.* New York: Kitchen Table: Women of Color Press, 1983.

Moya, Paula M. L. "Postmodernism, 'Realism,' and the Politics of Identity: Cherríe Moraga and Chicana Feminism." *Feminist Genealogies, Colonial Legacies, Democratic Futures.* Ed. M. Jacqui Alexander and Chandra Talpade Mohanty. New York: Routledge, 1997. 125–50. [Reprinted as chapter 2 in this volume.]

Perry, Donna. "Gloria Anzaldúa." *Backtalk: Women Writers Speak Out.* New Brunswick, NJ: Rutgers University Press, 1993. 19–42.

Scheman, Naomi. "Anger and the Politics of Naming." *Women and Language in Literature and Society.* Ed. Sally McConnell-Ginet, Ruth Borker, and Nelly Furman. New York: Praeger, 1980. 174–87.

Wahl, Wendy. "Bodies and Technologies: Dora, Neuromancer, and Strategies of Resistance." *Postmodern Culture* 3.2 (January 1993). http//muse.jhu.edu/journals/postmodern_culture/archive.html.

CHAPTER 8

Is There Something You Need to Tell Me?

Coming Out and the Ambiguity of Experience

William S. Wilkerson

In his essay "The Epistemic Status of Cultural Identity," Satya P. Mohanty develops a postpositivist realist theory of identity as an alternative to both essentialist and postmodernist understandings of identity. The essentialist theory of identity claims that the identity shared by members of a social group is stable and based on shared, self-evidently meaningful experiences, whereas the postmodernist understanding of identity claims that experience is fundamentally unreliable and socially constituted, such that it can be neither a source of knowledge nor a starting place for identity formation ("The Epistemic Status" 42). Mohanty effectively overcomes this antinomy by accepting the truth contained in each view. He thus claims that experience is not self-evidently meaningful but is rather partly constituted by social forces and by the very act of coming to understand it. Knowledge gained from experience is thus highly mediated by theoretical understandings of the world. This is the "postpositivist" element in his theory, and it is certainly a tenet many postmoderns would accept. Conversely, Mohanty maintains that there can be more and less accurate interpretations of experience and more and less accurate understandings of one's own identity and social position based on one's interpretation of experience. This is the "realist" element in this theory: one's identity may indeed be constructed, but it is not arbitrary; we can indeed strive for better and more accurate knowledge of ourselves and our world.

Mohanty draws one of his primary examples from the feminist

philosopher Naomi Scheman's discussion of consciousness raising. When a woman joins a consciousness-raising group, she discovers that her feelings of guilt and depression were in fact a mistaken interpretation of her deeper and more pervasive anger at the situation of being a woman in a sexist society. Her discovery of her anger is mediated by a theory of society, which organized and focused formally diffuse experiences and also legitimated her anger by explaining its source. Through organizing her diffuse experiences and making them seem legitimate, the theory of society actually shaped her experiences as much as it accurately represented and explained them. Thus her experience both provided a starting point for knowledge and was itself mediated by theoretical knowledge about society.

Since the coming out process of many of gays and lesbians parallels many of the features of consciousness raising, the realist theory also gives us insight into the development of lesbian and gay identity. A standard picture of the coming out process holds that a person has experiences of same-sex desire and homosocial emotional bonding that eventually motivate her or him to come out and adopt a gay/lesbian identity. Such a picture of coming out reinforces essentialist notions of identity in which experiences are taken as straightforward and unmediated sources of knowledge on which individuals can construct personal identities. Indeed, even the expression "coming out" is essentialist; it implies the revealing of an already present, but hidden, identity. Mohanty's realist theory of identity, on the other hand, would view coming out as the reinterpretation of homoerotic experiences, previously thought forbidden, as legitimate and positive. This reinterpretation is accomplished via nonhomophobic understandings of the world. The crucial point is that this change of values and self-understanding changes the character of the experiences, and so alters the very kind of experiences that motivated an individual to come out in the first place. Homoerotic experiences, therefore, would not only motivate coming out, but coming out would also reshape the experiences of desire as one accepts oneself in spite of homophobia.

In both of these cases, Mohanty's realist theory claims that identities are both constructed and discovered from experiences ("The Epistemic Status" 70). To avoid positivist-style experiential foundationalism, however, the experiences themselves cannot be self-evidently meaningful but must themselves be both "discovered and constructed." So the realist theory claims that both identity and the experiences that serve as material for the construction of identity are mediated by theoretical understandings of the world and one's place in it. It is this lack of given or self-evident meanings in experience that make us prone to error in our understandings of experience. Experience requires interpretation, and interpretation implies the space of possible error. However, someone might object to this aspect of the realist theory as follows: by claiming that there can be more and less accurate interpretations of experience, the realist theory faces a paradox when it comes to the structure of human experience. The realist must insist both that experiences have a meaning that should motivate specific identity claims and that this meaning itself changes in relation to changing understandings of identity, because experience is always mediated. However, if experience changes in relation to new identity, in what sense is a new identity an accurate reflection or interpretation of those previous experiences? With the case of coming out, this issue is particularly acute. Homoerotic experiences may motivate a person to come out, but once that person has come out, the experiences of homoerotic feelings are different, and not just different after coming out but different *retroactively*, such that previous elements of experience cohere together in new, meaningful patterns. "I was always gay," a gay man might say, even as he might also claim his desires only "made sense" on coming out. If being gay is an accurate identity to infer from one's experiences, we would want to say that one had "gay experiences" all along but didn't know it. But often, one's life and experience lack the organization granted by a self-reflective understanding of one's sexual identity, and so it does not seem right to say that one was gay all along. If one is not really yet having the experiences of someone who is gay, because one has not adopted such an identity and had it alter one's experience, then how can the interpretation that one is gay be more accurate? What makes it more accurate if the feelings and desires themselves lack the coherence necessary to really be those of a gay person? It is difficult to understand what a person experiences before coming out, and therefore it is difficult to say that accepting a lesbian or gay identity is an accurate interpretation of one's life up until that point.

The objection, then, is that the realist theory of identity has an incoherent view on the nature of human experience, in which it is both mediated and yet somewhat self-evident, and that this threatens the ability to claim that there can be more accurate interpretations of the meaning of experience.[1] The objection stems from the fact that a realist theory of

---

1. When I speak of the "meaning" of experience, I am referring to that "cognitive component" of experience that is available for reporting and making knowledge claims. "Experience" here denotes the subjective living through of an event.

254 William S. Wilkerson

identity like Mohanty's wants to claim both that it is possible to be wrong about something as intimate as one's experience (as in the case of being wrong about one's sexuality) and that it is possible to discover more accurate interpretations of experience (as when one comes out). To dispel this objection, we need to examine more closely how a postpositivist realist theory understands experience—both its structure and its relation to identity. Specifically, I want to argue that the picture of experience it offers is not so "weird" after all and that it is accurate to characterize human experience as both contextual and nonetheless subject to more and less accurate interpretations. Experiences do not have meanings apart from mediation, but they are not without latent meanings that can be interpreted, and, moreover, the accuracy of these interpretations can be measured by continued verification. A realist analysis of coming out would demonstrate precisely this point. First, therefore, I present some phenomenological considerations about experience, demonstrating how experience is not immediate and self-evident but rather mediated and ambiguous, such that it is possible both to be wrong about one's experience and to arrive at more accurate interpretations of experience. In the process, I contribute to a realist understanding of gay identity by developing a picture of coming out that shows how gay identity is tied to existing social and political structures as well as an accurate understanding of a "pregay" individual's experience.

In the second part of this chapter, I broaden the inquiry to show that the realist theory of experience, as discussed in the first part, can evade many of the standard criticisms that postmodernists have made against experience-based knowledge. I thus discuss the context of contemporary continental philosophy out of which many of these postmodernist views on experience emerged. After presenting some criticisms of the postmodernist understanding of experience, I discuss how the realist theory avoids the pitfalls of foundationalist epistemologies without having to go the route of postmodernism.

UNDERSTANDING COMING OUT ON A REALIST THEORY

A striking feature of many coming out experiences is that one works up the courage to tell a friend or relative about one's homosexuality only to find out that she already knew. In my case, several of my relatives, some of my friends, and every queer person I was acquainted with knew about me long before I began the process of coming out to them. Having lived within the queer community for some time now, I have no doubt that many of my queer friends were gossiping and speculating about me while I was still in denial, because I have partaken of that same delicious ritual with my queer friends too many times to count. While this produces many a humorous situation—"Bill, is there something you need to tell me?"—it also raises some rather difficult philosophical problems concerning self-knowledge and the epistemic status of bodily experience.

The discomfort that we feel about this situation has a number of sources. In a rather alarming way, it makes clear the extent to which we are not sovereign over the meaning of our most intimate bodily experiences. Typically, in the modern philosophical tradition of the West, knowledge of one's self and one's mental states is thought to be more easily had than knowledge of another's mental and affective life, and although Descartes thought that the mind is better known than the body, it certainly seems that no experience could be more intimate than one's own body and desires. The possible interpretations that can be placed on this experience would seem to be constrained by the immediacy with which one experiences one's own body. But the experience of coming out, and the experience of others knowing something about my own sexual orientation prior to my knowing it, seems to challenge this seemingly obvious notion. This challenge, in turn, threatens security in one's own sexuality. If one can be wrong about one's own sexuality, and another can be right about it, then it is at least possible that you could be wrong about *your* sexuality, and for the majority of straight people, even well-meaning ones, the possibility of being gay or lesbian or bisexual or transsexual is alarming indeed.

Both of these difficulties stem from a deep philosophical puzzle that is the same problem that the realist theory of identity touches on: how is the continued and long-term misapprehension of one's own most intimate experiences possible? What is the experience of this misapprehension like? Even more, this possibility might even call into question the ability to be right about the meaning of one's own experience at all. If it is possible to genuinely believe, either in spite of or because of one's experience, that one is straight, and then later that one is gay, and that one was in fact "gay all along," what, if anything, determines whether experience is "veridical" at all? The realist theory has a ready explanation for this: there are many distorted and ideological understandings of the world and aspects of our lives, such as race, gender, and sexuality, and when we misapprehend our experience, we do it under the influence of these inaccurate theories. Adopting theories that more accurately describe the world and our place in it as a member of particular social groups reorient our experiences and give us a more accurate understanding of who we are. But, if experience is so intimate and so obvious, how could we possibly even use the wrong theory in understanding it? To answer this question, I will turn to a brief examination of the structure of experience.

THE STRUCTURE OF EXPERIENCE

If we are led to think that coming out poses a puzzle with respect to experience, then this is because we have the view that experiences come neatly packaged, in relatively discrete units, and with largely or entirely self-evident meanings. Experience has been understood as the awareness or "living through" of some event, and under the influence of Cartesianism, the subjective element in this notion of experience leads us to think that we neither require external aids in deciding the meaning of the experience, nor that we can be inaccurate about that thing of which one is immediately aware. Naomi Scheman has an elegant image that captures this view: "on the surface of our stream of consciousness float leaves that are our sensations, thoughts and feelings, each unmistakably labeled" (23). Even a more Freudian picture does not effectively change this view, she claims, since it merely places some of the leaves at the bottom of the stream (repressed thoughts, feelings, etc.) and tries to infer the presence of these leaves by the subtle influences they have on the course of the stream. On either the Cartesian or Freudian picture, coming out is nearly inexplicable, because it is as hard to see how one could *not* be aware of one's sexual and emotional desires and needs—how, that is, one could miss such brightly colored leaves floating on the surface of the water—as it is to see how one could simply "submerge" these bright desires and needs and not have some awareness of them. Sex and love are simply not things we easily pass over.

Moreover, understanding coming out on the Cartesian/Freudian picture would remain within an experiential foundationalism, in which experiences provided an unambiguous and self-evident source of knowledge; in this case, desires would provide a self-evident basis for understanding that one is gay or lesbian.[2] Mohanty's version of realism is precisely *post-*

---

2. I understand experiential foundationalism here to denote a cluster of views that take first-person experiences as the ultimate source for knowledge. This view has a long history in philosophy, belonging in various forms to both empiricist and rationalist strains of thought. Typically, it assumes that experiential givens are immediate, atomic, and self-

positivist because it avoids positivism's commitment to experiential givens that serve as a source for knowledge and takes a more holistic view in which experience may be a source of knowledge, but in which knowledge itself mediates experience. Since both the Cartesian and the Freudian views take experiences as discrete and self-evident, perhaps the best course for understanding coming out would be to reject this view of experience, and hold that it is diffuse and ambiguous instead of discrete, and contextual instead of self-evident.

There are in fact many different reasons for rejecting such experiential givens. Refutations of the givenness of experience abound in recent philosophy. Hegel, for example, opened his *Phenomenology of Spirit* with a refutation of empiricist notions of simple sensations. In the analytic tradition from which Mohanty draws, one of the most famous and forceful rejections of self-evident experiences was given in Wilfrid Sellars's "Empiricism and the Philosophy of Mind." There, Sellars argued against the positivist notion that simple, atomic, perceptual experiences (like colors) founded our knowledge claims on the grounds that proffering and justifying linguistic knowledge claims was of a different order than perceptual experiences.[3] Many in the analytic tradition are also still engaged with refuting notions of "qualia"—which are not thought of as the foundation of knowledge but which are still taken to be ineffable, atomic, and self-evident components of any experience. In twentieth-century continental philosophy, another fruitful discussion of the relation between experiences and self-understanding and identity stems from the work of the French phenomenologist Maurice Merleau-Ponty, who offered an analysis of the relation between one's self-understanding and one's social position and available theories about society.[4] His analysis is noteworthy for arguing that experience is mediated by one's current tasks and social location while nonetheless providing a source of knowledge about one's identity. In what follows, I draw from all of these sources in arguing that experiences do not come in neat, self-evident packages that can be grasped all at once. Instead, experience is contextual and

---

evidently meaningful, since interpretation or mediation would mitigate the possibility for experience to play a role as an ultimate foundation.

3. This is found on pp. 164–70 of *Science, Perception and Reality*. Rorty takes this claim even further, arguing that the "language games" of giving and justifying reasons is itself socially and historically specific, such that our experience and its meaning is historically situated and mediated (*Philosophy* 173–212).

4. This discussion is located in the final chapter of the *Phenomenology of Perception*, although his analysis there relies heavily on the book's previous analyses of embodiment, experience, and subjectivity.

dispersed, and is subject to reflection and reorganization by the experiencing subject.

Following the experimental work of Gestalt psychologists, existential phenomenologists came to view experience as a structure in which we attend to certain focal elements within a background or context. The phenomenologists departed from the Gestaltists by broadening this view of experience beyond mere perceptual consciousness and by developing non-experimental, conceptual considerations to bolster their idea. For example, the very idea that I could have an experience of just some patch of color or light or other "simple impression" without a background is difficult to make sense of. In order for something to appear as a "patch of red," it must be distinguished from a background. It would not be identifiable as a *patch* of red were it not against something else that is at least not the same shade of red. This is true, not only of the visual, spatial aspects of an experience, but also of its temporal aspects. For example, philosophers were fond of discussing the experience of color one gets when one pushes against one's closed eye as an example of a pure experience. Yet, to distinguish this experience as that particular experience, it must at the least appear against a past in which it was not, and it is typically anticipated to end in the coming moments. Moreover, the color sensation is only analytically separate from the tactile sensation and the expectation of having the experience.

Being able to identify a particular experience implies being able to distinguish it from what it is not, for we would not say that one can identify an experience if one cannot distinguish it from different experiences. Also, reapprehending the experience means reidentifying it as the experience it is. However, if experience has a focus-context structure, then things are even more complex than this. Since a focus is made a focus by its contrast with a background, the conditions of identifying that focus include a background that is other than the immediate focus of my experience, be it a spatial or a temporal background. Immediate apprehension of an experience implies that there be no relation between what I apprehend and some third term. Thus the focus-context view of experience implies that any focal element of experience cannot be immediately apprehended, because it can only be apprehended in relation to a background or context that defines it as a focus.[5] Whatever we attend to most closely in our experience has defining features that lie outside of

---

5. This type of argument is similar to that made by Hegel in the opening of the *Phenomenology of Spirit,* where he argued that any perceptual atom, in order to be identified,

this aspect. Living through experience is not, therefore, a matter of strict coincidence between an experiencing subject and an experience; it is dispersed across time and space. I note the shapes and colors and sounds of my life among one another, and this means a thick now in which experience coheres together.

Moreover, because context is integral to the identity of the focus, the background context is not merely a passive element in our experience but is rather constitutive of the focus of experience. Returning to the example of a patch of some color, not only is the shape distinguished by having a background, but the very color we perceive is affected by the color of the background. A swatch of green may look quite different against a blue versus a yellow background. The experience of the color is neither immediate nor atomistic but requires a constitutive horizon and background to establish it as the color that it is. Similarly, the same chocolate may taste quite different in the midst of a cup of coffee versus a glass of champagne; the taste itself being partly constituted in our experience by the background of what we have just tasted.[6]

So far, this discussion focuses on simple percepts. Presumably, if there is a lack of immediacy at even this simplest level, then more complex and extended experiences would most certainly be mediated. This should not be taken to imply that more complex experiences are simply composed of the smaller ones, a view that would be reminiscent of the positivist picture in which experiential atoms compound to form more complex experiences. Instead, to fully endorse this figure/ground notion of experience, the "elements" of experience we analyze out of a larger field of experience are not simply atoms out of which the experience was "composed" but rather decontextualized elements of something that was an interrelated whole prior to analysis. As one example, our moods and emotional states are not merely an extra feeling laid over our ordinary thoughts and behaviors; they are part of a horizon that actually changes and molds our thoughts and behaviors, even as our behaviors and experiences reinforce our emotions. If I am angry, my anger is not just a reaction to frustrating happenings or disappointed expectations. Rather, my

---

must take on a relation to its context. In particular, to note a perception as here and now already implies a "not there and not then."

6. Such considerations are based on current themes in analytic philosophy, where a debate about "qualia"—intrinsic, subjective experiences—has raged over the last few years. People opposed to the idea that our experience is made up of qualia (e.g., Daniel Dennett) will argue that experiences are simply too dependent on their relation to the broader context of our experience to have any intrinsic or given properties.

anger has both a reactive and an anticipatory element, such that it causes happenings to be experienced as frustrating, as much as the happenings in turn cause my anger. When I am writing while angry and my pencil breaks, I may lash out in frustration, even though in a different mood I may simply get up and sharpen it and begin again. The experience is altered by the antecedent context of being angry, and being angry is not just an inner feeling but a whole style of being in the world. I may be able to distinguish and classify certain groups of my bodily feelings as anger, but these parts are never the whole story about my experience of anger. Similarly, any experience is not separable from my attentiveness to it in analyzing it as an experience. Reflection on an experience changes its character, for example, from an experience of "red, here, now" to one of red focused on as an element of an investigation of experience. Thus Husserl and his phenomenological followers were aware that to attend to an experience changes the character and feel of the experience itself.

Such phenomenological analyses show that our experiences are not simple, self-evident givens, not the "leaves" that Schemen describes, but rather complex wholes that take place within fields that condition their meaning. This means that apprehension of experiences is not immediate and that experiences have meaning only in relation to the broader context in which they are experienced.[7] A second feature of experience is that what we notice is not merely the result of passive perception or the mechanical action of experience upon us. Instead, our expectations and life histories polarize and structure our experience. Heidegger referred to this preexperiential context as the "fore-structure" of the understanding, by which he meant taken-for-granted cultural meanings and sedimented practices that guide the initial direction an interpretation may take. In Merleau-Ponty, this notion is described as the preconscious horizon of our embodiment: our habits of action and thought, our emotions, our feelings, exist on the edge of the horizon of awareness but have a profound impact on the character of our attention to things in the world. Just as anger may affect my relation to my environment, so sedimented

---

7. It is still open to the experiential foundationalist to object that focus-context of structure does not show that experience is not self-evidently meaningful and that it is not apprehended in an immediate moment. The objection would be that the entire focus-context structure can be grasped at once, as a self-evident whole. As a response, it should be pointed out that this would beg the question by ignoring the distinction between focus and context. The claim is not that our experience is like a picture and its frame that we can apprehend entirely and in one glance but rather that attention to experience is only one element within our overall situation, and that this situation affects both what we attend to and what we might infer from our experience.

ways of understanding what I should be thinking and feeling may affect how I actually do think and feel. For example, in simple race sensitivity training, one often begins by pointing out the degree to which we are trained to notice skin color from among all of the physical features that present themselves to us. We might just as easily notice hair color, eye color, whether or not someone is wearing glasses, but often we do not, because we have not been drilled from an early age to think that this is important. As a simpler example, musical training and ear training may profoundly affect that experience one has of music, changing it forever. Putting focal elements of experience under reflection and viewing them within different contexts, changing what we expect to find and what we seek, can change the character of experiences and allow new meanings and new patterns of experience to emerge. Similarly, discoveries about oneself and new understandings of one's identity and one's place in the world can happen when this preconscious horizon of expectations and self-understandings comes under increased scrutiny or examination.

Returning to the discussion of coming out can make this more clear. Before coming out, we can say that a "potentially gay person" had been repressing or denying his or her desire, but we do not have to view this desire as fully formed yet submerged and awaiting recognition and expression; it is not the submerged leaf waiting to surface. This view of denial is difficult to understand anyway. If the desire has its meaning fully contained within it, what could it possibly mean to desire something but deny this desire? If the desire is felt as a discrete and fully meaningful aspect of one's experience, what could possibly motivate one to refuse this meaning?

Rather than view the desire as there, but ignored, it makes more sense to say that the desire is experienced as a dispersed set of behaviors and feelings that a person lacks the ability to classify and group together. Before I came out, I was in denial about my feelings, and if you stop to think about it, the word "denial" expresses an experience that is ambiguous in its core—to deny is to both acknowledge and refuse. My life was dominated by sexual attraction and close emotional connections to people of the same gender while I was simultaneously trained from an early age to expect an attraction and interest in the opposite gender. I had neither acknowledged, accepted, nor acted on my sexual desire, and I was even at pains to come to elaborate rationalizations of my own feelings, yet I must have been aware of my feelings to formulate these rationalizations and to hold the experiences and feelings at a distance. To deny is to acknowledge precisely by refusing. In such a case, my body exerted its own pull on my behavior, striving to put me near a "new best friend" and the emotional and erotic high that being around him brought me. Hovering around that person at a party, watching for him as I walked across town or across campus, visiting that store where "my friend" worked when there was nothing I needed, having sexual fantasies about him without even realizing I was fantasizing, the desired person became the focus of an entire complex of behaviors and feelings, the meaning of which may have been quite obvious to an outside observer, but which I refused even as I engaged in them. (Perhaps it is by noting this pattern that queers can know about another person before that person does.) There was a whole pattern of feelings and actions that I would not consciously choose and that I refused to engage and reflect on, even though I found myself in the midst of these feelings all of the time. Nonetheless, given a social context in which such behavior might be completely unacceptable, in which such desires and behaviors are not even considered a possibility for myself or others, I was basically unable to view these disparate aspects of my life as meaning I was gay. I could not see the pattern that my feelings and behaviors formed.

It is precisely because experience is not self-evidently meaningful but rather contextualized, ambiguous, and subject to interpretation that this strange phenomenon of denial is possible. Just as the woman in Scheman's example had feelings but understood them via a patriarchal understanding of the world, on the far side of the coming out process I had feelings and experiences that did not have straightforward meanings and were mediated by a homophobic understanding of the world. Nowhere is the ambiguity of experience, and the degree to which its meaning is the result of interpretation, more apparent than in the abortive attempt of a closeted gay man to date women. An emotion as complex as love is certainly something with many aspects, some of which are mostly the subject of actual decisions (commitment) and some of which are mostly out of our control (parts of our sexual desire), and recognizing all of these elements together—seeing the pattern that makes it love—is not an automatic process but is something that one learns from reflection on one's experience and from cultural ideas about what love is. Which feelings and which decisions one is supposed to feel and make when one is in love is learned from a culture as much as from our own innermost feelings. Certainly, this is what we express when we tell young teenagers, with their raging hormones, that they do not yet really understand what love is, that they do not see the overall picture of how our culture understands the intricate relations among desire, emotion, intellect, and commitment. I learned an understanding of heterosexual romantic love from a combination of movies, television, the teachings of my church, and the example of my parents, and I applied it to my experience: piecing together something I genuinely believed to be love out of a limited sexual desire, a genuine enjoyment of another's company, and certain emotional warmth I felt for my female companions. I gave love an almost operational definition—whatever I was feeling when I was around women was love, and I am embarrassed now at how "canned" my sentiment was. But what choice did I have? I couldn't be gay, and certainly I had some feelings, and so I went on, performing whatever gestures had seemed romantic to me in movies and hurting many feelings in the process. Even as I broke dates with my "girlfriends" to spend time with whichever boy I was currently infatuated with, it did not occur to me until I was really ripe for coming out that what I felt for my male friends was what all the songs and stories were about. There was nothing self-evident or given about my feelings in the slightest, and it was a significant achievement for me, and for anyone who comes out, to reject standards and understandings of one's feelings and reorient one's life around an antihomophobic standard.

Thus I denied feelings even as I felt them, and I claimed that I had homosexual desires but that these desires were not the desires of a homosexual, because my understanding was that homosexuals were abnormal and practiced all sorts of degenerate behaviors that I had not the slightest desire to practice. Conversely, I continued to assume that whatever meager feelings I had for women were the feelings I was supposed to have. I thus adopted a heterosexual institution into my everyday existence, and it existed in a vaguely felt tension with other elements of my own experience. According to the homophobic understanding of the world, a person who does not fit with the homophobic picture of being homosexual could not be gay. Even if I were to acknowledge my desire, it was the additional *theoretical* realization that being gay is acceptable and natural and that the homophobic worldview is simply wrong that allowed me to acknowledge and categorize my own feelings and to accept a gay identity for myself. For me, this theoretical knowledge came, not just from reading about being gay, but through interaction with other gays who were stronger than I in their own self-acceptance. They helped me to see a pattern of experiences and feelings, both by pointing them out and by also celebrating them as true and right.[8]

---

8. I do not intend this description of coming out to cover all cases of coming out. Coming out stories can differ widely. Some people, for example, never come out but accept

This discussion of coming out might still seem to imply that experiences had a self-evident meaning that required no theoretical mediation, insofar as I claim that a desire was there in some sense, and that it was more accurate to trade my straight identity for a gay one. However, to adopt this "essentialist" understanding of coming out would be to return to the categories of experiential foundationalism in which experience is either simply there with its meaning (a person always had the desire of a homosexual) or not there at all (the person did not have the desires). However, there are times when how experiences fit together and what we should infer from them are simply unclear, because we lack the keys necessary to unlock their interrelation and see the meaning that emerges. Although, obviously, we also want to say that the experiences do have a specific meaning and that someone should come out and accept her or his sexuality. In these cases, perhaps we should say that experiences have "latent" or unrealized meaning.

To understand this recognition of the meaning of experience, consider what it is like to recognize a pattern.[9] Imagine staring at a sheet of paper with marks and swirls all over it and being told to find the pattern in it. After puzzling over it a bit, you notice certain repeating elements in a geometrical relation to each other. Now, in what sense is the pattern "really there"? On the one hand, you can now plainly see it, and its elements are perfectly obvious. On the other hand, the elements taken individually do not make up the pattern, it is only their relation to each other that makes the pattern. Moreover, the pattern required an act on your part to decode and find it. If nobody ever found it, we could not say it existed, but we would be equally hesitant to say that it did not exist. We should perhaps say that the pattern, until discovered, was latently or potentially there, and it was your effort that first brought it to light. Finally, once we recognized the pattern, it changed the experience of the sheet of paper. It is now very difficult for us not to notice that pattern on the paper, even though it is the same sheet of paper.

Experience and the act of interpreting it, I suggest, can be much like pattern recognition. Elements of our experience have meaning only in relation to each other, just like the elements of the pattern. This means

---

themselves (and reject homophobia) from the beginning. There are also other reasons for rejecting homophobia. A friend commented that he did not reject homophobic moral standards so much as the idea that morality really had anything to say about private, consensual sex at all. The interesting cases for a theory of experience, however, are like these cases I have described here.

9. I am inspired in this comparison by Dennett, "Real Patterns."

that foregrounded parts of experience have potential meanings that emerge in relation to other elements of experience that make up their context. This unfolding of experience is often the result of an act of interpretation and reflection on the part of the experiencer, just as the pattern requires an act of observation. Finally, once the pattern is recognized, that is, once the elements of our life experiences are recontextualized and seen afresh, the experiences themselves change, but only because they had that latent possibility to begin with. Meanings can be located within experience, but only with respect to future possible interpretations. Before these interpretations, the meaning held in this experience is felt and thought only vaguely or inaccurately or possibly not at all.

Any remaining discomfort with the "there/not there" quality of those experiences that motivate a change in identity results, I think, from remaining caught within a foundationalist notion that experience must be either self-evidently meaningful or not meaningful at all. This is exactly the kind of thinking that Mohanty and the realist theory of identity is urging us to move beyond. To recognize mediated knowledge as the only kind of knowledge we have is also to recognize that a more fluid, changing kind of experience with mediated and changing meanings is the only kind of experience that there is.[10]

Although my understanding of experience is based in part on phenomenological considerations, it is realist in precisely the sense that it also holds out the claim that there are more accurate understandings of experiences. Accurate interpretations of experiences are those that, through theoretical reflection, provide the most fruitful and long-lasting understanding of one's own identity. Our best test for the accuracy of an interpretation of experience, in other words, is whether or not it continues to provide coherent explanations of future experiences. Moreover, an interpretation of experience and the identity based on it are accurate precisely insofar as they are subject to continued verification over the course of one's life.[11] One's identity, on the realist theory, is not fixed and immutable, it can change as one's place in society and one's own experiences change, but there will be interpretations of experiences that take account of the most experiences and the most salient facts and continue to do so through the course of one's life.

10. This is similar to Merleau-Ponty's claim that we must recognize ambiguity as a fundamental feature of human experience, rather than simply see all experience as either fully there and meaningful or not meaningful at all.

11. See Moya 139.

To summarize, meaning in experience is taken up through theoretical reflection and becomes the source of new knowledge about oneself and one's place in the world. The act of reflection changes the character of these experiences, often radically, by noting how they fit together in new ways. Although the most coherent pattern of experience is the best interpretation, coherence is not the only standard of accuracy for judging one's understanding of one's identity. New interpretations of experience not only make sense of what has gone before, they are subject to constant verification as they stand through the future events in a person's life.

Coming out is neither the recognition of one's self-evident and immutable essence nor an arbitrary and fragmented reinterpretation but instead the simultaneous recognition and reordering of experiences along the lines of a new identity that is simultaneously discovered and constructed. But then what do we say about a person before he or she comes out? Is he or she gay or lesbian? And if coming out is *both* discovery and construction, then what sense does it make to view coming out as the revealing or discovery of one's gay identity? If one does not view oneself as homosexual, and if one had homosexual experiences but not the experiences of a homosexual, then it would seem that the identity is not really present and being revealed.

For this reason, I think it is more coherent to construe coming out as *transformation:* the development of a new identity based on a reinterpretation of experiences. This new identity reflects a new and more accurate understanding of who one is in the world and how one can act in the world. Coming out allows gays or lesbians to better organize salient aspects of their experience, to gain an understanding of themselves that will help them to understand their place in the world and to develop modes of life and personalities that stem from this new understanding.

Changing our understanding of coming out from revelation to transformation would have additional ramifications. We would begin to see that the supposed contrast between choice or nature is simply mistaken, insofar as coming out is change motivated by experience interpreted through explicitly political understandings of the world. So it is either both choice and nature (the experiences are not chosen, but the interpretation of them is) or neither choice nor nature (there is nothing necessary and natural in the experiences, and the identity is not chosen but constructed). Also, the debate about essentialism and social constructionism would be recast. By construing coming out as transformation, we can sensibly say that there were always people who were having homosexual experiences, although they may have chosen to organize these experiences in varying ways across cultures and historical epochs. Yet homosexuality, as a politically salient identity organized around a particular view of one's sexuality, is indeed a modern construct. So it is both real and constructed.

Moreover, as Mohanty correctly points out, these understandings that establish identity are not only theoretically mediated; this mediation is more often than not political in character ("The Epistemic Status" 51). This is particularly clear in the case of coming out. While some gays and lesbians would like to "just" *be* gay and not be "political" about it, the realist theory shows that this is an incoherent and inaccurate understanding of one's sexual identity. Insofar as a pre–coming out understanding of oneself is typically based on the idea that being lesbian or gay is simply wrong or unnatural, and insofar as this idea is a distorted and inaccurate ideology about what counts as sexual normalcy, the acceptance of an alternative theory about one's own sexual desire that claims that it is normal and acceptable is, by its very nature, oppositional. Modern lesbian and gay identity as such is political insofar as the act of coming out that so characterizes modern gay identity involves the rejection of homophobic standards.

Anyone who adopts a gay or lesbian identity but ignores the political implications of this action has not fully grasped the meaning of the coming out experience. Coming out is the recognition that one has been in error with respect to who one was, and that this error came about because of homophobic theories about sexuality and personhood prevalent in society. Once the transformation into a gay identity begins, one implicitly rejects homophobia and those parts and structures of society that maintain it. In this way, gay identity "refers" to existing social structures, reveals their relation to one's personal identity, and also condemns them as wrong.

MEETING THE OBJECTION

Mohanty's realist theory of identity is therefore able to meet the objection put forward at the beginning of this chapter. Because experience is contextual, it is neither immediate nor self-evident, and so both error and accuracy are possible. Interpretations of experience can be more or less accurate because there are more and less coherent and comprehensive understandings of one's own experience, understandings that take account of more salient features of the pattern or lattice of our experience. However, recognition and reinterpretation change these experiences and their meaning in precisely the way that recognizing a pattern involves a Gestalt-like switch in our perceptual field. Aspects of our experience thus motivate us to new interpretations, even as these new interpretations dialectically transform the motivating factors. We can assert that these interpretations are accurate in that they are based on latent meanings in the experience and in that the identity established from them is subject to future verifications.

On phenomenological reflection, therefore, we see that the picture of experience tucked into Mohanty's theory is not at all implausible; at the least it is no stranger than the actual phenomenon of pattern recognition. Moreover, it allows us to make sense of the way in which a person's identity and self-understanding can change, in light of the same experiences that previously had not motivated one to any strong stand with respect to oneself. Thus it is not a contradiction to assert that, for example, developing a gay identity reflects an accurate interpretation of one's experience, even if that experience is not yet the experience of a gay person, because one's pre–coming out experience is potentially that of a gay person, and fulfillment of this potential will both allow for a more coherent interpretation of previously ambiguous experiences and continue to be confirmed as the person lives out his or her life.

POSTMODERN[12] VIEWS ON EXPERIENCE AND KNOWLEDGE

As Mohanty points out (*Literary Theory* 203) postmodernist criticisms of identity and identity politics often stem from suspicions about the reliability of knowledge gained from experience. These postmodernist suspicions, in turn, are often based on Derridean criticisms of a theory of experience that, while peculiar to the continental tradition of phenomenology, do have a broader currency in the history of philosophy. Having shown that the realist theory of experience is accurate and fruitful for understanding the relation of experience and identity, I would now like to further demonstrate how its understanding of experience

12. Since none of the theorists I will be examining here identify as postmodernists (few, it seems, do identify as such), I justify this claim on the grounds that they hold many of the views that seem to characterize a broad movement that has come to be called postmodern. These views are a strident antifoundationalism, skepticism with regard to the capacity of reason to produce truth, a commitment to power and desire as constitutive in the formation of both knowledge claims and personal identities, and a belief in historicism.

evades altogether the standard postmodernist criticisms of experience. In what follows, I explain the phenomenological context to which Derrida is reacting, in order to clarify the specific nature of his criticisms. I then expound postmodernist views that expand on Derrida's arguments and argue that they lead to irresolvable incoherencies. Finally, I show how the realist theory does not so much respond to the difficulties with postmodernist epistemologies as simply sidestep the problems they raise.

HUSSERL AND DERRIDA

Phenomenology is a tradition specifically concerned with the nature and structure of human experience. Edmund Husserl's initial goal was to clarify the foundations of both philosophy and logic (and eventually the sum of human knowledge) through an understanding of the structure of our experience. The motivating idea was that experience was the point of access to the world and to knowledge and that by understanding the structure of experience, we could find the foundation for our knowledge of the world. The guiding light of Husserl's inquiry (in his middle period) was a notion of truth and evidence according to which an object of experience was in perfect correlation with itself, in "self-givenness." That is, we know truth from its experience of absolute coincidence between intention and intended object (*Cartesian Meditations* 11–14, 57–58). It is this ideal of perfect coincidence in the now that forms Husserl's "principle of principles" and which Derrida picks as the starting point for his criticism.

Derrida's deconstruction of Husserl in *Speech and Phenomena* is built around two related themes. First, Derrida launches an immanent critique of Husserl's theory of truth and evidence, claiming that it is inconsistent with Husserl's considered view on time. On the one hand, Husserl required full and immediate presence of the object of experience in order to ground his notion of evidence. This required the punctual view of time in which nows were fully self-contained. On the other hand, Husserl's investigations into the experience of time passage seem to reject this punctual view of time by insisting that experiencing something as present in the now requires the now to be related to my past experience and to future anticipations of that state of affairs (*The Phenomenology*). Thus Husserl, in his commitment to an accurate description of experience, thought that the immediacy required for evidence was not possible. However, he nonetheless held on to notions of perfect presence and punctual presents as criteria for his notion of evidence (Derrida 60–67).[13]

Second, Derrida argues that immediacy as such is impossible, because any sense or awareness of the present moment as the present moment is necessarily "divided" by its reference to nonpresent moments. Derrida's claim, while intricate, can be understood by noting his view that things are "ideal" insofar as they admit of the possibility of repetition and substitution. For example, the ideality of a sign consists in its ability to be reidentified through its various material instantiations. The punctual now must, like a sign, be iterable if we are to have a sense of this current now as it relates to previous and future nows. This means, however, that each now is split in its core by its reference to nows that are nonidentical with it—the future and past nows. This splitting or doubling of the now introduces otherness and absence into the very moment of the selfsame now, and reveals that the pure, simple presence of the now runs off into an infinity of otherness. Derrida then argues that the present moment in which the subject of experience is simultaneous with the object of experience must be reproduced in its connection to previous nows, so the perfect coincidence required for Husserlian evidence and experiential foundationalism is not possible.[14]

This all seems highly arcane, but it is essential to see that the view of experience as immediate and punctual is a part of the view of experiential foundationalism since Descartes. Derrida himself sees this point, noting that reliance on presence "defines the very element of philosophical thought, it is evidence itself, conscious thought itself, it governs every possible concept of truth and sense" (62). Any mediation would destroy the intimate connection between the experiencing and knowing subject and the object known and open space for interpretation and error. Thus most postmodern theorists accept such a refutation of givens within experience and then further assume that, since we can derive no accurate knowledge from experience, the category of experience should no longer serve as the starting point for explanations of identity formation or the history of social groups. For example, in *Essentially Speaking*, Diana Fuss

13. This criticism of Derrida's might be unfair to Husserl. Husserl's view of the now might have been that it was "broad" and constituted in relation to future and past moments, such that immediate presence really does not imply a punctual now. For a discussion of this ambiguity in Husserl, see Robert Sokolowski, *Husserlian Meditations,* esp. 165–67. For a discussion of how the problem relates to Derrida's criticism, see M. C. Dillon, *Semiological Reductionism,* esp. 43–46.

14. This argument is not fully articulated in one place, although most of it can be found in *Speech and Phenomena* 48–59, 67–69.

picks up the Derridean criticism of the metaphysics of presence (mediated through Jonathan Culler) and argues that experience cannot be simply an "unmediated real" (114). Instead, she claims that experience is "socially mediated" by language and discourse (25, 114). She then takes an additional step common to a postmodern perspective and claims that this mediation takes place via a distorting ideology, such that belief in the truth of experience is itself an ideological production.[15] Thus she claims that not even the experience women have of something as intimate as their own bodies is a reliable place to form an understanding of the category "woman." Fuss asserts that this does not rule out the place of experience in providing evidence, because it can still be used as "evidence of a sort" of the productions of ideology (118). Thus we can use experience to understand processes of identity formation and distortion but not to form a reliable understanding of identity.

Joan Scott, in "The Evidence of Experience," presents a similar account of experience. She argues that historians, even "historians of difference" who recover the hidden narratives of racial minorities, women, and lesbians and gays, view experience as incontestable evidence based on transparent and self-evident meanings, which these historians use as the foundation of explanation (775–77). For example, these historians might read the development of gay culture as the process of a transparently meaningful desire that has gradually created institutions to accommodate itself over time, and the gradual "coming out" of these institutions has challenged the repression of society (778). Scott argues, specifically, that we are wrong to interpret Samuel R. Delany's autobiographical reflections about coming to a "gay consciousness" on entering a bathhouse as his reflection on brute and transparently meaningful experiences of being black and gay in the early 1960s. Instead, she urges that we see his development as "the substitution of one interpretation for another" based on the recognition of the shifting uncertainties of representation itself (794). Scott argues that the foundationalist theory of experience and evidence is wrong simply *because* it does not attend to its own historicity and construction. While not made explicit, I believe her reasoning is based on the way in which some historians might assume that the meaning of an experience is intrinsic to that experience.

15. Fuss does not explain what she means by ideology. Since the discussion makes mention of Althusser, however, we can assume she means something like the rules and ideas of the established political and economic order that have some role in reproducing the relations of production.

This would mean, in turn, that its meaning is unrelated to issues of social and historical context, and thus could be said to be ahistorical.[16]

Scott proposes that we leave behind the idea of experience as a foundation, and even a beginning of our knowledge, and instead inquire about the production and constitution of experience and identities. Rather than use experience as the origin of our explanation, we should treat it as the object of our explanation. This is possible because, according to Scott, experience is a linguistic event that does not happen outside established meanings (793). Accordingly, experience cannot be understood apart from language, and since language is a social and historical creation, "historical processes, through discourse, position subjects and produce their experiences" (779). Thus, like Fuss, Scott claims that we can understand the processes that produce these discourses and produce the experiences of difference itself. This new explanation is the payoff for this switch of perspectives: we can understand something more basic and fundamental than simply differences in identity and perspective; we can now understand the *origin* of these differences.

PROBLEMS WITH POSTMODERNIST VIEWS ON EXPERIENCE

Postmodernists are right, I believe, to put forward and accept various criticisms of immediacy, givenness, and foundationalism. And in this, they are in some agreement with less radical critiques of these notions that belong to more "modern" views like those of Hegel, Merleau-Ponty, and Wittgenstein and, of course, the realist theory. The realist theory is also sympathetic to postmodern attention to power relations in the production of identity. The problem, however, is that the postmodernist view goes too far in its rejection of experience as a starting point for knowledge. By rejecting any possibility that experience gives us reliable knowledge and by claiming that it is totally historical and constituted, we are led into two aporias. First, we cannot distinguish ideology from truth, since all experience is the production of ideology. Second, it is unclear how we arrive at knowledge of the production of experience through ideology and discourse, if not from the very experience that we are supposed to reject.[17]

---

16. She presents no further argument that something's being ahistorical is a problem, although I accept such a premise.

17. I here understand "ideology" in a fairly narrow Marxist sense as those conceptions and ideas that help to maintain structures of domination and oppression. Although sometimes false, ideological conceptions are often distortions and partial truths.

The first of these points is illustrated by Fuss. Recall that she claimed experience is the product of an ideology. She is not clear, however, whether she wants to claim that *all* experience is an ideological production or merely some or most of it. If it is the former view that she endorses, then it is not possible to explain how we could actually come to have knowledge that our experience is the product of ideology. Knowledge and understanding of the world must come from some source. Presumably the source of most of it is our experience or what we infer and discover through reflection on that experience. (We certainly would not want to adopt nativism, and it is hard to see how language and discourse escape being part of our experience.) If all of that experience is somehow distorted or ideological, then we could never have experience that is not ideological. Ideology would then become total and inescapable, and capacity to distinguish it *as* ideology would therefore collapse.[18] If Fuss takes the latter view that only some of our experience is the product of ideology, then she owes us a story about how we can come to distinguish ideological from nonideological experience. Such a story would have to explain how there can be theory- and knowledge-mediated experience that can be more and less accurate, since Fuss would not want to revert back to the immediate view of experience that she takes herself to have transcended. This, in turn, would imply a concept of truth that did not rely on the notions of immediacy and presence she criticizes. No such account of truth or experience is to be found in *Essentially Speaking*.

Scott illustrates the second aporia: if discursive practices actually produce our experience and identity, then the origin and reliability of my knowledge of these discursive practices becomes highly questionable. If my knowledge of these identity- and experience-forming practices comes through experience, then it would seem that we are back to taking experience as the starting point for knowledge. This itself goes against Scott's basic thesis, and, even if she were to offer it as a response, she would face difficulties similar to those faced by Fuss. If my knowledge is not had through experience, then it seems we require a nonexperiential source of knowledge: either knowledge of these things would be innate (which is absurd), or knowledge of them would be an inference to the best explanation of the source of my experience. But if it is merely an inference from experience, by hypothesis, I could not have any way of testing my understanding of the source of my experience: no experi-

---

18. One is of course free to adopt such a position, but it would seem to eliminate the need for liberatory theory, since getting out from under ideology is simply impossible.

ence could prove it to be true or false, since I can have no experience of an unmediated reality. Theory about the origin of my identity and experience becomes conjecture.

If Fuss's and Scott's theories face similar difficulties, it is because they share the same, flawed assumption. Both assume as a starting point a false dichotomy between an absolute and self-evidently meaningful experience and an experience that is produced, contingent, and typically ideological. When the foundationalist view then fails, they are forced to take on the other view, which is equally as "totalizing" as the foundationalist view they leave behind. Fuss, for example, describes the contrast as existing between the view that either experience is "real and immediate presence and therefore . . . a reliable means of knowing," or it is "itself a product of ideological practices" and is therefore "fundamentally unreliable" (114). The possibility that experience can be both produced and mediated and nonetheless reliable (without, however, being foundational) never arises, and so we are left to wonder how the knowledge that experience is ideological can possibly be formed.

Although Scott also criticizes the foundationalist view, she is more nuanced in her understanding of possible alternatives, holding out that experience can be an interpretation (i.e., something produced) and something to be interpreted (i.e., something with some meaning of its own) (797). However, she never really examines the interrelation of these two elements, as is visible in her treatment of Delany's work and her understanding of what it might mean to have one's "consciousness raised." When she claims that Delany's raised consciousness is the result of the substitution of one interpretation for another, this implies that Delany, and by extension anyone changing her or his understanding, is basing this change of consciousness on *experience*. After all, claiming that it is a changed interpretation means that it is in fact an interpretation, and interpretation is always an interpretation of something. What else could it be an interpretation of, except Delany's experience? Scott, however, is basically silent on this question of what he is interpreting and *why* he might have preferred one interpretation over another. Instead, she shifts to a discussion of the inability of any representational medium to accurately capture any identity that is historically specific. The categories "black" and "gay" are not adequate to the task of understanding an identity that was both black and gay before either category had come to be fully articulated. Moreover, Delany views his identity as formed not only by racial and sexual categories but also by economic forces. Because all of these categories—racial, sexual, and economic—are the product of historically specific discourses, these categories are limited to these discourses and historicize the experience they mediate (794–95). But with this interpretation of consciousness raising, Scott commits herself to a contradictory position. On the one hand, she continues to assume that there is something not captured by the categories available to Delany, implying that his experience does have some meaning awaiting better interpretation; on the other, she claims that there is nothing beyond the available discursive structures to be understood, implying that there is nothing there but the production of historical discourses. So, on this postmodernist understanding, we seem to recognize that available understandings of the meaning of one's experience are inadequate while simultaneously implying that there is nothing in experience beyond the available understandings.

EVADING THESE APORIAS THROUGH REALISM

These investigations into postmodernism show that, even if the realist picture of experience as both meaningful and mediated seems troubling to those of us conditioned to think in foundationalist terms, the outright rejection of the possibility of experience-based truth claims leads to apparently insoluble difficulties. Namely, postmodern "epistemologies" like those I have examined undercut the very claims that they want to make about ideology and the production of ideology by prohibiting possible sources of knowledge about these facets of social life. Postmodernists are also unable to explain what would actually motivate someone to reexamine and change their self-understanding and identity. These two problems stem from an unwillingness to view experience in any other than two categories: totally mediated and therefore inaccurate or totally self-present and without outside mediation and influence.

Returning to the discussion of Derrida, we see that his own criticisms of notions of the total self-presence of experience were in fact launched against a very specific theory of experience: Husserl's theory of evidence. Derrida claims, nonetheless, that in attacking Husserl's theory, he is attacking the foundations of much of Western philosophy (4–5). About this he may be right: the insistence on immediacy of meaning and the self-givenness of experience has a long history in philosophy, turning up in the classical empiricists like Locke and Hume as well as in their later positivist decedents, and also in more "idealist" and rationalist strains of philosophy like Husserl's.[19] And his criticisms of this picture of immediacy are devastating indeed.

Regardless of how devastating they may be, however, they are also quite limited. For, if one releases the "principle of principles"—the assumption that evidence and truth is contained in the absolute presence of object and intuition—and adopts a different picture of experience and truth altogether, then one evades the Derridean criticism. Some philosophers in Derrida's own tradition of phenomenology have in fact done precisely this. Merleau-Ponty flatly refused to accept a picture of time and consciousness in which an object is experienced in an immediate now-point, and in which truth is contained in this coincidence. Instead, he viewed our experience of time as a complex and extended network of intentionalities, in which objects were experienced across time and experience was fluid and somewhat ambiguous. This allowed him to avoid the difficulties with foundationalist views of experience without falling prey to the difficulties that ensnare other postmodernists.

The realist theory of identity, it seems to me, evades Derridean criticisms in a similar fashion. Because it views experience as mediated from the start, it does not have to deal with the problems that arise from assuming immediacy and perfect self-presence in experience. However, because it starts with the idea that all experience is mediated, rather than with a rejection of foundationalism, it is not tempted to hold on to the antinomy that structures much of postmodernist thought: either knowledge must be absolutely grounded, or it will have no grounding at all.

Furthermore, the realist theory's willingness to regard mediated knowledge as the only kind of knowledge that we have grants it the leverage to distinguish ideological distortion from (mediated) truth. To see this, recall my earlier discussion of coming out. I described the process of coming out as having its source in a twofold recognition: on the one hand, a person notes the latent pattern in her or his life experience that had previously eluded them or had at best been noted only dimly; on the other, this recognition is spurred on by a rejection of homophobic institutions and ideals in the current society. This rejection itself is a form of theoretical mediation, insofar as contact with other, self-accepting gays and lesbians and an invigorating criticism of current gender relations in society make it possible. I claimed that these two points about coming

---

19. Even Descartes's insistence on an introspective truth criteria like "clear and distinct" ideas has a sort of immediacy tucked into it.

out mean that the acceptance of gay identity is a political act, one that condemns societal standards. Coming out, therefore, represents a rejection of an ideological and distorted view of a person's experience, a view that suppressed certain relevant patterns in one's life and which must be set aside as inaccurate in light of the more comprehensive view granted by the acceptance of gay identity. Thus, in the case of coming out, the interrelation of experience, mediation, and social structures allows one to recognize distorted understandings and the negative impact they have on one's life and to seek more accurate, more comprehensive, and ultimately freer understandings of one's own identity. The other essays in this volume demonstrate that this same is true of many other identities. The identities do not need to be fixed forever, but neither should they be viewed as solely the product of distorting outside forces. Instead, through continued examination and interaction with others in similar situations, more accurate and comprehensive views of one's place in the world can be gathered.

CONCLUSIONS

The realist theory, I have argued, has a robust and reasonable theory of experience, according to which experience can both be mediated and grant more and less accurate knowledge via reflections on the part of subjects who are willing to look closely at their experience. Moreover, this theory of experience is not one that is without precedence in the philosophical tradition. Indeed, I have drawn extensively on the work of Merleau-Ponty in developing some of the insights of the realist theory. This choice of Merleau-Ponty as an ally of the realist theory is apt in two important ways: as the "philosopher of the ambiguous," Merleau-Ponty sought to find middle grounds between many of the classical antinomies of philosophy. This included the realist/relativist antinomy, according to which knowledge must either be absolutely grounded or totally relativistic. The realist theory successfully skirts this antinomy as well. Also, Merleau-Ponty's work avoids many of the difficulties that led to the Derridean critique of experience and knowledge. I argued that, in a similar fashion, the realist theory evades the problematic ideas that led to postmodern epistemologies and so can stand apart from them. The realist theory is particularly important, however, in its ability to show that ideologically distorted understandings of identity and experience can be overcome through the very mediation that postmodernists think undercuts all possibility of knowledge.

WORKS CITED

Dennett, Daniel C. *Consciousness Explained*. Boston: Little, Brown, 1991.

———. "Real Patterns." *Journal of Philosophy* 89 (1991): 27–51.

Derrida, Jacques. *Speech and Phenomena*. Trans. David B. Allison. Evanston, IL: Northwestern University Press, 1973.

Dillon, M. C. *Semiological Reductionism*. Albany: State University of New York Press, 1995.

Fuss, Diana. *Essentially Speaking: Feminism, Nature & Difference*. New York: Routledge, 1990.

Husserl, Edmund. *Cartesian Meditations*. Trans. Dorian Cairns. Dordrecht: Kluwer Academic Publishers, 1993.

———. *Ideas Pertaining to a Pure Phenomenology and to a Phenomenological Philosophy*. Bk. 1. Trans. F. Kersten. Dordrecht: Kluwer Academic Publishers, 1982.

———. *The Phenomenology of Internal Time Consciousness*. Ed. Martin Heidegger. Trans. James Churchill. Bloomington: Indiana University Press, 1964.

Merleau-Ponty, Maurice. *The Phenomenology of Perception*. Trans. Colin Smith. London: Routledge and Kegan Paul.

Mohanty, Satya P. "The Epistemic Status of Cultural Identity: On *Beloved* and the Postcolonial Condition." *Cultural Critique* 24 (Spring 1993): 41–80. [Reprinted as chapter 1 in this volume.]

———. *Literary Theory and the Claims of History*. Ithaca: Cornell University Press, 1997.

Moya, Paula M. L. "Postmodernism, 'Realism,' and the Politics of Identity: Cherríe Moraga and Chicana Feminism." *Feminist Genealogies, Colonial Legacies, Democratic Futures*. Ed. M. Jacqui Alexandra and Chandra Talpade Mohanty. New York: Routledge, 1997. 125–50. [Reprinted as chapter 2 in this volume.]

Rorty, Richard. *Philosophy and the Mirror of Nature*. Princeton: Princeton University Press, 1979.

Schachter, S., and J. Singer. "Cognitive, Social, and Physiological Determinants of Emotional State." *Psychological Review* 69.5 (1962): 379–99.

Scheman, Naomi. *Engenderings: Constructions of Knowledge, Authority and Privilege*. New York: Routledge, 1993.

Scott, Joan. "The Evidence of Experience." *Critical Inquiry* 17 (1991): 773–97.

Sellars, Wilfrid. *Science, Perception and Reality*. Atascadero, CA: Ridgeview, 1963.

Sokolowski, Robert. *Husserlian Meditations*. Evanston, IL: Northwestern University Press, 1972.

CHAPTER 9

Reading "Experience"

*The Debate in Intellectual History
among Scott, Toews, and LaCapra*

John H. Zammito

To believe that you have your space and I mine, to believe, further, that
there can be no responsible way in which I can adjudicate between
your space—cultural and historical—and mine by developing a set
of general criteria that can have interpretive validity in both contexts
(because there can be no interpretation that is not simultaneously an
evaluation)—to believe both these things is also to assert something
quite large. Quite simply, it is to assert that all spaces are equivalent,
that they have equal value. . . . I cannot—and consequently need not—
think about how your space impinges on mine or how my history is
defined together with yours. . . . I end by denying that I need to take
you seriously.

Satya P. Mohanty,
Literary Theory and the Claims of History

In history, the principle cannot be that the stronger the misreading the
better, for here history does not emulate creative writing and is constrained by different norms of inquiry. At the very least, there is in history a basic distinction between the attempt to reconstruct the object
of inquiry, including its meaning or possibilities at its own time or over
time, and the entry into a dialogic exchange with it that tries to bring
out its potential in the present and for the future.

Dominick LaCapra,
"History, Language and Reading"

In an essay that continues to have repercussions in a wide variety of fields
such as literary theory, cultural studies, minority studies and feminism,
the historian Joan Scott has attacked the concept "experience" as a dangerously laden term whose presumed self-evidence abets the hegemonies

of orthodoxy.[1] One of the thrusts of her critique is to challenge the place of "experience" in methodological discussions of the practice of history. Scott writes: "'Experience' is one of the foundations that has been reintroduced into historical writing in the wake of the critique of empiricism. . . . It has recently emerged as a critical term in debates among historians about the limits of interpretation and especially about the uses and limits of post-structuralist theory for history" ("Evidence" 780). Her exasperation with the term and its use is vivid: "Experience is not a word we can do without, although it is tempting, given its usage to essentialize identity and reify the subject, to abandon it altogether" ("Experience" 37). In particular she condemns the intellectual historian John Toews for his use of the term. She elaborates: "Experience for Toews is a foundational concept. . . . Whatever diversity or conflict may exist among them, Toews's community of historians is rendered homogeneous by its shared object (experience)" (32). For Scott, such a community constitutes itself only by *repressing* conflicting interests: "As Ellen Rooney has so effectively pointed out . . . this kind of homogeneity can exist only because of the exclusion of the possibility that 'historically irreducible interests divide and define reading communities'" ("Evidence" 790).[2] Elsewhere, Scott charges that any effort to articulate some common standard tends toward the "establishment and protection of hegemonic definitions." She sees this as a mechanism for "the forcible exclusion of Others' stories" ("History in Crisis?" 681, 690).

Postmodernist theorists of history such as Scott often make gestures of acknowledgment that history is an "empirical" discipline, that "evidence matters," that there is a presumption of "referentiality" in our disciplinary practices.[3] Where the problem appears to lie is in establishing what exactly such gestures betoken. When others try to grasp them more determinately we risk being condemned for "reductionism," "positivism," or, worse still, political oppression.[4] But the time is long since

1. Joan Scott, "The Evidence of Experience," in *Critical Inquiry,* and in a shorter but more widely circulated version, "Experience," in Judith Butler and Joan Scott, eds., *Feminists Theorize the Political.* Subsequent references to these essays will be noted as "Evidence" and "Experience," respectively.

2. See Ellen Rooney, *Seductive Reasoning.*

3. See, e.g., Joan Scott, "History in Crisis?" 686; Dominick LaCapra, "History, Language and Reading" 826; and Frank Ankersmit, *History and Tropology* 194.

4. Dorothy Ross, for example, writes, "Although it is surely worthwhile to articulate professional norms such as impartiality and empirical grounding . . . these norms do not reach the deeper problems of historical contingency. Also, they can slide over into efforts at professional containment." She sees "standards of impartiality" being used as "a fixed basis for professional definition and hence . . . a tool for policing borders," i.e., as "part

past when representatives of new "theory" or—much more important—
of new social or cultural orientations have been marginalized or excluded.
Joan Scott's prominence in the profession is unquestioned. Dominick La-
Capra and Hayden White are the most influential historical theorists of
the current era. Feminist and minority history is a powerful and presti-
gious pursuit, as anyone attending current disciplinary conferences will
find obvious. The pathos of marginalization as an argument for the
benefits of radical "theory" is simply outdated. Now the question must
be about the relative merits of epistemological and ontological claims
for the future cognitive as well as political progress of the discipline.

Scott insists that she is eager to discuss "questions about how poststructuralism can study change, about the limits of textualizing for historians, about the uses of Freud and Lacan for thinking about subjectivity historically" ("The Tip of the Volcano" 443). Toews was trying to
enter into just such a discussion of the limits of postmodernist conceptions of historical method, only to have his contestation impugned as politically repressive. Ironically and ominously, Scott's response is a far more
blatant instance of the politically preemptive gesture that she imputes to
Toews. Not only is this contention contestable for its cognitive claims;
it is not even clear that it is consistent with its ostensible political criterion of democratization of historical practice if that has as one of its car-
dinal criteria free exchange of ideas. In that context, grasping each other's
language remains the indispensable undertaking if our dialogue is to have
any substance.[5] The question is whether there can be any standard that
is not spurious, and whether the disciplinary community can afford to
be without some shared standards. I contend that history as an empirical discipline must cultivate standards of evidential objectivity, but I add
emphatically that it is not in a position and is also under no obligation
to establish an absolute foundational grounding for these standards. They
are constituted in and by the discipline for the sake of its collective project.
It is always by situating appraisals and claims within the horizon of reception or influence, a tradition of discourse, that historians take up questions of validity. Raymond Martin offers us a reasonable point of de-

---

of a political program." (Afterword 706). Hans Kellner pushes the same political line: "The
debate is not really over narrative and 'science.' It is about power and legitimation in the
profession, not how best to present or conduct research." (*Language and Historical Representation* 122).

5. "In the absence of discussion of the foundational questions that separate them, contextualists and postmodernists cannot engage each other but merely hurl assertions and
counter-assertions, a linguistic turn indeed" (Hoopes, "Objectivity *and* Relativism Affirmed" 1554n).

parture: "If we reject, as I think we should, the ridiculous idea that in historical studies *anything goes,* then an essential and central part of our philosophical task is to determine what *stops* a historical interpretation; or, more modestly, in case nothing stops an interpretation cold, then our task is to discover what *slows one down*" ("Objectivity and Meaning" 32; original emphasis).

A good part of what Martin seeks is within reach when we see that the appraisal of historical interpretations is always already embedded in a *community of discourse.* How they are received is a function of the situation—the cognitive and also the normative expectations—of the interpreters. Marc Bevir notes aptly, "Objectivity arises from comparing and criticizing rival webs of interpretations in terms of facts. The basis for such a comparison of rival views exists because historians agree on a wide number of facts which collectively provide sufficient overlap for them to debate the merits of their respective views" ("Objectivity in History" 334). There is a set of procedural and normative standards by which historians practice such comparison and critique of interpretations. Bevir adverts to "criteria of accuracy, comprehensiveness, consistency, progressiveness, fruitfulness, and openness" (337). While we might choose somewhat different terms, expanding or contracting this list, the point is that no practicing historian is at all likely to take the set to be empty, though no one is likely to think that any of these criteria is unambiguous or not liable to mutual contestation (e.g., ranking). These are the terms of our disciplinary discourse. Their imprecision can neither be evaded nor turned into a justification for hyperbolic skepticism.

My motivation to dispute Scott's thesis arises equally from a concern to find some theoretical accommodation with the views of LaCapra, who has not only advocated the fruitfulness of the new postmodern approaches to intellectual history but also shown a serious regard for the elements of substance in more traditional approaches. To conceive an adequate postpositivist standard of empirical inquiry that could form a shared horizon of understanding for intellectual history, it is important to find some coordinates of "translation" between the theoretical vantage he represents and that of others like Toews who adopt a more hermeneutical approach. Unfortunately, LaCapra's recent effort to assess and relate the range of historical practices—"readings"—available to intellectual historians today is marred by his incorporation of Scott's indictment of Toews on experience ("History, Language and Reading" 821). Hence I propose to extricate Toews and the concept of experience from what I take to be the unreasonable accusations of Scott and defend a conception of historical practice that can reconcile hermeneutic-historicist concerns with those of LaCapra. My crucial recourse will be to Satya Mohanty's conception of "postpositivist realism."

LACAPRA'S VIEWS ON INTELLECTUAL HISTORY

With the "linguistic turn," that is, the premise that "language . . . is not a purely transparent medium," LaCapra believes that the "entire research paradigm" of history has been "placed in question" ("History, Language and Reading" 804). For him, the linguistic turn "mitigates the stark dichotomy between history and . . . critical and self-critical theory bearing on the practice of history itself" (803). He calls for "an active awareness that such issues as the subject-position(s) and voice(s) of the historian are an integral component of historiography complicating research and that the elucidation of one's implication in a contemporary network of research and methodological-theoretical-ideological controversy is not simply a dispensable matter of 'metahistory' or a specialized activity to be relegated to the 'think-piece'" (803). Such *historicization of the historical subject* makes it indeed unthinkable that we could return to the "naivety" of self-effacement *à la Ranke*.[6] LaCapra is certainly correct to insist that without reckoning with our own situatedness we compromise the prospects of meaningful research. Yet he is persuaded that what Martin Jay aptly terms "disintegral textualism" has neither established a clear consensus among postmodernists nor won over the historical discipline to a completely "textualist" self-conception.[7]

In his own theoretical writings, LaCapra has made some major contributions on behalf of the linguistic turn in historical method. He has argued that all sources have not merely a "documentary" but a "worklike" element.[8] Thus simple "documents" need not and should not always be "gutted" for information; read for their "worklike" elements, they can offer a richer harvest for historical interpretation. Even archival documents have "writerly" dimensions—that is, material most amenable to tropological analysis—and hence a *density* that only interpretation can penetrate. Conversely, "writerly" texts are vitally documentary; that is,

6. The phrase is from Gadamer, and it has been used effectively by Ankersmit to constate the essential issue between postmodernist and historicist approaches to historical writing. See Ankersmit 219–23.

7. See Martin Jay, "The Textual Approach to Intellectual History."

8. On the distinction of the "worklike" from the documentary, see LaCapra, *Rethinking Intellectual History*, esp. 29–30.

they embody and constitute the "real" of any given historical situation. This revisionist notion implies that the flow of causation should not simply be from context to text, as would seem to be the thrust of a *social* history of ideas. Literary works may well serve as the richest evidence for the complexity of the historical epoch in which they are embedded. "A fruitful reversal of perspectives would propose the complex text itself as at times a better model for the reconstruction of the 'larger context.' The relationship between text and context would then become a question of 'intertextual' reading, which cannot be addressed on the basis of reductionist oversimplifications that convert the context into a fully unified or dominant structure" (*History and Criticism* 128). Even more important is LaCapra's critique of naive notions of context. His argument undercuts the "notion of context as a synchronic whole, situated in time and place." Instead, he insists on "multiple, interacting contexts" (*Rethinking Intellectual History* 91, 344).[9] Accordingly, "texts interact with one another and with contexts in complex ways, and the specific question for interpretation is precisely how a text comes to terms with its putative contexts" (*History and Criticism* 128).

> The context itself is a text of sorts. . . . It cannot become the occasion for a reductive reading of texts. By contrast, the context itself raises a problem analogous to that of "intertextuality." For the problem in understanding context—and a fortiori the relation of context to text—is a matter of inquiry into the interacting relationships among a set of more or less pertinent contexts. Only this comparative process itself creates a "context" for a judgment that attempts to specify the relative importance of any given context. (*Rethinking Intellectual History* 95–96)

Yet nowhere in his own subtle handling of this question does LaCapra deny that documents *do* have constative aspects, that some references are reconstitutable. Sometimes, to invoke one of his favorite authors, a cigar is just a cigar.

While LaCapra clearly endorses "a concern for the work and play of the signifier or, more generally, for the way a text does what it does," he nonetheless honors "the insistence on thorough research, the importance of substantiating empirical statements, and the careful distinction between empirical and more speculative assertions—procedures that are ingrained as common sense in professional historiography" ("History, Language and Reading" 810). He cannot bring himself to repudiate them, and he

---

9. Hayden White launched the postmodern critique of context. See his "Historical Writing as a Literary Text," esp. 42–43.

even sees their value as "a check on more extravagant tendencies in reading and interpretation" (811). Still, his loyalties lie with more venture-
some interpretive styles, as emerges clearly in his defense of deconstructive reading practices: "In deconstructive reading, there is a pronounced
suspicion of synoptic or contextual reductionism, and virtually everything is to be found in nuance and the close reader's response to it." La-
Capra insists that Derrida's phrase, "il n'y a pas de hors-texte" (there is
nothing outside of the text), is not designed to foreclose the text but rather
"situates meaning and reference within a network of instituted traces or
a general trace-structure." The point is that "a text never simply con-
forms to its author's intentions, and its language is never fully transparent." Indeed, "deconstruction involves the analysis of the tensely related,
internally 'dialogized' forces in a text that place its author's explicit goals
or intentions in more or less extreme jeopardy" (812, 813).

Yet his dialogism is not simply linguistic; it is also historicist, for he
shows the same acuity about the resistance the *past* in the determinacy
of its traces offers to our constructions. For LaCapra, the "voice[s] of
the past" are not ventriloquistic "reality effects" of our own textual im-
mersion.[10] Against such a view he asserts: "The past has its own 'voices'
that must be respected, especially when they resist or qualify the interpretations we would like to place on them" (*Rethinking Intellectual History* 63–64). Historians must take cognizance of their essentially *dialogic*
relationship with the past: neither historian nor past exercises total hegemony. It is in this light that LaCapra finds Mikhail Bakhtin so important.[11] His own dedication to "dialogism" is the clear theoretical consequence of this.

That "the observer is constitutively implicated in the object of research" LaCapra analyzes in terms of Freud's notion of *transference*.[12]
LaCapra believes that Freudian notions like displacement and transference can have "great analogical value" in understanding the "repetition
with difference" of "the historical process in general." He writes, "The
turn to Freud may bring into prominence the role of transference as it
affects the historicity of the historian in entering into exchange with the
past, for, despite the importance of critical distance, the historian is never
in a position of total master over the object studied, and the concerns

10. As contrasted with Roland Barthes, "The Discourse of History" and "The Reality Effect."
11. See esp. "Bakhtin, Marxism, and the Carnivalesque," in *Rethinking Intellectual
History* 291–324.
12. LaCapra develops this idea in *Representing the Holocaust*.

agitating figures in the past may find their analogues in the work of the historian himself" (*Rethinking Intellectual History* 337). LaCapra contrasts this notion of transference to old-fashioned concerns with objectivity. Since "considerations at issue in the object of study are always repeated with variations—or find their displaced analogues—in one's account of it," following out the transference analogy in historical interpretation allows a discrimination along the lines of the therapeutic situation between "working through" and "acting out" the "repetition" experience (*History and Criticism* 72). He considers the former salutary while rejecting the latter as "phantasmatic" in its treatment of the displaced past as "a fully present reality" (*Soundings* 41).

LaCapra charges that "redemptive" historical reconstruction or hermeneutics threatens to revive that naive transparency both of the object and of the subject that twentieth-century criticism has debunked. He disputes the presumption that "the full meaning of a text or experience is . . . available to the interpreter" through contextualization, the "meaning-in-context of a past text." Worse still, he believes, is the *redemptive* motive itself—"a projective reprocessing of the past [in which] the meaning redeemed is typically that which one desires in the present"—for that involves "filling in or covering over traumas and gaps" in a spurious *Aufhebung*. LaCapra disdains this "harmonizing interpretation, especially when a neo-Hegelian frame of reference explicitly encourages a model of speculative, dialectical transcendence that is often combined with a phenomenological notion of experience as the foundation of meaning" ("History, Language and Reading" 819).

LaCapra concentrates his criticism of this "neo-Hegelian view," whereby "culture is a medium (or mediation) to make experience meaningful, and language is its primary means of accomplishing this (redemptive) feat," on Toews, but the sweep of his claim is wider, and all historical reconstruction of a contextualist-dialectical order seems to be implicated.[13] I propose to uphold historical reconstruction as a legitimate practice of empirical inquiry. To be sure, a Hegelianism "without reserve," one that proposes speculative transcendence, is problematic, but it hardly follows that *any* effort that seeks coherence or continuity along dialectical lines is *necessarily* specious. Two points should be made here. First, not every effort to be determinate (constative) makes pretense to

---

13. In a footnote, he assimilates my own views to those of Toews, with whom I do largely agree; thus this critique of Toews takes on contestatory salience for me. (La Capra, 803n, referring to my "Are We Being Theoretical Yet?")

"full meaning," to a totalizing, irrefutable account. To make a knowl-edge claim is not necessarily to practice "speculative transcendence." Contingency and fallibilism are essential features of any respectable his-torical empiricism. Second, the "phenomenological notion of experience" cannot be dismissed with a peremptory assertion. There is a substantial body of theoretical and empirical argument that buttresses the phe-nomenological approach. While hardly above criticism, it is a working basis for the interpretation of human affairs whose results are by no means inferior to those attained as yet by poststructuralism.

In sum, LaCapra envisions an "alternative conception of objectivity" that "would stress the importance of thorough research and accuracy, while nonetheless recognizing that language helps to constitute its ob-ject, historical statements depend on inferences from textualized traces, and the position of the historian cannot be taken for granted" ("History, Language and Reading" 804–5). In my view, these three premises are fully acceptable to hermeneutically oriented historians. That is, we ac-cept that language helps to constitute its object, rejecting only the view that it is solely constitutive of such objects. Similarly, we are sensitive to the textuality of the sources from which most of our historical inferences are drawn, and hence recognize the inevitably interpretive stance into which that puts us, as well as the levels of ambiguity through which we are removed from certainties. Finally, the acuteness of self-consciousness that LaCapra and other postmodernists have come to term "anxiety" is a tradition that had quite a history in the discipline of history before post-modernism, as the phrase "crisis of historicism" and all that it implies should betoken.[14] If there is, then, substantial accommodation from the side of hermeneutical-historicism to the position LaCapra outlines, I sub-mit there is a corresponding accommodation available from LaCapra's side. He refuses to "pander to a morbid delight in the aporias of current intellectual life . . . or indulge a facile equation of political radicalism and formal innovation in all its guises and under all conditions" (*History and Criticism* 112 and n). He concludes *History and Criticism* on that same note: "Fascination for discursive impasses and an obsessive interest in the aberrant and aleatory [represent] tendencies that threaten to identify all controlling limits with totalizing mastery and thus to undermine any conception of critical rationality" (141). He opens his third book once again with the same message: "The critique of totalization that has been

14. On the "crisis of historicism," see the recent study by Charles Bambaugh, *Hei-degger, Dilthey, and the Crisis of Historicism.*

so prominent in recent thought should not devolve into an indiscriminate reliance on techniques of fragmentation, decentering and associative 'play'" (*Soundings* 1).

Thus LaCapra demonstrates his fundamental allegiance to empirical historical practice. For him, historical practice is "constrained by different norms" than creative writing or literary criticism. He recognizes both historical reconstruction, which seeks "to reconstruct the object of inquiry, including its meaning or possibilities at its own or over time," and a "dialogic" approach concerned with contemporary or future relevance ("History, Language and Reading" 816). On this basis, it seems that there are considerable possibilities for a rapprochement between the sort of position that Toews represents and the one that LaCapra is hewing out. But there remains the stumbling block of Toews's notion of experience and Scott's political allegations about it.

"EXPERIENCE" IN THE PRACTICE OF INTELLECTUAL HISTORY

In one of the most important review essays of the 1980s for intellectual historians, Toews offered a measured and critical appraisal of the so-called linguistic turn in our discipline.[15] LaCapra describes it accurately as "the avenue through which many historians came to understand— and react to—the so-called linguistic turn in historiography." As he notes, Toews offered a "consistently high" discussion that made some powerful and persuasive points. Nonetheless, LaCapra suggests that the "definition, relations, and history" of Toews's key operating terms—meaning, experience, and language—"may be more problematic than Toews allows" ("History, Language and Reading" 821). Above all, he concentrates on Toews's notion of *experience*.

His rhetoric here proves puzzlingly equivocal. First, LaCapra writes that Toews developed a "sophisticated, well-developed argument," in which "one of the merits [was] to introduce unexpected intricacies into one's conception of 'experience.'" (One needs to pause over these words in anticipation of the balance of the controversy. Scott would have it that Toews never even reflected on his term!) After such a positive beginning, however, LaCapra shifts over to the attack, suggesting that "perhaps to some extent" Toews may be guilty by association with "other quarters [in which] it has become something of a scare word that intimidates op-

---

15. John Toews, "Intellectual History after the Linguistic Turn."

ponents[,] . . . a means of authenticating one's own position or argument . . . [in which] it often functions as the blackest of black boxes" (823). What is LaCapra insinuating here? How does this guilt by association work? For whom has it been a "scare word that intimidates opponents" and to what ends, in what conflicts? Where does Toews anywhere endorse these "others" who operate the "black box"? None of this can be discerned from *Toews's* text. LaCapra is in fact "reading" another: that of Scott. It remains to be seen whether Scott is right to charge that Toews's notion is unexamined or undefined, or LaCapra fair in linking Toews's argument with an invocation of "the blackest of black boxes."

We must consider Toews's original essay once again. He began by recognizing that most intellectual and cultural historians by the early 1980s accepted the necessity of taking up the "linguistic turn." Thus most historians had determined to "adapt traditional historical concerns for extralinguistic origins and reference to the semiological challenge" ("Intellectual History" 882). But to *adapt* is not to *abandon*. There were elements of established historical practice that remained essential to the conduct of inquiry. It was in trying to characterize what remains indispensable in these traditional historical concerns that Toews invoked the concept of *experience*. Historians were concerned—Toews used Martin Jay as his example—to discriminate "which among a variety of linguistic theories of meaning a historian should choose" ("Intellectual History" 881). This is a vital point: the postpositivist theoretical world is pluralist; there are many very different views of the impact of language on knowledge. Thus, within the analytic philosophy of language, there is the opposition of W. V. O. Quine or Donald Davidson to the views of John Austin, John Searle, and the intentionalist program, or in the continental tradition, there is the French poststructuralist appropriation of Ferdinand de Saussure to contest both the structuralists and the hermeneuticists, each with their own linguistic views. Some of these theoretical postures make more place for the conduct of empirical inquiry. Others take so hyperbolic a stance on language as to render conventional inquiry hopeless. What concerned Toews was "semiological theory of meaning in its extreme form [which] would seem to imply that language not only shapes experienced reality but constitutes it, that different languages create different, discontinuous, and incommensurable worlds, that the creation of meaning is impersonal, operating 'behind the backs' of language users whose linguistic actions can merely exemplify the rules and procedures of languages they inhabit but do not control" (882). As we will see from Scott's own arguments, these positions are not straw men of Toews's invention. Jay has demonstrated how one can move from Derrida's idea that the "trace" undermines *full* transparency to the implication that language renders reference in any discourse *opaque*.[16] Jay formulates this in fluent poststructuralist idiom: "Our reconstructions are themselves figurally charged, rhetorically constructed texts, which are allegorizing at a distance from the phenomena they purpose to reconstruct" ("Textual Approach" 85).[17] What postmodernists like Paul de Man, Hans Kellner, James Clifford, and Frank Ankersmit develop are various theories of linguistic opacity.[18]

Toews recognized that language is not a mere result but a causal engine of experience: "The 'experience' that generates the revising and transforming procedures of creative consumption is never 'raw' but 'always already' constituted in meaning" ("Intellectual History" 885). Invoking LaCapra and Roger Chartier, however, Toews introduced the crucial complication: "Meanings are never simply inscribed on the minds and bodies of those to whom they are directed or on whom they are 'imposed' but are always reinscribed in the act of reception" (883–84).[19] Toews described J. G. A. Pocock's complex theory of linguistic contextualization as one model of how this dialectic could be conceived. Pocock had pro-

---

16. The move from Derrida to this hyperbole is made particularly by Paul de Man. See de Man, *Allegories of Reading*. LaCapra has always been skeptical of de Man. See LaCapra, "History, Language and Reading," esp. 812–16.

17. Jay elaborates:

> Once meaning is recognized as entangled in the linguistic web of rhetorical devices which necessarily mediate it, it is impossible to posit its full historical recovery as a hermeneutic goal. . . . No amount of attention paid to reconstructing their illocutionary force, pace Skinner, will allow us to recall their intentionality, for prior to grasping how speech acts perform, we must make sense of their constative or locutionary meaning, which we cannot do without becoming entangled in the web of rhetorical, that is tropological, devices affecting our reading of them. ("Texual Approach" 83)

Jay offers the following reassurance: "Rather than denying the importance of referentiality in the name of a pure interplay of diacritical sign systems, as deconstruction is sometimes alleged to be doing, it should be understood as stressing its [that is to say, referentiality's] inevitability" (84). Yet he noticeably evades any mention of the social or the material in these remarks. Referentiality is never, it would appear, more than to other texts. If I understand Jay correctly, he sounds here amazingly like Paul de Man in suggesting that we never get out of the tropology of texts. Jay's own practice, of course, demonstrates that he does not really hold such a view, and that suggests further that his articulation of the "textualist" view is not representative of his own position.

18. De Man, *Allegories of Reading*; Clifford, "On Ethnographic Authority" and "On Ethnographic Allegory"; Kellner, *Language and Historical Representation*; Ankersmit, *History and Tropology*. I have addressed myself to this issue of hyperbole and opacity in "Are We Being Theoretical Yet?" and in "Ankersmit's Postmodern Historiography."

19. Toews invokes LaCapra's *Rethinking Intellectual History* and *History and Criticism*, as well as Chartier's "Intellectual History or Sociocultural History?"

posed three dimensions of reconstruction. First, he identified established discursive structures—"relatively stable conventions, usages, idioms, rhetorics or vocabularies." (Pocock now refers to these as "languages.") The point is that "many such languages may and usually do coexist . . . and any given text may participate in a number of languages." Pocock maintained that historical significance largely resided in how these "languages" were deployed in particular circumstances: "the specific linguistic performances or 'speech-acts'" involved. Toews noted that this was where the "creativity of reception" manifested itself. "The conditions that make a discourse possible are a plurality of languages and the existence of speakers who have access to these languages and are thus able to engage in creative linguistic performances." Historical interpretation reached its ultimate level in offering *explanations* of these particular reinscriptions of the available languages: "the innovations and transformations that individual speech acts perform on inherited languages must ultimately be situated in a history of experience and related to it in a 'diachronous, ambivalent and problematic' manner" (891–92).[20] That, I submit, represents a formulation of historical reconstruction that is responsive to the constitutive role of language in subjectivity and in social reality.

Moving from his discussion of Pocock to a more general perspective, Toews asserted: "Understanding change in the history of meaning requires a contextual analysis that is more than intertextual, that connects meanings to experience, that does not lose sight of the fact that 'living individuals' and not only texts are participants in the history of discourse" (897). Thus Toews claimed that the historical practice of intellectual history involves taking up "the problems of sustaining the dialectical unity of and difference between meaning and experience (as all historians must) in the wake of the linguistic turn" (882). "In spite of the relative autonomy of cultural meanings, human subjects still make and remake the worlds of meaning in which they are suspended. . . . [T]hese worlds are not creations *ex nihilo* but responses to, and shapings of, changing worlds of experience ultimately irreducible to the linguistic forms in which they appear" (882). The appeal to agency and to the materiality of context both stand, in my view, indispensably at the center of the historian's task, and "experience" is the theoretical term Toews invokes to identify them. What is at issue in Toews's formulation is the *dialectical* relation he postulates between meaning and experience. For his critics, Toews appears

20. See Allan Megill, "Recounting the Past."

to have granted too much essentialism to the two elements, allowing an ontological duality that his epistemology could not then contain. But a more hermeneutic, post-Hegelian conception of dialectic, which Toews explored in his own research and which I take him to be advocating here, is fully consistent with a postpositivist approach, as developed, for example, by Satya Mohanty or Anthony Giddens. Indeed, a Hegelian, dialectical approach (without, of course, his commitment to the Absolute) has been operative in the most creative social theory in the tradition of Marx and in the tradition of hermeneutics.

Finally, Toews demonstrated his sensitivity to the "historicization of the historical subject" by noting the further hermeneutic problematic for the interpreting historian: "Knowledge of the experience to which discourse responds and which it transforms into meaningful experience is itself only accessible through the mediation of texts: experience is not simply given but already worked over and mediated by language and thus as much an object of interpretation as the texts in the history of discourse" (892). This results in what Giddens has called a "double hermeneutic," that of the inquirer dealing with the subject material from his own situatedness, and that intrinsic to the matter investigated, since that is itself always already interpreted by its subjects.[21]

I have cited Toews so fully in order to carry out one of LaCapra's own injunctions for contestatory discourse, to provide enough citation to let the text's voice speak against the interpreter's ("History, Language and Reading" 826). I believe I have demonstrated that Toews fulfills each of the three demands that LaCapra proposed for his new, postpositivist standard of objectivity and that his usage of "experience" in this regard is perfectly appropriate.

Why, then, does LaCapra find fault with Toews's idea of experience? There are several considerations. LaCapra raises a number of substantive objections to Toews's notion of experience. First, he notes that *trauma* seems to spring the frame of both the phenomenological and the commonsense model of experience.[22] Indeed, psychological "opacities" are an important problem in reconstructing histories of experience, but the

---

21. See Anthony Giddens, *New Rules for the Sociological Method.* It is noteworthy that this interpretation is affirmed by Habermas but rejected by Rorty. Gloria Warnke, in "Hermeneutics and Social Science," defends the notion of a double hermeneutic. On Giddens as an exemplary theorist for intellectual historians caught up in the contextualist/poststructuralist polarization, see Stephen Collins and James Hoopes, "Anthony Giddens and Charles Sanders Peirce."

22. LaCapra's ideas on trauma take up the insights of Cathy Carruth, *Unclaimed Experience.*

very existence of such *categories* as "trauma" suggests that we are not utterly without resources, and that to employ them we must use other "experiences" to give us purchase on the repressed ones. While certainly there have been individual and collective traumas—most urgently, the Holocaust—that tax the resources of historical reconstruction, it remains that we can either fall mute or take up the laborious task of piecing together across the silenced and the unspeakable some approximation of the *experience* of trauma. If the latter exposes the enormous difficulty of the undertaking, it does not in my view discredit it.

Second, LaCapra argues that history must take into account what was not personally experienced, the "traces of others' experiences." Either I fail to understand what he means, or LaCapra has failed to understand what Toews in fact *proposed* in the most important passage involving experience in his essay. No individual experience adequately registers everything of importance in a historical context, and ever since Thucydides historians have painstakingly sought corroborating evidence. It hardly undermines the materiality and indispensability of experience to insist that historians must seek out its *plurality*. A historian works precisely to meld the experiences of many into one narrative. That is contingent on the limitations of his or her own experience, to be sure, and in many instances there will be conflicting accounts of experience that will call for difficult appraisals of the relative trustworthiness of evidence. Yet in every step of this procedure, both for the agent of inquiry and in terms of the objects of that inquiry, experience is an indispensable feature in the historical accounting.

Third, LaCapra holds that experience has been so "commodified" in postmodern culture that "meaningful experience" has become a cloying cliché. Even if we agree with this diagnosis, I suggest, LaCapra has hardly provided us with any idea of an appropriate response. Should we, since it has been "commodified" into a cliché, abandon the term? That would certainly be a precedent that would wreak havoc on our language, since experience is hardly unique in this "commodification." Is not the more prudent and critical recourse to seek to extricate the analytically essential elements of the concept "experience" from the banal and the illicit usages into which it may have fallen? The fastidiousness with which LaCapra seems to wish to distance himself from all things clichéd and "commodified" seems misplaced. In any event, I fail to see that anything in Toews's essay plays up to or instantiates such usage, and thus this is just a red herring.

Ultimately, LaCapra proclaims: "Experience in and of itself neither authenticates nor invalidates an argument or point of view" ("History, Language and Reading" 822). That proposition is not self-evident. Of course we can take the phrase "in and of itself" in so abstract and absolute a sense that it discredits what it modifies. But what does "experience *in and of itself*" really mean? Would the pure phenomenality of my experience of fire by personal contact have no bearing on my appraisal of someone else's argument that it burns? Would seeing the scars of victims of political torture not persuade us to attend to the arguments of Amnesty International? Similarly, we could construe "authenticates or invalidates" as implying some absolute certainty of evaluative efficacy. This, too, would discredit the notion. But ordinary life hardly seems to be restricted to such all-or-nothing epistemological gambits. When I step outside to see whether it is raining, I do feel that I can "authenticate or invalidate" someone's claim that it is. Juries every day weigh evidence and reach judgments. In the more sophisticated context of historical interpretation, experience matters in adjudicating contested claims, and historians *do* reach conclusions about evidential aptness. The recent upheavals in the historiography of the French Revolution provide a striking instance of such complex assessments. In short, I fail to see that LaCapra's hyperbolic recourses are incumbent on the user of the concept "experience" in empirical practice. Rather, its invocation signifies a concern for evidential verification that not only *can* but indeed *should* provide (contingent and fallible) warrant for claims. Without the appeal to some warranting instance in experience, it is unclear how we can ever get beyond simply arbitrary assertions, where the force of argument loses out to the argument of force.

That experience matters hardly means we cannot subject experiential claims to rigorous investigation and disputation. Experience is a human category; it entails the inevitably personal, first-person order of all claims to knowledge, and in just that measure their contingency and fallibility. Yet that by no means discredits them. To be too proud to take experience seriously is to set oneself apart in a rather remote absolute. The posture that dismisses experience is a "view from nowhere." The essential point is that first-person is ultimately how each of us must come to recognize evidence, to construct the narrative of our experience. In a court of law, the attestation of witnesses, the whole idea of evidence, is grounded in *first-person* experience. But as the film *Rashomon* unforgettably illustrates, experience always signifies an *emergent,* not an *essence:* it makes determinate claims even as it is constructed by and within a web of social and linguistic forces. That can render the "same" event radically variant in the experience of divergent witnesses. Yet we can read their readings—contingently, fallibly—to reconstruct more plausible versions, our own selective filters contested or nuanced by those of our judging peers. Objectivity requires experience, but it rarely recognizes it as *one* individual's attainment. At the same time, it is essential to recognize learning, acknowledgment of error, changing one's mind, as elements in experience. Experience is a process, negotiated socially, which *can* lead to better insight. Holding out for such a dialectical, empirical notion of learning and of degrees of objectivity and warrant seems certainly a defensible position.

LaCapra is carrying to hyperbole a skepticism whose more measured use is surely granted by all but the most obtuse of interpreters. But at the hyperbolic extremity to which he carries it, his claim becomes preposterous. Why would he press it so far? I suggest that he is embroiled in someone else's argument here. Our clue is a passage in which LaCapra allows "experience" to be acceptably invoked only by "victims" whose subject-position "should be respected." Here we get to the essentially contested issue. What lies behind this line is a debate that has been raging not so much in historical epistemology as in ethnic and minority studies. The context we need is not to be found in Toews but rather in Scott, whose essay "Experience" in fact proposes to dispute the politics of identity and its claims for recognition and respect based on experience of cultural and ethnic difference because they are grounded in a self-defeating "essentialism." Thus her essay begins with an exegesis and critique of Samuel Delany's account of his vision of gay empowerment through the experience of a thronging bathhouse. She charges that Delany naturalizes and essentializes identity, and therefore succumbs to structures of meaning determination that affirm the very power system from which his "conversion experience" was supposed to begin liberating him.

As Paula Moya has demonstrated, the core of the debate about "experience" has been between poststructuralist critics like Scott and "activists of color" (or sexuality) for whom experience and identity have been "primary organizing principles" of theoretical self-understanding, mobilization, and political practice. The poststructuralists insist that any invocation of experience *must* be "essentialist" and therefore "politically repressive" ("Postmodernism, 'Realism'").[23] They therefore set out to "delegitimate *all* accounts of experience," as Linda Alcoff puts it (127).[24] Michael R. Hames-García has spelled out the result in his chap-

23. See also Diana Fuss, *Essentially Speaking*.
24. Linda Alcoff, as cited in Moya, "Postmodernism, 'Realism'" 127.

ter in this volume: "poststructuralism increases the sense of homelessness" for such minorities because "it removes the epistemological ground on which one can claim that one 'belongs' within a group (or that someone else does not) and of making normative demands for inclusion, acknowledgment, and legitimacy." Ironically, this postmodernist stratagem is aimed at liberation, but it cannot conceive of any experience or identity that is not a subjection to "Power." Contesting this, Moya's interpretation of Cherríe Moraga (and of her own identity formation) stresses the progressive potential in experience and identity as mediated and learned. Rejecting essentialism, she nonetheless insists on the importance of identity for knowledge and of experience for identity. "Identities have more or less epistemic validity to the extent that they 'refer' outward to the world, that they accurately describe and explain the complex interactions between the multiple determinants of an individual's social location" ("Postmodernism, 'Realism'" 138). Citing Mohanty, she insists that "'granting the possibility of epistemological privilege to the oppressed might be more than a sentimental gesture'" because "the key to claiming epistemic privilege for people who have been oppressed in a particular way stems from an acknowledgment that they have [unique] experiences . . . that can provide them with information we all need to understand how hierarchies of race, class, gender, and sexuality operate" (141). That this is an empirical matter and subject to criticism is inherent in the view Moya brings to the notion of experience: there is always the "possibility of error and of accuracy in interpreting experience," yet "experience in its mediated form contains a 'cognitive component' through which we can gain access to knowledge of the world" (137–38). That brings us directly to a critical engagement with the views of Joan Scott.

SCOTT'S POSTSTRUCTURAL "HISTORICISM"

Recognizing that Toews wished to query poststructuralist ideas, Scott sets out to preempt any such dialogue. As her opening contestatory move, she denies that Toews exercised any critical scrutiny of his terms: "'Experience,' in Toews's usage, is taken to be so self-evident that he never defines the term [and] this allows it to function as a universally understood category—the undefined word creates a sense of consensus by attributing to it an assumed, stable, and shared meaning" ("Evidence" 788). We are less impressed with this criticism when we ask how many of Scott's own terms (e.g., "political") get explicitly defined in her text, when we proceed further to argue that any sophisticated lexicality involves a whole host of nuances and connotations to be discriminated by the linguistic context of the utterance, and when finally we recall that Toews in fact made a sustained effort to clarify what he meant by experience—as La-Capra himself attested.[25] Nevertheless, Scott insists on a nefarious *political* implication, which Ellen Rooney helped her to discern, a covert strategy to repress difference within the historical profession.

Beyond this "political exposé," there are two prongs to Scott's attack. First, she questions the hypostasis of "individuals" as objects of historical inquiry. She insists, "Talking about experience [uncritically] leads us to take the existence of individuals for granted (experience is something people have) rather than ask how conceptions of selves (of subjects and their identities) are produced" ("Evidence" 782). Thus "we need to attend to the historical processes that, through discourse, position subjects and produce their experiences. It is not individuals who have experience, but subjects who are constituted through experience" (779). Scott's fundamental argument is, "When experience is taken as the origin of knowledge, the vision of the individual subject (the person who had the experience or the historian who recounts it) becomes the bedrock of evidence on which explanation is built. Questions about the constructed nature of experience, about how subjects are constituted as different in the first place, about how one's vision is structured—about language (or discourse) and history—are left aside" (777). Instead, she proposes that historians follow poststructuralism in "trying to understand the operations of the complex and changing discursive processes by which identities are ascribed, resisted, or embraced, and which processes themselves are unremarked and indeed achieve their effect because they are not noticed. To do this a change of object seems to be required, one that takes the emergence of concepts and identities as historical events in need of explanation" (792). Scott denies that this entails a "new form of linguistic determinism," since "subjects are constituted discursively, but there are conflicts among discursive systems, contradictions within any one of them, multiple meanings possible for the concepts they deploy." Similarly she denies that this abandons subjective agency; instead, it sees the agency of subjects "created through situations and statuses conferred on them" (793). That is, "subjects are constituted discursively and experience is a

25. On the undefined character of "political," see Fuss, *Essentially Speaking:* "Politics is precisely the self-evident category in feminist discourse—that which is most irreducible and most indisputable. . . . [I]t tenaciously resists definition" (36).

linguistic event (it doesn't happen outside established meanings), but neither is it confined to a fixed order of meaning" (793).

There is an obvious contradiction in these last contentions. If something cannot happen outside established meanings, how is it not confined to a fixed order of meaning? Either/or: Scott cannot have it both ways. And the fact of the case is that we create new meanings all the time. How can we? Why should we? The answer, Scott notwithstanding, is new *experience*. We learn, we discover our errors, we change our minds, we change our descriptions. Remarkably, some of the most brilliant work on just this theme has been offered by the postpositivist theory of metaphor.[26] Moreover, this whole question puts the emphasis on the dynamic, on change, a feature that is central to a more authentic (i.e., *dialectical*) conception of "historicism" than the radical *elenchus* of all concepts that Scott offers as her notion.[27]

Of course, much that Scott proposes makes perfect sense. But there is an element of hyperbole that compromises the plausibility of the argument and renders it into an intransigence that is difficult to reconcile with empirical practice. Note first the deliberately passive grammatical constructions with reference to the subject. Precisely what Scott seeks rhetorically to evade or undermine is the very idea of agency. While no historian is so "naive" as to presume the full transparency of consciousness in a conflicted self or the full efficacy of intentions in a resistant physical and social world, the scope of agency is precisely what is at the core of historical inquiry as an empirical pursuit. To see the various constraints and constructions within which it proceeds is indubitably a task for the historian. To leave it out as an essential element is to have a *Hamlet* in which one has deliberately erased the Prince of Denmark. "Experience is at once always already an interpretation *and* something that needs to be interpreted" ("Evidence" 797; original emphasis). To be sure! Toews *said* as much, and I suggest that any reasonable contextualist intellectual historian recognizes this and incorporates it in historical practice.[28] The issue is first whether experience can serve as a concept through which agents construe themselves and second whether the historian's own procedures have some accessible correlative evidence (experience) on the basis of

26. On the postpositivist theory of metaphor, see the collection *Metaphor and Thought* edited by Anthony Ortony.

27. Charles Altieri, "Temporality and the Necessity for Dialectic." See also Reed Way Dasenbrock, "Accounting for the Changing Certainties of Interpretive Communities."

28. In chapter 10, Linda Alcoff puts it as bluntly as the case warrants: "No one believes that the meaning of an experience is transparent, theory-neutral, or uninterpreted."

which other historians may judge the plausibility and illumination of proposed interpretations. These are *empirical* matters, not transcendental ones. We are historians, and our skepticism must be of a different order from that of philosophers, or rhetoricians pretending to be philosophers.

Stipulative pantextualism ("experience is a linguistic event") is what is at issue. No sufficient case has yet been offered for abandoning the physical determinacy and the causal relations involved in social and material forces in history (which, of course, may be sedimented in or mobilized by linguistic forms). One need hardly be a reductive materialist to insist these represent real problems for historical interpretation. The assertion that "experience is a linguistic event" is dogmatic. It begs all the theoretical questions that Toews was trying to bring into consideration: *real* questions, not ideological distraction. It may well be, to offer an off-hand instance, that I can tell you about listening to Mozart only in words, but I deny that listening to Mozart is a linguistic event. (It is *not* a sufficient rebuttal to urge that "Mozart" and "music" are culturally inherited terms. These might guide or shape but cannot entirely *constitute* the actual event.)[29] Of graver import, victims may only explain what pain or humiliation felt like in words (and they are often paltry in that endeavor) but I deny that what befell them were merely "linguistic events."

More generally and technically, that facts are "theory laden" does *not* signify that all there is, is theory.[30] This global misconception of empirical inquiry appears to be the essential issue in contest between contextualism and poststructuralism. It is a dishearteningly widespread practice among postmodernists crudely to collapse *empirical inquiry* into "positivism." Chris Lorenz has correctly suggested that what creates this confusion is that postmodernism conflates the search for *knowledge* with the search for *certainty;* that is, it imputes "Cartesian anxiety" to *every* effort at empirical determination.[31] The "opacity" of language invoked by poststructuralism is thus merely an inversion of foundationalist absolutism.[32] But, "recognition of the fact that historical knowledge does not have a certain and uniform foundation in facts or logic [need] not

29. On the importance of abstract music as a category of experience in the controversy between philosophy and postmodernism, see Andrew Bowie, *Aesthetics and Subjectivity* (34 passim).

30. See Larry Laudan, *Beyond Postivism and Relativism;* Philip Kitcher, "The Naturalists Return"; Steven Shapin, "Here and Everywhere."

31. Chris Lorenz, "Historical Knowledge and Historical Reality." On "Cartesian anxiety," see Richard Bernstein, *Beyond Objectivism and Relativism.*

32. Bevir recognizes that "the role of theories in observation does not mean that facts depend solely on theories, as idealist epistemologies claim" ("Objectivity in History" 333).

lead to the epistemological skepticism of the relativists, but to fallibilism
and contextualism. Contextualists recognize that all knowledge is relative to specific epistemic contexts. And fallibilists recognize that all claims
to knowledge are corrigible" ("Historical Knowledge" 306). That is essentially what it means to call historical practice *empirical*. Empirical
knowledge assuredly has its problems. I would be astounded to find a
single historian who believes that one can achieve *apodeictic certainty*
by this method. Yet the claim to knowledge is not and need not be a claim
to absolute certainty. "The limitations of knowledge are not failures of
it" (Cavell 241). Ambiguity is not necessarily indeterminacy (Vickers
169). Contingency and fallibility just are the conditions of real human
knowing. Thus, as Wilkerson puts it, experience is "constructed, but . . .
not arbitrary," or as Alcoff puts it, "experience is epistemologically indispensable but never epistemically sufficient."[33] Wilkerson, in this volume, caps the argument:

> The postmodern view goes too far in its rejection of experience as a starting
> point for knowledge. . . . [W]e are left with two aporias. First, we cannot dis-
> tinguish ideology from truth, since all experience is the production of ideol-
> ogy. Second, it is unclear how we arrive at knowledge of the production of
> experience through ideology and discourse, if not from the very experience
> that we are supposed to reject. . . . [I]f discursive practices actually produce
> our experience and identity, then the origin and reliability of my knowledge
> of these discursive practices becomes highly questionable.

There is a profound incongruity in the way Scott proposes the empirical inquiry, because she undercuts its epistemology at the outset.

In her second line of attack, Scott argues that the postulation of "experience" is a device to shield the historical inquirer from scrutinizing the
vexed subjectivity of his or her own situatedness. Scott writes, "The question of where the historian is situated—who he is, how he is defined in
relation to others, what the political effects of his history may be—never
enters the discussion" ("Evidence" 783). For Scott, the concept of experience "provides an object for historians that can be known apart from
their own role as meaning makers and it then guarantees not only the objectivity of their knowledge, but their ability to persuade others of its importance" ("Experience" 32). But it is by no means the case—and Toews
was quite explicit about this—that the invocation of experience as a
methodological concept entails the suppression of self-consciousness in

---

33. Wilkerson, "Is There Something You Need to Tell Me?" this vol.; Alcoff, cited in
Moya, "Postmodernism, 'Realism'" 148.

the historian. The idea of the historicization of the historical subject was in fact articulated in the *hermeneutical* tradition, by Hans Georg Gadamer, and is not the monopoly of poststructuralists. More generally, the endeavor to persuade others of the importance of one's claim is hardly a sinister matter: it is the substance of human discourse. Rhetoric must not be confused with obfuscation. Of course, historians resort to claims of warrant in their efforts to persuade others. What is new or problematic in that? What else is Scott doing? As to "guarantees" of objectivity, we must once again insist on an empirical, not an absolute, standard of what such "guarantees" signify, and against Scott raise the issue whether we can reasonably dispense with any evidential warrant in empirical practice. If not, then we need concepts about the qualifying forms of such evidential warrant, and experience has a place in that discourse.

Scott concludes: "Deciding which categories to historicize is inevitably political, necessarily tied to the historian's recognition of his or her stake in the production of knowledge" ("Evidence" 797). (What a relief to see a feminine pronoun!) When "all categories of analysis [are taken] as contextual, contested and contingent [they] open consideration of what Dominick LaCapra has referred to as the 'transferential' relationship between the historian and the past. . . . [T]hey historicize both sides of that relationship" (796). LaCapra's notion of transferentiality is indeed one of the best approaches we have to the problem of the historian's subjectivity, but its complexity should not be reduced to the "inevitably political . . . stake" the historian has in "the production of knowledge." Politics is important, but it is not everything; the determinations that guide a historical inquiry involve more than one's political concerns or values, though these are hardly remote from the matter. More generally, there is something askew in the totalizing that is operative in Scott's notions of "historicizing" and the "political." She proposes a radical "historicizing"— "a historicizing that implies critical scrutiny of all explanatory categories usually taken for granted, including the category of 'experience'" (796). In the form she gives it, the radical "historicizing" Scott proposes is impossible: there is no standpoint outside all our terms; we can only judge some while holding others stable. That is the powerful lesson of Quine's concept of the web of beliefs.[34] While it is true that nothing in that web is sacrosanct, and that modulating any element in it reverberates through

---

34. Willard V. O. Quine and J. S. Ullian, *The Web of Belief.*

the entire web, we can only work on the web from within it (or, to use Quine's favorite metaphor, we can only repair our ship at sea). Finally, what makes it possible for us to communicate at all, to have a community in which to dispute politically, is that we can and we do *share experiences,* both sensually and in symbolic rearticulation.

"'Politics,'" Scott writes, "is . . . not the antithesis of professionalism but its expression" ("History in Crisis?" 690). Earlier in the same essay Scott writes, "History is inherently political. There is no single standard by which we can identify 'true' historical knowledge. . . . Rather, there are contests, more and less conflictual, more and less explicit, about the substance, uses, and meanings of the knowledge that we call history" (681). The question is how this politics should be conducted, and whether there is anything worthwhile in the effort to construct commonalities after, and because we have deconstructed, hegemonies. The problem with the kind of move that Scott and Rooney make is that, although it legitimately underscores the existence of political divisions within our discursive community, it seems to allow no dialogic way to achieve any measure of mutual understanding and accommodation. That "often (not always, but often)" exclusionary politics have operated in the discipline or in the society at large is not to be denied ("History in Crisis?" 686). Yet even Scott posits that it does not necessarily follow that this is always the case. Moreover, there is something lost in preempting the very possibility of mutual recognition. That postulates, as Linda Alcoff puts it, that "negation, resistance, and destabilization are the only self-respecting moves." Alcoff questions this assumption, arguing "although all identities require a social context and external mediation, they are not all fundamentally a submission to a pernicious power." On the contrary, Alcoff, in this volume, holds out the prospect that "the project of creating identity within community is, at least potentially, collective, even democratic, and just, and not unremittingly authoritarian." Scott recognizes that as a discursive community we "share a commitment to accuracy and to procedures of verification and documentation," but she insists that they are not invariant, that "the knowledge we produce is contextual, relative, open to revision and debate, and never absolute" ("History in Crisis?" 686). The point I wish to cling to is that we share such a commitment at all. That standards are indispensable is precisely why we cannot totally abandon the notion of evidential warrant, and why we need a concept like experience to help us in its characterization. Just for that reason, in the context of what she herself terms "a particularly heated period of interpretive conflict," we have a need to be able to find those places where our separate discourses *overlap,* where at least a *measure* of "translation" is possible. That is what the (critical) reinvocation of terms such as "objectivity," "empiricism," and "experience" signifies in disciplinary conversation today. It is that, and not the "policing of borders," that is involved in the effort to achieve what Scott dismisses as renewed foundations.

POSTPOSITIVIST REALISM

One of the most balanced and careful efforts to sketch out how, in the context of our politicized, postpositivist disciplinary practices, we may nonetheless seek a rigorous sense of standards comes from Satya Mohanty. He establishes that the idea of competing rationalities raises a "nagging question: how do we negotiate between my history and yours?" Very simply, we cannot afford "to leave untheorized the question of how our differences are intertwined and, indeed, hierarchically organized" ("'Us and Them'" 13). Mohanty insists that "to the extent that our initial interest in relativism was motivated by a political respect for other selves, other spaces, other contexts, relativism seems now to be an unacceptable theoretical position" (15). Relativism becomes a vehicle for new and subtler forms of ethnocentric condescension or political paralysis. This outcome, with all its political implications, can be seen in the complacent relativism of Richard Rorty.[35] Mohanty is suggesting that the wider syndrome of postmodern relativism in fact results in annulling by fiat the very possibility of genuine dialogue. We are faced, in Mohanty's view, with an inescapable task: "how do we conceive the other, indeed the Other, outside of our inherited concepts and beliefs so as not to replicate the patterns of repression and subjugation we notice in the traditional conceptual frameworks?" The only hope for the success of such an enterprise is to be very careful about our question: "Just how other, we need to force ourselves to specify, is the Other?" (*Literary Theory* 121).[36] We need not leap to the view that there is no commonality through which to bridge and to adjudicate: "We need to respect other cultures

35. See David Hollinger's recognition of this danger in Rorty in "How Wide the Circle of the 'We'?" On the problems with Rorty's ethnocentrism, see his exchange with Clifford Geertz: Geertz, "The Uses of Diversity," and Rorty, "On Ethnocentrism." See also Herbert Dreyfus, "Holism and Hermeneutics"; Charles Taylor, "Understanding in Human Science."
36. That question cannot be asked naively, in ignorance of "institutions of 'cultural translation' which exist in a matrix of unequal languages and asymmetrical access to the institutions of discourse and power" (*Literary Theory* 123).

not as insular and impenetrable wholes but rather as complex webs of beliefs and actions" (133). To get past this impasse of global "incommensurability" Mohanty urges that we recognize with Donald Davidson that "an interpretation of the Other is dependent on an acknowledgment of common ground" (138).[37]

For Mohanty, it is precisely the category of *human agency* that represents the essential commonality from which we must set out: human agency as "not merely the capacity to act purposefully but also to *evaluate* actions and purposes in terms of larger ideas we might hold about, say, our political and moral world" ("'Us and Them'" 22) It is this, he continues, "which enables us to be critically and cumulatively self-aware in relation to our actions . . . and makes possible the sociality and the historicality of human existence" (*Literary Theory* 139). Mohanty connects this claim to a cross-cultural commonality with the Kantian notion that rational agency is universal and grounds claims about the dignity of every individual (199). But Mohanty means this as social theory, not speculative ethics: "Such claims (about agency, and the model of rational capacity it implies) are no less 'objective' for being culturally and 'theoretically' mediated" (200). On this basis questions regarding "the reason underlying different practices and different choices . . . become not only intelligible but also *necessary*" (141; original emphasis). That is what postpositivist realism is about: "On the realist view I have been advocating . . . when we strive for objectivity in inquiry (whether in the academic disciplines or in everyday life), we seek to produce an account of the socially based distortions as well as the socially based insights that constitute our presuppositions, including our most sophisticated 'theories'" (201).

This entails a radically different conception of what it means to impute rationality to human agents. Postpositivist realism, as Mohanty conceives it, stresses the "need to focus on the cognitive successes and failures of finite—as opposed to ideal—epistemic agents" (114n). Not certainty but learning, acknowledging error, changing one's mind, become the crucial matters for inquiry. "It would be seriously debilitating for critical analysis to confuse a minimal notion of rationality as a cognitive and practical human capacity with the grand a priori foundational

37. See Davidson's crucial essay, "On the Very Idea of a Conceptual Scheme." This is a classic rebuttal of the exaggerated claims in Thomas Kuhn's original formulation of his paradigm theory. For a measured restatement of the issues, see Gerald Doppelt, "Kuhn's Epistemological Relativism."

structure that has traditionally been called reason" (117). But that has
been the basic penchant of poststructuralism: "poststructuralist views
about the relation between experience and knowledge in fact turn out
to be mirror images of the idealist figure they were meant to dislodge"
(113). The kind of radical "historicizing" that Scott proposes leaves empirical inquiry *and the indispensable negotiation of difference* without
purchase in the concrete situation. As Mohanty puts it:

> The move from the rejection of an empiricist or positivist (or even idealist)
> model of objective knowledge to the opposite extreme, the adoption of a full-
> blown skepticism about knowledge, is fairly typical. Postmodernist skeptics
> implicitly assume that the only kind of objective knowledge that can be con-
> ceived at all is positivist (or idealist). When they find this conception (the aper-
> spectival knower or the subject of Hegelian absolute knowledge) defective for
> one reason or another, they assume that a thoroughgoing skepticism is war-
> ranted. (42n)

Social construction of knowledge need not deny a causal role for the world
in that knowledge. As Moya puts it, "When the realist says that something is 'real,' she does not mean to say that it is not socially constructed;
rather, her point is that [it] is *not* only socially constructed" ("Postmodernism, 'Realism,'" 180n; original emphasis). As Mohanty insists, "The
world exists independently of our knowledge of it; it is not paradigm
specific. But significant portions of it, namely, the social and cultural aspects of it, including much of the natural world, are also causally affected
by our actions, our theories, and our knowledge-gathering procedures:
we do not only 'discover' reality; we 'make' it as well" (*Literary Theory*
193). Mohanty explicitly terms this a "dialectical view of knowledge and
the social organization of inquiry" (193). Complex, concrete, dynamic,
and mediated, a dialectic of experience has the potential for contingent
objectivity.

   Mohanty interprets the crucial concept of experience in this light:
"there is nothing particular to experience as such which warrants its rejection on epistemological grounds." That is, "experience can be 'true'
or 'false,' can be evaluated as justified or illegitimate in relation to the
subject and his world, for 'experience' refers very simply to the variety
of ways humans process information." It can "yield reliable and genuine
knowledge," and it can be involved in "real mystification" (204–5). Assuredly, "'personal experience' is socially and 'theoretically' constructed,
and it is precisely in this mediated way that it yields knowledge" (206).
That is, "constructedness does not make it arbitrary or unstable in advance" (211). As Alcoff has argued, we must understand experience as

a process, as recursive and interpretive even as it is causally engaged with a constraining otherness. She writes, "This process always involves a kind of mediation or interpretation. . . . The meaningfulness of an experience is not understood as attached to an event, after the fact, but as in the event itself" (this vol.). She cites Gadamer as having taken a similar stance. Similarly, Wilkerson holds that "phenomenological analyses show that our experiences are not simple, self-evident givens . . . but rather complex wholes that take place within fields that condition their meaning" (this vol.). Only this dialectical reconception can lift us out of the frozen polarities of the postmodernist/essentialist standoff, with its all or nothing epistemology and will-o'-the-wisp ontology. And only this reconception takes due warrant of our actual practices of learning and changing. As Wilkerson writes, "Putting focal elements of experience under reflection and viewing them within different contexts, changing what we would expect to find and what we seek, can change the character of experiences and allow new meanings and new patterns of experience to emerge" (this vol.).

It is along these lines, as well, that I believe key theorists of the "interpretive turn" in social science—Charles Taylor, Clifford Geertz, Jürgen Habermas, and Anthony Giddens, to name only a few—have been working to make concrete a theory of social and cultural practice that is both politically and hermeneutically sensitive, without tripping over into poststructuralist hyperbole.[38] LaCapra himself suggests that "more moderate advocates" like Geertz might authenticate empirical reconstruction. He includes Taylor in this vein as the sponsor of a combination of the hermeneutic approach with a "phenomenological notion of experience." Hence LaCapra would appear to be at least somewhat amenable to the "interpretive turn" in social thought.

CONCLUSION

I accept the question just as Scott phrased it: "How can we maintain a disciplinary organization, with some commitment to shared standards and at the same time tolerate diversity in membership and profound dif-

---

38. See the volumes edited by Paul Rabinow and William Sullivan, *Interpretive Social Science* and *Interpretive Social Science: A Second Look*; Norma Hahn et al., eds., *Social Science as Moral Inquiry*; and David Hiley, James Bohman, and Richard Shusterman, eds., *The Interpretive Turn*. On the social theory of the interpretive turn, see esp. Kenneth Baynes, "Rational Reconstruction and Social Criticism."

ferences in method, philosophy, and interpretation? What would a genuinely democratic history look like?" ("History in Crisis?" 692). The line of my answer I take from someone closer to her own camp: Peter Novick. Having documented with severity the lapses of objectivity in the American historical profession over most of its existence, Novick nevertheless offers a remarkable summation: "With all its faults, the organized American historical profession, particularly in recent decades, has been the most ideologically open, the least exclusionary, of any such body in the world" ("My Correct Views" 703).

That hardly means we are now fully democratic. If I may borrow a turn of phrase from Immanuel Kant, we are not yet a democratic discipline but a discipline in pursuit of democratization. Our disciplinary matrix is our *only* basis for situating and adjudicating disputes. It is unquestionably *for us* to reach understanding; it cannot be imported from outside our common practices and our mutual contestations. It can only be constituted in them. Like democracy in society, democracy in our discipline is woefully imperfect. Like democracy, we could call it the worst political system (for intellectual life) except for all the others that have been tried. That is because, like actual political democracy, it has a (blemished) record of and a (diffident) interest in expanding participation in discourse and decision. Finally, like democracy, it is up to its members to make it better. There is no transcendent vantage, no unsituated knowing possible in the controversies over "paradigms" in our discipline. But that does not mean that we cannot try clearly to establish what the governing principles of our respective stances may be and where the "essentially contested issues" lie between us.[39] And it also does not mean that we cannot try to build bridges of understanding among us. Though it is not plausible to suppose that anything approaching full "consensus" can ever be achieved, the search for understanding across difference, with consensus as a "regulative ideal" (what Habermas would call the "ideal speech situation"), ought not always and already be understood as a hegemonic appropriative strategy.

What objectivity can mean in a postpositivist age is just the responsible undertaking of disciplinary discourse within these standards. It is what Allan Megill has termed "*disciplinary* objectivity," but, in light of everything that we have seen about the "historicization of the historical subject," our disciplinary objectivity as historians is incorporating within

39. See W. B. Gallie, "Essentially Contested Concepts."

308 John H. Zammito

it what Megill distinguishes as "dialectical objectivity" as well ("Four Senses" 5). Dialectical objectivity is just that recognition of the situatedness and structuration of the interpreter in any enterprise of objectification, "the claim that subjectivity is indispensable to the constituting of objects" (8). The discipline should welcome the theoretical perspicuity that comes of the historicization of the historical subject, especially as this fuels the further democratization of our practices. But this does not and should not preclude the dialogic search for commonality of critical appraisal, for an internal, postpositivist standard of objectivity.

WORKS CITED

Alcoff, Linda. "The Elimination of Experience in Feminist Theory." Paper delivered at the Women's Studies Symposium, Cornell University, February 3, 1995.
Altieri, Charles. "Temporality and the Necessity for Dialectic: The Missing Dimension of Contemporary Theory." *New Literary History* 23 (1992): 133–58.
Ankersmit, Frank. *History and Tropology: The Rise and Fall of Metaphor.* Berkeley: University of California Press, 1994.
Bambaugh, Charles. *Heidegger, Dilthey, and the Crisis of Historicism.* Ithaca: Cornell University Press, 1995.
Barthes, Roland. "The Discourse of History." *The Rustle of Language.* Berkeley: University of California Press, 1989. 127–40.
———. "The Reality Effect." *The Rustle of Language.* Berkeley: University of California Press, 1989. 141–48.
Baynes, Kenneth. "Rational Reconstruction and Social Criticism: Habermas's Model of Interpretive Social Science." *Philosophical Forum* 21.1–2 (Fall–Winter 1989–90): 122–45.
Bernstein, Richard. *Beyond Objectivism and Relativism: Science, Hermeneutics, and Praxis.* Philadelphia: University of Pennsylvania Press, 1983.
Bevir, Marc. "Objectivity in History." *History and Theory* 33 (1994): 328–44.
Bowie, Andrew. *Aesthetics and Subjectivity: From Kant to Nietzsche.* Manchester: Manchester University Press, 1990.
Carruth, Cathy. *Unclaimed Experience: Trauma, Narrative, and History.* Baltimore: Johns Hopkins University Press, 1996.
Cavell, Stanley. *The Claims of Reason.* Oxford: Oxford University Press, 1979.
Chartier, Roger. "Intellectual History or Sociocultural History? The French Trajectories." *Modern European Intellectual History: Reappraisals and New Perspectives.* Ed. Dominick LaCapra and Steven Kaplan. Ithaca: Cornell University Press, 1982. 13–46.
Clifford, James. "On Ethnographic Allegory." *Writing Culture: The Poetics and Politics of Ethnography.* Ed. James Clifford and George Marcus. Berkeley: University of California Press, 1986. 98–121.
———. "On Ethnographic Authority." *Representations* 1 (1983): 118–46.
Collins, Stephen, and James Hoopes. "Anthony Giddens and Charles Sanders

Peirce: History, Theory, and a Way Out of the Linguistic Cul-de-Sac." *Journal of the History of Ideas* 56 (1995): 625–49.

Dasenbrock, Reed Way. "Accounting for the Changing Certainties of Interpretive Communities." *Modern Language Notes* 101.5 (1986): 1022–41.

Davidson, Donald. "On the Very Idea of a Conceptual Scheme." *Inquiries into Truth and Interpretation.* Oxford: Clarendon Press, 1984. 183–98.

de Man, Paul. *Allegories of Reading.* New Haven: Yale University Press, 1979.

Doppelt, Gerald. "Kuhn's Epistemological Relativism: An Interpretation and Defense." *Inquiry* 21 (1978): 33–86.

Dreyfus, Herbert. "Holism and Hermeneutics." *Review of Metaphysics* 34 (1980): 3–23.

Friedlander, Saul, ed. *Probing the Limits of Representation.* Cambridge, MA: Harvard University Press, 1992.

Fuss, Diana. *Essentially Speaking: Feminism, Nature & Difference.* New York: Routledge, 1989.

Gallie, W. B. "Essentially Contested Concepts." *Philosophy and the Historical Understanding.* 2d ed. New York: Schocken, 1968. 157–91.

Geertz, Clifford. "The Uses of Diversity." *Michigan Quarterly Review* 25 (1986): 105–23.

Giddens, Anthony. *New Rules for the Sociological Method.* New York: Basic-Books, 1976.

Hahn, Norma, Robert Bellah, Paul Rabinow, and William Sullivan, eds. *Social Science as Moral Inquiry.* New York: Columbia University Press, 1983.

Hiley, David, James Bohman, and Richard Shusterman, eds. *The Interpretive Turn: Philosophy, Science, Culture.* Ithaca: Cornell University Press, 1991.

Hollinger, David. "How Wide the Circle of the 'We'? American Intellectuals and the Problem of the Ethnos since World War II." *American Historical Review* 98 (1993): 317–37.

Hoopes, James. "Objectivity *and* Relativism Affirmed: Historical Knowledge and the Philosophy of Charles S. Peirce." *American Historical Review* 98 (1993): 1545–55.

Jay, Martin. "The Textual Approach to Intellectual History." *Fact and Fiction: German History and Literature, 1848–1924.* Ed. Gisela Brude-Firnau and Karin MacHardy. Tübingen: Francke, 1990. 77–86.

Kellner, Hans. *Language and Historical Representation: Getting the Story Crooked.* Madison: University of Wisconsin Press, 1989.

Kitcher, Philip. "The Naturalists Return." *Philosophical Review* 101 (1992): 53–114.

LaCapra, Dominick. *History and Criticism.* Ithaca: Cornell University Press, 1985.

———. "History, Language and Reading: Waiting for Crillon." *American Historical Review* 100.3 (June 1995): 799–828.

———. *Representing the Holocaust: History, Theory, Trauma.* Ithaca: Cornell University Press, 1994.

———. *Rethinking Intellectual History.* Ithaca: Cornell University Press, 1983.

———. *Soundings in Critical Theory.* Ithaca: Cornell University Press, 1989.

Laudan, Larry. *Beyond Positivism and Relativism: Theory, Method, and Evidence.* Boulder, CO: Westview Press, 1996.

Lorenz, Chris. "Historical Knowledge and Historical Reality: A Plea for 'Internal Realism.'" *History and Theory* 33 (1994): 297–327.

Martin, Raymond. "Objectivity and Meaning in Historical Studies." *History and Theory* 32 (1993): 25–50.

Megill, Allan. "Four Senses of Objectivity." *Rethinking Objectivity*. Ed. Allan Megill. Durham: Duke University Press, 1994. 1–20.

———. "Recounting the Past: 'Description,' Explanation and Narrative in Historiography." *American Historical Review* 94 (1989): 627–53.

Mohanty, Satya P. *Literary Theory and the Claims of History*. Ithaca: Cornell University Press, 1997.

———. "'Us and Them': On the Philosophical Bases of Political Criticism." *Yale Journal of Criticism* 2.2 (1989): 1–31.

Moya, Paula M. L. "Postmodernism, 'Realism,' and the Politics of Identity." *Feminist Genealogies, Colonial Legacies, Democratic Futures*. Ed. M. Jacqui Alexander and Chandra Talpade Mohanty. New York: Routledge, 1997. 125–50. [Reprinted as chapter 2 in this volume.]

Novick, Peter. "My Correct Views on Everything." "AHR Forum on Novick's *That Noble Dream*." *American Historical Review* 96 (1991): 699–703.

Ortony, Anthony, ed. *Metaphor and Thought*. 2d ed. Cambridge: Cambridge University Press, 1993.

Quine, Willard V. O., and J. S. Ullian. *The Web of Belief*. 2d ed. New York: Random House, 1978.

Rabinow, Paul, and William Sullivan, eds. *Interpretive Social Science: A Reader*. Berkeley: University of California Press, 1979.

———. *Interpretive Social Science: A Second Look*. Berkeley: University of California Press, 1987.

Rooney, Ellen. *Seductive Reasoning: Pluralism as the Problematic of Contemporary Literary Theory*. Ithaca: Cornell University Press, 1989.

Rorty, Richard. "On Ethnocentrism: A Reply to Clifford Geertz." *Michigan Quarterly Review* 25 (1986): 525–34.

Ross, Dorothy. Afterword to "AHR Forum on Novick's *That Noble Dream*." *American Historical Review* 96 (1991): 704–8.

Scott, Joan. "The Evidence of Experience." *Critical Inquiry* 17 (Summer 1991): 773–97.

———. "Experience." *Feminists Theorize the Political*. Ed. Judith Butler and Joan Scott. New York: Routledge, 1992. 22–40.

———. "History in Crisis? The Others' Side of the Story." *American Historical Review* 94 (1989): 680–92.

———. "The Tip of the Volcano." *Comparative Studies in Society and History* 35 (1993): 438–43.

Shapin, Steven. "Here and Everywhere: Sociology of Scientific Knowledge." *Annual Review of Sociology* 21 (1995): 289–321.

Taylor, Charles. "Understanding in Human Science." *Review of Metaphysics* 34 (1980): 24–38.

Toews, John. *Hegelianism: The Path toward Dialectical Humanism, 1805–1841*. New York: Cambridge University Press, 1980.

———. "Intellectual History after the Linguistic Turn: The Autonomy of Meaning and the Irreducibility of Experience." *American Historical Review* 92 (1987): 879–907.

Vickers, Brian. *Appropriating Shakespeare: Contemporary Critical Quarrels.* New Haven: Yale University Press, 1993.

Warnke, Gloria. "Hermeneutics and Social Science: A Gadamerian Critique of Rorty." *Inquiry* 28 (1985): 339–57.

White, Hayden. "Historical Writing as a Literary Text." *The Writing of History: Literary Form and Historical Understanding.* Ed. Robert H. Canary and Henry Kozicki. Madison: University of Wisconsin Press, 1978. 42–43.

Zammito, John. "Ankersmit's Postmodern Historiography: The Hyperbole of Opacity." *History and Theory* 37 (1998): 330–46.

———. "Are We Being Theoretical Yet?" *Journal of Modern History* 65 (1993): 783–814.

CHAPTER 10

Who's Afraid
of Identity Politics?

Linda Martín Alcoff

This volume is an act of talking back, of talking heresy. To reclaim the term "realism," to maintain the epistemic significance of identity, to defend any version of identity politics today is to swim upstream of strong academic currents in feminist theory, literary theory, and cultural studies. It is to risk, even to invite, a dismissal as naive, uninformed, theoretically unsophisticated. And it is a risk taken here by people already at risk in the academy, already assumed more often than not to be uninformed and undereducated precisely because of their real identities.

Of course, identity is today a growth industry in the academy, across the humanities and social sciences, influencing even law and communication studies. The constitutive power of gender, race, ethnicity, sexuality, and other forms of identity has, finally, suddenly, been recognized as a relevant aspect of almost all projects of inquiry. However, as I shall discuss in this chapter, simultaneous to this academic commodification of identity is an increasing tendency to view identity as politically and metaphysically problematic, some have even said pathological. So, on the one hand, the theoretical relevance of identities has become visible, while, on the other, many theorists are troubled by the implications of

I am very grateful to Paula Moya and Michael Hames-García for their helpful comments and suggestions on this chapter. In formulating my argument, I have also benefited very much from discussions with Robert Gooding-Williams, Dan Holliman, Tom McCarthy, Linda Nicholson, Ramon Saldívar, Paul Taylor, and Iris Young.

the claim that identity makes a difference. Increasingly, then, the attachment to identity has become suspect.

If identity has become suspect, identity politics has been prosecuted, tried, and sentenced to death. To espouse identity politics in the academy today risks being viewed as a member of the Flat-Earth Society. Like "essentialism," identity politics has become the shibboleth of cultural studies and social theory, and denouncing it has become the litmus test of academic respectability, political acceptability, and even a necessity for the very right to be heard.

In contrast, there has been a noticeable thaw regarding the term "essentialism." What was once perfunctorily denounced at the start of every paper in feminist theory has recently been tentatively examined by a few theorists for possible signs of validity. Christine Battersby, Elizabeth Grosz, and Teresa de Lauretis have pointed out that it is only the Aristotelian concept of essence that has been used in the feminist debates, that is, the idea of a fixed and stable feature common to all members of a natural kind. De Lauretis and Battersby have argued in favor of using Locke's concept of nominal essences, which allows essences to be contingent on language use and thus variable, while other feminists, such as Susan Babbitt, have defended nondeterministic naturalist accounts of essentialism as consistent with feminism's liberatory aims as well as with the heterogeneity of women's experiences. Babbitt shows that the problem for feminism is not the concept of essentialism but the deterministic account of gender, which is sometimes associated with it but which is not inherent to the concept. On scrutiny it turns out, then, that essentialism itself entails no commitment to ahistorical, prelinguistic, transcendent truths, and the denunciations of essentialism were based on an inadequate exploration of the concept, its history, and its variable meanings. I believe it is time we reassess identity politics in the same light.

One of the problems is that identity politics is nowhere defined—nor is its historical genesis elaborated—by its detractors. So the very thing we are discussing is surprisingly vague. Identity politics is blamed for a host of political ills and theoretical mistakes, from overly homogenized conceptions of groups to radical separatism to essentialist assumptions. But what are its own claims? In what is probably its locus classicus, the Combahee River Collective's "Black Feminist Statement" of 1977, identity politics emerges as a belief in the relevance of identity to politics, such that, for example, one might justifiably assume that those who share one's identity will be one's most consistent allies. Such a claim does not assume that identities are always perfectly homogeneous or that identity groups are unproblematic: the very formation of the Combahee River Collective was motivated by the founders' concerns with the racism in the white-dominated wing of the women's movement, the sexism in the male-dominated wing of the Black Liberation movement, and the heterosexism that was virulent everywhere. But they did assume that identities *mattered,* and that they were in some sense *real.*

In this volume, Satya P. Mohanty and Paula M. L. Moya have carefully unpacked and analyzed the philosophical assumptions behind claims of identity as well as claims about its political and epistemological importance. For many theorists in the humanities today, the key issue boils down to one: are identities in any sense real? If identities are simply products of ideology, false consciousness, Power, or the Law of the Father, one might well wonder why a politics of liberation would want to defend identities rather than deconstruct them. And moreover, many wonder what it can mean to call *anything* real in this post-Foucauldian moment, identities or anything else. What can it mean to make truth claims about the political realities of experience, of history, and of the liberatory aspirations of oppressed peoples? Epistemic skepticism can weaken political determination and give comfort to political cynicism, and to overcome this the question of realism must be broached directly.

Michael R. Hames-García and others here argue convincingly that the wholesale critique of identity and the repudiation of all forms of realism are based on a mistake; legitimate causes of concern have been mistakenly attributed to realist views of identity, such that, now, *all* claims of identity have become suspect, no matter how they are formulated or what their political implications are purported to be. Acknowledging multiplicity and the mediated character of experience entails only that *some* accounts of identity are mistaken. But somehow a concern with overly homogenizing, radically separatist, deterministic approaches to the politics of identity has led to a situation in which *all* identity claims have become suspect, and the links among identity, politics, and knowledge have become so nebulous that it looks as if none exist at all. This position, when examined carefully, is in fact specious. William S. Wilkerson's chapter on the possibility of being mistaken even about one's sexuality shows that one can repudiate the absolute authority of one's claims about the meaning of one's own experience without forsaking the ability to draw knowledge from experience, and it is precisely the epistemic distinctions engendered by a postpositivist realism that make such discriminating judgments possible.

In this chapter my aim is to provide further defense for the realist account of identity and for its corresponding claims about identity politics. First, I consider how advisable it is to use the word *realist*. Next, I consider the current philosophical attacks on identity and present a counterdiagnosis that would situate the true "problem of identity" elsewhere than it is generally situated today. And finally, I turn to the question of identity's epistemic and political relevance.

REALISMS

No one here disputes the fact that identity categories are cultural negotiations, nor is anyone unaware that group identities obscure internal heterogeneity (and thus it is not the case, as Hames-García explains, that as soon as I declare I am gay I have no more need to define my politics). None of us believe that the meaning of an experience is transparent, theory-neutral, or uninterpreted or that political commitments follow immediately from social location. In fact, Caroline S. Hau provides a defense of political intellectuals on the basis of their ability to develop an accurate account of the world and not on the basis of their social identity, suggesting that the postmodernist repudiation of the intellectual engagé assumes precisely the unmediated character of social location that they would purportedly oppose.

Thus the authors here can hardly be said to deny the constitutive impact of theory and social context on truth. Yet we also want to claim that identities refer outward to objective and causally significant features of the world, that they are thus nonarbitrary, and that experience provides both an epistemic and a political basis for understanding. But do we really need the word *realism*? Isn't this being intentionally provocative as well as inviting misinterpretation?

In contrast to literary circles, any participant to the conversations within analytic epistemology and metaphysics will know that, today, the term "realism" admits of multiple meanings. There is classical realism, commonsense realism, naive realism, scientific realism, internal realism, pragmatic realism, critical realism, contextual realism, moral realism, and alethic realism, and each of these terms will itself admit of multiple philosophical interpretations![1] The core idea of realism is often thought to be that it is possible for human beings to have knowledge that is about the world as it is, that we are not caught in the "prison house of language"

---

1. For discussions and/or defenses of these various forms, see Alston; Lynch; Elgin; Wright; Putnam; Archer et al.; Sayre-McCord.

to such an extent that we can know nothing about the world at all. But once one thinks about it, this core idea is compatible with some very different metaphysical accounts of the world and of the character of human knowledge.

For example, though realism is compatible with positivism, or the belief that we can *completely* step outside of language and present facts in pure form, as in "red patch here now," it does not entail positivism. Very few philosophers continue to hold such a view; indeed, the logical positivists themselves abandoned this view by the 1930s and went on to develop coherentist accounts of knowledge, as well as radical forms of empiricism, and to inspire critical realism. Nor does the core idea behind realism even entail that one must be an ontological absolutist, or to hold, in other words, that there is only one true story of the world. Even such diverse epistemologists as the pragmatist Hilary Putnam and the foundationalist William P. Alston agree that ontological pluralism turns out to be compatible with realism. Ontologies can be thought of as models of reality useful in science (or in social theory) that approximate the world as it is, thus capturing some truth about it, without enjoying a one-to-one correspondence with categories of entities as they exist completely independently of human languages or human practices. On this view, ontologies might be understood as justified on the grounds of some sort of utility function, but different ontologies can coexist that have different uses, such as folk psychology (which presumes that such things as "minds" exist) and physicalism (which denies the existence of any nonmaterial entity).[2]

Ironically, as Mohanty points out, it is a *positivist* error to assume that this more complicated picture of human knowledge leads us to skepticism, or that to allow multiple ontologies is to say that ontologies have nothing to do with the way the world is. That is, because positivism holds out for pure, "out of theory" experiences, because it raises the bar so ridiculously and unnecessarily high for what can count as knowledge, unless we can base all of science on statements like "red patch here now," and unless we can fool ourselves into believing that such statements are uncontaminated, the positivist says we must opt for skepticism (Babbitt 142). But to believe that some of our knowledge captures the way the world really is does not require us to hold that history, language, or even social stratification is irrelevant to epistemology. This is because knowl-

2. See esp. Lynch.

edge is contingent on a historical development of theoretical commitments
that itself could have been otherwise. Susan Babbitt makes use of Stephen
Jay Gould's account of evolutionary theory here to conceptualize what
such an account of knowledge as contingent can mean:

> [Gould] points out that people repeatedly misinterpret evolution . . . as move-
> ment in a certain, predictable direction—as a "ladder of progress." Instead he
> suggests that if we were able to rewind life's tape—thoroughly erasing every-
> thing that has actually happened—to some time in the past, there is no reason
> at all to think the replay would be anything like the actual history of life. Each
> replay would demonstrate radically different evolutionary directions. This does
> not mean, though, that evolution is senseless and without meaningful pat-
> tern. . . . Each step proceeds for cause, but no finale can be specified from the
> start, and none would ever occur a second time in the same way. (143–44)

Babbitt appropriates this account of evolution for thinking about knowledge as a whole, and specifically how one can juxtapose the historical contingency of knowledge to its ability to correspond to the real world. Knowledge claims are contingent on theories that are themselves contingent in
the sense that they might have developed otherwise. But to say that they
might have developed otherwise is not to say that they convey nothing
about reality, no more than saying that our biological history could have
developed otherwise is to say that evolutionary theory is disproved.

The sort of postpositivist realism invoked in this volume will thus be
more familiar in analytic philosophy circles than in literary theory circles. I do not mean to imply that such a form of realism is currently dominant in analytic philosophy, or even that all philosophers will want to
grant the honorific title "realism" on the actual views defended here.[3] I
wish that were the case, but it is not. However, it is the case, within the
context of philosophy, that the word *realism* is known to admit of many
different formulations and that foundationalists and positivists have no
copyright on it.

Aside from the question of how the word signifies in various disciplinary discourses, the critical issue here is that a claim of realism in no way
presupposes that the real can be drained of its human contributions. This
makes even less sense in regard to claims within social theory than to claims
within science: even in the natural sciences, work must necessarily proceed through linguistic formulations of historically embedded theoretical
traditions. Unless one thinks that language is a transparent medium, or

3. See, e.g., Schmitt, which is a review of my book *Real Knowing*. Note also my "Reply to My Critics," esp. 296–98.

that the "facts" discerned through elaborately staged experiments are theory-neutral, the reality that science pictures is most properly understood to be a composite. As Putnam, with some exasperation, puts it, "If one must use metaphorical language, then let the metaphor be this: the mind and the world jointly make up the mind and the world" (*Reason, Truth and History* xi).[4] The ability to neatly distinguish the "human" part and the "world" part is not required before one can assert that the knowledge we have is really about the world: we know that we cannot find evidential support for any theory whatever, and that well-supported theories yield predictions and enhance practical success, and thus we know that the knowledge we have is not merely, or exclusively, self-reflection.

But in regard to the objects of social theory there is a double hermeneutic, for here one is engaged in the linguistic analysis of linguistic beings and linguistic behavior. Social identities are real (or not) within the social world, but this is not to say that social identity is infinitely plastic, malleable to opportunistic specifications, or *merely* linguistic. As John H. Zammito says, "We accept that language helps to constitute its object, rejecting only the view that it is solely constitutive of such objects." Just as we can understand the object of scientific knowledge to be, in some sense, "human and world," and thus acknowledge the human element in science, so too should we recognize the "world" aspect of the objects of social theory. Social identities are often carried on the body, materially inscribed, perceived at a glance by well-disciplined perceptual practices, and thus hardly the mere epiphenomena of discourse. This, some poststructuralists will argue, is not their claim. Of course, identities are real in the sense of being lived, of having real effects, and of constituting key features of our shared reality, they say. However, identities are produced through domination itself and as such should be transgressed against and subverted. In the next section I turn to these arguments.

PROBLEMS WITH IDENTITY

Many theorists express a worry that the very concept of identity involves domination because it presumes sameness, thus excluding difference, and because it presumes some *haecceity,* or essential core. Traditionally in philosophy, to share an identity is to be indiscernible or to share every property. This is not the ordinary language understanding of identity, of

---

4. See also Rouse; Alcoff, *Real Knowing.*

course, in which it is common to talk about national identity or ethnic identity even while one assumes that there are differences between the individuals who might share such an identity as well as similarities that such individuals may share with those in another identity group. Identity is conceived as something common to a group, but what this something is can be variously spelled out: for example, it might be something that is socially based and historical rather than stable and inherent. The concept "linked fate," used by social scientists to signify a felt connection to others of one's identity group based on the belief that their fate will impinge on one's own, operates to tie individuals together on the basis of being subject to a certain kind of treatment, which of course does not entail any concept of an essential core. The worry that identity *entails* an ahistorical essentialism or that it posits an absolute sameness seems to me to be the sort of worry Wittgenstein said philosophers develop when we let language go on holiday. It is based on a conflation of contextually based meanings and standards.

But there is a more legitimate worry, in my view, about the individual's relationship to group categories of identity. Is identity inherently constraining? Moreover, if the genealogy of identity is based on something like the concept of linked fate that I mentioned earlier, then it looks as if identity is something created by oppression that our goal should be to dismantle rather than celebrate or build a politics around.

This is the sort of worry that has motivated an interest in poststructuralist and psychoanalytic accounts of identity. Famously for Foucault, the moment of subjectification—-the moment at which we attain the status of subject—is simultaneously the moment of subjection. Only as subjects can we be made subject to the Law and subject to disciplinary strategies that produce docile bodies. Only when we conceive of ourselves as possessing a "self" can this self become the focal point of the self-monitoring practices embedded in the Panopticon. Foucault was particularly concerned with group categories of identity that work to integrate individuals "by a conscience or self-knowledge" under a unified condition with "a set of very specific patterns" ("Subject and Power" 214, 221). Despite Foucault's late attempts to develop an account of an ethical relation to one's self, he never considered the possibility of refashioning an ethical relation with a collectivity of others, presumably because he viewed such formations as the inevitable product of discipline.[5]

---

5. And the ethical relation with the self Foucault explored—when he talks about the cultivation of the self, the care of the self, or techniques of the self—stops firmly short of

Derrida has argued that making demands in the name of a subject (i.e., woman) will replicate structures of domination by stipulatively unifying that which in reality cannot be unified.[6] This does not preclude the justifiable use of identity claims in all cases for Derrida, but he does suggest that at best we should approach identity as a strategy, through a strategic essentialism, a temporary utilization rather than deep commitment, and/or an ironic attitude. We should use identity categories only in ways that will work ultimately to subvert them.

And, of course, in a Freudian model, identity attachments are the symptom of a certain ego dysfunction. As Ernesto Laclau puts it, "the psychoanalytic category of identification" explicitly asserts that there is "a lack at the root of any identity; one needs to identify with someone because there is an originary and insurmountable lack of identity" (3). The more one expresses an insistence on identity, then, the more one is evidently suffering from this lack. Freud argued that the effort to overcome the unavoidable disunity of the self through a collective identification or group solidarity may itself be the sign of a pathological condition caused by "the inability of the ego to regain autonomy following the loss of an object of desire."[7]

In her book *The Psychic Life of Power,* Judith Butler, building on Althusser as well as Freud and Foucault, argues that interpellation never identifies that which existed before but calls into existence a subject that becomes subject only through its response to the call.[8] Moreover, like Jean-Paul Sartre, Butler holds that there always remains a psychic excess beyond that which is named and out of which agency becomes possible. This is not to say that agency would preexist the process of subjectivation; the appearance of an excess itself is only made possible by the process of naming that tries to accurately and fully identify the self. In other words, interpellation, or naming, creates an identity the inadequacy of which produces the excess, where agency is possible; it is on the basis of the excess that one resists the imposition of the identity, but it is only because one has an identity that one can act. Subjectivation is nec-

creating collective categories of identity or ways of being in a public domain that might reconfigure the collective imaginary.

6. See esp. his "Women in the Beehive" and "Deconstruction and the Other." There is a useful critical discussion of Derrida's views on this topic in both Gates and Steele.

7. Steinberg n.p.

8. See her *Gender Trouble,* esp. pt. 1; and *The Psychic Life of Power,* esp. introd. and chaps. 3 and 4.

essary for agency because it creates the subject who then can act, but at the same time it misnames that subject and inscribes it into Power.

> Called by an injurious name, I come into social being, and because I have a certain narcissism that takes hold of any term that confers existence, I am led to embrace the terms that injure me because they constitute me socially. The self-colonizing trajectory of certain forms of identity politics are symptomatic of this paradoxical embrace of the injurious term. As a further paradox, then, only by occupying—being occupied by—that injurious term can I resist and oppose it, recasting the power that constitutes me as the power I oppose. (104)

For Butler, social categories of identity make resistance possible but always fail to identify accurately, and thus by this very fact create the need for resistance. Accepting identities is tantamount to accepting dominant scripts and performing the identities Power has invented. Identities are not and can never be accurate representations of the real self, and thus interpellation always in a strict sense fails in its representational claim even while it succeeds in inciting and disciplining one's practice. The question Butler then poses for herself in this book is, when we are interpellated in this way by Power, why do we respond? Why do we turn toward the identifying, subjectivating source rather than away from it? This question is especially troubling to Butler in regard to oppressed identities, for example, racial and sexual, in which case the turn toward them is even more pathological. Yet interpellation is the price for recognition.

> The desire to persist in one's own being requires submitting to a world of others that is fundamentally not one's own (a submission that does not take place at a later date, but which frames and makes possible the desire to be). Only by persisting in alterity does one persist in one's "own" being. Vulnerable to terms that one never made, one persists [i.e., continues as a subject] always, to some degree, through categories, names, terms, and classifications that mark a primary alienation in sociality. (*Psychic Life* 28)[9]

---

9. I doubt that Butler's account of Foucault is accurate on this point. Her aim in this book is not to follow faithfully Foucault, and she in fact argues that his accounts lead to postulations about the psyche that he himself could not follow up (a claim I do agree with). Nonetheless, she is taking Foucault as support for her global anti-identitarianism. And here, like others, I suspect that Foucault's view of the subject and even of identity is more complex, given that he does call for the reformulation of subjectivities and thus sounds a good deal less pessimistic about subjectivity, surprisingly, than does Butler herself.

Also, I realize that it may appear at this point that we are talking about two concepts rather than one: identity, on the one hand, and subjectivity, on the other. One might think of identity as one's public self, based on publicly recognized categories, and of subjectivity as one's lived self, or true self, or thinking self, etc. However, this neat separation doesn't

The fundamental idea in Butler's work, as in Derrida's, Freud's and Foucault's, is that social naming is alienating and that its source is some form of pernicious Power.

Butler's analysis is strikingly consistent with Sartre's distinction between the for-itself and its ego, though in some cases she gives different reasons for the separation than does Sartre. For the Sartre of *Being and Nothingness,* when we are identified, for example, as "the homosexual" or "the heterosexual" we are recognized by our past choices, choices that can be transcended in the future. Thus identifications in a sense never hit their mark, they never identify the real self but only its historic trail.

When we organize on the basis of these identities we are unwittingly, naively, remaining caught in Power's clutches. Wendy Brown argues, in *States of Injury,* that "this truth" some feminists think we need "has been established as the secret to our souls not by us but by those who would discipline us through that truth" (42). When we organize around identity, or what she names our "wounded attachments," we are compulsively repeating a painful reminder of our subjugation and maintaining a cycle of blaming that continues to focus on our oppression rather than to seek ways to transcend it.[10] Freud suggested that a compulsion to repeat traumatic events from the past was motivated by our desire to gain control over and thus master the event. But he knew that this repetition-compulsion maintains the power of the event over us by making it the organizing focus of our actions and choices. Parallel to Nietzsche's claim that "man" would rather will nothingness (or nihilism) than to will nothing at all, Butler and Brown hold that those who embrace their identity-categories are saying in effect, "I would rather exist in subordination than not exist" (Butler, *Psychic Life* 7). Butler concludes from this that subjectivity itself is thus irretrievably bound up with melancholia.

STRATEGIC ESSENTIALISM

Although identities are, then, according to these theorists, both pernicious and metaphysically inaccurate, in another sense they are, or seem to be, unavoidable. Certainly identities are needed in the political arena so that movements can make demands "in the name of" and "on behalf

---

quite work: Butler takes herself to be critiquing identity and subjectivity (i.e., the modernist account of subjectivity) in the same breath, because to some extent on her and Foucault's view they are created simultaneously. Or, identity is the price we pay for subjectivity.

10. I discuss Brown's arguments in more detail in "Becoming an Epistemologist."

of" women, Latinos, gays, and so on. The political solution to this paradox widely accepted among feminist theorists and many others today is strategic essentialism, first formulated by Gayatri Spivak, which pairs an antirealist account of identity with a pragmatic acceptance of the necessity of using identity categories to advance political claims in the public domain (*In Other Worlds* 205).[11] Thus, although one "knows" that identity is not real, that its purported homogeneity is an illusion, one can still deploy identity in the public domain as a way to displace hegemonic knowledges and structures of oppression.

But "strategic essentialism" produces a politically pernicious elitism and even vanguardism when it operates to divide the "knowing" theorists who deploy identity strategically and the "unknowing" activists who continue to believe in identity. It also accepts a certain theoretical incoherence between one's political practice and one's theoretical commitments. Like Nietzsche, I believe that any such strategic account is ultimately unworkable: a claim can only be taken seriously—and thus have its strategic effects—when it is taken as truth in a real and not merely strategic sense. Despite these problems, strategic essentialism is considered by many to be the best possible position given the specious character of identity claims.

The acceptability of strategic essentialism rests heavily on the acceptance of the account of identity I summarized above. But is this description of identity formation and its necessary link to Power truly convincing? Of course, if we try to resist it some would have a ready diagnosis of our resistance: we are pining for a lost fixity and compulsively focused on the source of our own victimization.[12] But the arguments themselves strain our credibility. If we move away from Leibniz, there *are* concepts of identity that can handle internal heterogeneity in the way the identity is made manifest in various individuals and that avoid presuming to capture the whole person in any given category or set of categories. Such concepts can be developed from the ordinary usage of the term.

Moreover, it seems obvious that one would need to make distinctions between kinds of processes in which identities are formed, all of which may not be coercive impositions. Although Foucault, Butler, and Brown are right about some aspects of some identities or subjectification processes, they are not obviously right about *all such aspects of all such processes.* In contrast to their analysis, for example, the social theorist

11. For Spivak's reconsidered view on the topic, see her "In a Word. Interview."
12. For such diagnoses, see Brown and also Gitlin.

Manuel Castells explains identity as a generative source of meaning, necessarily collective rather than wholly individual, and useful not only as a source of agency but also as a meaningful narrative (7). Similarly, Satya Mohanty argues that identity constructions provide narratives that explain the links between group historical memory and individual contemporary experience, that they create unifying frames for rendering experience intelligible, and thus they help to map the social world.

In contrast to the work by philosophers that tends to homogenize the variety of processes in which identities are constructed, recent work by sociologists and historians on identity seem generally better at noting the differences. Good work is emerging that looks very specifically at the development of a white identity, a pan-Latino identity, pan-African identity, and others. Castells, for example, distinguishes nationalist narratives that aim toward legitimizing identity, from resistance movements that affirm the oppressed by reinforcing their boundaries so as to exclude the oppressors, and both of these from projects that seek to reconstruct existing identity categories toward a transformation of overall social structures. Because Butler and others collapse these processes into a single account, it is easier for them to render a uniform political valence for all social identity.[13]

It is also the case that theories of identity can take into account psychoanalytic insights without Butler's pessimistic conclusions. The Mexican philosophers Samuel Ramos and Leopoldo Zea both employ existentialist and psychoanalytic accounts in order to explore identity as a form of mediation between self-knowledge, on the one hand, and national and cultural realities, on the other.[14] For them, identity has no purchase on individual life unless it is taken up and given material interpretation, and this process necessarily involves a creative appropriation by the individual. What Butler sees as our being "forced" to adhere to this subjectivating process, Zea and Ramos, along with Mohanty, envision as a process by which the individual develops a meaningful self. To the extent there is oppression in this process, it is because the social context disallows or severely curtails the possibilities of meaning making and not because the individual is forced to make meaning in the first place.

13. Although she supports some movements for recognition, the influential left-wing theorist Nancy Fraser also holds that socialism will "require[] that all people be weaned from their attachment to current cultural constructions of their interests and identities." See her *Justice Interruptus* esp. 31.

14. See Ramos; Schutte; Zea, *The Latin American Mind* and *The Role of the Americas in History*.

Strategic essentialism, then, is not justified on its own terms. Even if identity were such a dangerous fiction that we had to deploy it only with great care, strategic essentialism invites elitism and courts incoherence. Moreover, it is far from clear that identities, in all cases, are either fictional or dangerous, in which case strategic essentialism is unnecessary. A prima facie case can be made that the critiques of identity are based on over-generalizations of human experience and social praxis. The uniform negative valence given to identity, as rooted in domination and always alien to the self, has failed to answer the challenge posed by accounts that understand identity as a process of meaning making. These alternative accounts get no consideration in Butler's work, or in Brown's, Derrida's, or others. Which makes one wonder why the critique has become so influential, why there is so much worry and consternation—both political and philosophical—about claims of identity, and why the consensus seems to be that identity must be overcome. In my view, a counterdiagnosis is in order, and I offer one in the next section.

A GENEALOGY OF THE PROBLEM

To understand the current aversion to identity, one would need to retrace the development of the philosophical treatment of identity in modern, Western philosophy. Charles Taylor's *Sources of the Self* is undoubtedly the best recent attempt to do this and to engage in what he calls a project of historical retrieval: to retrieve those forgotten or less remembered aspects of modernity's thinking about the self, such as, for example, important elements of a critique of atomism. Taylor also tries to reveal the background or hermeneutic horizon that lies behind our current universalist moral intuitions. It seems to me that it is just such an approach that is needed to understand the current critique of identity.[15]

Taylor's history shows that the modern moral ideal of autonomy or of the disengaged self is a development from the ancient ideal of "mastery of self," found both in Plato and in the Stoics, that was the central criterion of moral virtue and behavior worthy of citizens. Mastery of self signals the dominance of reason over emotion but also precludes mastery by another and thus yields autonomy. In the modern period this ethical motivation for autonomy is largely replaced by an epistemological

15. For a history of the modern development of racial and cultural identity, see, e.g., Eze; Faull; Goldberg; Anderson; West; Omi and Winant; Gregory and Sanjek.

one. The ideal of autonomy becomes a cornerstone aspect of the scientific worldview's ideal of the "disengaged self, capable of objectifying not only the surrounding world but also his own emotions and inclinations, fears and compulsions" (21). Given this, it might seem that the distrust of cultural or social identity is justified by its conflict with reason: if a strong attachment to identity disallows disengagement or the objectification of one's culture and one's people, even an imaginative disengagement, for the purposes of reflective critique, then one cannot gain critical distance, and thus one's allegiance to it cannot be rational.

However, the current philosophical discourses that distrust identity are not restricted to those who follow within this Platonic and, later, Kantian tradition in which autonomy so conceived is a necessary condition of rationality. Butler and Foucault, for example, follow the Hegelian break with this tradition, in which Hegel scoffs at the very possibility of a total disengagement from culture or history. But what is interesting about Hegel in this regard is that his formulation of the relation between self and other succeeds at both contradicting and confirming the value of autonomy.

Hegel moves away from a self-enclosed conception of identity—of an identity that is fundamentally the product of an autogenous process—to a conception of identity as dependent on recognition. This transformation inaugurated a new problematic of identity that can be seen throughout much of Western philosophy but especially clearly in the work of Hegel, Freud, Sartre, and Foucault, figures who have each influenced all parties to the identity politics debate. Retracing the steps of this developing conversation will shed light on how identity has become relegated to the sphere of the pathological and chimerical.

Hegel's writings inaugurate a critical shift in thinking about the self, toward understanding the self as a kind of process rather than objectively describable or static. In *The Phenomenology of Spirit* Hegel attempts to describe the moments of the shifting, evolutionary trajectory of the self as it is manifest simultaneously in Spirit and in the sense of the historical human self. Though Hegel imagines this process as exemplifying a discernable, developmental teleology, he departs from the previous pursuit of timeless substances. For Hegel, the appearance of discrete stable objects is epiphenomenal on a more fundamental metaphysical state of incessant change that inheres in all that is real. Geist itself is a process of self-knowing and self-realization whose essential nature is not to be found in an originary moment or final end state but in the very movement itself. "Perfectibility [the key feature of Absolute Spirit] is something almost as undetermined as mutability in general; it is without aim and purpose and without a standard of change. The better, the more perfect toward which it is supposed to attain, is entirely undetermined" (*Reason in History* 68).

Hegel's famous description of the developmental trajectory of "man's" subjectivity, which moves through stages of consciousness in which the core is fundamentally altered through its negotiations and struggles with an external environment, is based on his claim that there exists an explicit parallelism between the unfolding and indeterminate "circuit" of activity that constitutes Life in general and that which constitutes self-consciousness. Thus the human self has the potential to participate in this open-ended, undetermined formative process that constitutes the rational Real. Hegel makes self-determination parasitic upon a process ontology within an open dialectic. If man is to be self-determining, he must be defined only by his capacity to objectify and negate whatever is given and to exist within a dynamic context that is itself indeterminate.In this move from being to becoming, Hegel moves radically away from Kant's theory of constitutive categories and even from Hume's psychologistic account of the self and lays the groundwork simultaneously for what seems to be a more thorough concept of self-determination as well as for a tremendous anxiety created by the very indeterminacy and formlessness of our inner essence. To the extent that Hegel then goes on to give a larger role to the social in the formation of the self, the potential harm or interference of that social realm on the self is all the greater.

Anticipating Sartre, one might say, Hegel describes the process of development that self-consciousness undergoes as primarily one of negation, the negation of the independent object that confronts it, and he makes this a necessary step toward its own self-certainty and thus its being for-itself. The negation that inaugurates the process by which self-consciousness develops is only the initial moment toward the sublation of the Other, a sublation that has a double meaning and is a kind of double gesture, involving both the repudiation of the Other and its absorption. He says, "Self-consciousness . . . must set itself to sublate the other independent being, in order thereby to become certain of itself as true being, secondly, it thereupon proceeds to sublate its own self, for this other is itself" (*Phenomenology of Mind* 229). What is curious about this account is that, on the one hand, the self is presented as fundamentally social because an individual can only achieve self-consciousness and thus become a subject and a moral agent after recognition from the Other and thus, in a certain sense, after it has been absorbed by the social. This represents an important turn in Western metaphysical accounts of the self. But, on the other hand, Hegel goes on to describe the attitude of self-consciousness as a negation and sublation of the Other who *is, or has become, one's self.* The potential power that the Other may have to constitute the self, in that self-consciousness or subjectivity requires recognition, is thereby dissolved. As Allen Wood, without any qualms, puts it, Hegel's account holds that otherness "can be overcome" (45). We are dependent on the Other only to the extent that achieving our independence requires a certain process of engagement with the Other and cannot be achieved by "Stoical aloofness" or an attempt to flee. But the sublation itself works to separate rather than to entwine: "through sublation," Hegel tells us, self-consciousness "gets back itself, because it becomes one with itself again through the cancelling of *its* otherness; but secondly, it likewise gives otherness back again to the other self-consciousness, for it was aware of being in the other, it cancels this its own being in the other and thus lets the other again go free" (*Phenomenology of Mind* 229–30). This is a model of temporary engagement with the aim of separation and mutual noninterference: as Mitchell Aboulafia says, "Hegel's self-consciousness . . . attempt[s] to use the strategy of negating that which is other in order to deny the intrusion of otherness" (109). The presence of the Other is the occasion or prompt of the development of self-consciousness; it is not its ground, nor does it make a substantive contribution to the content of one's self. Hegel seems anxious to avoid such an outcome: the dependence of self-consciousness on the Other is dissolved almost immediately.

Of course, in Hegel's mature political philosophy and ethical theory there emerges a different and arguably better account of intersubjective relations that, in fact, "shreds . . . the subjectivistic, atomistic, and moralistic foundations of modern liberalism" and promotes "communitarian principles," as Wood puts it (258). Hegel argues that individual self-actualization is best maximized through collective institutions and the pursuit of shared goals, a clearly more robust account of interdependence than the one he gives in the *Phenomenology.* Only in the sphere of morality does one have relations with others and through this become a moral subject or a subject with moral agency; only insofar as one is constituted by the Other does one acquire specific social identities, both objectively and subjectively, on the basis of which collective interests that motivate rational action and judgment can even be developed. This is much more robust than the position in the *Phenomenology* where self-consciousness is produced by a negation or an overcoming of the Other's otherness. In the *Philosophy of Right,* it is the otherness of the Other that constitutes one's social identity and through which moral subjectivity is achieved. Thus it is here where Hegel begins to displace the classical liberal core/periphery model of the self with a more holistic model in which the self's very internal capacities are preconditioned by external relations. Consciousness itself becomes an emergent entity of a social and historical process rather than a kind of presocial thinking substance that could conceivably exist entirely on its own. The locus of agency, in particular, is not simply internal to the self.

Hegel has thus greatly influenced current discourses on identity, relocating the source of identity outside the "core" or internal self and making it dependent for its substantive features and capacities on culturally and historically variable external elements. But it is important to note here that Hegel both inaugurates a constitutive self/Other relation and manifests an anxiety about this very dependence and integration. It is this double gesture that can be traced out through subsequent developments in Western thought.

Freud offers what is in some respects an expansion of this notion, without the liability of Hegel's metaphysical commitment to an Absolute Spirit inhabiting the process of development. Freud's account emphasizes the individual or microlevel process and avoids presuming the inevitability of a higher synthesis as the outcome. The ego develops through negotiations between multiple, conflicting, inner drives, on the one hand, and the outpouring of stimuli from the external world, on the other. The self or subsequent identity that is created through this process contains sedimented features that are in some sense internal, but Freud's hallmark was to understand these features not as intrinsic, presocial, or ontologically self-sufficient but as fundamentally generated through interpersonal interaction, especially, of course, during infancy.

Jacques Lacan's linguistic interpretation of Freud's characterization of the genealogy of the self had the effect of integrating wider cultural and historical forces in the process, as did also the theorists organized around the Frankfurt school who extended the Freudian account of the unconscious and of the subject-in-process in order to describe and explain collective, cultural phenomena. Freud himself had used the unconscious to explain larger social tendencies, as in *Totem and Taboo,* but did not incorporate language to the same extent as Lacan or the idea of a collective social self as did Erich Fromm.

Given the influence of these later accounts, an analysis of the self could no longer be restricted to early family dynamics for a given individual.

This effected a move outward from the "internal" self and exacerbated the tendency toward determinism that had already reached a troubling dimension in Freud. What sense of individual agency could possibly be efficacious in a subjectivation process involving such large social structures? The problem of determinism thus came to dominate theoretical debates over the self in the twentieth century, creating various positions both within and between structuralism, Marxism, and existentialism and inspiring new free will debates in Anglo-American philosophy. The traditional philosophical problem of "free will" was originally a theological concern, but in the twentieth century it became reformulated within the domain of the social and psychological sciences as a problem about determinism in the secular world.

Sartre's account of the self, though enormously at odds in different respects with both Hegel's and Freud's, is also contiguous with the Hegelian tradition in that he acknowledges the Other's power to give or withhold recognition and even characterizes this interrelationship as a kind of death struggle. Even in his early work, Sartre recognizes that one of the most important constraints on the self involves the look of the Other and the subsequent felt alienation of the self. Our being-for-others puts an absolute limit on our freedom, that is, on the meaning and valuation of ourself within domains of projection configured by the Other.

It was Sartre who provided an ingenuous answer to the problem of determinism. He sharply separated the "real" self, which is the pure ability to nihilate the given, and the ego or more substantive self, which consists of the historical sedimentation of states through which we have built up a substantive self and by which we would ordinarily identify a specific individual. That is, in one sense for Sartre the self is a mere capacity, in particular, the capacity to negate or go beyond whatever is presented to consciousness, including the given material environment, social context, as well as one's own individual history. The substantive self or ego is formed through such acts of nihilating the given. But the essential feature of *être-pour-soi*, that which demarcates it from *être-en-soi* and that which causes all its existential difficulties, is its freedom to negate the given.

Thus, unlike Freud, Sartre erects an impenetrable border between the substantive self of the ego, which consists of the pattern of past choices, and the core self or the for-itself, which is simply a capacity to nihilate the given. This distinction allows Sartre to hold on to a strong version of agency while recognizing the facticity of our unchosen situations, since the capacity to negate remains unaffected by the substantive self. But in this account, identity is positioned outside the real self. "It is not that I do not wish to be this person or that I want this person to be different. But rather . . . [i]t is a 'representation' for others and for myself, which means that I can be he only in *representation*. But if I represent myself as him, I am not he; I am separated from him as the object from the subject" (103; original emphasis). Identity is a feature of the ego, which is coextensive with one's past, or in its public manifestation identity is a feature of one's situation, which imposes limited and often oppressive categories and is subject to a total negation. This is why Sartre had such trouble, even in his later writings, acknowledging ethnic or racial identity; in both *Anti-Semite and Jew* and "Black Orpheus" he reduces Jewish and black identity to the construction of oppressors.

What should be highlighted here, and what has for too long been lost in debates over Sartre's belief in radical freedom, is that the distinction Sartre draws between identity and the for-itself allows Sartre to hold, in effect, the Other at bay, such that the recognition by the Other vital to the development of subjectivity has purchase only on the ego or past self and not on the real or core self. Sartre found the power of the Other to know me in a way I cannot know myself very discomforting: "The Other *looks* at me and as such he holds the secret of my being, he knows what I *am*. Thus the profound meaning of my being is outside me, imprisoned in an absence. The Other has the advantage over me" (473; original emphasis). However, by separating the for-itself from the ego or substantive self, the power that the Other has over me is deflated. The Other knows only the object that I act to represent, but I can negate this at will. Thus the Other is not in a position to know me as subject, or to constitute me, but only that past self from which I am already separated. The essential character of the for-itself is to be "remote-from-itself" (55). The for-itself "must be able to put himself *outside of* being, and by the same stroke weaken the structure of the being of being" (59; original emphasis).

Notice also that the defining activity of the for-itself, and that which alone can secure its freedom, is the ability to negate, to destroy, to change, and to imagine what is not, capacities that Sartre called the *negatités*. That which is given to me, and thus by definition is not something I myself have made, must be challenged, thwarted, and rebuffed precisely in order to establish my own reflective consciousness, my own power. "Man's *relation* to being is that he can modify it" (59–60; original emphasis). Not accept, absorb, or augment being but modify, and thus alter it.

In its broad strokes, it is this sort of ontology of the self that is presupposed, I want to argue, in the philosophical and political critiques of identity that take it to be an a priori political danger and a metaphysical mistake on the grounds that identities commit the individual to social categories. These critiques conceptualize identity as outside the core self, as public and as imposed, and they hold that identity never provides a fair or adequate represention. It is this ontology that makes all substantive representations of the self inadequate and even equates the very attempt to represent with the attempt to oppress. The excess that escapes all representation is thought to be one's real self, one's capacity to negate, and the seat of purposeful action and choice. It is only the excess that is free, uncontainable, indeterminate, too fluid to be characterized in substantive terms. But the idea of transcending one's identity, of never being fully contained within it, returns us to a Sartrian for-itself that is itself defined as transcendence.[16]

Thus, from Hegel's inaugurating moment of recognizing the constitutive power of recognition itself, of bringing the Other center stage into the formation of the self, Western philosophy has struggled with this alien internal presence, has struggled to find the means to offset its power of determination. The Other, from Hegel to Foucault, is accorded the power to recognize, to name, even to constitute one's identity. This is why the look of the Other produces nausea and even terror, as our own capacity of determination drains away in Sartre's famous metaphor. And as Lewis Gordon has argued, racism's attempt to constrain, imprison, and deny nonwhite subjectivity is precisely motivated by this desire to deflect the look of the nonwhite Other: "The white body is expected not to be looked at by black bodies. . . . There was a period in the American South when, for blacks, looking a white in the eye carried the risk of being lynched" (102). If the look of the Other *generally* has a terrifying power, the look of the Other *whom one has colonized and enslaved* must be deflected at all costs. An identity that has been grounded on racist, vanguard narratives— an identity that gains its very coherence through supremacy—can literally not survive the Look of the colonized Other whose recognition must necessarily be accusatory. Luce Irigaray has shown a similar effect of female presence in a masculine order where masculine subjectivity is predicated on the erasure of women. The power of the Other to constitute the self must lead, in such situations, precisely to the death struggle that Hegel envisioned.

In classical liberalism, developed against the backdrop of European

---

16. I am not of course arguing here that Sartre/Foucault comprise a coherent philosophy, only that one can trace a common thread.

colonial expansion, that which originates outside of me must be fought against, it is assumed, else my very selfness, my ownness to my self, will be at stake. The human self is essentially a reasoning self, but reason requires autonomy or the ability to gain critical distance and to pass independent judgment on anything external. The idea of being constituted by others threatens such a self with dissolution. The neo-Hegelian tradition we have just retraced starts from a different place but effectively ends in the same view. To submit to our being-for-others as if this were an inescapable truth about ourselves is to commit bad faith. The essential self is the capacity to resist, to transcend and to exceed all attempts at representation. This is an Oedipal scene written into a phenomenological ontology of being, and it has unconsciously constituted the very meaning of "autonomy" and "freedom" in Western political traditions.[17]

We can find a similar scene, in a very different play, written into more recent treatments of identity given by Foucault and Althusser, the one ascribing it to ideology and the other locating it in the movements of Power. But in both cases the answer turns out to be the same as for Sartre: resistance to identity is somehow both metaphysically and politically mandated, insofar as it is possible (which in the estimation of Foucault and Althusser is far less than in Sartre's). Foucault and Sartre were theoretical adversaries, and Foucault's deterministic account of discursive formations and his repudiation of intentionality were aimed directly against Sartrian existentialism. However, a close look at Foucault's treatment of the self reveals an almost indistinguishable account of the separation between identities, which are discursively constituted and imposed, and the basic capacities of self-transformation that Foucault assumes in his ethics of the self. Like Sartre's privileging of the negatités, Foucault privileges resistance—and especially resistance to identity—as the central feature of contemporary political struggles in his call to replace sexual identity with bodies and pleasures and "to refuse what we are" ("Subject and Power" 216).

The difference between modern and postmodernist accounts is simply in their degree of optimism about the extent to which the individual can negate the given and resist an external Power. Postmodernists are much less sanguine about the efficacy of individual agency. But in both modern and postmodern accounts it is striking that negation, resistance, and destabilization of what comes to the individual from the social—

17. See, e.g., Hartsock; Lloyd.

whether that social is discourse, disciplinary mechanisms, the Law of the Father, or cultural traditions—are normatively privileged; this makes sense only given the prior assumption that what comes to the individual from the social is necessarily constraining and pernicious or that the individual must be the final arbiter of all value.

But why make this assumption? Why assume that giving any prerogative to the parent/community/society or the discourse/episteme/socius is in every case and necessarily psychically pernicious and enabling only at the cost of a more profound subordination? Why assume that if I am culturally, ethnically, sexually identifiable that this is a process akin to Kafka's nightmarish torture machines in the penal colony? Wilkerson's chapter provides a vivid example of the way in which the Other's privileged knowledge of us can be at times quite helpful, and how accepting the Other's knowledge can enhance rather than inhibit the process of gaining autonomy. Minh T. Nguyen and Moya show ways in which group identities not only allow for meaning making but also for a fuller discernment of one's environment. So why is it assumed so easily that accepting social categories of identity is a form of subordination?

My diagnosis points to a fear of the power of the Other as providing the missing premise to make this argument compelling. There is much reason to think that this fear itself is situated, not existentially primordial. The colonizers and the dominant need to deflect the reflection they see in their victims' eyes, and the victims themselves need to be able to transcend the oppressors' representations. Thankfully, however, these do not exhaust the possible relationships that can exist between self and Other. Nor do they exhaust the genealogies of social categories of identity.

POLITICS AND IDENTITIES

It may be that the most important difference between the critics of identity and the authors whose essays are collected here concerns not what identities are as much as the normative and epistemological implications of identity, which is to say it is about the politics of identity. Both might agree that in a certain sense identities are real, insofar as they have real effects and correlate to real experiences, but they surely disagree over whether identities are politically healthy or reliable sources of truth.

On Mohanty's view, identities are politically and epistemically significant because of their correlation with experience. Although he understands experience to be theoretically mediated, he still maintains that experience is the basis of knowledge, meaning not just what is taken to be true but what *is* true (or likely to approximate the truth). Mohanty argues that the infinite plasticity of meaning and the irreducibility of difference are belied by the fact that we, for any given we, share a world from which we can negotiate across our differences toward a fallible and partial but mutual understanding of the features of that world. Transcending difference does not happen through the application of abstract universal principles, or by forcing the Other to accept what we "know" to be the unmediated truth, but through a shared activity in a shared context. Thus do we achieve knowledge. Identities are not an unsurpassable block against achieving such understanding but the location from which each must work, given the fundamental way in which our identities will limit and shape our possibilities, our desires, questions, and perceptions.

None of these claims suggest that those with the same identity will have the same set of experiences, or that the same experience will always yield the same understanding, but it is absurd to deny the importance of experience or identity, or to say that it would be better if we could just deconstruct all identities as soon as possible. This would make sense only if identities are conceived of as solipsistic bubbles that forever separate us, or as limiting constraints foisted on us by dominant structures. Because the practice of mediating experience is always a social practice, acknowledging the role of identity in knowledge and experience does not lead to solipsism. To say that we have an identity is just to say that we have a location in social space, a hermeneutic horizon that is both grounded in a location and an opening or site from which we attempt to know the world. Understood in this way, it is incoherent to view identities as something we would be better off without.

In the last section, I argued that the recent Western qualms about identity are rooted in a fear of the Other's power over the self. But if identity is defined simply as something like social location—a definition that would certainly render plausible the claim that identity has epistemic salience—how does the Other have power over one's social location? And if the Other does have such power, doesn't this compromise or at least complicate identity's epistemic role?

To answer these questions, it will be helpful initially to distinguish two different senses or aspects of identity that are often conflated. These aspects are interconnected and interdependent but metaphysically distinguishable:

(1) Public identity, or that identity which one has in a public space such as on a street or in a census form, and by which one is hailed, in-

terpellated, and categorized. This identity is external, visible, and under only limited individual control. It is what I am seen as, though I may be seen as something different in different cultural contexts. It is produced through social mechanisms of categorization and learned modes of perception. It is used by those around me, consciously and unconsciously, to interpret the meanings of my actions and utterances, with more or less accuracy and goodwill.

(2) Subjectivity, also sometimes involved in discussions of identity, especially when the link between identity, politics, and epistemic authority is being explored. Subjectivity refers to my own sense of myself, my lived experience of my self, or my interior life.[18]

My public identity and my lived self may be at some significant odds from each other. Fanon calls this a corporeal malediction, that is, the disequilibrium induced by the experience of having one's subjectivity and one's identity, or one's first-person self and one's third-person self, seriously at odds with one another.[19] Richard Rodriguez relates just such an experience when he says, "My face could not portray the ambition I brought to it" (1). Here the "I" and the face—that is, the subjectivity and the visible, public identity—are at odds. One of the questions prompted by a realist account is what such a lack of correspondence between public identity and subjectivity means: does it always imply that one side or the other is "mistaken"? Should my own sense of self always trump public attributions? Or are we really talking about two different entities, or two different aspects of a single entity, which can each be described correctly or incorrectly but without being determined by the other? (I will henceforth use the general term "identity" to refer to both public identity and subjectivity, but I will make distinctions between the different aspects of identity by use of these latter categories.)

Western common sense has it that we have more individual control over our subjectivity than we have over our public identity, especially if the former is thought to be "internal" and the latter "external," but this "internal/external" terminology is misleading. Our sense of ourselves, our capacities and aspirations, is made possible by our public identity. Hegel was right to argue that without some social recognition for our

18. Subjectivity in this sense is not to be contrasted with objectivity; my use of "subjectivity" refers to a lived experience of self, rather than a biased or interested perspective as often associated with the word.

19. See Fanon. Weiss very helpfully develops and explains Fanon's view, esp. 26–33.

status as thinking subjects, our very capacity for subjectivity is stunted. Without a social space, such as a civil society or neighborhood or perhaps a family, in which the individual can operate as a free, moral, decision-making agent, the individual cannot become a moral agent, indeed, is not a moral agent. Slavery rendered impossible Sethe's, and other slaves', ability to make moral decisions regarding the welfare of their children: mothers could not oversee their upbringing, provide resources, keep their children nearby, or even protect them from the worst kind of daily violence. Sethe's act of murder, which Morrison based on a real event, was itself the only *analectical* act possible to her, that is, the only act that could take her and her child beyond the terms of possibility within her located present.[20] For this reason it was unintelligible to those around her. Thus, in a sense, it was the only *act* that was possible to her as a moral agent.

This is part of Mohanty's claim in saying that identity denotes location: identities are indexical entities and thus only real *within* a given location. But this also means that the "internal" is conditioned by, even constituted within, the "external," which is itself mediated by subjective negotiation. Subjectivity is itself located. Thus the metaphysics implied by "internal/external" is, strictly speaking, false.

But there is a distinction between the sense one has of oneself as seen by others and of one's own self-perception, or between one's third-person and first-person selves (though both of these are dynamic and contextual). Fanon argued that the corporeal malediction produced by the disjuncture between one's own "tactile, vestibular, kinesthetic, and visual experience" (Fanon 111) and the racial parameters that structure one's identity must be reconciled; one cannot live in permanent disequilibrium. One might weather intermittent contradictions of this sort but not uninterrupted ones. Fanon believed, and lived experience confirms, that one cannot easily tolerate a serious and sustained conflict between a first-person and a third-person identity without it producing pathological effect.

The inevitable interdependence and connection between one's public identity and one's lived sense of self, and the felt need to pursue a coherence between one's first-person and third-person selves, does not mean that the self can ever achieve perfect coherence. But it is also a mistake to assume that we are all incoherent to the same degree, or that one per-

---

20. For an explanation of this term invented by Enrique Düssel, see Barber.

son's struggle with multiple racial identities is essentially the same as the universal struggle individuals have to integrate their multiple selves. There are significant differences in the scope, depth, and daily difficulties of various forms of heterogeneity and disequilibrium.

Belief in a sharp boundary between the inner and outer self no doubt contributes to the prevalent view that one should be able to psychologically "pull yourself up by your own bootstraps," ignore social rejection, and believe in yourself. In contrast to this view, Bernard Williams explains that shame in the face of an internalized Other—an Other that need only be imagined but that embodies a genuine social reality—provides "through the emotions a sense of who one is and of what one hopes to be, it mediates between act, character and consequence" (102). His is essentially a development of the Hegelian account, to the extent that the formation of a substantive subjectivity operates through a mediating process seeking recognition in some respected or desired external other. Shame is simply one of the effects, and symptoms, of this necessary dependence on elements outside the self.

These are specific and contextually produced difficulties, not global ones inherent in having an identity itself. The mediation of self performed by social context can also produce more positive and even joyful emotions associated with self-assurance, connection with others, shared sensibilities, and simply the serenity that follows when one feels oneself *understood*. The perniciousness of identity-based forms of oppression, such as racism and sexism, lies not in the fact that they impose identities but in that they flatten out raced and sexed identities to one dimension, and they disallow the individual negotiation and interpretation of identity's social meanings. Racism, as Eduardo Mendieta has put it, feels as if one finds oneself in the world ahead of oneself, the space one occupies as already occupied. One's lived self is effectively dislodged when an already outlined but very different self appears to be operating in the same exact location, and when only that projection from others receives their recognition. In the extreme, no true intersubjective interaction is possible in such a space; agency is eclipsed by an a priori schema onto which all of one's actions and expressions will be transferred. Though this operates as a kind of identity in the sphere of social intercourse, it is not a real identity: there is no identifying with such flattened, predetermined identities, and there is no corresponding lived experience for the cardboard cutout. Even the conservative, antifeminist woman is not really seeing herself as the sexist sees her, but choosing to take up the traditional role as her own space of activity. In the sexist's representation, there is no space in which she can operate as a critical and moral agent, where she can make choices, or where intersubjective interaction is possible.

Real identities are indexed to locations in which experience and perception occur and from which an individual acts. Consider, in this light, Robert Gooding-Williams's recent formulation of black identity. Gooding-Williams argues that "being racially classified as black—is a necessary but not a sufficient condition of being a black person" (23). The third-person interpellation, the public identity, must be designated black; one cannot simply negate the modes and norms of description in one's social world or reinvent new ones at will. But Gooding-Williams does not give this public inscription the last word. He argues that "one becomes a black person only if (1) one begins to identify (to classify) *oneself* as black and (2) one begins to make choices, to formulate plans, to express concerns, etc., in light of one's identification of oneself as black" (23; original emphasis). This definition highlights the individuals' negotiation and their subjectivity. That is, black identity involves both a public self and lived experience, which means that it is produced out of the modes of description made possible in a given culture but it is also dependent on any given individual's active self-understanding. Gooding-Williams uses this definition to make sense of the sort of experience he says is "described time and again in the letters and literature of black persons," such as Du Bois's experience in his youth of only coming to the realization that he is "different from the others" after he has his visiting card refused by whites. Though he was classified prior to this experience as a black person, at least in some contexts, Du Bois did not have a black identity in the full sense by Gooding-Williams's definition.

A realist account would argue here that there is a fact of the matter about Du Bois's identity. When he comes to recognize his different treatment, Du Bois is recognizing a fact about his environment it seems impossible to deny, that is, that he has a public identity in North America as a black person. Like Wilkerson, he is recognizing a truth about himself that preexisted this recognition, and thus in that sense it is an objective truth even though the full or meaningful sense in which he has a black identity is only developed postrecognition. Gooding-Williams's motive, I suspect, in requiring self-understanding is not to repudiate the significance of the public identity but to recognize that this is not all there is to one's identity. Identity, on his account, and arguably in everyday parlance, is necessarily something that is one's own. In the newspaper this morning it was argued that gun control legislation threatens the very identity of those who have grown up in communities where hunting is a central part of the culture. In this familiar usage of the term, identity is not simply that which is imposed but is integral to the individual's sense of himself, his place, and his culture. Advocates of gun control who ignore this are likely to fail. We also use identity to talk not only about how one is *identified,* but how one *identifies with* the new Latina on the city council, the working mother in the soap opera, the child victim in the sexual abuse reported in the newspaper, each on the basis of some aspect of one's lived experience. In identifying *with,* one can come to identify *as* more self-consciously.

The idea of making choices, formulating plans, and expressing concerns in light of one's identification of oneself as African American, Latina, or otherwise is a key component of the rationale behind the original concept of identity politics. It should be obvious that one's identity in this full sense, one's positional consciousness, will play a role in one's actions, particularly as these involve political contestations. Recently at an Anti-Violence Peace Rally in downtown Syracuse, the speakers *spoke as* young people facing daily violence in the public schools, *as* African Americans and Latinos with a different relationship to gun violence than middle-class whites (for whom the problem of school violence might be newer), and *as* U.S. citizens feeling the responsibility to oppose publicly their government's military policy in Kosovo. This wasn't about claiming authenticity, or an incontestable epistemic privilege based on identity, or "creating" divisions, but about sharing multiple, overlapping, but sometimes very different perceptions and analyses of crises in our shared world. In each case, their identity made a difference in what they knew about and how they approached a problem that we all face. The rally organizers recognized that identities had important epistemic and political roles to play precisely in ensuring and enhancing solidarity.

Both the kind of role identity plays and the degree to which it plays a role at all are entirely variable. The particular meaning and significance of one's identity is interpreted in many different ways, and one may take one's racial identity, for example, as more or less central to one's life. Yet to be black, that is, to self-identify as black in Gooding-Williams's sense, cannot be understood as merely something that befalls one, something that cannot touch the "real self" of an individual as if that were prior to all identities. One makes sense of one's identity based on one's experience, which is itself a function of interpellation. And, against Althusser, to respond to interpellation by accepting the hail, even in the context of racialized identities, is not simply to capitulate to power but to actively engage in the construction of a self. To the policeman I have the option of saying "You have the wrong person," of accepting his recognition, or, as in the "I am Spartacus" variant, reinterpreting his interpellation to accept it in a way he is not intending. All of these options involve my interpretive agency, including the option of acceptance. But the "I" that chooses among these options is always already socially located.

Somehow the process by which identity has been pathologized and all forms of realism have been demonized needs to be unraveled, for these claims are far from obvious when pressed. To self-identify even by a racial or sexed designation is not merely to accept the sad fact of oppression but to understand one's relationship to a historical community, to recognize one's objective social location, and to participate in the negotiation of the meaning and implications of one's identity. The word *real* here is not meant to signify an identity that is nondynamic, noncontingent, or not the product of social practices and modes of description. Rather, the word *real* works to counter a view that interpellations of social identity are always chimeras foisted on us from the outside or misrepresentations.

A realistic identity politics, then, is one that recognizes the dynamic, variable, and negotiated character of identity. It is one that acknowledges the variability in an identity's felt significance and cultural meaning. Yet it is also one that recognizes that social categories of identity often helpfully name specific social locations from which individuals engage in, among other things, political judgment. What is there to fear in acknowledging that?

WORKS CITED

Aboulafia, Mitchell. *The Mediating Self: Mead, Sartre, and Self-Determination.* New Haven: Yale University Press, 1986.

Alcoff, Linda Martín. "Becoming an Epistemologist." *Making Futures: Explorations in Time, Memory, and Becoming.* Ed. Elizabeth Grosz. Ithaca: Cornell University Press, 1999.

———. *Real Knowing: New Versions of the Coherence Theory.* Ithaca: Cornell University Press, 1996.

———. "Reply to My Critics." *Social Epistemology* 12.3 (July–September 1998): 289–305.

Alston, William P. *A Realist Conception of Truth.* Ithaca: Cornell University Press, 1996.

Anderson, Benedict. *Imagined Communities.* London: Verso, 1993.

Archer, Margaret, Roy Bhaskar, Andrew Collier, Tony Lawson, and Alan Norrie, eds. *Critical Realism: Essential Readings.* London: Routledge, 1999.

Babbitt, Susan E. *Impossible Dreams: Rationality, Integrity, and Moral Imagination.* Boulder, CO: Westview Press, 1996.

Barber, Michael D. *Ethical Hermeneutics: Rationalism in Enrique Düssel's Philosophy of Liberation.* New York: Fordham University Press, 1998.

Battersby, Christine. *The Phenomenal Woman: Feminist Metaphysics and the Patterns of Identity.* New York: Routledge, 1998.

Brown, Wendy. *States of Injury: Power and Freedom in Late Modernity.* Princeton: Princeton University Press, 1995.

Butler, Judith. *Gender Trouble: Feminism and the Subversion of Identity.* New York: Routledge, 1990.

————. *The Psychic Life of Power: Theories in Subjection.* Stanford: Stanford University Press, 1997.

Castells, Manuel. *The Information Age: Economy, Society, and Culture.* Vol. 2: *The Power of Identity.* Malden, MA: Blackwell, 1997.

Combahee River Collective, "The Combahee River Collective: A Black Feminist Statement." *Capitalist Patriarchy and the Case for Socialist Feminism.* Ed. Zillah R. Eisenstein. New York: Monthly Review Press, 1979. 362–72.

de Lauretis, Teresa. "Upping the Anti (sic) in Feminist Theory." *Conflicts in Feminism.* Ed. Marianne Hirsch and Evelyn Fox Keller. New York: Routledge, 1990.

Derrida, Jacques. "Deconstruction and the Other." *Dialogues with Contemporary Continental Thinkers—The Phenomenological Heritage.* Manchester: Manchester University Press, 1984.

————. "Women in the Beehive." *Men in Feminism.* Ed. Alice Jardine and Paul Smith. New York: Routledge, 1989.

Elgin, Catherine Z. *Between the Absolute and the Arbitrary.* Ithaca: Cornell University Press, 1997.

Eze, Emmanuel Chukwudi, ed. *Race and the Enlightenment: A Reader.* Cambridge: Blackwell, 1997.

Fanon, Frantz. *Black Skin, White Masks.* Trans. Charles Lam Markmann. New York: Grove Press, 1967.

Faull, Katherine M., ed. *Anthropology and the German Enlightenment.* Lewisburg, PA: Bucknell University Press, 1995.

Foucault, Michel. "The Subject and Power." *Michel Foucault: Beyond Structuralism and Hermeneutics.* Ed. Hubert L. Dreyfus and Paul Rabinow. 2d ed. Chicago: University of Chicago Press, 1982.

Fraser, Nancy. *Justice Interruptus: Critical Reflections on the "Postsocialist" Condition.* New York: Routledge, 1997.

Gates, Henry Louis, Jr. "The Master's Pieces: On Canon Formation and the African American Tradition." *The Politics of Liberal Education.* Durham: Duke University Press, 1992.

Gitlin, Todd. *The Twilight of Common Dreams: Why America Is Wracked with Culture Wars.* New York: Henry Holt, 1995.

Goldberg, David Theo. *Racist Culture: Philosophy and the Politics of Meaning.* Cambridge: Blackwell, 1993.

Gooding-Williams, Robert. "Race, Multiculturalism, and Justice." *Constellations* 5.1 (January 1998): 18–32.

Gordon, Lewis. *Bad Faith and Antiblack Racism*. Atlantic Highlands, NJ: Humanities Press, 1995.

Gregory, Steven, and Roger Sanjek, eds. *Race*. New Brunswick: Rutgers University Press, 1994.

Grosz, Elizabeth. *Space, Time, and Perversion: Essays on the Politics of Bodies*. New York: Routledge, 1995.

Hartsock, Nancy. *Money, Sex, and Power*. New York: Longman, 1983.

Hegel, G. W. F. *The Phenomenology of Mind*. Trans. J. B. Baillie. New York: Harper and Row, 1931.

———. *Reason in History*. Trans. Robert S. Hartman. Indianapolis, IN: Bobbs-Merrill, 1953.

Laclau, Ernesto. Introduction. *The Making of Political Identities*. Ed. Ernesto Laclau. New York: Verso, 1994.

Lloyd, Genevieve. *The Man of Reason: "Male" and "Female" in Western Philosophy*. Minneapolis: University of Minnesota Press, 1984.

Lynch, Michael P. *Truth in Context: An Essay on Pluralism and Objectivity*. Cambridge, MA: MIT Press, 1998.

Omi, Michael, and Howard Winant, eds. *Racial Formations in the United States: From the 1960s to the 1980s*. New York: Routledge, 1986.

Putnam, Hilary. *The Many Faces of Realism*. LaSalle, IL: Open Court, 1987.

———. *Reason, Truth and History*. New York: Cambridge University Press, 1981.

Ramos, Samuel. *Profile of Man and Culture in Mexico*. Trans. Peter G. Earle. Austin: University of Texas Press, 1962.

Rodriguez, Richard. *Days of Obligation: An Argument with My Mexican Father*. New York: Viking, 1992.

Rouse, Joseph. *Knowledge and Power: Toward a Political Philosophy of Science*. Ithaca: Cornell University Press, 1987.

Sartre, Jean-Paul. *Being and Nothingness: A Phenomenological Essay on Ontology*. Trans. Hazel Barnes. New York: Simon and Schuster, 1956.

Sayre-McCord, Geoffrey, ed. *Essays on Moral Realism*. Ithaca: Cornell University Press, 1988.

Schmitt, Frederick F. "Realism, Antirealism, and Epistemic Truth." *Social Epistemology* 12.3 (July–September 1998): 267–88.

Schutte, Ofelia. *Cultural Identity and Social Liberation in Latin American Thought*. Albany: State University of New York Press, 1993.

Spivak, Gayatri. "In a Word. Interview," With Ellen Rooney. *differences* 1.2 (Summer 1989): 124–54.

———. *In Other Worlds: Essays in Cultural Politics*. New York: Methuen, 1987.

Steele, Meili. *Theorizing Textual Subjects: Agency and Oppression*. Cambridge: Cambridge University Press, 1997.

Steinberg, Michael. "'Identity' and Multiple Consciousness." Paper delivered at the colloquium "Identity: Do We Need It?" Internationales Forschungszentrum Kulturwissenschaften, Vienna, Austria, May 1995.

Taylor, Charles. *Sources of the Self: The Making of Modern Identity*. Cambridge, MA: Harvard University Press, 1989.

Weiss, Gail. *Body Images: Embodiment as Intercorporeality*. New York: Routledge, 1999.

West, Cornel. *Prophecy Deliverance!* Philadelphia: Westminster Press, 1982.
Williams, Bernard. *Shame and Necessity.* Berkeley: University of California Press, 1993.
Wood, Allen W. *Hegel's Ethical Thought.* Cambridge: Cambridge University Press, 1990.
Wright, Crispin. *Realism, Meaning and Truth.* 2d ed. Cambridge: Blackwell, 1993.
Zea, Leopoldo. *The Latin American Mind.* Trans. James H. Abbott and Lowell Dunham. Norman: University of Oklahoma Press, 1963.
———. *The Role of the Americas in History.* Ed. Amy Oliver. Trans. Sonja Karsen. Savage, MD: Rowman and Littlefield, 1992.

Contributors

LINDA MARTÍN ALCOFF is Professor of Philosophy, Political Science, and Women's Studies at Syracuse University. She is the author of *Real Knowing: New Versions of the Coherence Theory* (Cornell), coeditor of *Feminist Epistemologies* (Routledge), and editor of *Epistemology: The Big Questions* (Blackwell). She is currently working on a book titled *Visible Identities: Race, Gender, and the Self* (forthcoming, Oxford) and is coediting *Thinking from the Underside of History*, with Eduardo Mendieta, a collection of essays on the philosophy of Enrique Düssel.

MICHAEL R. HAMES-GARCÍA is Assistant Professor of English at the State University of New York at Binghamton, where he teaches courses in Chicana/o literature, U.S. Latina/o literature, American literature, and literary theory. He has written articles on U.S. Latina/o literature and is at work on a book, *Justice and the Politics of Freedom: Race, Law, and Writings from U.S. Prison Movements*.

CAROLINE S. HAU is Associate Professor of Southeast Asian Studies at Kyoto University. She is the editor of *All the Conspirators*, the Filipino American writer Carlos Bulosan's posthumous novel, and *Intsik: An Anthology of Chinese Filipino Writing*, both published in the Philippines.

BRENT R. HENZE is a doctoral student in the Rhetoric Program at the Pennsylvania State University. His research focuses on the emergence of scientific institutions and publics, particularly on the formation of biological and ethnological research methods in the early nineteenth century.

AMIE A. MACDONALD is Assistant Professor of Philosophy at John Jay College/City University of New York. She teaches courses in political philosophy, multicultural feminism, and philosophy of law. She is currently coediting, with Susan Sánchez Casal, an anthology titled *The Feminist Classroom for the Twenty-first Century: Pedagogies of Power and Difference* (forthcoming, Garland).

SATYA P. MOHANTY is Professor of English at Cornell University. He teaches courses in critical theory, twentieth-century literature, and colonial and postcolonial studies. He is the author of *Literary Theory and the Claims of History* (Cornell) and is currently working on two books: *Are Values Always Political? On Criticism and Evaluation* and *Multicultural Values: The Ethics and Aesthetics of Social Diversity.*

PAULA M. L. MOYA is Assistant Professor of English at Stanford University, where she teaches courses in American literature, U.S. Latina/o and Chicana/o literature, and minority and feminist theoretical perspectives. She has published articles on Chicana feminism and feminist theory and is currently working on a book titled *Learning from Experience: Realist Theory and Chicana/o Identity.*

MINH T. NGUYEN is a doctoral candidate in English at Cornell University. She is currently working on her dissertation project, which examines the epistemic and ethical dimensions of Asian American literature and ethnic studies. In particular, her project focuses on the cognitive link between emotions and objective knowledge.

WILLIAM S. WILKERSON received his Ph.D. in Philosophy at Purdue University in 1997 and is Assistant Professor of Philosophy at the University of Alabama in Huntsville. He has published articles in the areas of twentieth-century continental philosophy and philosophy of mind and is currently coediting an anthology titled *New Critical Theory: Essays on Liberation.*

JOHN H. ZAMMITO is Associate Professor of History and German and Chair of History at Rice University. His major publications include *The Great Debate: "Bolshevism" and the Literary Left in Germany, 1917–1933* (Peter Lang) and *The Genesis of Kant's Critique of Judgement* (Chicago). He is currently working on two books, *Are We Being Theoretical Yet? "Theory" and Historical Practice* and *Parting Ways: Kant, Herder, and the Split of Anthropology from Philosophy, 1762–1773.*

Index

Aboulafia, Mitchell, 328
accuracy. *See under* error
agency: determinism and, 330–34; identity and, 338–39; individual, 233–34; individual, and collectivity, 230, 238, 240–42, 242–45; interpellation and, 340–41; interpretation of experience and, 236–37, 242–45; political struggle and, 229–31; representation and, 237–42; social location and, 235–36. *See also* authority
Alcoff, Linda Martín: and coherence theories of truth, 107; and community and identity, 302; and experience, 212, 295, 298n28, 300, 305–6; on feminism and postmodernism, 69; and identity, 119
Alston, William P., 316
Althusser, Louis, 271n15, 333
ambiguity, of experience, 216–65. *See also* uncertainty
Ankersmit, Frank, 283n6, 290
Anthony, Louise M., 173n4
Anzaldúa, Gloria: and identity, 230–31; and marginality, 245n; misappropriation of, 87; and multiplicity, 78n8, 106–7; and *This Bridge Called My Back*, 240
Appiah, Kwame Anthony, 33n4, 215–16
Asian American studies and literature: experience and, 189; normative component of, 202; objectivity and, 172–74; postmodernism and, 171–73, 174–

76; values and, 190. *See also* Kogawa, Joy
authority: interpretive, 232–34; to represent others, 233; to speak for others, 3–4, 134–36, 148–52, 164–65, 244. *See also* agency; representation

Babbitt, Susan, 313, 317
Baker, Houston, 33n4
Bakhtin, Mikhail, 285
Baldwin, James, 106–7
Bambara, Toni Cade, 239
Barad, Karen, 107, 119n21
Battersby, Christine, 313
Beloved: community in 44–55, 234; freedom and, 47; infanticide in, 53–54, 61, 337; memory and "rememory" in, 43–55; moral debate in, 44–55; moral growth in, 55, 58–59; motherhood and slavery in, 51–54, 61; objectivity and, 61–62; revisionary historiography and, 53–54; sympathy and broadening of consciousness in, 45–47; trust and emotional labor in, 45, 50–51
Bevir, Marc, 282
bias. *See* error; objectivity; theoretical mediation
black churches, 211
black colleges, 209–10
Black Panther Party, 211
Boggs, Grace Lee, 190–91
Bordo, Susan, 249n8

Bowie, Andrew, 299n29
Boyd, Richard N., 40, 107, 162
Brown, Wendy, 8n11, 322, 323, 325
Butler, Judith: and agency, 320–21; and
    autonomy, 326; and Cherríe Moraga,
    70, 76–77; and experience and iden-
    tity, 68; on Foucault, 321–22n9; and
    identity, 7n10, 76–79, 320–22, 323–
    25; and misappropriation of women
    of color, 7on11; and normative political
    claims, 115, 117; and race, 80n11
Butler, Octavia, 106–7

Cabral, Amilcar: on intellectuals and
    "the masses," 144–47, 150n31; and
    political education, 162; and political
    struggle, 150; and representation,
    151; writings of, 135n5, 138n12,
    141n14
Calhoun, Craig, 5n6, 14
Castells, Manuel, 324
Chavez, Linda, 85n19
Cheah, Pheng, 143n17, 165n47
Cherniak, Christopher, 164n46
Cheung, King-Kok, 175–76
Chicanas: Chicano Movement and,
    88–90; as cyborgs, 71–72; feminism
    and, 89–90; identity and, 84–85;
    lesbian, 89. See also Chicano identity;
    Hispanic identity; identity; Mexican
    American identity; Moraga, Cherríe
Chicano identity, and multiplicity, 105–
    6, 113–14, 118. See also Chicanas;
    Hispanic identity; identity; Mexican
    American identity
Chinese Revolution, 137–41
Clifford, James, 290
cognitivism. See knowledge; postpositivist
    realism; realism
Combahee River Collective, 313–14
coming out. See under gay/lesbian
    identity
consciousness, transformation of, 149,
    151–52, 162–64, 180–89, 246–49,
    261, 266–67. See also gay/lesbian
    identity, coming out and; moral
    growth
consciousness raising: experience and,
    252; feminist, 33–38, 41, 184, 233;
    interpretation of experience and, 242–
    45; Japanese Canadian identity and,
    186
constructivism, 155, 159n39. See also
    postmodernism; postpositivist realism;
    theoretical mediation
Cuban Revolution, 146–47
Culler, Jonathan, 31, 271

cultural nationalism, 88–90
cyborg identity, 71–72, 74–76

Davidson, Arnold, 179–80
Davidson, Donald, 107, 304
Debray, Regis, 133
decolonization, 63–64, 141–47. See
    also identity-based political struggle;
    political struggle
deconstruction, 5, 285
Delany, Samuel R., 271, 274–75, 295
de Lauretis, Teresa, 313
de Man, Paul, 48n13, 290
Dennett, Daniel, 259n6
Derrida, Jacques: and experience, 270–
    71, 275–76; on Husserl, 269–70; and
    identity, 320, 322, 325; and language,
    290; and strategic essentialism, 320
Descartes, René, 255
de Sousa, Ronald, 37
Díaz del Castillo, Bernal, 73
difference, 67–68, 78. See also
    multiplicity
Dirlik, Arif, 137, 140–41n14
discourse, 121n23. See also theoretical
    mediation
Du Bois, W. E. B., 215n19, 339
Dunye, Cheryl, 214n18

emotions: epistemic value of, 33–39, 156,
    162, 183–89; evaluation of, 38, 158;
    experience and, 33–43; identity and,
    188–89; interpretation of, 184–86;
    love and justice and, 199–200; objec-
    tivity and, 187–88, 200–202; theoreti-
    cal mediation and, 33–43, 186–87;
    values and, 198–202. See also trust
empiricism. See positivism
epistemic privilege, of the oppressed, 58–
    62, 80–81, 86–87, 211–12
epistemology: naturalized, 154; as
    political, 41; as social process, 156.
    See also knowledge
error: accuracy and, 159–61; ideology
    and, 150; knowledge and, 13, 42–43,
    110, 146, 192–93; objectivity and,
    42n12, 109–10, 136–37, 159–60,
    192–93; as object of inquiry, 160;
    political struggle and, 165; poststruc-
    turalism and, 115–16; representation
    and, 152; status of, in intellectual
    praxis, 135, 141; truth and, 165.
    See also truth
essentialism, 7n8, 80n12; agency and,
    232, 236; criticisms of, 3–4, 35–36,
    217, 220–21, 232; experience and,
    264; identity and, 231–32, 251, 252;

identity-based political struggle and,
2n2, 232; postmodernism and, 30;
racial program housing and, 215;
reconsideration of, 313; strategic,
9n13, 57–58, 116–17, 217, 221, 320,
322–25. *See also* foundationalism;
positivism
experience: accuracy and, 265; agency
and, 291; ambiguity of, 261–65;
Cartesian view of, 256–57; commodification and, 293; context and,
258, 291; criticisms of, 30–32, 68,
269–72, 279–80, 292–95, 296–301;
emotions and, 33–43; epistemic status
of, 33–43, 58, 81, 153, 156–59, 173,
176–79, 182–85, 187–89, 253–54,
298–300; error and, 150, 255; existential phenomenology and, 258–61;
fallibility and, 294; foundationalism
and, 256, 260n7, 269–70; Freudian
view of, 256–57; historical inquiry
and, 184–87, 288–96; identity and,
82; ideology and, 152–53, 272–75;
interpretation and, 186–88, 233–34,
236–37, 240–45, 248–49, 253–54,
255–56, 258, 263–65, 267–68, 274–
75, 298–300; knowledge and, 38–39,
57, 59–60, 152–53, 161–64, 178–
89, 246–49, 256–57, 296; language
and, 289–92, 299; "latent" meaning
in, 264–65; multiplicity and, 293;
representation and, 3–4; social construction of, 38, 290; social location
and, 81–82, 91–92, 236, 238–39,
246–49; as social process, 295; theoretical mediation and, 33–43, 82–83,
92, 182, 251–54, 256–57, 260, 262,
264–66, 334–35; trauma and, 292–
93; truth and, 159, 276; values and,
190, 198–202. *See also* identity

fallibility, 13, 42–43. *See also* error
Fanon, Frantz: and corporeal malediction, 336, 337; on intellectuals and
"the masses," 141–43, 150n31; and
political education, 162; and political
struggle, 150; and representation, 151;
writings of, 135n5, 138n12, 141n14
feminism: critiques of epistemology and,
192; identity and, 217; objectivity
and, 135n6; sexuality and, 95n28;
standpoint epistemology and, 39,
246n7. *See also* Chicanas; consciousness raising; identity; identity-based
political struggle; Moraga, Cherríe
Feyerabend, Paul, 155
Flax, Jane, 172n1

Foucault, Michel: and autonomy, 326;
and discourse, 115n13; and identity,
319, 323, 333; and power, 115; and
resistance, 333; and subjectivity and
identity, 321–22n9
foundationalism, 107–8. *See also*
essentialism; positivism
Frankfurt school, 329
Fraser, Nancy, 324n13
Freire, Paulo, 162n42
Freud, Sigmund, 243n5, 320, 322,
329–30
Fromm, Erich, 329
Fuss, Diana: and essentialism, 80n12;
and experience, 57n17, 270–72,
273–75; and identity-based political
struggle, 30n1; and politics, 297n25

Gadamer, Han Georg, 301
Garcia, Robert, 124–25
gay/lesbian identity: coming out and,
252–57, 261–64, 266–67, 268, 277;
denial and, 261–63; essentialism and,
252, 264; multiplicity and, 105–7;
philosophical problems concerning,
255–56; political nature of, 267;
theoretical mediation and, 252–54,
263–64, 266–67, 268; as transforma-
tion, 266–67. *See also* Chicanas; femi-
nism; heterosexual identity; identity;
Moraga, Cherríe
Gestalt psychology, 258
Giddens, Anthony, 292
Goellnicht, Donald C., 174–75, 176n10
Gooding-Williams, Robert, 339, 340
Gordon, Lewis, 332
Gould, Stephen Jay, 317
Gray, John, 231–32
Gray, William, 207n8
Grosz, Elizabeth, 313
Guinea-Bissau, national liberation
struggle in, 144–47

Hames-García, Michael R.: and identity,
295–96, 314; and identity-based
political struggle, 315; and mutuality,
196n37; and strategic essentialism, 217
Haraway, Donna: on Cherríe Moraga,
70; and Chicana identity, 71–72;
and identity, 75–76, 78–79; and La
Malinche, 74; and objectivity and
fallibility, 42n12; and women of color,
74–76
Harding, Sandra, 39, 112–13, 212,
246n7
Harstock, Nancy, 246n7
Hau, Caroline, 193, 315

Hegel, G. W. F.: and autonomy, 326; and experience, 257; and perception, 258–59n5; and recognition, 336–37; and the self, 123, 326–29, 332

Heidegger, Martin, 260

Henderson, Mae, 48n13

hermeneutics. *See* historical interpretation

heterosexual identity, 246. *See also* gay/lesbian identity; identity

The Hidden Law: Chicano identity and, 105–6, 113–14; expansion of solidarity and, 105–6; HIV status and, 106; homophobia and, 105–7; moral truth and culpability and, 113–14; multiplicity and, 118, 122, 125; multiplicity and restriction and, 104–7; sexuality and, 105–7

Hirst, R. J., 153–54

Hispanic identity, 84–86. *See also* Chicanas; Chicano identity; identity; Mexican American identity

historical interpretation: adjudication of, 181–87, 294–95; community of discourse and, 282; context and, 284; deconstruction and, 285; as dialogic, 285, 288; experience and, 179–85, 287; fallibility and, 287, 294–95; as historical reconstruction, 286–88; language and, 287, 290–91; limits on, 285, 287–88, 299; the "linguistic turn" and, 283–87; procedural and normative standards and, 282; situatedness and, 283; trauma and, 292–93. *See also* history

history: decolonization and, 144–45; democratization of, 307–8; experience and, 280; objectivity and, 59–60; postmodernism and, 174, 280–88, 296–303; shared standards, discipline of, 281–85, 287–88, 289, 298–303, 306–7. *See also* historical interpretation

Hollinger, David, 303n35

homophobia, 105–6, 262–63

hooks, bell, 221

House of Color, 122–25

Husserl, Edmund, 260, 269–70, 275–76

Hutcheon, Linda, 174

identification, imaginative, 246, 248–49

identity, 11–12, 14, 15; agency and, 340–41; benefits of, 214n18, 324, 334–35, 340–41; criticisms of, 1–4, 68–70, 76, 216, 312–13, 318–22; cyborg, 71–72, 74–76; debates about, 1–4, 29; epistemic status of, 8–9, 71,

83–86, 209–10, 334–35; essentialism and, 3, 10, 30, 231–32, 251, 252, 313, 322–25; experience and, 82–83, 177, 340; evaluation of, 22–23, 56–57, 85; heterosexual, 246; Hispanic, 84–86; Jewish, 217–18; language and, 318; material effects of, 92; Mexican American, 83–85, 94–95; moral inquiry and, 209–10; multiplicity and, 103–7, 110–12, 119–27, 218, 318–19, 337–38; philosophical treatment of self and other and, 325–34; political, 57n16, 207, 217–19; political struggle and, 86–87, 186–87; postmodernism and, 8, 10–11, 30, 319–23, 325; public, and subjectivity, 335–41; racial, and constitutive meaning, 219; racial, as inessential, 218–19; as real, 56, 339; reference and, 84; revision of, 83–84, 185, 261–67; significance of, 8–9, 69, 312–13; social location and, 78–79, 81–82; solidarity and, 125–27, 340; theoretical mediation and, 8–9, 43, 54–55, 125, 156–57; verification of, 84; victimization and, 211. *See also* Chicanas; Chicano identity; feminism; gay/lesbian identity; identity-based political struggle; Japanese Canadians; race; social location

identity-based political struggle: criticisms of, 312–13; defense of, 313–15; knowledge and, 62–64; moral universalism and, 60–64; political necessity of, 62–64; solidarity and, 125–27. *See also* decolonization; feminism; identity; political struggle

ideology, 149–50, 160, 272–74

intellectuals, role of: alienation and, 137–38, 142, 144; decolonization and, 135, 141–47; epistemic authority and, 136, 152; epistemic reliability and, 134–35; error and, 141; in political struggle, 133–34, 137–41, 147–52; and representation of "the people," 138–52, 162–65; social location and, 137–38

interests: conflicting, 280; determination of, 163, representation of, 233. *See also* authority; representation

interpretation: of experience, 83–84; as social, 233–34

Irigaray, Luce, 332

Itsuka (Kogawa), 178, 184–89, 195, 198–99

Japanese Canadians, experience of, 176, 181, 184–85, 196–97, 199. *See also* identity; Kogawa, Joy

Jardine, Alice A., 31n2
Jay, Martin, 283, 290
Jenkins, Keith, 9–10n13
Jewish community, 210n12
Jewish identity, 217–18. *See also* identity

Kahneman, D., 160n41
Kanefsky, Rachelle, 179n16
Kaye/Kantrowitz, Melanie, 217–18
Kellner, Hans, 281n4, 290
Kim, Elaine, 221
knowledge: accuracy and, 157–61; the
   body and, 91–92; Buddhist meditation
   and, 194n33; colonialism and, 145–
   46; contextualism and, 299–300; as
   contingent, 317; evaluation of, 152–
   53; fallibility and, 165, 299–300;
   identity-based political struggle and,
   62–64; ideology and, 162n43; love
   and, 187–88, 199–202; as mediated
   by identity, 86; nonpropositional, 192;
   political struggle and, 86, 137–47;
   social location and, 160–61; as social
   practice, 161–62; revisability of,
   182–83; theoretical mediation and,
   137, 145, 152–53, 156–60, 256–57,
   334–35. *See also* objectivity; theoretical mediation
Kogawa, Joy: and doubt, 198–200;
   and emotions, 184–89, 193–201;
   and experience, 178–89; and history,
   178–87; and knowledge, 187, 193–
   201; and normative values, 178, 191–
   202; postmodern interpretations of,
   174–76, 179; and trust, 195, 198–
   99. Works: "Is There a Just Cause?"
   193–202; *Itsuka,* 178, 184–89, 195,
   198–99; *Obasan,* 174–76, 178–84,
   187. *See also* Japanese Canadians
Kuhn, Thomas, 155, 304n37

Lacan, Jacques, 329
LaCapra, Dominick: on de Man, 48n13;
   and experience, 292–95; and hermeneutics, 306; and historical reconstruction, 286–87, 288; and hyperbole,
   295; and intellectual history, 283–
   88; and objectivity, 59–60, 287–88,
   292; and postmodernism, 282–83;
   on Toews, 286, 288–89, 292–94, 297
Laclau, Ernesto, 39–40n10, 116, 320
La Malinche, 72–74
Lazarus, Neil, 150n29
Lehrer, Keith, 195n34
lesbian identity. *See* Chicanas; gay/les-
   bian identity; Moraga, Cherríe
Levine, George, 16

Lewis, Philip, 135n6
Livingstone, Paisley, 16, 173n3
Lorde, Audre, 37n8, 106–7, 126–27
Loreto, Paola, 180n18
Lugones, María: and identity, 104n3,
   111, 120–22; and Latino stereotypes,
   221; and solidarity, 120–22

The Maltese Falcon (novel), 113
Mao Zedong: and contradiction, 138;
   and error, 141; on intellectuals and
   "the masses," 137–41, 150n31, 161–
   62; and political education, 162; and
   political struggle, 150; and repre-
   sentation, 151; on social location, 138;
   writings of, 135n5, 138n12, 141n14
Martin, Raymond, 281–82
Marx, Karl, 150n30, 212, 272n17
Megill, Allan, 307–8
memory, partiality of, 180–81
Mendieta, Eduardo, 338
Merleau-Ponty, Maurice, 257, 260,
   265n10, 276
mestizaje, 73
Mexican American identity, 83–85,
   94–95. *See also* Chicanas; Chicano
   identity; Hispanic identity; identity
Meyerson, Denise, 162n43
Middle Passage, 43, 49–54. See also
   Beloved
Mills, Charles, 218
Mohanty, Chandra Talpade, 57n16, 217
Mohanty, Satya P.: and agency, 233,
   304–5; and causation, 159n38; and
   community, 234; and cultural diversity, 222; and emotions, 186; and
   evaluation of theories, 161; and
   experience, 153, 212, 232–33, 238,
   251–54, 267–68, 305; and identity,
   11–12, 84n17, 109, 209, 219n29,
   230, 231, 251–54, 267, 314, 324,
   334–35, 337; and knowledge, 156,
   265, 316; and minimal rationality,
   304–5; and moral growth, 121n24;
   and oppositional struggle, 86, 110;
   and postmodernism, 268; and realism,
   107, 177, 190n24, 292; and reference,
   157–58; and relativism, 303–4; and
   social constructivism, 305
Moody-Adams, Michelle, 192n28
Moraga, Cherríe: and agency, 236; and
   Chicana feminism, 90; and collectivity,
   238–42; and empathy, 248–49; and
   experience, 93–97; and identity, 69,
   95, 124, 214n18, 230–31; and lesbianism, 93–95; and marginality,
   245n6; misappropriation of, 70, 92;

Moraga, Cherríe *(continued)*
  and multiplicity of oppressions, 77–
  78; and oppression, 97–98; and social
  location, 79, 93–95; and theoretical
  mediation, 92; and "theory in the
  flesh," 91–92, 234–37, 239–40; and
  Third World feminism, 67, 90–92;
  and *This Bridge Called My Back*,
  240–41; treatment of La Malinche
  by, 74; and whiteness, 93–95, 98;
  and women's movement, 95–96, 243.
  See also Chicanas
moral growth, 38, 41, 60–62, 201.
  See also consciousness; values
Morris, Aldon D., 211n15
Morrison, Toni. See *Beloved*
Mouffe, Chantal, 39–40n10, 116
Moya, Paula M. L.: on Cherríe Moraga,
  235–37; and Chicana identity, 234–
  37; and experience, 212, 235–36, 238–
  39, 295–96; and identity, 111n9,
  177n11, 216, 230, 314, 334; and
  realism, 107; and social construction,
  305
Mujeres Activas en Letras y Cambio
  Social (MALCS), 69
multiculturalism, 29, 220
multiplicity: challenges posed by, 105–
  7; Chicano identity and, 105–6, 113–
  14; conflicting interests and, 280; of
  experience 293; identity and, 110–
  12, 119–27; interests and, 104, 121,
  122–25; as mutual constitution, 103–
  4, 106; restriction and, 104–7, 110;
  sexual identity and, 105–7, 113–14;
  verification and revision and, 111–12.
  See also difference
Murdoch, Iris, 200–201n42

National Association for the Advance-
  ment of Colored People (NAACP),
  211
Nava, Michael. See *The Hidden Law*
Nguyen, Minh T., 334
Niagara Movement, 211
Nietzsche, Friedrich, 31n2, 36n7
Novick, Peter, 307
Nussbaum, Martha, 38n9

Obasan (Kogawa), 174–76, 178–84, 187
objectivity: Asian American literature
  and, 172–74; bias and, 12–13, 173;
  cultural diversity and, 222; deconstruction and, 5; emotions and,
  187–88, 200–202; error and, 192–93;
  experience and, 295; foundationalism
  and, 173; knowledge and, 5; opposi-

tional struggle and, 40–41, 110,
  164–65; as social practice, 39–41;
  theoretical mediation and, 12–14,
  136–37, 159–60; values and,
  200–202. *See also* knowledge
Omi, Michael, 171
oppositional struggle. *See* political
  struggle
Outlaw, Lucius, 214, 218

Palumbo-Liu, David, 172
Peirce, C. S., 13
phenomenology, 258–61, 269–72
Pines, Christopher, 150n30
"El Plan de Santa Bárbara," 88n21
Pocock, J. G. A., 290–91
political education: Cuban Revolution
  and, 146–47; political struggle and,
  139–41, 145–47, 151–57, 162;
  popular consciousness and, 142
political struggle: collectivity and, 137–
  38; error and, 165; experience and,
  240; identity and, 186–87; knowledge
  and, 86–87, 133–35, 137–41, 161–62,
  186–87; objectivity and, 164–65;
  political education and, 151–52, 162;
  role of outsiders in, 245–49; values
  and, 191. *See also* decolonization;
  identity-based political struggle
popular consciousness: decolonization
  and, 141–47; generalizing of, 134–35,
  139, 141–43, 146–47, 165; ideology
  and, 149; political education and, 139;
  political struggle and, 141–43
positivism, 108–9, 148, 158, 316–17.
  See also essentialism; foundationalism
postmodernism, 6n7, 171–72, 268n12;
  agency and, 333–34; Asian American
  studies and, 171–73; criticisms of,
  9n13, 11, 57–58, 68–69, 74–79,
  150–52, 175–76, 272–75; difference
  and, 68; empirical inquiry and, 299–
  300; essentialism and, 30; experience
  and, 30–31, 68–69, 158, 177n13,
  189, 268–69, 270–75, 296; feminism
  and, 68–69; foundationalism
  and, 68–69; foundationalism and,
  32–33, 36, 193n31, 299–300; history
  and, 280–88, 296–303; identity and,
  8, 68–70, 71–72, 74–79, 251; normative judgments and, 116–17; objectivity and, 42n12, 135–36, 173; relativism and, 303–4; and truth and, 174–76.
  See also poststructuralism
postpositivist realism, 11n15, 12n16;
  agency and, 233–45, 304–5; Asian
  American studies and, 190; coming
  out and, 252–57, 261–64, 268, 176–

77; empirical vs. metaphysical questions and, 108n6; epistemic privilege and, 58–60, 60–61; error and, 109–110, 159–60, 165; evaluation of theories and, 116–17, 157–64; experience and, 32–43, 55, 58, 60, 81, 153, 177–79, 251–54, 255–57, 267–68, 305–6; fallibility and, 42–43; history and, 282–83; identity and, 11–12, 14, 55–64, 81–87, 125–27, 177, 208, 251–54, 255–56; knowledge and, 41–43, 265, 276–77; minimal rationality and, 164, 304–5; moral truth and, 112–13; moral universalism and, 60–64; multiplicity and, 110–13, 119–21; objections to, 253–54; objectivity and, 12–14, 41–43, 58–59, 158–60, 173–74; oppositional political struggle and, 86–87, 110, 161; positivism and, 107, 109; postmodernism and, 57–58, 153; reference and, 55–56, 157–61, 164–65; representation and, 136–37; social location and, 87; solidarity and, 120; theoretical mediation and, 109, 136–37, 252–54, 276–77, 317–18; theory-independent reality and, 108, 315–16; truth and, 119–20, 155, 165; uncertainty and, 192–97; universalism and, 303–5. See also realism; reference
poststructuralism, 5n6, 114n12; agency and, 297–98; criticisms of, 115–18, 322–35; empirical inquiry and, 299–300; error and, 117; experience and, 31, 289–90, 295, 297–301; foundationalism and, 118, 299–300; historical inquiry and, 296–303; hyperbole and, 306; identity and, 4–7, 297, 319–23, 325; language and, 289–90; multiplicity and, 114–15; normative judgments and, 115–17; objectivity and, 135–36; political struggle and, 115–17, 147–52; representation and, 147–51; theoretical mediation and, 116–18; truth and, 117. See also postmodernism
psychoanalysis: historical interpretation and, 285–86; identity and, 319, 320–22, 324
Putnam, Hilary, 107, 316

qualia, 257, 259n6
Quine, W. V. O, 32n3, 107, 301–2

race, 73, 94–95, 216n23, 218–19. See also identity
racial democracy, 205, 219–20
racial program housing: benefits of, 207,

215, 219, 221–23; at Brown University, 207; controversy over, 206–8, at Cornell University, 207–8, 222; criticisms of, 208–9, 214, 216–17; epistemic diversity and, 212; epistemic power and, 214; insurgent academic disciplines and, 221; legality of, 208; political identities and, 207, 219; racial justice and, 213. See also self-segregation
racism: incidents of, on college campuses, 205–6; racial identity and, 206n2; in United States, 212n17, 213
Ramos, Samuel, 324
realism: history of, 153–55; ontological pluralism and, 316; positivism and, 316; varieties of, 315–16. See also postpositivist realism
reference: accuracy of, 157–61; causal theory of, 12, 56n15, 108, 157, 159, 164; theoretical mediation and, 159n40
representation, 148–53, 163, 237–42. See also authority
Riggs, Marlon, 214n18
Rodriguez, Richard, 336
Roman, Leslie, 107
Rooney, Ellen, 297, 302
Rorty, Richard, 257n3, 303
Ross, Dorothy, 280n4

Sartre, Jean-Paul, 320, 322, 330–33
Scheman, Naomi: and consciousness raising, 242–45; and emotions, 33–38, 184, 186; and experience, 233, 252, 256
Scott, Joan: and agency, 297–98; and coming out, 271; and difference, 305; and discourse, 297–98; and experience, 33, 68, 177n13, 189, 271–72, 273–75, 279–80, 295, 296–301; and history, 280–81; and hyperbole, 298; and identity, 297; and identity-based political struggle, 295; and misappropriation of women of color, 70n1; and politics, 301–3; and radical "historicizing," 301; and shared standards, 302–3; on Toews, 280–81, 288–89, 296–303
Sekyi-Otu, Ato, 141n14
self-segregation: benefits of, 210–11; imposed segregation vs., 213–14; integration vs., 212–13; moral inquiry and, 210; racial justice and, 213; role of, in U.S. civil rights movement, 210–11; white, 206, 212-13. See also racial program housing

Sellars, Wilfrid, 257
sexuality. *See* Chicanas; Chicano identity; feminism; gay/lesbian identity;
   identity; Moraga, Cherríe
Silko, Leslie Marmon, 214n18
Simon, Caroline, 200n42
Singer, Linda, 69
Sivanandan, A., 57n16
skepticism, 179n17. *See also* postmodernism; poststructuralism
slavery, 112. See also *Beloved*
Smith, Barbara Hernstein, 13n18
Sneed, Pamela, 122–23
social location: agency and, 235–36;
   epistemic status of, 85; experience
   and, 81–82, 91–92, 236, 238–39;
   hermeneutical tradition and, 301;
   identity and, 78–79; knowledge
   and, 160–61; as social interest, 39.
   See also identity
Southern Christian Leadership Conference (SCLC), 211
Southern Poverty Law Center, 211
Spelman, Elizabeth, 106
Spivak, Gayatri Chakravorty: on Deleuze,
   148–49, 151; on Foucault, 148–49,
   151; and ideology, 136, 150–51; and
   native agency, 149n28; and normative
   evaluation, 116; and political education, 151–52; and political struggle,
   151–52; and representation, 136, 147–
   52; and role of intellectuals, 147–52;
   and strategic essentialism, 323; and
   transformation of consciousness,
   151–52
Steele, Shelby, 209, 211, 220
Steward, Helen, 159n38
Student Non-Violent Coordinating
   Committee (SNCC), 211

Takagi, Dana Y., 171, 189n23
Tan, Amy, 214n18
Taylor, Charles, 63n18, 325–26
Taylor, Jocelyn, 123
theoretical mediation: constructivism
   and, 155; emotions and, 186–89;
   experience and, 256–57, 267–68;
   knowledge and, 145, 152–53, 156–

60, 265, 276–77, 299–300; objectivity
   and, 136–37, 159–60; poststructuralism and, 116–18; reality and, 317–18;
   reference and, 159n40; truth and, 109.
   See also knowledge
Third World feminism. *See under*
   Moraga, Cherríe
This Bridge Called My Back (Anzaldúa
   and Moraga, eds.), 67, 238–42
Toews, John, 281, 288–93, 298–99
trust, 194–95, 201–2. *See also*
   emotions
truth: correspondence theory of, 12, 155;
   domination and, 110; error and, 165;
   evaluation of, 196; experience and,
   276; justification and, 154–55
Tversky, A., 160n41

uncertainty, epistemological, 191–200.
   See also ambiguity
United Negro College Fund, 211
universalism, 60–62, 303–5

values: emotions and, 198–202; evaluation of, 197–202; experience and,
   192, 198–202; facts and, 14, 40–41;
   normative theories and, 190–202;
   objectivity and, 14, 200–202; social
   location and, 192; theoretical mediation and, 197–98
vulnerability, 194–97, 201–2

Wahl, Wendy, 243n5
Warnke, Gloria, 292n21
West, Cornel, 209–10, 214n18
White, Hayden, 284n9
Wilkerson, William S.: and experience,
   300, 306, 314; and the other, 334;
   and truth, 339
Williams, Bernard, 338
Wittgenstein, Ludwig, 111
Wong, K. Scott, 189n23
Wood, Allen, 328

Yarbro-Bejarano, Yvonne, 87

Zammito, John H., 318
Zea, Leopoldo, 324

Text: 10/13 Sabon
Display: Sabon
Composition: Integrated Composition Systems
Printing and binding: Sheridan Books